SEVENTH EDITION

MANAGEMENT MISTAKES AND SUCCESSES

Robert F. Hartley
Cleveland State University

JOHN WILEY & SONS, INC.

ACQUISITIONS EDITOR	Jeff Marshall
MARKETING MANAGER	Charity Robey
SENIOR PRODUCTION EDITOR	Patricia McFadden
SENIOR DESIGNER	Kevin Murphy
PRODUCTION MANAGEMENT SERVICES	Hermitage Publishing Services

This book was set in New Caledonia by Hermitage Publishing Services and printed and bound by Courier Westford. The cover was printed by Lehigh Press.

This book is printed on acid-free paper. ∞

ISBN 0-471-20368-8

Printed in the United States of America

10 9 8 7 6 5 4 3 2 1

This seventh edition marks the twentieth anniversary of *Management Mistakes*. Who would have thought that interest in mistakes would have been so enduring.

I doubt that anybody has used all the editions. If anyone has, going back to 1983, I would really like to hear from you. I know that many of you are past users, though, and hope you will find this seventh edition with its new and updated cases a worthy successor to earlier editions. It is always difficult to abandon interesting cases that have stimulated student discussions and provided good learning experiences. But newer case possibilities are ever competing for inclusion. Examples of good and bad handling of problems and opportunities are always emerging.

For new users, I hope the book will meet your full expectations and be an effective instructional tool. Although case books abound, you and your students may find this somewhat unique and very readable, a book that can help transform dry and rather remote concepts into practical reality, and lead to lively class discussions, and even debates amid the arena of decision making.

NEW TO THIS EDITION

In contrast to the early editions, which examined only notable mistakes, and based on your favorable comments about recent editions, I have again included some well-known successes. While mistakes provide valuable learning insights, we can also learn from successes, and we can learn by comparing the unsuccessful with the successful.

In this seventh edition we have added two new sections. The last decade has seen a rash of firms salivating to merge or make acquisitions, and many of these turned out disastrous to employees and shareholders alike. We have devoted Part I to three such cases. Managing Change and Crises has received considerable attention of late, and Part II looks at how three such firms fumbled their extreme challenges, while one became the classic masterpiece in handling a crisis of the worst kind: loss of life. Again, we have included cases dealing with great comebacks, the truly inspiring examples of firms coming back from adversity. We have also tried where appropriate to present in Late-Breaking News sections the most recent developments as we go to publication.

Some of you have asked that I identify which cases would be appropriate for the traditional coverage of topics as organized in most management texts. With many cases it is not possible to truly compartmentalize the mistake or success strictly according to each topic. The patterns of success or failure tend to be more pervasive. Still, I think you will find the following classification of cases by subject matter to be helpful. I thank those of you who made this and other suggestions.

Table 1 Classification of Cases by Major Management Topics

Topics	Most Relevant Cases
Merger Mania	Daimler/Chrysler, Snapple, Maytag, Boeing
Crisis Management	Scott Paper, Herman Miller, Perrier, Johnson & Johnson, Met Life, Maytag, United Way, ADM, Boeing, Firestone/Ford
Great Comebacks	Continental Airlines, Harley Davidson, IBM
Planning	Euro Disney, Coca-Cola, Vanguard, Southwest Airlines, Scott Paper, Boston Beer, Office Max, IBM
Leadership/Execution	High-Tech Excesses, Boeing, Southwest Airlines, Continental Airlines, Harley Davidson, IBM, Boston Beer, ADM, Johnson & Johnson, Scott Paper, Maytag, Perrier, Herman Miller, United Way, Met Life, Firestone/Ford
Control	United Way, Met Life, McDonald's, Maytag, Boeing, Firestone/Ford
Global Applications	Euro Disney, McDonald's, Boeing, Maytag, ADM, Harley Davidson, Daimler/Chrysler, Perrier
Customer Service	Vanguard, Southwest Airlines, Continental Airlines, Office Max, Met Life, Harley Davidson
Nonprofit/Nonproduct	United Way, Disney, Airlines
Entrepreneurial	Boston Beer, Office Max, High-Tech
Social and Ethical	United Way, Met Life, ADM, Johnson & Johnson, Daimler/Chrysler, Firestone/Ford, Scott Paper

TARGETED COURSES

As a supplemental text, this book can be used in a variety of courses, both undergraduate and graduate, ranging from principles of management to strategic management. It can also be used in courses in business ethics and organizational theory. It certainly can be used in training programs and even for those nonprofessionals who look for a good read about well-known firms and personalities.

TEACHING AIDS

As in the previous editions, this edition contains a plethora of teaching aids within and at the end of each chapter. Some of these will be common to several cases, and illustrate that certain successful and unsuccessful practices tend to cross company lines.

Information Boxes and Issue Boxes are included within each chapter to highlight relevant concepts and issues. Learning insights help students see how certain practices—both errors and successes—cross company lines and are prone to be either traps for the unwary or success modes. Discussion Questions and Hands-On Exercises encourage and stimulate student involvement. A recent pedagogical feature is the Team Debate Exercises, in which formal issues and options can be debated for each case. Invitation to Research suggestions allow students to take the cases a step further, to investigate what has happened since the case was written. In the final chapter, the various learning insights are summarized and classified into general conclusions.

An Instructor's Manual written by the author accompanies the text to provide suggestions and considerations for the pedagogical material within and at the ends of chapters.

ACKNOWLEDGMENTS

In this anniversary edition it seems fitting to acknowledge all those who have provided encouragement, information, advice, and constructive criticism through the years since the first edition of these *Mistakes* books. I hope you all are well and successful, and I truly appreciate your contributions. I apologize if I have missed anybody, and would be grateful to know such so I can rectify this in future editions. I would also appreciate updates of present affiliations.

Beverlee Anderson, University of Cincinnati; Y.H. Furuhashi, Notre Dame; W. Jack Duncan, University of Alabama-Birmingham; Mike Farley, Del Mar College; Joseph W. Leonard, Miami University (OH); Abbas Nadim, University of New Haven; William O'Donnell, University of Phoenix; Howard Smith, University of New Mexico; James Wolter, University of Michigan—Flint; Vernon R. Stauble, California State Polytechnic University; Donna Giertz, Parkland College; Don Hantula, St. Joseph's University; Milton Alexander, Auburn University; James F. Cashman, University of Alabama; Douglas Wozniak, Ferris State University; Greg Bach, Bismark State College; Glenna Dod, Wesleyan College; Anthony McGann, University of Wyoming; Robert D. Nale, Coastal Carolina University; Robert H. Votaw, Amber University; Don Fagan, Daniel Webster University; Andrew J. Deile, Mercer University; Samuel Hazen, Tarleton State University; Michael B. McCormick, Jacksonville State University.

Also: Barnett Helzberg, Jr. of the Shirley and Barnett Helzberg Foundation. My colleagues from Cleveland State: Dean Ephraim Smith, Donald Scotton, Ram Rao, Sanford Jacobs, Andrew Gross, and Benoy Joseph. From Wiley, Richard Blander, Tim Kent, Ellen Ford, Brent Gordon, and Jeff Marshall.

Robert F. Hartley
Professor Emeritus
Cleveland State University
Cleveland, Ohio
RFHartley@aol.com

CONTENTS

CHAPTER ONE

Introduction

*I*n this seventh edition, we have added seven new cases. Six cases have been dropped to make room for the new entries, with the rest revamped and updated, and in some instances, reclassified. Many of these cases are as recent as today's headlines; some have still not come to complete resolution.

In accordance with your expressed preferences, we have kept the format of the last several editions by examining not only notable mistakes but also some notable successes. We continue to seek *what can be learned*—insights that are transferable to other firms, other times, and other situations. What key factors brought monumental mistakes for some firms and resounding successes for others? Through such evaluations and studies of contrasts, we may learn to improve the "batting average" in the intriguing, ever-challenging art of decision making.

We will encounter examples of the phenomenon of organizational life cycles, with an organization growing and prospering, then failing (just as humans do), but occasionally resurging. Success rarely lasts forever, but even the most serious mistakes can be (but are not always) overcome.

As in previous editions, a variety of firms, industries, mistakes, and successes are presented. You will be familiar with most of the organizations, although probably not with the details of their situations.

We are always on the lookout for particular cases that bring out certain points or caveats and that give a balanced view of the spectrum of management problems. We have sought to present examples that provide somewhat different learning experiences, where at least some aspect of the mistake or success is unique. Still, we see similar mistakes occurring time and again. The prevalence of some of these mistakes makes us wonder how much decision making has really improved over the decades.

Let us then consider what learning insights we can gain, with the benefit of hindsight, from examining these examples of successful and unsuccessful management practices.

LEARNING INSIGHTS

Analyzing Mistakes

In looking at sick companies, or even healthy ones that have experienced difficulties with certain parts of their operations, we are tempted to be unduly critical. It is easy

1

to criticize with the benefit of hindsight. Mistakes are inevitable, given the present state of decision making and the dynamic environment facing organizations.

Mistakes can be categorized as errors of omission and of commission. *Mistakes of omission* are those in which no action was taken and the status quo was contentedly embraced amid a changing environment. Such errors, which often typify conservative or stodgy management, are not as obvious as the other category of mistakes. They seldom involve tumultuous upheaval; rather, the company's fortunes and competitive position slowly fade, until management at last realizes that mistakes having monumental impact have been allowed to happen. The firm's fortunes often never regain their former luster. But sometimes they do, and we have devoted Part III to the intriguing and inspiring topic of Great Comebacks, describing the cases of Continental Airlines, Harley Davidson, and IBM, all of which fought back successfully from adversity.

Mistakes of commission are more spectacular. They involve bad decisions, wrong actions taken, misspent or misdirected expansion, and the like. Although the costs of the erosion of competitive position coming from errors of omission are difficult to calculate precisely, the costs of errors of commission are often fully evident. We have devoted the premier position, Part I, to a particularly costly type of errors of commission, those involving unwise mergers and acquisitions. But errors of commission are seen in many other cases throughout the book. Looking at a few such examples, we see that the costs associated with the misdirected efforts of Met Life in fines and restitution totaled nearly a hundred million dollars. With Euro Disney, in 1993 alone the loss was $960 million; it improved in 1994 with only a $366 million loss. With Maytag's overseas Hoover Division, the costs of an incredibly bungled sales promotion brought it a loss of $315 million (10.4% of revenues) in 1992, with losses continuing to mount after that.

Although they may make mistakes, organizations with alert and aggressive management show certain actions or reactions when reviewing their own problem situations:

1. Looming problems or present mistakes are quickly recognized.

2. The causes of the problem(s) are carefully determined.

3. Alternative corrective actions are evaluated in view of the company's resources and constraints.

4. Corrective action is prompt. Sometimes this requires a ruthless axing of the product, the division, or whatever is at fault.

5. Mistakes provide learning experiences. The same mistakes are not repeated, and future operations are consequently strengthened.

Being slow to recognize emerging problems leads us to think that management is lethargic and incompetent or that controls have not been established to provide prompt feedback at strategic control points. For example, a declining competitive position in one or a few geographical areas should be a red flag to management that something is amiss. To wait months before investigating or taking action may mean a permanent loss of business. Admittedly, signals sometimes get mixed, and complete information may be lacking, but procrastination cannot be easily defended.

Just as problems should be quickly recognized, the causes of these problems—the "why" of the unexpected results—must be determined as quickly as possible. It is premature, and rash, to take action before knowing where the problems really lie. To go back to the previous example, the loss of competitive position in one or a few areas may reflect circumstances beyond the firm's immediate control, such as an aggressive new competitor who is drastically cutting prices to "buy sales." In this situation, all competing firms will likely lose market share, and little can be done except to stay as competitive as possible with prices and servicing. However, closer investigation may reveal that the erosion of business was due to unreliable deliveries, poor quality control, uncompetitive prices, or incompetent sales staff.

With the cause(s) of the problem defined, various alternatives for dealing with it should be identified and evaluated. This may require further research, such as obtaining feedback from customers or from field personnel. Finally the decision to correct the situation should be made as objectively and prudently as possible. If drastic action is needed, there usually is little rationale for delaying. Serious problems do not go away by themselves: They tend to fester and become worse.

Finally, some learning experience should result from the misadventure. The president of one successful firm told me:

> I try to give my subordinates as much decision-making experience as possible. Perhaps I err on the side of delegating too much. In any case, I expect some mistakes to be made, some decisions that were not for the best. I don't come down too hard usually. This is part of the learning experience. But God help them if they make the same mistake again. There has been no learning experience, and I question their competence for higher executive positions.

Analyzing Successes

Successes deserve as much analysis as mistakes, although admittedly the urgency is less than with an emerging problem that requires remedial action lest it spread.

Any analysis of success should seek answers to at least the following questions:

Why were such actions successful?
- Was it because of the nature of the environment, and if so, how?
- Was it because of particular research and planning efforts, and if so, how?
- Was it because of particular engineering and/or production achievements, and if so, can these be adapted to other aspects of our operations?
- Was it because of any particular element of the strategy—such as service, promotional activities, or distribution methods—and if so, how?
- Was is because of the specific elements of the strategy meshing well together, and if so, how was this achieved?

Was the situation unique and unlikely to be encountered again?
- If not unique to the situation, how can we use these successful techniques in the future or in other operations at the present time?

ORGANIZATION OF THE BOOK

In this seventh edition we have added two new sections. The last decade has seen a rash of firms salivating to merge or make acquisitions, and many of these were disasters to stockholders. We have devoted Part I to three cases on the Perils of Merger Mania.

Change and Crisis Management has received considerable attention of late, and Part II looks at how four firms handled such extreme situations. Three fumbled, and one became the classic masterpiece in handling a crisis of the worst kind: loss of life.

We have continued two earlier additions that many of you approved of: Great Comebacks, and Entrepreneurial Adventures. We can learn much from examining how great adversity was finally turned to success. Polls of students show that interest in entrepreneurship has never been greater, and Entrepreneurial Adventures gives us two intriguing cases with their challenges and triumphs. Otherwise, we have categorized cases under traditional management functions of planning and control, but have combined the organization and leadership functions under "execution." Finally, social responsibility and ethical concerns can hardly be ignored in the close scrutiny of business practices today.

Perils of Merger Mania

The merger of Chrysler with the huge German firm, Daimler, maker of Mercedes, was supposed to be a merger of equals. But Chrysler management soon found this not so, as top Chrysler executives were replaced by executives from Stuttgart, Germany. Problems of assimilation and coordination plagued the merger for years. Adding to the problems, the industry and the economy soured.

Snapple, a marketer of noncarbonated fruit-flavored and iced tea drinks, was acquired by Quaker Oats in late 1994 for $1.7 billion. As sales declined and losses mounted, it soon became apparent to all but the president of Quaker that far too much had been paid for this acquisition. No strategy changes were able to turn Snapple around. In 1997, Snapple was sold for $300 million, a loss of $1.4 billion in only three years.

The problems of Maytag's Hoover subsidiary in Great Britain almost defy belief. The subsidiary, acquired in the late 1980s, was allowed to operate under very loose reins from corporate Maytag. In 1992 it planned a promotional campaign so generous that it was overwhelmed with takers; it was unable either to supply the products or to grant the prizes. Maytag was left to foot the bills while trying to appease irate customers and stockholders, to the tune of over $300 million.

Change and Crisis Management

Albert Dunlap had gained a well-deserved reputation of being the premier hatchet man, the one who would come into a sick organization and fire enough people to make it temporarily profitable—they called him "Chainsaw Al." Somehow, with Sunbeam this seemingly proven downsizing strategy did not work. Dunlap himself was fired by the board of directors.

Herman Miller, maker of top-of-the-line office furniture, had long been extolled in management books and classrooms for successfully melding good business operations and altruistic employee and environmental relations. In recent years, however, demand for its high-priced products dwindled and harsh realities pitted altruism against viability.

Perrier, the bottled-water firm, encountered adversity when traces of benzene were found in some of its product. Responsibly, it ordered a sweeping recall of all bottles in North America and a few days later in the rest of the world, while the company sought to correct the problem. For five months the product was off the market, thereby giving competitors an unparalleled windfall and savaging its market share. Added to this was public recognition that the claims regarding purity of its product were false.

Johnson & Johnson exemplified a superb example of crisis management under the most severe circumstances: loss of life directly connected with its flagship product, Tylenol. J&J became a role model on how to "keep the faith" with its customers, putting their best interests ahead of the firm's and in the process enhancing a public image as a responsive and caring firm.

Great Comebacks

The comeback of Continental Airlines from extreme adversity and devastated employee morale to become one of the best airlines in the country is an achievement of no small moment. New CEO Gordon Bethune brought human relations skills to one of the most rapid turnarounds ever, after a decade of raucous adversarial relations.

In the early 1960s, Harley Davidson dominated a static motorcycle industry. Suddenly, Honda burst on the scene and Harley's market share dropped from 70 percent to 5 percent in only a few years. It took Harley nearly three decades to revive, but now it has created a mystique for heavy motorcycles and gained a new type of user.

In a previous edition, we classified IBM as a prime example of a giant firm that had failed to cope with changing technology. Along with many other analysts, we thought the behemoth could never rouse itself enough to again be a major player. But we were wrong, and IBM resurrected itself to become a premier growth company.

Planning Blunders and Successes

In April 1992, just outside Paris, Disney opened its first European theme park. It had high expectations and supreme self-confidence (critics called it arrogance). The earlier Disney parks in California, Florida, and, more recently, Japan, were spectacular successes. But the rosy expectations soon turned out to be a delusion as a variety of planning miscues finally showed Disney that Europeans, and particularly the French, were not carbon copies of visitors elsewhere.

The classic miscalculation of Coca-Cola in changing the flavor and tampering with the heritage of its major product showed flawed planning—this despite the use of extensive research. Although the situation eventually worked out, embarrassed executives had to make a major improvisation.

Vanguard just became the largest mutual fund company, overtaking Fidelity. Vanguard's strategy was to walk a road less traveled, downplaying marketing and shunning the heavy advertising and overhead of its competitors. It provided investors with better returns through far lower expense ratios, and relied on word of mouth and unpaid publicity to gain new customers, while old customers continued to pour money in. Its momentum was ever increasing.

Leadership and Strategy Execution

By the end of the millennium, high-tech excesses—dot.coms, tel.coms, and others— characterized most Nasdaq stocks. Investors disregarded lack of profits and, mesmerized by wild speculations of future promise, bid up stock prices to absurd valuations. In the euphoria of such instant multimillionaires, spending frenzies abounded, until this balloon burst. The situation was similar to that of the Savings & Loan industry of a decade earlier. When will entrepreneurs and investors learn?

Boeing represents an interesting dilemma: too much business. It was unable to cope with a deluge of orders in the mid- and late 1990s. Months, and then years went by, as it tried to make its production more efficient.

Last in this section we examine the outstanding success of Southwest Air. It found a window of opportunity in being the lowest-cost and lowest-price airline, a situation that somehow no competitor could match. Now its strategic plan threatened major airlines in all their domestic routes.

Control Weaknesses and Strengths

United Way of America is a not-for-profit organization. The man who led it to become the nation's largest charity perceived himself as virtually beyond authority. Exorbitant spending, favoritism, conflicts of interest—these went uncontrolled and uncriticized until investigative reporters from the *Washington Post* publicized the scandalous conduct. Amid the hue and cry, contributions nationwide drastically declined.

Met Life, the insurance firm, whether through loose controls or tacit approval, permitted an agent to use deceptive selling tactics on a grand scale, and enrich himself in the process. Investigations of several state attorneys general forced the company to cough up $100 million in fines and restitutions.

Although it would seem that maintaining high standards and controls for indepedent franchises would be more difficult than controlling company-owned outlets, McDonald's refutes this notion. Since its beginning, McDonald's was the epitome of tightly controlled operations, insisting on the highest standards of cleanliness, product quality and freshness, and customer service, with its growth pattern continuing almost unabated for nearly four decades. Now it has difficulties maintaining such controls and is no longer the same paragon, but is showing great strength and adaptability in international markets.

Entrepreneurial Adventures

OfficeMax, an office-supply category-killer chain, grew to $2.5 billion in sales in only a few years. The dedication and creative efforts of its founder can serve as a model for any would-be entrepreneur who aspires to make it big. Yet, it is number three in its industry and the heady years of growth may be over.

Boston Beer burst on the microbrewery scene with Samuel Adams beers, higher priced even than most imports. Notwithstanding this—or maybe because of it—Boston Beer became the largest microbrewer. It showed that a small entrepreneur can compete successfully against the giants in the industry, and do this on a national scale.

Lapses in Ethical and Social Responsibility

ADM presents a paradox. It was a successful firm, but its success was tarnished by unethical practices and even illegal price-fixing schemes that sent some of its major executives to prison. A dictatorial CEO also fostered political cronyism.

Product safety lapses that result in injuries and even loss of life of users are among the worst ethical and social responsibility abuses. Worse even is when such risks are allowed to continue for years. Ford Explorers equipped with Firestone tires experienced more than 200 deaths from tire failures and vehicle rollovers. After revelations about the accidents surfaced in the media, Ford and Firestone each blamed the other for the deaths. Eventually, a host of lawsuits led to massive recalls and billions in damages.

GENERAL WRAP-UP

When possible, we have depicted the major personalities involved in these cases. Imagine yourself in their positions, confronting the problems and facing choices at their points of crisis or just-recognized opportunities. What would you have done differently, and why? We invite you to participate in the discussion questions, the hands-on exercises, and, yes, the debates appearing at the ends of chapters. There are also discussion questions for the various boxes within chapters. We urge you to consider the pros and cons of alternative actions.

In so doing you may feel the excitement and challenge of decision making under conditions of uncertainty. Perhaps you may even become a better future executive and decision maker.

QUESTIONS

1. Do you agree that it is impossible for a firm to avoid mistakes? Why or why not?
2. How can a firm speed up its awareness of emerging problems so that it can take corrective action? Be as specific as you can.

3. Large firms tend to err on the side of conservatism and are slower to take corrective action than smaller ones. Why do you suppose this is so?

4. Which do you think is likely to be more costly to a firm, errors of omission or errors of commission? Why?

5. So often we see the successful firm eventually losing its pattern of success. Why is success not more enduring?

PART
ONE

PERILS OF
MERGER MANIA

CHAPTER TWO

DaimlerChrysler: Merger of Equals?

It was supposed to be so right, almost a merger made in heaven, some said at the beginning. Chrysler was the smallest but since 1994 the most efficient U.S. auto producer, with the highest profit margin. Now its productivity and innovative strength would be blended with the prestige of Daimler's legendary Mercedes-Benz. Furthermore, Chrysler during one of its periodic crises had sold off its international operations to help raise needed money, and this merger would increase international exposure in a big way and mate it with a rich partner. The instigator, Juergen Schrempp of Daimler, was lauded for his intentions of building a new car company that would have global economies of scale.

Of course, there were two cultures involved, German and American. But in the executive offices, decision making would be shared, with Chrysler's CEO, Robert Eaton, being a co-chairman with Schrempp.

So in November 1998 this merger of "equals" was finalized. And the s___ hit the fan.

CHRYSLER BEFORE THE MERGER

During the last several decades, Chrysler had had a spotted history:

Some said Lee Iacocca performed a miracle at Chrysler. He became president of an almost-moribund firm in November 1978. It was so bad he turned to Washington to bail out the company, and obtained federal loan guarantees of $1.5 billion to help it survive. By 1983, Iacocca had brought Chrysler to profitability, and then to a strong performance for the next four years. He paid back the entire loan seven years before it was due. Like a phoenix, the reeling number-three automaker had been given new life and respectability. Some said Iacocca should be president of the United States, that his talents were needed in the biggest job of all.

Iacocca turned to other interests in the latter half of the decade, and by 1988 the company was hurting again. To a large extent the new problems reflected capital deprivation: Sufficient money had not been invested in new car and truck designs.

11

This lack of funds was the result of a 1987 acquisition of American Motors. Corporation (AMC). The crown jewel of this buyout was the Jeep line of sport-utility vehicles that appealed to younger, more affluent buyers than the older, lower-income customers of Chrysler. Still, Chrysler found itself saddled with the substantial inefficiencies that had bedeviled AMC.

An aging Iacocca again turned his full attention back to the car business, now seven years after retiring his company's horrendous bank debt. He staked company resources on four high-visibility cars and trucks: a minivan, the Jeep Grand Cherokee, LH sedans, and a full-size pickup. Fearful that the company might not survive until the new models came out, especially if a recession were to occur before then, Iacocca instituted a far-reaching austerity program, which cut $3 billion from the company's $26 billion annual operating costs.

By 1992 the company was riding high. Iacocca retired on December 31, 1992, with a job well done. As he said on TV, "When it's your last turn at bat, it sure is nice to hit a home run."[1] Robert Eaton, formerly with GM of Europe, replaced Iacocca as Chrysler chairman.

As it moved to the millennium, Chrysler prospered because of a combination of innovative designs, segment-leading products, and rising sales throughout the auto industry. See Table 2.1 for the sales and net profit statistics of these golden years for Chrysler relative to its two U.S. competitors, General Motors and Ford.

AFTER THE MERGER

Seldom has a merger turned out worse, and so quickly. Perhaps because of morale problems and too much attention given to smoothing relations between Detroit and Stuttgart, the bottom line of Chrysler was wracked. Or maybe the problems at Chrysler had been latent, below the surface, and only needed the disruption of a massive takeover to emerge. Or could the problems have been triggered by an unwise dictation by the company's German master?

On November 16, 1998, Daimler-Benz issued an additional $36 billion of its stock to buy Chrysler. This when added to the $48 billion value of its existing stock brought total market value of DaimlerChrysler to $84 billion. Early in December 2000, barely two years later, a collapsing DaimlerChrysler stock had a market value of only $39 billion, less than Daimler alone was worth before the deal.

Chrysler was bleeding money. During the second half of 2000, Chrysler lost $1.8 billion and went through $5 billion in cash, this at a time when GM and Ford were still doing well.

By 2000, Eaton was long gone, along with nine other top Chrysler executives, including the renowned designer, Thomas Gale. Then in November 2000, Eaton's successor, James Holden, a Canadian, the last high-level non-German remaining, was also given the ax. His replacement was Daimler executive Dieter Zetsche, 47, a tall German with a walrus mustache. Zetsche brought with him Wolfgang Bernhard, 39,

---

[1] Alex Taylor III, "U.S. Cars Come Back," *Fortune* (November 16, 1992), p. 85.

TABLE 2.1 Sales and Profit Comparisons, Big Three U.S. Automakers, 1993–1998 (millions of dollars)

	1993	1994	1995	1996	1997	1998
Ford						
Sales	108,521	128.439	137,137	146,991	153,637	144,416
Net Profit	$2,529	5,308	4,139	4,371	6,920	6,579
	2.3%	4.1%	3.0%	3.0%	4.5%	4.5%
GM						
Sales	138,220	154,951	168,829	164,069	173,168	161,315
Net Profit	$2,466	5,659	6,933	4,668	5,972	3,662
	1.8%	3.7%	4.1%	2.8%	3.4%	2.3%
Chrysler						
Sales	43,600	52,235	53,195	61,397	61,147	NA
Net Profit	$(2,551)	3,713	2,025	3,529	2,805	NA
	(5.9)%	7.1%	3.8%	5.7%	4.6%	

Sources: Company public records. NA=Not applicable because of merger with Daimler.

Commentary: After a poor year in 1993—a $2.5 billion loss—Chrysler really bounced back, making a profit of $3.7 billion, which was over 7 percent of sales, far above that of its two major competitors. Chrysler continued the strong showing with multibillion-dollar profits from 1994 on. In 1995 its 3.8 percent profit was well above Ford, but slightly less than GM; in 1996 and 1997 its profit margin again was the best. While we do not have specific figures in 1998, we know that this was also a good year. The collapse came in 1999.

Note: These are total company sales, the bulk of which are autos/trucks. But with nonvehicle diversifications, the sales will be somewhat overstated for autos/trucks.

an intense young man, an engineer with an MBA from Columbia who was a stickler for cost-cutting, as chief operating officer. It could have been worse: Zetsche could have brought a big team from Germany instead of only one other man. Still, indignation surfaced at this putting German executives in top positions at this old American firm—a firm that had played an important part in defeating the Germans in World War II.

Eaton and the rest of the Chrysler hierarchy had found to their dismay that this was not a merger of equals, despite Chairman Schrempp's 1998 statements to the contrary not only to Chrysler top management but also to the SEC (Securities and Exchange Commission), and the inclusion of the Chrysler name in the corporation name. In reality, Chrysler had become only a division of Daimler. In interviews with the media, Schrempp admitted that such subjugation of Chrysler had always been his intention, this a duplicity of no small moment.[2]

Later we will analyze why the merger so quickly proved a disaster, at least in the short and intermediate term. In the longer term, maybe: maybe not.

[2] For example, "A Deal for the History Books: The Auto Takeover May Be Remembered for All of the Wrong Reasons," *Newsweek* (December 11, 2000), p. 57.

Jurgen Schrempp

DaimlerChrysler Chairman, Jurgen Schrempp, a trim 56, had an untarnished reputation going into the Chrysler merger. He began his career with Mercedes as an apprentice mechanic nearly 40 years before, and had moved steadily upward. Now he acknowledged that he faced "outstanding" challenges with Chrysler. But he pointed out, "Five years ago in 1995, Daimler-Benz posted a loss of 6 billion marks [$3 billion]. We turned it around in a matter of two years. I think we have the experience and know-how to attend to matters, and if necessary we'll do that at Chrysler ... Our aim is to be the No. 1 motor company in the world."[3]

Still, there were those who thought he destroyed Chrysler, that "he didn't realize it was the people who counted, not the factories, which were old, or the sales and profits, which could come and go."[4] So, Schrempp either forced or encouraged key people to leave, and some would say these departures were of the heart and soul of Chrysler. His duplicity in misleading top Chrysler management and shareholders that this was to be a merger of equals could hardly be viewed as anything but ambitious conniving.

During the merger finalization, it was predicted that Chrysler would earn more than $5 billion in 2000, this being what it earned in 1998. In late 1999, however, Chrysler President James Holden reduced this prediction to only $2.5 billion because of having to spend billions retooling for new model introductions at a time when an economic slowdown seemed to be looming.

The reduced profit expectation coming so soon after the merger was unacceptable to Schrempp, and he pressured Chrysler to pump up earnings for the first half of the year by building 75,000 more cars and trucks than could readily be sold, with these quickly shipped to dealers. (The accepted accounting practice was to consider a car as revenue to Chrysler when it reached a dealer's lot, not when it was sold by the dealer.) As a result, Chrysler was just short of its $2.5 billion target in the first half of 2000.

Not surprisingly, the inventory buildup resulted in showrooms overflowing with old model minivans, just as new models began arriving in August. With car sales in general now slowing because of the economy, Chrysler had to cut prices even on popular minivans, and it was necessary to increase rebates up to $3,000 on the old models. These price cuts destroyed the profitability of Chrysler all the more since the company in its optimism after record profits in the 1990s had upgraded its cars and trucks, expecting to charge more for them. But with competition increasing and car pricing turning deflationary, such price hikes did not hold up, and this and the rebates severely affected profits in the third and fourth quarters. (See the following Information Box for a discussion of rebates.)

Schrempp Takes Action

With the huge losses in the second half of 2000, Schrempp sent Zetsche to Detroit with simple instructions: "My orders were to fix the place."[5] On his first day Zetsche

---

[3] Williams J. Holstein, "The Conquest of Chrysler," *U.S. News & World Report* (November 27, 2000), p. 54.

[4] Jerry Flint, "Free Chrysler!" *Forbes* (October 30, 2000), p. 132.

[5] Alex Taylor III, "Can the Germans Rescue Chrysler?" *Fortune* (April 30, 2001), p. 109.

INFORMATION BOX

REBATES

A rebate is a promise by a manufacturer to return part of the purchase price directly to the purchaser. The rebate is usually given to consumers, although it can be offered to dealers instead in the expectation that they will pass some or all of the savings along to consumers.

Obviously, the objective of a rebate is to increase sales by giving purchasers a lower price. But why not simply reduce prices? The rebate is used instead of a regular markdown or price reduction because it is perceived as being less permanent than cutting the list price. This can give more promotional push by emphasizing the savings off the regular price, but only for a limited time. Rebates can be effective in generating short-term business, but they may affect business negatively once the rebate has been lifted.

Come to be expected

Do you see any dangers with rebates from the manufacturer's viewpoint? As a consumer, would you prefer a rebate to a price reduction, or does it make any difference?

---

fired the head of sales and marketing. Then in two months he developed a three-year turnaround plan. It called for cutting 26,000 jobs (29% of the workforce), reducing the cost of parts by 15 percent, and closing six assembly plants. Zetsche projected a breakeven point by 2002 and an operating profit of $2 billion in 2003.[6] This would still be well below the operating profit of Chrysler in 1993–1997, before the merger, as shown in Table 2.1.

His colleague from Stuttgart, Wolfgang Bernhard, organized engineers and procurement specialists into 50 teams to find ways to save money on parts. Suppliers were told to reduce prices by 5 percent as of January 2001, with a further 10 percent reduction over the next two years. Some companies such as Robert Bosch GmbH, the world's second-largest parts maker, and Federal Mogul, said they would not cut prices. Zetsche observed, "If they do not support us to get to the 15 percent, we have to consider that in our future decisions."[7]

Bernhard also focused attention on improving quality as a way to cut costs. In particular, the four-wheel drive trucks showed up poorly on quality surveys. The company began rigorously evaluating new models for quality while they were still in the design stage, so that parts or manufacturing processes could be changed before too much money had been committed.

Zetsche began to direct much of his attention to bringing back standout designs that Chrysler had been noted for in the 1990s. Of late, design and engineering

---

[6] *Ibid.*

[7] "Daimler Threatens to Drop Some Suppliers," Bloomberg News as reported in *Cleveland Plain Dealer* (February 28, 2001, p. 6C).

efforts, such as the 2001 minivan and the 2002 Ram, seemed more evolutionary than revolutionary, with leadership allowed to slip while Toyota and Honda became stronger competitors.

Despite increased competition, Zetsche had a unique asset that should help his company regain the edge: the prestige and competence of Mercedes-Benz technology. Mercedes previously had feared diluting its premium brand, but now it was directed to share components with Chrysler. New rear-wheel versions of the Chrysler Concorde and 300M coming out in 2004 and 2005, for example, were planned to make use of Mercedes electronics, transmissions, seat frames, and other parts. "If Zetsche can sprinkle some Mercedes magic on the Chrysler brand without damaging the premium status of Mercedes, Chrysler has a shot at doing well in the future."[8]

To his credit, Zetsche worked hard to overcome the anti-German feelings that initially followed his and Bernhard's arrival. To stem the potential brain drain, he persuaded many senior Chrysler executives to stay. And the drastic cutback of workers and closing of factories before long came to be viewed as necessary cost-cutting to keep the company viable. Even UAW President Steve Yokich endorsed these actions: "[Otherwise] I don't think there would be a Chrysler."[9]

Other Problems for Schrempp   *And MITSUBISHI*

Two other major problems confronted Schrempp. In October 2000, despite misgivings by Chrysler executives, he acquired 34 percent of Mitsubishi Motors, with the option to up that to 100 percent after three years. Hardly had the deal been finalized than Mitsubishi admitted it had misled consumers about product quality for decades. It also announced that losses for the last six months had nearly doubled. Schrempp reacted by installing a turnaround expert as chief operating officer at Mitsubishi and he was accompanied by dozens of Japanese-speaking Daimler executives. All the while the new chief executive, Takashi Sonobe, was quoted as saying that he, not the German team, remained in charge and that he saw no need for big changes. This was a contest of wills.[10]

DaimlerChrysler's Freightliner, the leading North American heavy-truck maker, was also struggling as the North American market hit one of the steepest slumps in a decade. After an aggressive growth policy that involved acquisitions of other truck makers and a heavy investment in a facility for reconditioning used trucks to sustain Freightliner's sale-buyback strategy, demand for new and used heavy trucks plummeted 50 percent, and prices fell sharply. It was expected that Schrempp would install a German national as head of this unit.[11]

---

[8] Detroit manufacturing consultant Ron Harbour, as reported in *Fortune* (April 30, 2001), p. 110.

[9] Taylor, p. 107.

[10] Holstein, "The Conquest of Chrysler."

[11] Joseph B. White, "Head of Truck Maker Freightliner Is Leaving Post," *Wall Street Journal* (May 25, 2001), p. A4.

PROGNOSIS

As of mid-2001, many observers were pessimistic of the probabilities of Schrempp resurrecting Chrysler any time soon. In the long term, perhaps; but they questioned whether creditors and shareholders would tolerate a long period of profit drain by Chrysler and low share prices for DaimlerChrysler stock. Rumors were that Deutsche Bank, DaimlerChrysler's largest shareholder, was getting ready to oust Schrempp, and that Chrysler would be broken up into smaller pieces and sold off.[12]

Still, friendly German banks and shareholders might be more patient than Wall Street. DaimlerChrysler was the first German company to be listed on the New York Stock Exchange, and such a listing subjected Schrempp to the impatience of the international financial markets and the markets' obsession with meeting quarterly earnings expectations. In an age of volatile markets, failure to meet such expectations often resulted in a company's stock price collapsing. This bothered Schrempp: "I don't think [it] is advantageous: focusing on quarterly results. It might well be that because we increase our spending, investment, whatever, for a very good reason, that I might occasionally miss what they [investors] expect from me."[13]

Schrempp could have another worry imperiling his job if Chrysler did not improve soon. The third largest holder of DaimlerChrysler stock was the Las Vegas takeover tycoon Kirk Kerkorian, a powerful man with a reputation for being easily offended. Rumors were that Schrempp did not make himself available to see Kerkorian, but instead went to his ranch in South Africa.[14]

Chrysler executives, much as they might dislike Schrempp, could be worse off if he should be ousted. Mercedes executives ruled in the headquarters at Stuttgart, and without Chrysler's main supporter, Schrempp, Chrysler could not be sure it would receive the resources needed to make a comeback. It could be broken up and sold, or left withering within DaimlerChrysler's empire.[15]

ANALYSIS

This case illustrates the downside of mergers and acquisitions, as will the next two cases.[16] The causes of these problems are diverse, although certain commonalities occur time and again.

We will examine the salient factors that led to the collapse of Chrysler soon after the merger under (1) those mainly Daimler's fault, (2) those Chrysler's fault, and (3) the externals that made the situation worse. Then we will examine this whole concept of a "merger of equals." Can there really be a merger of equals?

---

[12] "Can the Germans Rescue Chrysler?, pp. 106–107.

[13] Holstein, p. 69.

[14] Reported in "A Deal for the History Books," p. 57.

[15] See Robyn Meredith, "Batman and Robin," *Forbes* (March 5, 2001), pp. 67, 68; and Jerry Flint, "Free Chrysler," *Forbes* (October 30, 2000), p. 132 for more discussion of these scenarios.

[16] We use the terms *mergers* and *acquisitions* somewhat similarly, but will consider *merger* as closer to the idea of equals coming together, while *acquisition* suggests a larger firm absorbing a smaller one.

Daimler's Contribution to the Problem

The Morale Factor

Different cultures are often involved when a merger or acquisition takes place, even among seemingly similar firms. For example, one business culture may be more conservative and the other aggressive and even reckless; one may be formal and the other informal; one culture may insist on standard operating procedures (SOPs) being followed, while the other may be far less restricted; one may be dominated by accountant or control mentalities, which emphasize cost analysis and rigidity of budgets, and the other by the sales mentality, which seeks maximum sales production and flexibility of operations even if expenses sometimes get out of line. Such differences impede easy assimilation.

This assimilation challenge for divergent corporate cultures becomes all the more difficult when different nationalities are involved, for example, Germanic versus American. National pride, and even prejudice, may complicate the situation.

It is hardly surprising that this mammoth merger of a proud German firm and an American firm with a long heritage should present morale problems. Especially with one party misled as to the sharing of leadership, the seeds were laid for extreme resentment. Some of this resentment among rank-and-file workers could even go back to World War II.

But there were other obstacles to a smooth melding of the two firms. Daimler had to adjust from being an old-line German firm to becoming a huge international firm confronted with a diversity of cultures. "The German instinct is for hierarchy, order, planning. Daimler executives use Dr. or Prof. on their business cards. Many wear dark three-piece suits. Chrysler, by contrast, was known for a freewheeling creativity."[17]

Chrysler's company culture had been highly successful in the very recent past, as shown in Table 2.1 and in Table 2.2, which presents the gain in market share or competitive position during the 1990s. This rather unrestrained-by-rules culture seemed to many to be the key to innovative thinking and technical leadership. With the merger it was not only being challenged but repudiated and supplanted by Germans who little appreciated the contributions of designers like Bob Lutz, who came up with products customers wanted that were not engineered at great cost and research. "The daring and imagination of the old Chrysler [is] buried under German management."[18]

Schrempp's Major Blunder

A miscalculation by Schrempp little more than a year after the merger was to have drastic consequences. His order to produce and ship out 75,000 more older-model vehicles than could reasonably be sold before the new models came out, thus beefing up sales and profits for the first half of the year, resulted in huge imbalances of

---

[17] Holstein, p. 56.
[18] Flint, p. 132.

TABLE 2.2 Chrysler's Market Share of the Big Three U.S. Automakers, 1991–1998

	Chrysler's Sales Percentage of U.S. Car/Truck Automakers
1991	12.2
1992	13.7
1993	15.0
1994	15.6
1995	14.8
1996	16.5
1997	15.8
1998	NA

Be Careful of Market Share!

Sources: Calculated from publicly reported sales figures; 1998 figures not applicable due to merger in November.

Commentary: The improvement in Chrysler performance in the middle and late 1990s is clearly evident. Market share improvement of even .05 percent translates into a gain in competitive position. And here we see a gain of more than 4.0 percent in 1996 and 3.6 percent in 1997. You can see how the improving performance of Chrysler in the latter years of the 1990s would be attractive to Daimler.

inventories in the last half and destroyed year-2000 results as well as the early months of 2001. This overproduction was perhaps the trigger that brought Chrysler its huge losses and even jeopardized the soundness of Schrempp's acquisition decision.

Chrysler's Contribution

Arguments could be raised that Chrysler had grown fat and inefficient after its years of success in the last half of the 1990s, that it was on the verge of a drastic decline in profits even if Daimler had not come on the scene to stir things up. By 1999, Chrysler showrooms were saddled with aging models, including the important minivans that were in their fifth year. While still the leader in minivan sales, Chrysler was losing market share to competitors with newer models, including the Honda Odyssey.

The prosperity of Chrysler in the mid-1990s may have reflected not so much inspired management as a combination of good luck factors: innovative designs and segment-leading products, yes, but also rising sales throughout the auto industry and a groundswell of demand for high-profit minivans and pickup trucks. Maybe the success of those years paved the way for the disaster that came shortly after Daimler took over. The great demand for vehicles like the Ram pickup truck, Jeep Grand Cherokee, and Dodge Durango brought a heady confidence that these good times would be lasting. Accordingly, Chrysler projected market share to increase to 20 percent by 2005, far above anything ever attained before. (See Table 2.2 for market share achievements during the heady days in the 1990s. You can see from this that attaining a 20% market share was not very close.) So Chrysler spent heavily on refurbishing plants and buying new equipment. It went from having the fewest workers per point of market share in 1996 to the most by 1999. It was spending money extravagantly and its entrepreneurial culture was operating unchecked. "The company lost its purpose and lost its direction," former chief engineer François Castaing said.[19]

The uncontrolled entrepreneurial culture led to poor communication and coordination, with each team buying its own components such as platforms and parts for the different cars, and thus not taking advantage of economies of scale. For example, the Durango and the Jeep had different windshield wipers, and Chrysler's five teams specified three different kinds of corrosion protection for the rolled steel used to reinforce plastic bumper surfaces.[20]

Other lapses of good judgment included continuing production of old-model minivans as it was switching production to the new one, thus flooding the market. This yielding to the pressure of Schrempp was, as we have seen earlier, a major factor in the disastrous 2000 results. Could Chrysler executives have protested more vigorously? The practice of the old management to introduce new models in batches rather than spreading them over several years brought a feast or famine situation: very good years, and rather bad years in between.

External Factors

Certainly the merger was consummated at a time when the auto industry, and the economy in general, was on the threshhold of a downturn. Chrysler apparently miscalculated such an eventuality, spending heavily for costlier models just before demand turned down, and its brands were not strong enough to command higher premiums from customers. By early 2001, Chrysler was outspending all other major automakers on rebates and other incentives.

Chrysler also seemed to be oblivious to the threat of competitors during its golden years. Despite this heavy use of incentives, Chrysler lost market share for the first three months of 2001: a 14.2 percent market share versus 15.1 percent for the same three months in 2000.

Can There Really Be a Merger of Equals?

In reality there is seldom a merger of equals. Unless the two parties actually recapitalize themselves with new stock—and this is seldom done—there is always an acquirer and an acquiree. Even if both parties to the merger have equal seats on the board of directors, still the acquiring firm and its executives are more dominant. Even if the name of the new, combined firm is completely changed, this does not assure a merger of equals. For example, in a well-publicized merger "of equals" in 2000 between Bell Atlantic and GTE, the name *Verizon* was created. But no one was fooled: Bell Atlantic was in charge. Furthermore, there can be no true merger of

---

[19] As quoted in "Can the Germans Rescue Chrysler?", p. 109.
[20] *Ibid.*

equals if one firm owns more of the consolidated stock (usually reflecting its larger size) than the other, and this is almost always the case. Daimler was certainly the larger firm in this merger, having paid $36 billion for Chrysler while its own shares just before the merger had a market value of about $48 billion.

How important is this merger of equals to the executives of acquired firms? Apparently to many it is not of major consequence as long as they get a good price for their stake, or as long as they believe the acquiring firm will honor their importance. Occasionally a merger negotiation will fall apart over the issue of who will be in charge. Take the example of Lucent and Alcatel of France, two of the world's biggest makers of communications equipment: At the last minute on May 29, 2001, Henry B. Schacht, chairman of Lucent, called off the merger talks. "It started to feel more like an acquisition than a merger," one of the Lucent participants explained. They could not accept the probability that Alcatel would be in charge.[21]

WHAT CAN BE LEARNED?

Mergers are no panacea. For years, in recurrent cycles of exuberance and caution, businesses have tried to solve the problem of growth with mergers and acquisitions. What you didn't have you could acquire, faster and better than developing it yourself, so the reasoning went. The term *synergy* became widely used, especially in the 1980s, to tout the great benefits and advantages of such mergers and acquisitions. (The following Information Box describes in more detail this concept of synergy.)

Wall Street dealmakers, investment bankers, and lawyers reap the bonanza from merger activities, but many of these mergers do not work out as well as expected, and some are even outright disasters, as we will examine in the next two cases.

We have seen the cultural conflict in the DaimlerChrysler merger. But this is just one of the things that can go wrong. Many acquisition seekers are so eager to get the target company because it has strength in market share or access to strategic technologies, or because it will make their firm so much bigger in its industry (with all the glamor and prestige of large size for the executives involved) that they are prepared to pay well, and often too much. Funds for such borrowing are usually readily available, heavy debt has income tax advantages, and profits may be distributed among fewer shares so that return on equity is enhanced. But all too often the best of the acquired human assets are soon sending out resumes to prospective new employers, and the assimilation and effective consolidation of the two enterprises may be years away. Furthermore, acquiring companies may be left with mountains of debt from overambitious mergers and acquisitions, thus greatly increasing the overhead to cover with revenues before profits can be realized.

[21] For more details, see Seth Schiesel, *New York Times,* reported in *Cleveland Plain Dealer* (June 3, 2001), p. 1H.

INFORMATION BOX

SYNERGY

Synergy results from creating a whole that is greater than the sum of its parts, that can accomplish more than the total of individual contributions. In an acquisition, synergy occurs if the two firms, when combined, are more efficient, productive, and profitable than they were as separate operations before the merger. Sometimes this is referred to as $2 + 2 = 5$.

How can such synergy occur? If duplication of efforts can be eliminated, if operations can be streamlined, if economies of scale are possible, if specialization can be enhanced, if greater financial, technical, and managerial resources can be tapped or new markets made possible—then a synergistic situation is likely to occur. Such an expanded operation should be a stronger force in the marketplace than the individual single units that existed before.

The concept of synergy is the rationale for mergers and acquisitions. But sometimes combining causes the reverse: negative synergy, where the consequences are worse than the sum of individual efforts. If friction arises between the entities, if organizational missions are incompatible, if the new organizational climate creates fearful, resentful, and frustrated employees, then synergy is unlikely, at least in the short and intermediate term. Furthermore, if because of sheer optimism or an uncontrolled acquisitive drive more is paid for the acquisition than it is really worth, then we have a grand blunder. Could that have been the case with the Chrysler acquisition, in addition to the culture problem?

Do you think a typical committee or group has more synergy than the same individuals working alone? Why or why not?

Cultural differences should be considered in mergers and acquisitions. These differences—in perceptions, in customs, in ways of doing things, in prejudices—often are not given enough heed. The acquiring firm expects to bulldoze its culture on the acquired firm (despite how this may affect pride and willingness to cooperate). As we saw with the Daimler merger with Chrysler—in reality a merger of unequals—arrogance and resentments surfaced.

Should the acquiring company express its dominance quickly, or should it try to be as soothing as possible? Morale will probably not be savaged in a soothing takeover, but there can be serious problems with this approach also. We will see in Chapter 4, Maytag's English adventure, that permitting an acquisition's nationals to continue operating with little control can be a disaster waiting to happen.

How much can you trust? Both parties to a merger negotiation may express a commitment to equality. But such lip service may prove a façade. Even if executive positions are as evenly balanced as possible, one person may be a more dominant personality than the other, perhaps by dint of bigger stock ownership.

Consequently, the merger of equals becomes in name only, with any equal standing of the acquired firm existing only at the convenience of the acquirer.

Another way to bring together two companies. There is another way to bring together the strengths of two companies without the huge costs and without the morale and coordination problems of mergers and acquisitions. Strategic alliances, also called partnering, are increasingly being used by companies seeking to stimulate growth. See the following information box.

The danger of cannibalization. Cannibalization occurs when a new product takes away sales from an existing product. This is likely to occur whenever a new product is introduced, but flooding the market with the old product just before a new model introduction, as Daimler pressured Chrysler to do, is asking for headaches, and worse. DaimlerChrysler found that it took both massive rebates of the old models and well as substantial price reductions of the new ones to move the inventory—all of this destructive to profitability. The same scenario had confronted computer makers and other firms at the cutting edge of new technology. When do you let go the old model without jeopardizing lost sales in the interim?

INFORMATION BOX

STRATEGIC ALLIANCES

Some are calling this the most powerful trend to sweep American business in a century. Strategic alliances can take many forms—outsourcing, information sharing, Web consortia, joint marketing. The most extreme is a corporate partnership "wherein two proudly independent companies together spawn a new company in many ways independent of its parents." Indicative of the importance attached to this alternative to mergers and acquisitions (M&As) by major firms is the creation of a new major executive position by Coca-Cola: President of New Business Ventures, with Steven Heyer as the first outsider to be brought in as an operating president in more than 20 years. He was president of Turner Broadcasting Systems. One of his first actions was to meld Coke's noncarbonated beverages into a new joint venture with Procter & Gamble's snacks, such as Pringles chips and drinks. This partnership would start off with sales of $4 billion.

Of an estimated 10,000-plus new strategic alliances formed in 2000 were such major firms as IBM, Kmart, Wal-Mart, Pfizer, Eli Lilly, Dow Chemical, Xerox, Cisco, Microsoft, AOL, and Intel, as well as many young companies.

Critics of such partnerships raise the objection that they are likely to dissolve into disruptive squabbles in the absence of a hierarchical corporate structure. Do you think this is the Achilles heel of such new business structures? If so, is this downside worse than the negatives of M&As?

Sources: Matthew Schifrin, "Partners or Perish," *Forbes* (May 21, 2001), pp. 26–28; and James W. Michaels, "Don't Buy, Bond Instead," *Forbes* (May 21, 2001), p. 20.

We do not advocate stopping production of the older model when the new model is first announced. But it seems judicious to reduce production in the months after the announcement. Then if the newer, technologically advanced model should be more attractive, shouldn't it command a higher price than the older version? DaimlerChrysler's problems in 2000 were aggravated in that the new models were not so much technologically superior, as having expensive options that some buyers found not worth the extra money.

Let us not denigrate the desirability of cannibalizing. As products are improved, they should be brought to the marketplace as soon as possible, and not held back because there may be some cannibalization. The temptation to hold back is there, especially when the new product may have a lower profit margin than the product it is supplanting, perhaps because of competition and higher costs. Invariably, the firm that restrains an innovation because of fear of cannibalizing a high-profit product winds up making the arena attractive for competitors to gain an advantage. *Fear of cannibalization should not impede innovation.*

LATE-BREAKING NEWS

Coca-Cola and Procter & Gamble announced on September 27, 2001 that they were abandoning plans to create the $4.2 billion joint venture combining their juice and snack businesses, described in the "Strategic Alliances" Information Box. A Coke spokesman said the proposition had not proven economically attractive: "The economics of distribution of goods on trucks yields better returns through beverages than through chips." The unraveling of the deal would probably hurt P&G since it would have to deal with underperforming Pringles and Sunny Delight on its own, and might well decide to get out of this business.

Meantime, Coke was moving ahead on another joint venture, with Nestle SA of Switzerland, to develop and market coffees and teas.

* * *

Latter 2001 results for DamlierChrysler show no change for the better. The financial turnaround plan laid out earlier in the year appears scuttled as losses accelerate. Through the end of August, Chrysler spent an average $2,289 a vehicle in customer incentives, more than either Ford or GM. Despite this, market share fell below 14 percent.

* * *

A study by consulting firm Booz Allen & Hamilton, which examined 78 deals over a two-year period, found that 53 percent of those mergers fell short of their expectations. Where the acquiring company purchased a target company of comparable size, the failure rate was 67 percent.

Sources: Betsy McKay and Emily Nelson, "Coke and P&G End Plans to Form Venture for Their Juices and Snacks," *Wall Street Journal* (September 27, 2001), p. B4; Janet Whitman, "Mergers Often Look Better on Paper, Consultant's Study of 78 Deals Finds," Dow Jones News, as reported in *Cleveland Plain Dealer*, August 4, 2001, p. H3; and Jeffrey Ball, "DaimlerChrysler Turnaround Seems to Be Going in Reverse," *Wall Street Journal*, October 11, 2001, p. B4.

CONSIDER

Can you think of other learning insights?

QUESTIONS

1. Do you think Schrempp was wise to replace the top Chrysler executives? Why or why not?

2. How could Chrysler boss Robert Eaton have been so naive as to permit himself to be ousted from power in a negotiation that he actively campaigned for and accepted? Do you see any way he might have protected his position in the merger?

3. How specifically can a firm protect itself from the extreme risks of cannibalization?

4. Do you think the cultural problems could have been largely avoided in this merger? How?

5. Dieter Zetsche was sent from Stuttgart headquarters to fix all-American Chrysler, after a disastrous year 2000. On his first day in Detroit he fired the head of sales and marketing. Discuss the advisability of such a quick action, considering as many ramifications and justifications as possible.

6. Evaluate the desirability of rebates rather than regular markdowns or price cuts.

7. Do you personally think the use of Mercedes parts in Chrysler vehicles would diminish the prestige of the Mercedes brand? Would it help Chrysler that much?

8. Do you think good times can ever be lasting in the auto industry? Why or why not?

HANDS-ON EXERCISES

1. You are one of Chrysler's largest suppliers of certain parts. You are shocked at the decree by the new management of Chrysler that you must cut your prices by 5 percent immediately, and another 10 percent within two years. What do you do now? Discuss and evaluate as many courses of action as you can. You can make some assumptions, but be specific.

2. Place yourself in the position of Robert Eaton, CEO of Chrysler before the merger, and now "co-chairman" with Jurgen Schrempp. You have just been told that your services are no longer needed, that the co-chairman position has been abolished. What do you do at this point? Try to be specific and support your recommendations.

3. You are Steve Yokich, president of the United Auto Workers. You had initially endorsed the plans of Dieter Zetsche to cut costs severely, including laying off 26,000 workers and closing six plants. You had been convinced

that such downsizing was necessary to save Chrysler. Now many of your union members are storming about such arbitrary cuts. They are castigating you for supporting these plans, and you may be ousted. Discuss your actions.

TEAM DEBATE EXERCISES

1. In this case we have the great controversy of German top executives replacing American ones. Debate the desirability of such replacments versus keeping most of the American incumbents. I would suggest dividing into two groups, with one being as persuasive as possible in arguing for bringing in fresh blood from German headquarters, and the other strongly contesting this. Be prepared to attack your opponents' arguments, and defend your own.

2. Debate the desirability of mergers and acquisitions versus strategic alliances or partnerships. You may need to do some research on these two strategic alternatives. Consider the pros and cons and debate their desirabilities under different situations, such as size of firms, technological differences, and so on.

INVITATION TO RESEARCH

What is the situation with DaimlerChrysler today? Has the DaimlerChrysler stock bounced back to values before the merger? Are Chrysler cars and trucks gaining market share? Is Jurgen Schrempp still Chairman? Is Zetsche still heading up the Chrysler operation?

CHAPTER THREE

Snapple: A Sorry Acquisition

*I*n late 1994, Quaker Oats CEO William D. Smithburg bought Snapple Beverage Company for $1.7 billion. Many thought he had paid too much for this maker of non-carbonated fruit-flavored drinks and iced teas. But in a similar acquisition eleven years before he had outbid Pillsbury to buy Stokely–Van Camp, largely for its *Prior* Gatorade, then a $90 million sports drink. Despite criticisms of that purchase, *Success* Gatorade went on to become a billion-dollar brand, and Smithburg was a hero. He was not to be a hero with Snapple.

THE COMPANY, QUAKER OATS

Quaker Oats had nearly $6.4 billion in fiscal 1995 sales, of which $1.7 billion was from foreign operations. Its brands were generally strong in particular grocery products and beverage areas. In hot cereals, generations had used Quaker oatmeal, and it was still the number-three selling brand in the overall cereal category. Quaker's ready-to-eat cereals included Cap'n Crunch and Life brands. The firm was a leading competitor in the fast-growing rice cake and granola bar categories, and also in rice and pasta with its Rice-A-Roni, Pasta Roni, and Near East brands. Other products included Aunt Jemima frozen products, French toast, pancake mixes, and syrups; Celeste frozen pizza; as well as grits, tortilla flour, and corn meal.

With the purchase of Snapple, sales of its beverage operation would approach $2 billion or about one-third of total corporate sales. Gatorade alone accounted for $1.3 billion worldwide in fiscal 1995 and growth continued with sales in the United States increasing 7 percent over the previous year, while overseas the gain was a whopping 51 percent. In order to help pay for the Snapple acquisition, several mature but still moneymaking units were divested, including pet foods and chocolates.

THE SNAPPLE ACQUISITION

The Snapple brand had a modest beginning in 1972 in Brooklyn, NY, and its beverages were initially sold to health-food stores. As the healthy lifestyle became popular among certain segments of the general public, Snapple's sales for a time increased as much as 60 to 70 percent a year, especially in the Northeast and West Coast. In 1992,

TABLE 3.1   Snapple's Sales Growth, 1993–1996

	1993	%	1994	%	1995	%	1996	%
			Sales Growth (millions of dollars)					
1st quarter			$134		$112	–12%		
2nd quarter	$130		243	+87%	200	–18%	180	–10%
3rd quarter	203		191	– 6%				–20%
4th quarter	118		105	–11%				

Source: 1995 Quaker Annual Report, and various 1996 updates.

Note: While we do not have complete information for all the quarters, still the negative sales since the second quarter of 1994—before the Snapple acquisition—can be readily seen: Every quarter since then has seen losses from the same quarter the preceding year.

it was purchased for $27.9 million by Boston-based Thomas H. Lee Co., which took the now-trendy brand public and built it up to almost $700 million in sales.

Unlike Gatorade, however, Snapple faced formidable competitors, including Coke's Fruitopia and Pepsi's joint venture with Lipton, which used low prices to capture 31 percent of the iced-tea market. Snapple's growth rate had turned to declines by December 1994 when, in an outpouring of supreme confidence in his own judgment, Smithburg bought Snapple for $1.7 billion. Before long, many said he had paid about $1 billion too much. Table 3.1 shows the quarterly sales results of Snapple since June 1993 before the acquisition, and after the acquisition.

William Smithburg

At the time of the purchase, Smithburg was 56 years old, but looked younger. He liked to wear suspenders stretched tightly over muscular shoulders that he had developed from years of tournament handball. He had been CEO at Quaker Oats since 1981 and had evolved from a flashy boy wonder to a seasoned executive. He was also a fitness buff, and perhaps this colored his zeal for products like Gatorade and Snapple.

His interest in fitness developed as a result of a childhood bout with polio. While he recovered with no permanent damage, the experience shaped his life: "As soon as I started to walk and run again, I said, 'I have to stay healthy,' and it just became part of my life."[1] In his long tenure as CEO, that passion shaped Quaker, too. The company developed extensive fitness programs, including a heavily subsidized health club at headquarters. Quaker's product line, also, had increasingly emphasized low-fat foods compatible with the healthy lifestyle.

Indicative of Smithburg's personality, after graduating from DePaul University in 1960 with a BS degree in economics and marketing, he defied his

---

[1] Greg Burns, "Crunch Time At Quaker Oats," *Business Week* (September 23, 1996), p. 72.

father by quitting his first job only three days later. He decided to enroll in Northwestern's business school.

With an MBA in hand he joined the Leo Burnett ad agency, and later, McCann Erickson. After five years of ad agency experience, he went to Quaker as brand manager for frozen waffles in 1966. There it took him ten years to become executive vice president of U.S. grocery products, Quaker's biggest division. Five years later in 1981 he became CEO, and was named chairman two years after that.

The same year he became chairman, he acquired Stokely–Van Camp, overbidding Pillsbury's $62-per-share bid with a $77 offer, which carried a price tag of $238 million. His own investment banker considered this too steep, and critics in the business press abounded. But Smithburg had done his homework, and his intuition was prescient. He recognized the potential in Stokely's Gatorade, a sport drink meant to replenish lost salts and fluids of athletes. "I'd been drinking Gatorade myself, and I knew the product worked."[2] A $90 million brand in 1983, by 1996 this was a $1.3 billion brand and held 80 percent of the growing sport-drink market.

Somehow, Smithburg did not do his homework well with Snapple, despite its seeming similarity to Gatorade.

Rationale for the Snapple Purchase

Snapple was the largest acquisition in Quaker's history. The *Quaker Oats 1995 Annual Report* discussed the rationale for this purchase and the "growth opportunity it offers to shareholders":

> Snapple appeals to all ages with its incomparable flavor variety in premium iced teas and juice drinks. Current sales are concentrated in the Northeast and West Coast. So, the rest of the country presents fertile territory for developing the brand. Because of its excellent cold-channel distribution, the Snapple brand has taught us a great deal about reaching consumers outside our traditional grocery channels. We can apply this knowledge to Gatorade thirst quencher, thereby enhancing its availability as well.[3]

So, Smithburg saw great opportunity to expand distribution of Snapple geographically from its present regional concentration. He thought it had wide appeal and that it could enhance sales of the already highly successful Gatorade.

Snapple beverages held good regional market positions in both the premium ready-to-drink tea and single-serve juice-drink categories. It was seemingly well positioned if consumer preferences continued to shift to all-natural beverages—and away from highly carbonated, artificially flavored, and chemically preserved soft drinks. Apparently not the least of the reasons for Smithburg's infatuation with Snapple was that it had a "sexy aura," even though problems were already emerging when he bought it. He liked to contrast it with Quaker's pet food: Pet food "was a dead, flat business with five or six big companies beating their brains out in it."[4] So, it was not

---

[2] *Ibid.*, p. 74.

[3] *Quaker Oats 1995 Annual Report*, p. 6.

[4] Burns, p. 74.

Sell off pet food

surprising that the pet food business, which had been acquired less than nine years before, was sold a few months after Snapple was acquired.

Other speculations as to why Smithburg chased Snapple, besides misreading the growth potential, were that he wanted to make Quaker, which was a hotly rumored acquisition candidate, less vulnerable to a takeover. Some even speculated that Smithburg became bored with Quaker and sought the excitement of a splashy deal.[5]

PROBLEMS

One would think that Snapple's resemblance to Gatorade would bring instant compatibility and efficiencies in marketing the two brands. After all, with the proven success of Gatorade, Quaker had become the third-largest beverage company, after only Coca-Cola and Pepsi. And, like Gatorade, Snapple was a flavored, noncarbonated drink. Surely this was a compatible marriage. *Looks Good*

But this was not the case. Only after it bought Snapple did Quaker fully realize that both Snapple's production and distribution systems were completely different from Gatorade's.

Quaker's production and distribution of Gatorade was state of the art. Its computers were closely integrated with those of its largest distributors and automatically kept these distributors well stocked, but not overstocked, with Gatorade.

The advertising of Gatorade was also markedly different. Several hundred million dollars a year was spent for Gatorade, with highly successful ads featuring Chicago Bulls star, Michael Jordan (Jordan was also a personal friend of Smithburg). Snapple's advertising, on the other hand, had run out of steam and was notably ineffective.

The production, distribution, and marketing efforts of Snapple at the time of the purchase were haphazard. Bottling was contracted to outsiders, and this resulted in expensive contracts for excess capacity when demand slowed. Snapple's 300 distributors delivered directly to stores; Gatorade's distributors delivered to warehouses. Quaker's efforts to consolidate the two distribution systems only created havoc. It tried to take the supermarket accounts away from Snapple distributors and give them to Gatorade, directing that the Snapple people concentrate on convenience stores and mom-and-pop retailers. Not surprising, Snapple distributors refused this downsizing of their operations. Eventually, Quaker backed down. But efforts at creating coordination and distribution efficiencies for 1995 were seriously delayed.

At the same time, Quaker failed to come up with a new business plan for Snapple in time for the peak 1995 season, which began in April. Tim Healy, president of a Snapple distributor in Chicago, noted, "there was no marketing plan, no initiatives, and no one to talk to [at Quaker]."[6]

The result was that 1995 sales of Snapple fell 9 percent, and there was a $100 million loss.

---

[5] *Ibid.*

[6] Scott McMurray, "Drumming Up New Business: Quaker Marches Double Time to Put Snap Back in its Snapple Drink Line," *U.S. News & World Report* (April 22, 1996), p. 59.

CORRECTIVE EFFORTS, 1996

As the dismal results of 1995 became widely publicized, Quaker faced the urgent need to vindicate the purchase of Snapple and somehow resurrect its failing fortunes. To aid the distributors, the company streamlined operations to reduce from two weeks to three days the time it took to get orders from bottlers to distributors. To do so, it coordinated its computers with the top 50 distributors, who represented 80 percent of Snapple's sales, so that it could replenish their inventory automatically, the way it was doing with Gatorade.

The company also introduced some packaging and product changes that it hoped would be more appealing both to dealers and to customers. It brought out 32- and 64-ounce plastic bottles of Snapple for families, along with 12-packs and 4-packs in glass bottles. It reduced the number of flavors from 50 to 35 and made taste improvements in some of the retained flavors. At the same time seasonal products were introduced, such as cider tea for Halloween.

To develop distributor enthusiasm, a two-day meeting had been held in San Diego. Quaker brought in comedian Bill Cosby to entertain and General Norman Schwarzkopf to motivate with a stirring speech on leadership. Then distributors were told that highly visible Snapple coolers would be placed in supermarkets, convenience stores, and schools—just like Coke and Pepsi.[7]

The weakness in the 1995 advertising also received, hopefully, corrective action. Quaker enlisted the creativity of Spike Lee, who had designed hyperkinetic TV commercials for Nike. While the campaign kept Snapple's "Made from the best stuff on earth," the new ads focused on Snapple's hope to become America's third choice in soft drinks, behind Coke and Pepsi, with such slogans as, "We want to be No. 3," and "Threedom = freedom." The goal of the advertising campaign, Smithburg explained, was to maintain Snapple's "funky" image while broadening its appeal beyond the East and West Coast markets.[8]

Still, sales languished. In late July, a huge nationwide sampling campaign was undertaken. In a $40 million effort, millions of bottles of the fruit-juice and ice-tea lines were given away during the height of the selling season, hopefully to spur consumer interest regardless of cost.

RESULTS OF 1996 EFFORTS

Unfortunately, the results of the summer giveaways were dismal. Instead of gaining market share during the important summer selling months, Snapple lost ground.

Snapple tea sales fell 14 percent, and juice sales fell 15 percent. This compared poorly with industry tea sales, which also dropped, but only 4 percent, and industry juice sales, which fell 5 percent during a particularly cool summer in the Northeast.[9]

---

[7] Zina Moukheiber, "He Who Laughs Last," *Forbes* (January 1, 1996), p. 42.

[8] *Ibid.*, p. 60.

[9] "Snapple Continues to Lose Market Share Despite Big Giveaway," *Wall Street Journal* (October 8, 1996), p. B9.

Relentless media scrutiny even found fault with the way in which Snapple was being given away. One critic observed the sampling at a New Jersey concert in which 16-ounce cans were handed out only 20 feet from the entrance in front of signs prohibiting food or drink beyond the gate. Most people barely had time to taste the drink before throwing it away. Furthermore, "for its brand undermining efforts, Quaker gets no consumer research either. Solution: In exchange for the self-serve sample, ask a few short … questions."[10]

The reputation of Smithburg was being eroded, his early success with Gatorade not enough to weather more current adversity. Online, cybercritics assailed him. In conference calls with financial analysts, he was peppered with barbed questions about this $600 million beverage for which he paid $1.7 billion. "Even my dad," Smithburg laughed, "he says, 'What are you doing with Snapple?'"[11]

Under pressure, Smithburg cast off president and chief operating officer Philip Marineau, whom he had been grooming as heir apparent for many years. This departure was widely interpreted to be the result of Snapple's failure to justify its premium pricing, with Marineau the scapegoat. Nine months later, Donald Uzzi was replaced as president of Quaker's North America beverages unit. His successor was Michael Schott, former vice president of sales of Nantucket Nectars, a small, privately held drink maker.

Some critics assumed that Smithburg's job was in jeopardy, that he could not escape personal blame for the acquisition snafu. Still, the past success of Smithburg with Gatorade continued to sustain him. The board of directors remained supportive, although they denied him any bonus for 1995. What made the continued loyalty of the board more uncertain was Quaker's stock price, which had fallen 10 percent since just before the acquisition, even as the Standard & Poor's 500-stock index had climbed to new highs.

If Snapple could not be revitalized, Smithburg had several options regarding it. All of these, of course, would be admissions of defeat and that a major mistake was made in acquiring Snapple. Any one of them might cost Smithburg his job.

One option would be to spin off the ailing Snapple to shareholders, perhaps under the wing of the booming Gatorade. Smithburg was no stranger to such maneuverings since he had divested retail, toy, and pet-food operations in his years as CEO. An outright sale could probably only be made at bargain-basement prices and would certainly underscore the billion-dollar mistake of Smithburg's purchase. A less extreme option would be to draw back from attempts to make Snapple a national brand, and keep it as a regional brand in the Northeast and West Coast where it was well entrenched.

Perseverance

By early 1997 Smithburg still had not given up on Snapple. Quaker Oats announced it was pumping $15 million into a major four-month sweepstakes promotion for Snapple's

[10] Gabe Lowry, "They Can't Even Give Snapple Away Right," *Brandweek* (September 30, 1996), p. 16.

[11] Burns, p. 71.

diet drinks, this to start right after the new year when consumers might be more concerned with undoing the excesses of the holiday season and when competitors would be less likely to advertise chilled drinks in cold weather. The theme was to be "Escape with Taste," and among other winners would be 50 grand-prize trips to the refurbished Doral Resort and Spa in Miami. If the campaign developed any momentum, it should carry over to a retooled image campaign planned immediately afterward in the spring.

This promotion was the first from new president Mike Schott, and it built on one product category that managed to grow 16 percent in convenience stores during the previous summer, even as core juices and teas slid drastically. The promotion plan was well received by distributors: "This one [promotion] is wonderfully thought out," one distributor said. "Diet drinks in the first quarter? It's a no-brainer."[12]

Since being named the brand's president late in the year, Schott had been visiting distributors to build up relations, offer greater support, and dispel rumors that Snapple was going to retrench to a regional brand. Still, Snapple's sales and profits showed no rebound.

On March 27, 1997, Smithburg finally threw in the towel; he sold the ailing Snapple to Nelson Peltz, chief executive of the smallish Triarc Cos., owner of RC Cola and Arby's restaurants. The price was shockingly low, only $300 million, or just over half of Snapple's $550 million in sales—this for a brand for which Smithburg had paid $1.7 billion only three years before. The founder of Snapple, Leonard Marsh, who had previously sold his controlling interest, said that "they stole the company."[13]

Undoubtedly, Quaker was desperate to sell the money-draining Snapple, but at such a fire-sale price? As it turned out, the company had few options. Major suitors, such as PepsiCo, Coca-Cola, and Procter & Gamble, only wanted to consider a Snapple purchase along with Gatorade, Smithburg's crown jewel and most profitable brand.

On April 24, 1997, The *Wall Street Journal* reported that Quaker Oats had posted a $1.11 billion quarterly loss reflecting the final resolution of the Snapple affair, and that William Smithburg was stepping down. "Many investors have been asking for a long time why he hasn't stepped aside sooner," said one food-industry analyst.[14]

ANALYSIS

Beyond doubt the price paid for Snapple was wildly extravagant. Demand was slumping, distribution inefficiencies had surfaced, and the advertising had run out of steam. We can understand Smithburg's reasoning that he had bought Gatorade at a high price and turned it into a winner. Why shouldn't he do the same thing with Snapple? The price paid for Gatorade, $238 million for sales of $90 million at the time, was roughly comparable to the $1.7 billion for Snapple sales of almost $700 million.

[12] Gerry Khermouch, "Snapple Diet Line Gets $15 mil Push," *Brandweek* (November 4, 1996), p. 1.

[13] I. Jeanne Dugan, "Will Triarc Make Snapple Crackle?" *Business Week* (April 28, 1997), p. 64.

[14] Michael J. McCarthy, "Quaker Oats Posts $1.11 Billion Quarterly Loss," *Wall Street Journal* (April 24, 1997), pp. A3, A12.

But we can surely fault Smithburg for not demanding that his subordinates analyze more thoroughly the compatibility of the two operations. There should have been no surprises after the sale that the distribution systems of Gatorade and Snapple were not compatible and maybe could not be made so. Furthermore, it seems only reasonable to expect for a purchase of this magnitude that adequate research and planning would also have been done concerning the promotional efforts of Snapple, whether they were adequate for the coming year or whether changes needed to be made, and, if so, what changes. Should not stockholders expect that rather solid business plans would be in place before the acquisition was finalized by Quaker? Without such, the decision to let go of $1.7 billion seems rather like decision making by hunch and intuition. Perhaps it was.

The spinning of wheels in 1996, after the disastrous 1995, suggests that Smithburg had fallen prey to the decision-making error called *escalating commitment*. This is a resolution to increase efforts and resources to pursue a course of action that is *not* working, to be unable to "call it quits."[15]

See the following Information Box for advice by John Schermerhorn on not being trapped in an escalation commitment.

throw good
after good. *See No Evil*
$ of

INFORMATION BOX

HOW TO AVOID THE ESCALATION TRAP

When should we call it quits, admit the mistake, and leave the scene as gracefully as possible, amid the cries of critics and the debris of sunk costs in a hopeless cause, and even embarrassment and shame and possible ouster by a board of directors tormented by irate investors? John Schermerhorn offers these guidelines to avoid staying in a lost cause too long:[16]

1. Set advance limits on your involvement in a particular course of action, and stick to them.
2. Make your own decisions; others may also be prone to escalation.
3. Carefully consider why you are continuing this course of action; unless there are sufficient reasons to continue, don't.
4. Consider the costs of continuing, and the savings in costs as a reason to discontinue.
5. Be on guard for escalation tendencies, especially where a big commitment has already been made.

Do you think Drucker's idea of an escalating commitment and Schermerhorn's suggestions for avoiding it have any downsides? In other words, when do you call it quits?

---

[15] Peter F. Drucker, "The Global Economy and the Nation-State," *Foreign Affairs*, vol. 76 (September–October 1997), pp. 159–171.

[16] John R. Schermerhorn, Jr., *Management*, 6th ed. (New York: Wiley, 1999), p. 67.

You can imagine how the big commitment that had already been made for Snapple would have stimulated the escalating commitment to the fullest: "We have too much invested for this for fail."

If the product life cycle of Snapple had peaked before the Quaker purchase, this would account for the inability of Quaker management to reverse the downward trend of sales and profits. But such a possibility should surely have been considered before the acquisition decision. (See the following Information Box for a discussion of the product life cycle.)

One would think that the best minds in a major corporation, and any outside consultants used, should have been able to bring Snapple to more healthy national and

---

INFORMATION BOX

THE PRODUCT LIFE CYCLE

Just as people and animals do, products go through stages of growth and maturity—that is, life cycles. They are affected by different competitive conditions at each stage, ranging often from no competition in the early stages to intense competition later on. We can recognize four stages in a product's life cycle: introduction, growth, maturity, and decline.

Figure 3.1 depicts three different product life cycles. Number 1 is that of a standard item in which sales take some time to develop and then eventually begin a slow decline. Number 2 shows a life cycle for a product in which a modification of the product or else the uncovering of a new market rejuvenates the product so that it takes off on a new cycle of growth (the classic examples of this are Listerine, originally sold as a mild external antiseptic, and Arm & Hammer Baking Soda, which was repositioned as a deodorizer). Number 3 shows the life cycle for a fad item or one experiencing rapid technological change and intense competition. Notice its sharp rise in sales and the abrupt downturn.

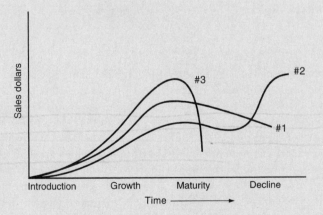

Figure 3.1   The product life cycle.

(continues)

THE PRODUCT LIFE CYCLE *(continued)*

Which life cycle most closely represented Snapple at the time of the acquisition? Snapple was definitely on a downward trend, which began the summer before Quaker purchased it, and this downward trend continued and even accelerated through 1995 and 1996. (See Table 3.1.) This suggests that Snapple had reached the maturity stage of its life cycle. As an admittedly trendy product, its curve in the worst scenario would resemble stage 3, the fad. An optimistic scenario would see a stage 2-curve, with strong efforts in 1997 bringing a rejuvenation. Perhaps the more likely life cycle is something akin to stage 1, with a slow downturn continuing for a lengthy period while aggressive efforts fail to stem the decline in an environment of more intense competition and less eager demand.

Do you agree with this prognosis? Why or why not?

international sales, or at least to a more profitable situation, even if the product life cycle had become less favorable. But in high-stake, near-crisis situations, prudent judgment may be abandoned as money is flung about in desperate efforts to turn things around. Often such merely aggravates the situation, as was the case with the expensive and poorly planned $40 million sampling effort and the $15 million sweepstakes program.

Finally, it is worth emphasizing again that in the acquisition quest, extensive homework should be done. These are *major* decisions. Hundreds of millions of dollars, even billions, are at stake if an unwise acquisition has to be divested a few years later. In addition, there is the management time taken up with a poorly performing product line at the expense of other responsibilities.

UPDATE

Quaker's Gatorade remained a great strength of the company, having an estimated 78 percent of the sport-drink market. This made Quaker an attractive acquisition. In 2000, Coca-Cola was interested in buying Quaker, but faced a sticker price of $16 billion that its board of directors, among them Warren Buffett, one of the country's most astute investors, decided to reject.

Just a few months later, PepsiCo bid $14.02 billion, which Quaker accepted. The deal was expected to close by the end of June 2001, but federal antitrust enforcers continued to raise objections. Federal Trade Commission concern was that this merger would give Quaker's Gatorade brand even greater dominance once it became part of Pepsi's powerful distribution network. Coca-Cola's Powerade brand share was only 15 percent of the sport-drink market, while Pepsi's All-Sport, which the company agreed to sell, was a distant third. Opponents of the deal argued that it would enable Pepsi to gain too much clout with retailers, particularly convenience stores where Gatorade and other Pepsi products such as Mountain Dew were already strong. As this is written, FTC approval was still pending, although the deal had already been approved by several foreign regulators, including the European Union's antitrust authority.[17]

WHAT CAN BE LEARNED?

The illusion of compatibility. Bad acquisition decisions—in which the merger or acquisition turns out to be a mistake—often result from miscalculating the mutual compatibility of the two operations. Expectations are that consolidating various operations will result in significant cost savings. For example, instead of two headquarters' staffs, these can be reduced perhaps to a beefed-up single one. Sometimes even certain aspects of production can be combined, allowing some facilities to be closed for greater cost efficiencies. Computer operations, sales forces, and distribution channels might be combined. But for these combinations and consolidations to be feasible, the two operations essentially should be compatible.

As we saw in the case, the distribution channels of Snapple and Gatorade were not compatible, and efforts to consolidate brought serious rancor from those who would be affected. Quaker had failed to do its homework and probe deeply enough to determine the real depth of compatibility, not merely assuming compatibility because of product similarities.

Certainly we see many acquisitions and mergers of dissimilar operations: These are called *diversifications*. Some of these have little or no compatibility, and may not provide significant opportunities for reducing costs. Instead, they may be made because of perceived growth opportunities, to lessen dependence on mature products, to smooth out seasonality, and so on. Unfortunately, many of these dissimilar diversifications prove to be disappointing, and are candidates for divestiture some years later.

The acquisition contest. Once an acquisition candidate is identified, negotiations sometimes become akin to an athletic contest: Who will win? Not infrequently, several firms may be drawn to what they see as an attractive would-be acquisition, and a bidding war commences. Sometimes management of the takeover firm strongly resists. So, the whole situation evolves into a contest, almost a game. And aggressive executives get caught up in this game and sometimes overreach themselves in their struggle to win. No matter how attractive a takeover firm might be, if you pay way too much for it, this was a bad buy.

The paradox of perseverance: When do we give up? We admire people who persevere despite great odds: the student who continues with school even though family and work commitments may drag it out for ten years or more; the athlete

---

[17] John R. Wilke and Betsy McKay, "PepsiCo Cites FTC for Further Delay of Quaker Deal," *Wall Street Journal* (June 11, 2001), p. B6.

who never gives up; the author who has a hundred rejection slips, but still keeps trying. So, how long should we persevere in what seems totally a losing cause? Isn't there such a thing as futility and unrealistic dreams, so that constructive efforts should be directed elsewhere? The engima of futility has even been captured in classic literature with Don Quixote, the "Man from LaMancha," tilting his lance at windmills.

The line is blurred between perseverance and futile stubbornness, the escalating commitment of Peter Drucker. Circumstances vary too much to formulate guidelines. Still, if a direct assault continues to fail, perhaps it is time to make an end run.

When should a weak product be axed? Weak products tend to take up too much management, sales force, and advertising attention, efforts that could better be spent making healthy products better and/or developing replacements. Publicity about such products may even cause customer misgivings and tarnish the company's image. This suggests that weak and/or unprofitable products or divisions ought to be gotten rid of, provided that the problems are enduring and not a temporary aberration.

Not all weak products should be pruned, however; rationale for keeping them may be strong. In particular, the weak products may be necessary to complete a line to benefit sales of other products. They may be desirable for customer goodwill. Some weak products may enhance the company's image or prestige. Although such weak products make no money in themselves, still their intrinsic value to the firm may be substantial. Other weak products may merely be unproven, too new in their product life cycle to have become profitable; in their growth and maturity stage they may contribute satisfactory profits. Finally, possibly a new business strategy will rejuvenate the weak product. That is the hope, and the proffered justification for keeping a weak product when its demise is overdue.

So, where did Snapple fit into this theoretical discussion? The only justification for procrastination would seem to be that business strategy alternatives to turn around the brand had not been exhausted. In the meantime, the image of Quaker Oats in the eyes of investors, and the reflection of this in stock prices, was being savaged.

Be cautious with possible fad product life cycles. With hindsight, we can classify Snapple's popularity as a short-term phenomenon. But it was heady and contagious while it lasted. Snapple transformed iced tea into a new-age product by avoiding the need for preservatives and adding fruit flavors and introducing innovative wide-mouth, 16-ounce bottles. It also used Howard Stern, with his cult following, as its spokesman.

The public offering of stock in 1993 was sensational. The original offering price was to be $14, but this was raised to $20; in the first day of trading the stock closed at $29. Two years later, Quaker paid $1.7 billion for a company whose founders paid just $500 to acquire the name. But the euphoric life cycle was turning down, and the cult following was distracted by imitators, such as Arizona Iced Tea, Mystic, and Nantucket Nectars, as well as Coke and Pepsi through alliances with Nestea and Lipton.

Perhaps what can be learned is that product life cycles are unpredictable, especially where they involve fad or cult followers who may be as fickle as the wind, and where imitation is easy. To bet one's firm on such an acquisition can be risky indeed. But in truth, Smithburg had faced a similar situation with Gatorade, and won big. The moral: Decision making under uncertainty can be a crap game. But prudence suggests a more cautious approach.

CONSIDER

Can you think of any other learning insights?

QUESTIONS

1. Why do you think the great Snapple giveaway was ineffective?
2. Do you think Snapple could have been turned around? Why or why not?
3. Do you think the premium retail price for Snapple was a serious impediment? Why or why not?
4. "Pouring more money into a lost cause is downright stupid. Smithburg has got to go." Discuss.
5. "This isn't a case where a guy has gone from a genius to a dummy. Who's better at running the company?"[18] Discuss this statement.
6. "What's all the fuss about? Snapple is doing great on our college campus. It's a success, man." Do you agree? Why or why not?
7. Do you drink Snapple? If not, why not? Is so, how often, and how well do you like it?
8. Do you think Snapple should have been sold for $300 million? Why or why not?

HANDS-ON EXERCISES

Before

1. A major decision is at hand. You are a vice president of the beverage operation at Quaker. William Smithburg is proposing the acquisition of Snapple for some huge sum. Before this decision is made, you have been asked to array any contrary arguments to this expensive acquisition, in other words, to be a devil's advocate (one who takes a contrary position for the sake of argument and clarification of opposing views). What concerns would you raise, and how would you defend them?

[18] Investor quote in Burns, p. 74.

After

2. It is late 1996. You are the assistant to Michael Schott, who has just been named president of Snapple. He asks you to formulate a strategic plan for resurrecting Snapple for 1997. What do you propose? Be as specific as you can, and be prepared to defend your recommendations.

TEAM DEBATE EXERCISE

The acquisition of Snapple is accomplished. Now begins the assimilation. A major debate has ensued regarding whether Snapple should be consolidated with Gatorade, or whether it should remain an independent entity. Debate the two positions as persuasively as possible. Be sure to identify any assumptions made.

INVITATION TO RESEARCH

What is the situation with Snapple and with Smithburg today? Has Snapple prospered under its new ownership? Is Smithburg running any company? Has Quaker been acquired, and, if so, by whom and at what price?

CHAPTER FOUR

Maytag: Leaving a Foreign Subsidiary Free as a Bird

Hadley took over after the debacle was underway.

The atmosphere at the annual meeting in the little Iowa town of Newton had turned contentious. As Leonard Hadley faced increasingly angry questions from disgruntled shareholders, the thought crossed his mind: "I don't deserve this!" After all, he had only been CEO of Maytag Corporation for a few months, and this was his first chairing of an annual meeting. But the earnings of the company had been declining every year since 1988, and in 1992, Maytag had had a $315.4 million loss. No wonder the stockholders in the packed Newton High School auditorium were bitter and critical of their management. But there was more. Just the month before, the company had the public embarrassment and costly atonement resulting from a monumental blunder in the promotional planning of its United Kingdom subsidiary.

1993

Hadley doggedly saw the meeting to its close, and limply concluded: "Hopefully, both sales and earnings will improve this year."[1]

THE FIASCO

In August 1992, Hoover Limited, Maytag's British subsidiary, launched this travel promotion: Anyone in the United Kingdom buying more than 100 UK pounds' worth of Hoover products (about $150 in American dollars) before the end of January 1993 would get two free round-trip tickets to selected European destinations. For 250 UK pounds' worth of Hoover products, they would get two free round-trip tickets to New York or Orlando.

The deal → $375

A buying frenzy resulted. Consumers had quickly figured out that the value of the tickets easily exceeded the cost of the appliances necessary to be eligible for them. By the tens of thousands, Britishers rushed out to buy just enough Hoover products to qualify. Appliance stores were emptied of vacuum cleaners. The Hoover factory in Cambuslang, Scotland that had been making vacuum cleaners only three days a week was suddenly placed on a 24-hour, seven-days-a-week production

Duh !!

[1] Richard Gibson, "Maytag's CEO Goes Through Wringer at Annual Meeting," *Wall Street Journal* (April 28, 1993), p. A5.

41

↑ $ Costs

schedule—an overtime bonanza for the workers. What a resounding success for a promotion! Hoover managers, however, were unhappy.

Why Not?

Hoover had never expected more than 50,000 people to respond. And of those responding, it expected far less would go through all the steps necessary to qualify for the free trip and really take it. But more than 200,000 not only responded but qualified for the free tickets. The company was overwhelmed. The volume of paperwork created such a bottleneck that by the middle of April only 6,000 people had flown.

P.R. ∴
DISASTER

Thousands of others either never got their tickets, were not able to get the dates requested, or waited for months without hearing the results of their applications. Hoover established a special hotline to process customer complaints, and these were coming in at 2,000 calls a day. But the complaints quickly spread, and the ensuing publicity brought charges of fraud and demands for restitution. This raises the issue of loss leaders—How much should we use loss leaders as a promotional device?—discussed in the following Issue Box.

Maytag dispatched a task force to try to resolve the situation without jeopardizing customer relations any further. But it acknowledged that it's "not 100 percent clear" that all eligible buyers will receive their free flights.[2] The ill-fated promotion

---

ISSUE BOX

SHOULD WE USE LOSS LEADERS?

Leader pricing is a type of promotion with certain items advertised at a very low price—sometimes even below cost, in which case they are known as loss leaders—in order to attract more customers. The rationale for this is that such customers are likely to purchase other regular-price items as well with the result that total sales and profits will be increased. If customers do not purchase enough other goods at regular prices to more than cover the losses incurred from the attractively priced bargains, then the loss-leader promotion is ill advised. Some critics maintain that the whole idea of using loss leaders is absurd: The firm is just "buying sales" with no regard for profits.

While UK Hoover did not think of their promotion as a loss leader, in reality it was: They stood to lose money on every sale if the promotional offer was taken advantage of. Unfortunately for its effectiveness as a loss leader, the likelihood of customers purchasing other Hoover products at regular prices was remote, and the level of acceptance was not capped, so that losses were permitted to multiply. The conclusion has to be that this was an ill-conceived idea from the beginning. It violated these two conditions of loss leaders: They should stimulate sales of other products, and their losses should be limited.

Do you think loss leaders really are desirable under certain circumstances? Why or why not?

---

[2] James P. Miller, "Maytag U.K. Unit Find a Promotion Is Too Successful," *Wall Street Journal* (March 31, 1993), p. A9.

[handwritten: $30 mill charge in 1 quarter]

was a staggering blow to Maytag financially. It took a $30 million charge in the first quarter of 1993 to cover unexpected additional costs linked to the promotion. Final costs were expected to exceed $50 million, which would be 10 percent of UK Hoover's total revenues—this for a subsidiary acquired only four years before that had yet to produce a profit.

Adding to the costs were problems with the two travel agencies involved. The agencies were to obtain low-cost space available tickets, and would earn commissions selling "packages," including hotels, rental cars, and insurance. If consumers bought a package, Hoover would get a cut. However, despite the overwhelming demand for tickets, most consumers declined to purchase the package, thus greatly reducing support money for the promotional venture. So, Hoover greatly underestimated the likely response, and overestimated the amount it would earn from commission payments. *[handwritten: WHY ??]*

If these cost-overruns added greatly to Maytag and Hoover's customer relations and public image, the expenditures would have seemed more palatable. But with all the problems, the best that could be expected would be to lessen the worst of the agitation and charges of deception. And this was proving to be impossible. The media, of course, salivated at the problems and were quick to sensationalize them: *[handwritten: MEDIA CIRCUS]*

> One disgruntled customer, who took aggressive action on his own, received the widest press coverage, and even became a folk hero. Dave Dixon, claiming he was cheated out of a free vacation by Hoover, seized one of the company's repair vans in retaliation. Police were sympathetic: they took him home, and did not charge him, claiming it was a civil matter.[3]

Heads rolled also. Initially, Maytag fired three UK Hoover executives involved, including the president of Hoover Europe. Mr. Hadley, at the annual meeting, also indicated that others might lose their jobs before the cleanup was complete. He likened the promotion to "a bad accident ... and you can't determine what was in the driver's mind."[4]

The issue receiving somewhat less publicity was why corporate headquarters allowed executives of a subsidiary such wide latitude that they could saddle parent Maytag with tens of millions in unexpected costs. Did not top corporate executives have to approve ambitious plans? A company spokesman said that operating divisions were "primarily responsible" for planning promotional expenses. While the parent may review such outlays, "if they're within parameters, it goes through."[5] This raises the issue, discussed in the following Issue Box, of how loose a rein foreign subsidiaries should be allowed. *[handwritten: lack of control]*

---

[3] "Unhappy Brit Holds Hoover Van Hostage," *Cleveland Plain Dealer* (June 1, 1993), p. D1; and Simon Reeve and John Harlow, "Hoover Is Sued Over Flights Deal," *London Sunday Times* (June 6, 1993).

[4] Gibson, "CEO Goes Through Wringer," p. A5.

[5] Miller, "Maytag UK Unit," p. A9.

ISSUE BOX

HOW LOOSE A REIN FOR A FOREIGN SUBSIDIARY?

In a decentralized organization, top management delegates considerable decision-making authority to subordinates. Such decentralization—often called a "loose rein"—tends to be more marked with foreign subsidiaries, such as UK Hoover. Corporate management in the United States understandably feels less familiar with the foreign environment and more willing to let the native executives operate with less constraints than it might with a domestic subsidiary. In the Maytag/Hoover situation, decision-making authority by British executives was evidently extensive, and corporate Maytag exercised little operational control, being content to judge performance by ultimate results achieved. Major deviations from expected performance goals, or widespread traumatic happenings—all of which happened to UK Hoover—finally gained corporate management attention.

Major advantages of extensive decentralization or a loose rein are: First, top management effectiveness can be improved since time and attention is freed for presumably more important matters; second, subordinates are permitted more self-management, which should improve their competence and motivation; and third, in foreign environments, native managers presumably better understand their unique problems and opportunities than corporate management, located thousands of miles away, possibly can. But the drawbacks are as we have seen: Parameters within which subordinate managers operate can be so wide that serious miscalculations may not be stopped in time. Since top management is ultimately responsible for all performance, including actions of subordinates, it faces greater risks with extensive decentralization and giving a free rein.

"Since the manager is ultimately accountable for whatever is delegated to subordinates, then a free rein reflects great confidence in subordinates." Discuss.

BACKGROUND ON MAYTAG

Maytag is a century-old company. The original business, formed in 1893, manufactured feeder attachments for threshing machines. In 1907, the company moved to Newton, Iowa, a small town 30 miles east of Des Moines, the capital. Manufacturing emphasis turned to home-laundry equipment, and wringer-type washers.

A natural expansion of this emphasis occurred with the commercial laundromat business in the 1930s, when coin meters were attached to Maytag washers. Rapid growth of these coin-operated laundries took place in the United States during the late 1950s and early 1960s. The 1970s hurt laundromats with increased competition and soaring energy costs. In 1975, Maytag introduced new energy-efficient machines, and "Home Style" stores that rejuvenated the business.

The Lonely Maytag Repairman

For years Maytag reveled in a coup, with its washers and dryers enjoying a top-quality image, thanks to decades-long ads in which a repairman laments his loneliness

TABLE 4.1   Maytag Operating Results, 1974–1981
(in millions)

	Net Sales	Net Income	Percent of Sales
1974	$229	$21.1	9.2%
1975	238	25.9	10.9
1976	275	33.1	12.0
1977	299	34.5	11.5
1978	325	36.7	11.3
1979	369	45.3	12.3
1980	346	35.6	10.2
1981	409	37.4	9.1

Average net income percent of sales: 10.8%

Source: Company operating statistics.

Commentary: These years show a steady, though not spectacular growth in revenues, and a generally rising net income, except for 1980. Of particular interest is the high net income percentage of sales, with this averaging 10.8 percent over the 8-year period, with a high of 12.3 percent.

because of Maytag's trouble-free products.[6] The result of this dependability and quality image was that Maytag could command a price premium: "Their machines cost the same to make, break down as much as ours—but they get $100 more because of the reputation," grumbled a competitor.[7]

During the 1970s and into the 1980s, Maytag continued to capture 15 percent of the washing machine market, and enjoyed profit margins about twice that of competitors. Table 4.1 shows operating results for the period 1974–1981. Whirlpool was the largest factor in the laundry equipment market, with a 45 percent share, but this was largely because of sales to Sears under the Sears brand.

Acquisitions

For many years, until his retirement December 31, 1992, Daniel J. Krumm had influenced Maytag's destinies. He had been CEO for 18 years and chairman since 1986, and his tenure with the company encompassed 40 years. In that time, the home-appliance business encountered some drastic changes. The most ominous occurred in the late 1980s with the merger mania, in which the threat of takeovers by hostile raiders often motivated heretofore conservative executives to greatly increase corporate indebtedness, thereby decreasing the attractiveness of their firms. Daniel Krumm was one of these running-scared executives, as rumors persisted that the company was a takeover candidate.

[6] Jesse White, the actor who first portrayed this repairman, died in early 1997.
[7] Brian Bremmer, "Can Maytag Clean Up Around the World?" *Business Week* (January 30, 1989), p. 89.

TABLE 4.2   Maytag Operating Results, 1989–1992

	Revenue	Net Income	% of Revenue
	(000,000)		
1989	$3.089	131.0	4.3%
1990	3,057	98.9	3.2
1991	2,971	79.0	2.7
1992	3,041	(315.4)	(10.4)

Source: Company annual reports.

Commentary: Note the steady erosion of profitability, while sales remained virtually static. For a comparison with profit performance of earlier years, see Table 4.1 and the net income to sales percentages of this more "golden" period.

POISON PILL

Largely as a defensive move, Krumm pushed through a deal for a $1 billion buyout of Chicago Pacific Corporation (CPC), a maker of vacuum cleaners and other appliances with $1.4 billion in sales. As a result, Maytag was burdened with $500 million in new debt. Krumm defended the acquisition as giving Maytag a strong foothold in a growing overseas market. CPC was best known for the Hoover vacuums it sold in the United States and Europe. Indeed, so dominant was the Hoover brand in England that many people did not vacuum their carpets, but "hoovered the carpet." CPC also made washers, dryers, and other appliances under the Hoover brand, selling them exclusively in Europe and Australia. In addition, it had six furniture companies, but Maytag sold these shortly after the acquisition.

Krumm had been instrumental in transforming Maytag, the number-four U.S. appliance manufacturer—behind General Electric, Whirlpool, and Electrolux—from a niche laundry-equipment maker into a full-line manufacturer. He had led an earlier acquisition spree in which Maytag had expanded into microwave ovens, electric ranges, refrigerators, and freezers. Its brands now included Magic Chef, Jenn-Air, Norge, and Admiral. The last years of Krumm's reign, however, were not marked by great operating results. As shown in Table 4.2, revenues showed no gain in the 1989–1992 period, while income steadily declined.

Trouble

Although the rationale for internationalizing seemed inescapable, especially in view of a recent wave of joint ventures between U.S. and European appliance makers, still the Hoover acquisition was troublesome. While it was a major brand in England and in Australia, Hoover had only a small presence in Europe. Yet, this was where the bulk of the market was, with some 320 million potential appliance buyers.

The probabilities of the Hoover subsidiary being able to capture much of the European market were hardly promising. Whirlpool was strong, having ten plants there in contrast to Hoover's two plants. Furthermore, Maytag faced entrenched European competitors such as Sweden's Electrolux, the world's largest appliance

Too Much entrenched Competition

maker; Germany's Bosch-Siemens; and Italy's Merloni Group. General Electric had also entered the market with joint ventures. The fierce loyalty of European to domestic brands raised further questions as to the ability of Maytag's Hoover to penetrate the European market without massive promotional efforts, and maybe not even then.

Australia was something else. Hoover had a good competitive position there, and its refrigerator plant in Melbourne could easily be expanded to include Maytag's washers and dryers. Unfortunately, the small population of Australia limited the market to only about $250 million for major appliances.

Australia

Britain accounted for half of Hoover's European sales. But at the time of the acquisition its major appliance business was only marginally profitable. This was to change: After the acquisition it became downright unprofitable, as shown in Table 4.3 for the years 1990 through 1992, as it struggled to expand in a recession-plagued Europe. The results for 1993, of course, reflected the huge loss from the promotional debacle—hardly an acquisition made in heaven.

recession

Maytag's earlier acquisitions also were becoming soured. Its acquisitions of Magic Chef and Admiral were diversifications into lower-priced appliances, and these did not meet expectations. But they left Maytag's balance sheet and its cash flow weakened (see Table 4.4). Perhaps more serious, Maytag's reputation as the nation's premier appliance maker became tarnished. Meanwhile, General Electric and Whirlpool were attacking the top end of its product line. As a result, Maytag found itself in the number-three or -four position in most of its brand lines.

Cheap appliances hurt image

TABLE 4.3 Operating Results of Maytag's Principal Business Components, 1990–1992

	Revenue (000,000)	Income[a] (000)
1990		
North American Appliances	$2,212	$221,165
Vending	191	25,018
European Sales	497	(22,863)
1991		
North American Appliances	2,183	186,322
Vending	150	4,498
European Sales	486	(865)
1992		
North American Appliances	2,242	129,680
Vending	165	16,311
European Sales	502	(67,061)

Source: Company annual reports.

[a] This is operating income, that is, income before depreciation and other adjustments.

Commentary: While these years had not been particularly good for Maytag in growth of revenues and income, the continuing, and even intensifying, losses in the Hoover European operation had to be troublesome. And this is before the ill-fated early 1993 promotional results.

TABLE 4.4   **Long-Term Debt as a Percent of Capital from Maytag's Balance Sheets, 1986–1991**

Year	Long-Term Debt/Capital
1986	7.2%
1987	23.3
1988	48.3
1989	46.8
1990	44.1
1991	42.7

Source: Company annual reports.

Commentary: The effect of acquisitions, in particular that of the Chicago Pacific Corporation, can be clearly seen in the buildup of long-term debt: In 1986, Maytag was virtually free of such commitments; two years later its long-term debt ratio had increased almost sevenfold.

ANALYSIS

Flawed Acquisition Decisions

The long decline in profits after 1989 should have triggered strong concern and corrective action. Perhaps it did, but the action was not effectual as the decline continued, culminating in a large deficit in 1992 and serious problems in 1993. As shown in Table 4.2, the acquisitions brought neither revenue gains nor profitability. One suspects that in the rush to fend off potential raiders in the late 1980s, the company bought businesses it might never have under more sober times, and that it also paid too much for these businesses. Further, they cheapened the proud image of quality for Maytag.

Who Can We Blame in the UK Promotional Debacle?

Corporate Maytag management was guilty of a common fault in their acquisitions: It gave newly acquired divisions a loose rein, letting them continue to operate independently with few constraints: "After all, these executives should be more knowledgeable about their operations than corporate headquarters would be." Such confidence is sometimes misguided. In the UK promotion, Maytag management would seem as derelict as management in England. Planning guidelines or parameters were far too loose and undercontrolled. The idea of subsidiary management being able to burden the parent with $50 million of unexpected charges, and to have such erupt with no warning, borders on the absurd.

Finally, the planning of the UK executives for this ill-conceived travel promotion defies all logic. They vastly underestimated the demand for the promotional offer and they greatly overestimated paybacks from travel agencies on the package deals. Yet, it took no brilliant insight to realize that the value of the travel offer exceeded the price of the appliance—indeed, 200,000 customers rapidly arrived at this conclusion—and that such a sweetheart of a deal would be irresistible to many, and that it could prove to be costly in the extreme to the company. A miscalculation, or complete naivete on the part of executives and their staffs who should have known better?

How Could the Promotion Have Avoided the Problems?

The great problem resulting from an offer too good could have been avoided, and this without scrapping the whole idea. A cost-benefit analysis would have provided at least a perspective as to how much the company should spend to achieve certain benefits, such as increased sales, greater consumer interest, and favorable publicity. See the Information Box for a more detailed discussion of the important planning tool of a cost-benefit analysis.

INFORMATION BOX

COST-BENEFIT ANALYSIS

A cost-benefit analysis is a systematic comparison of the costs and benefits of a proposed action. Only if the benefits exceed the costs would we normally have a "go" decision. The normal way to make such an analysis is to assign dollar values to all costs and benefits, thus providing a common basis for comparison.

Cost-benefit analyses have been widely used by the Defense Department in evaluating alternative weapons systems. In recent years, such analyses have been sporadically applied to environmental regulation and even to workplace safety standards. As an example of the former, a cost-benefit analysis can be used to determine if it is socially worth spending X million dollars to meet a certain standard of clean air or water.

Many business decisions lend themselves to a cost-benefit analysis. It provides a systematic way of analyzing the inputs and the probable outputs of particular major alternatives. While in the business setting some of the costs and benefits can be very quantitative, they often should be tempered by nonquantitative inputs to reach the broadest perspective. Schermerhorn suggests considering the following criteria in evaluating alternatives:[8]

Benefits: What are the "benefits" of using the alternatives to solve a performance deficiency or take advantage of an opportunity?

Costs: What are the "costs" to implement the alternatives, including direct resource investments as well as any potential negative side effects?

Timeliness: How fast will the benefits occur and a positive impact be achieved?

Acceptability: To what extent will the alternatives be accepted and supported by those who must work with them?

Ethical soundness: How well do the alternatives meet acceptable ethical criteria in the eyes of multiple stakeholders?

What numbers would you assign to a cost-benefit analysis for Maytag Hoover's plan to offer the free airline tickets, under an assumption of 5,000 takers? 20,000 takers? 100,000 takers? 500,000 takers? (Make any assumptions needed as to costs.) What would be your conclusions for these various acceptance rates?

---

[8] John R. Schermerhorn, Jr., *Management*, 6th ed. (New York: Wiley, 1999), p. 61.

A cost-benefit analysis should certainly have alerted management to the possible consequences of various acceptance levels, and of the significant risks of high acceptance. However, the company could have set limits on the number of eligibles: perhaps the first 1,000, or the first 5,000. Doing this would have held or capped the costs to reasonably defined levels, and avoided the greater risks. Or the company could have made the offer less generous, perhaps by upping the requirements, or by lessening the premiums. Such more moderate alternatives would still have made an attractive promotion, but not the major uncontrolled catastrophe that happened.

FINALE

Pull out

Maytag's invasion of Europe proved a costly failure. In the summer of 1995, Maytag gave up. It sold its European operations to an Italian appliance maker, recording a $135 million loss.

Even by the end of 1996, the Hoover mess was still not cleaned up. Hoover had spent $72 million flying some 220,000 people and had hoped to end the matter. But the fight continued four years later, with disgruntled customers who never flew taking Hoover to court. Even though Maytag had sold this troubled division, it still could not escape emerging lawsuits.

Update—Leonard Hadley

In the summer of 1996, Leonard Hadley could look forward and backward with some satisfaction. He would retire the next summer when he turned 65, and he had already picked his successor. Since assuming the top position in Maytag in January 1993 and confronting the mess with the UK subsidiary his first few months on the job, he had turned Maytag completely around.

He knew no one expected much change from him, an accountant who had joined Maytag right out of college. He was known as a loyal but unimaginative lieutenant of his boss, Daniel Krumm, who died of cancer shortly after naming Hadley his successor. After all, he reflected, no one thought that major change could come to an organization from someone who had spent his whole life there, who was a clone so to speak, and an accountant to boot. Everyone thought that changemakers had to come from outside, like Al Dunlap of Scott Paper and Sunbeam (described in Chapter 5). Well, he had shown them, and given hope to all number-two executives who resented Wall Street's love affair with outsiders.

Within a few weeks of taking over, he'd fired a bunch of managers, especially those rascals in the UK who'd masterminded the great Hoover debacle. He determined to get rid of foreign operations, most of them newly acquired and unprofitable. He just did not see that appliances could be profitably made for every corner of the world, because of the variety of regional customs. Still, he knew that many disagreed with him about this, including some of the board members who thought globalization was the only way to go. Still, over the next 18 months he had prevailed.

follower → leader

He chuckled to himself as he reminisced. He had also overturned the decades-long corporate mindset not to be first to market with new technology because they would "rather be right than be first." His "Galaxy Initiative" of nine top-secret new products was a repudiation of this old mindset. One of them, the Neptune, a front-loading washer retailing at $1,100, certainly proved him right. Maytag had increased its production three times and raised its suggested retail price twice, and still it was selling like gangbusters. Perhaps the thing he was proudest of was getting Maytag products in Sears stores, the seller of one-third of all appliances in the United States. Sears's desire to have the Neptune was what swung the deal.

As an accountant, he probably should be focusing first on the numbers. Well, 1997 was certainly a banner year with sales up 10.9 percent over the previous year, while profitability as measured by return on capital was 16.7 percent, both sales and profit gains leading the industry. And 1998 so far was proving to be even better, with sales jumping 31 percent and earnings 88 percent.

He remembered the remarks of Lester Crown, a Maytag director: "Len Hadley has—quietly, softly—done a spectacular job. Obviously, we just lacked the ability to evaluate him [in the beginning]."[9]

Leonard Hadley retired on August 12, 1999. He knew he had surprised everyone in the organization by going outside Maytag for his successor. He was Lloyd Ward, 50, Maytag's first black executive, a marketing expert from PepsiCo, and before that Procter & Gamble, who had joined Maytag in 1996 and was currently president and chief operating officer.

Hadley's choice of successor proved to be flawed, or maybe Ward was just a victim of circumstances mostly beyond his control. After 15 months, Ward left citing differences with Maytag's directors amid sorry operating results. Hadley came out of retirement to be interim president and CEO. Some 3,400 Maytag workers, a quarter of Newton's population, roared when they heard the news. They had feared the company would be moved to either Chicago or Dallas, or that it would be sold to Sweden's Electrolux. Hadley assured them that such would never happen as long as he's at the helm.[10]

15 mo. on the job

HAKE

WHAT CAN BE LEARNED?

Again—beware overpaying for an acquisition. Hoping to diversify its product line and gain overseas business, Maytag paid $1 billion for Chicago Pacific in 1989. As it turned out, this was far too much, and the debt burden was an albatross. Hadley conceded as much: "In the long view, it was correct to invest in these businesses.

[9] Carl Quintanilla, "Maytag's Top Officer, Expected to Do Little, Surprises His Board," *Wall Street Journal* (June 23, 1998), pp. A1, A8.

[10] "Maytag Chief Quits as Profits Plummet," *Cleveland Plain Dealer* (November 10, 2000), p. 3C; and Emily Gersema, "Maytag Re-hires Former CEO After Time of Internal Turmoil, *Wall Street Journal* (January 15, 2001), p. 3H.

But the timing of the deal, and the price of the deal, made the debt a heavy burden to carry."[11]

Zeal to expand, and/or the desire to reduce the attractiveness of a firm's balance sheet with heavy debt and thus fend off potential raiders, do not excuse foolhardy management. The consequences of such bad decisions remain to haunt a company, and the ill-advised purchases often have to be eventually sold off at substantial losses (as we saw in the previous case). The analysis of potential acquisition candidates must be soberly and thoroughly done, and rosy projections questioned, even if this means the deal may be soured.

In decision planning, consider a worst-case scenario. There are those who preach the desirability of positive thinking, confidence, and optimism—whether it be in personal lives, athletics, or business practices. But expecting and preparing for the worst has much to commend it, since a person or a firm is then better able to cope with adversity and to avoid being overwhelmed, and more likely to make prudent rather than rash decisions.

Apparently the avid acceptance of the promotional offer was a complete surprise; no one dreamed of such demand. Yet, was it so unreasonable to think that a very attractive offer would meet wild acceptance?

In using loss leaders, put a cap on potential losses. Loss leaders, as we noted earlier, are items promoted at such attractive prices that the firm loses money on every sale. The expectation, of course, is that the customer traffic generated by such attractive promotions will increase sales of regular profit items so that total profits will be increased.

The risks of uncontrolled or uncapped loss leader promotions are vividly shown in this case. For a retailer who uses loss leaders, the loss is ultimately capped as the inventory is sold off. With UK Hoover there was no cap. The solution is clear: Attractive loss leader promotions should be capped, such as the first 100 or the first 1,000 or for one week only. Otherwise, the promotion should be made less attractive.

Beware giving too loose a rein, thus sacrificing controls, especially of unproven foreign subsidiaries. Although decentralizing authority down to lower ranks is often desirable and results in better motivation and management development than centralization, it can be overdone. At the extreme, where divisional and subsidiary executives have almost unlimited decision-making authority and can run their operations as virtual dynasties, then corporate management essentially abdicates its authority. Such looseness in an organization endangers cohesiveness; it tends to obscure common standards and objectives; and it can even dilute unified ethical practices.

Such extreme looseness of controls is not uncommon with acquisitions, especially foreign ones. It is easy to make the assumption that these executives were operating successfully before the acquisition and have more firsthand knowledge of the environment than the corporate executives.

---

[11] Kenneth Labich, "Why Companies Fail," *Fortune* (November 14, 1994), p. 60.

Still, there should be limits on how much freedom these executives should be permitted—especially when their operations have not been notably successful. In Maytag's case, the UK subsidiary had lost money every year since it was acquired. Accordingly, one would expect prudent corporate management to have condoned less decentralization and insisted on tighter controls that it might otherwise.

The power of a cost-benefit analysis. For major decisions, executives have much to gain from a cost-benefit analysis. It forces them to systematically tabulate and analyze the costs and benefits of particular courses of action. They may find that likely benefits are so uncertain as to not be worth the risk. If so, now is the time to realize this, rather than after substantial commitments have already been made.

Without doubt, regular use of cost-benefit analyses for major decisions improves executives' batting averages for good decisions. Even though some numbers may have to be judgmental, especially as to probable benefits, the process of making this analysis forces a careful look at alternatives and most likely consequences. For more important decisions, input from diverse staff people and executives will bring greater power to the analysis.

CONSIDER

What other learning insights can you add?

QUESTIONS

1. How could the promotion of UK Hoover have been better designed? Be as specific as you can. *limits / sliding scale*

2. Given the fiasco that did occur, how do you think Maytag should have responded? *Blew a PR opportunity*

3. "Firing the three top executives of UK Hoover is unconscionable. It smacks of a vendetta against European managers by an American parent. After all, their only 'crime' was a promotion that was too successful." Comment on this statement. *More damage to image*

4. Do you think Leonard Hadley, the Maytag CEO for only two months, should be soundly criticized for the UK situation? Why or why not?

5. Please speculate: Why do you think this UK Hoover fiasco happened in the first place? What went wrong? *No CB analysis. No contingency plan.*

6. Evaluate the decision to acquire Chicago Pacific Corporation (CPC). Do this both for the time of the decision, and for now—after the fact—as a post mortem. Defend your overall conclusions.

7. Use your creativity: Can you devise a strategy for UK Hoover to become more of a major force in Europe?

8. Evaluate the reflections of Hadley in the summer of 1998. Do you agree with all of his convictions and actions? Why or why not?

HANDS-ON EXERCISES

1. You have been placed in charge of a task force sent by headquarters to England to coordinate the fire-fighting efforts in the aftermath of the ill-fated promotion. There are neither enough productive capacity nor enough airline seats available to handle the demand. How would you propose to handle this situation? Be as specific as you can and defend your recommendations.

2. As a staff vice president at corporate headquarters, you have been charged to develop companywide policies and procedures that will prevent such a situation from ever occurring again. What would you recommend?

TEAM DEBATE EXERCISE

How tightly should you supervise and control a foreign operation? This Maytag example suggests very tightly. But is this an aberration, unlikely to be encountered again? Debate the issue of very tight controls versus relative freedom for foreign operations.

INVITATION TO RESEARCH

How has Maytag done since Leonard Hadley came back to replace his chosen successor, Lloyd Ward? Is Maytag's headquarters still in Newton, Iowa? Is Maytag still independent or has it been acquired? Can you find further information on the Hoover operation?

PART TWO

CHANGE AND CRISIS MANAGEMENT

CHAPTER FIVE

Scott Paper, Sunbeam, and Al Dunlap

Al Dunlap was hired in July 1996 by two large Sunbeam investors to turn Sunbeam around. He had gained a reputation as a turnaround artist extraodinaire, most recently from his efforts at Scott Paper. His philosophy was to cut to the bone, and the press frequently called him "Chainsaw Al." He met his comeuppance with Sunbeam. In the process, his philosophy came under bitter attack. But was his strategy all that bad?

ALBERT J. DUNLAP

Dunlap wrote an autobiography, *Mean Business*, of his business philosophy and how it had evolved. He grew up in the slums of Hoboken, the son of a shipyard worker, and was imbued with the desire to make something of himself. He played football in high school and graduated from West Point. A former army paratrooper, he was known as a quick hitter, a ruthless cost cutter, a tough boss. But he got results, at least short-term.

In 1983, he became chief executive of Lily Tulip Co., a maker of disposable cups that was heavily in debt after a buyout. Dunlap quickly exhibited the management philosophy that was to make him famous. He slashed costs, decimating the headquarters staff, closing plants, and selling the corporate jet. When he left in the mid-1980s, the company was healthy. In the latter 1980s. Dunlap became the number-one operations man for Sir James Goldsmith, a notorious raider of corporations. Dunlap was involved in restructuring Goldsmith's acquisitions of Crown-Zellerbach and International Diamond. In 1991, he worked on a heavily debt-laden Australian conglomerate, Consolidated Press Holdings. Two years later, after his "chainsaw approach," Consolidated Press was 100 divisions lighter and virtually free of debt.

By now Dunlap was a wealthy man, having made close to $100 million on his various restructurings. Still, at 56, he was hardly ready to retire. When the board of Scott Paper heard that he was available, they wooed him, even purchasing his $3.2 million house in Florida from him.

SCOTT PAPER—A SICK COMPANY— AND DUNLAP'S RESULTS

An aged Scott Paper was reeling in the early 1990s. Per-share earnings had dropped 61 percent since 1989 on flat sales growth. In 1993, the company had a $277 million loss.

Part of the problem stemmed from Scott's commercial paper division, S. D. Warren. In 1990, the company spent to increase capacity at Warren. Unfortunately, the timing could not have been worse. One of the worst industry slumps since the Great Depression was just beginning. Three subsequent "restructurings" had little positive effect.

Table 5.1 shows the decline in sales from 1990 through 1993. Table 5.2 shows the net income and loss during these four years. Of even more concern was Scott's performance relative to the major competitors Procter & Gamble and Kimberly-Clark during these four years. Table 5.3 shows the comparisons of profits as a percent of sales, with Scott again showing up most poorly. Undoubtedly this was a company needing fixing.

In characteristic fashion, Dunlap acted quickly once he took over as chief executive officer on April 19, 1994. That same day to show his confidence and commitment, he invested $2 million of his own money in Scott. A few months later, after the stock had appreciated 30 percent, he invested another $2 million.

Only hours on the job, Dunlap offered three of his former associates top positions in the company. On the second day, he disbanded the powerful management committee. On the third day, he fired 9 of the 11 highest-ranking executives. To

TABLE 5.1   Sales of Scott, 1990–1993 (billions)

1990	$3.9
1991	3.8
1992	3.9
1993	3.6
Total change, 1990–1993	(7.7%)

Source: Company annual reports.

Commentary: The company's deteriorating sales come at a time of great economic growth and advancing revenues for most firms.

TABLE 5.2   Net Income of Scott and Percent of Sales, 1990–1993

	(millions)	% of sales
1990	$148	3.8%
1991	(70)	(1.8)
1992	167	4.3
1993	(277)	(7.7)

Source: Company annual reports.

Commentary: The company's erratic profit picture, culminating in the serious loss of 1993, deserved deep concern, which it received.

TABLE 5.3   Profit as a Percentage of Sales: Scott, Kimberly-Clark, and Procter & Gamble, 1990–1993

	1990	1991	1992	1993
Scott	3.8%	(1.8%)	4.3%	(7.7%)
P&G	6.6	6.6	6.4	(2.1)°
Kimberly-Clark	6.8	7.5	1.9	7.3

Source: Company annual reports.

° Extraordinary charges reflecting accounting changes.

Commentary: Scott again shows up badly against its major competitors, both in the low percentage of earnings to sales and their severe fluctuations into earnings losses.

ISSUE BOX

HOW SOON TO INTRODUCE DRASTIC CHANGES?

Some new administrators believe in instituting major changes as quickly as possible. They reason that an organization is expecting this and is better prepared to make the adjustments needed than it ever will be again. Such managers are often referred to as gunslingers. who "shoot from the hip." Other managers believe in moving more slowly, gathering more information, and taking action only when all the pros and cons can be weighed. But sometimes such delays can lull an organization into a sense of false calm, and make for even more trauma when the changes eventually come.

Relevant to the issue of moving swiftly or slowly is the health of the entity. If a firm is sick, in drastic need of help, we would expect a new manager to move more quickly and decisively. A firm doing well, although perhaps not as well as desired, reasonably should not require such drastic and abrupt disruption.

It has always baffled me how a fast-acting executive can acquire sufficient information to make the crucial decisions of who to fire and who to retain and what operations need to be pruned and which supported—all within a few days. Of course, operating statistics can be studied before formally taking charge. But the causes of the problems or successes—the whys—can hardly be understood so soon.

Boards, investors, and creditors want a fast turnaround. Waiting months before taking action to fix a sick company is not acceptable. However, not all companies are easily fixable. For example, Borden, a food and chemical conglomerate, has gone through the fifth restructuring in six years, with little improvement. But maybe Borden needed an Albert Dunlap, the person with a clear vision and a willingness to clean house. And, yes, a supportive board.

Do you think Dunlap acted too hastily in his initial sweeping changes? Playing the devil's advocate (one who takes an opposing view for the sake of debate), support a position that he did indeed act far too hastily.

complete his blitzkrieg, on the fourth day he destroyed four bookshelves crammed with strategic plans of previous administrations.

Can such drastic and abrupt changes be overdone? Should change be introduced more slowly and with more reflection? See the Issue Box on the previous page for a discussion of this.

At the annual meeting in June, barely two months after assuming command, Dunlap announced four major goals for the first year. First, he vowed to divest the company of nonstrategic assets, most notably S. D. Warren, the printing and publishing papers subsidiary, that had received major expansion funding only a few years before. Second he would develop a core team of accomplished senior managers. Third, Scott was to be brought to "fighting trim" through a one-time-only global restructuring. Last, he promised to develop new strategies for marketing Scott products around the world.

In one of the largest relative restructurings in corporate America, more than 11,000 positions out of a total of 25,900 were eliminated around the world. This included 71 percent of the headquarters staff, 50 percent of the salaried employees, and 20 percent of the production workers. Such draconian measures certainly cut costs. But were they overdone? Might such cuts potentially have detrimental long-term consequences? Please see the following Issue Box for a discussion of this.

In addition to cutting staff, Dunlap sought to reduce other costs, including outsourcing some operations and services. If these could be provided cheaper by other firms, then they should be farmed out. Dunlap announced that with the restructuring completed by year-end, pre-tax savings of $340 million were expected.[1]

ISSUE BOX

HOW DEEP TO CUT?

Bloated bureaucratic organizations are the epitome of inefficiency and waste, whether in business corporations or in governmental bodies, including school systems. Administrative overhead might even exceed actual operating costs. But remedies can be overdone, they can go too far. In Scott's case, was the axing of 11,000 employees out of 25,900 overdone?

Although we are not privy to the needed cost/productivity records, we can raise some concerns. Did the massive layoffs go well beyond fat and bloat into bone and muscle? If so, future operations might be jeopardized. Another concern ought to be: Does an organization owe anything to its loyal and long-standing employees, or should they simply be considered pawns in the pursuit of maximizing profits? Where do we draw the line between efficiency and responsibility to faithful employees? And even to the community itself?

You may want to consider some of these questions and issues. They are current in today's downsizing mindset.

---

[1] The New Scott, 1994 Annual Report, p. 5.

By late fall of 1994, Dunlap's plans to divest the company of nonstrategic assets bore fruit. S. D. Warren was sold for $1.6 billion to an international investment group. Other asset sales generated more than $2 billion, with as much as $3 billion expected when completed. This enabled Dunlap to lower debt by $1.5 billion and repurchase $300 million in Scott stock. This led to the credit rating being upgraded.

The results of Dunlap's efforts were impressive indeed. Second-quarter earnings rose 71 percent; third-quarter earnings increased 73 percent, the best quarterly performance for Scott in four years. Fourth-quarter earnings were 159 percent higher than in 1993, establishing an all-time quarterly record. For the whole year, net income increased 82 percent over the previous year. And the stock price performance since April 19, when Dunlap took over, stood at the top 1 percent of major companies traded on the New York Stock Exchange.[2]

Still, the cost-slashing was not helping market share. In the fiscal year ended April 2, 1995, Scott's bath-tissue sales in key U.S. markets slipped 1 percent, while in paper towels, Scott lost 5.2 percent in sales.[3]

On July 17, 1995, Dunlap's efforts to make Scott an attractive acquisition candidate were capped by Kimberly-Clark's $7.36 billion offer for the firm. In the process, Dunlap himself would be suitably rewarded, leaving far richer than after any of his seven previous restructuring efforts. But Dunlap insisted, "I am still the best bargain in corporate America."[4]

THE SUNBEAM CHALLENGE

Sunbeam is a maker of blenders, electric blankets, and gas grills. These old-line products had shown little growth potential, and revenues and profits languished. After the well-publicized turnaround success of Dunlap, it was not surprising he was courted for the top job at Sunbeam, and he entered the fray with gusto.

The day he was hired, Sunbeam stock rose 50 percent, "on faith." It eventually rose 300 percent. With his customary modus operandi he terminated half of Sunbeam's 12,000 employees and cut back its product offerings. Gone were such items as furniture and bed linens, and efforts were concentrated on things like grills, humidifers, and kitchen appliances. In 1996, he took massive writeoffs amounting to $338 million, of which almost $100 million was inventory.

In 1997, it looked like Dunlap was accomplishing another of his patented "miracles." Sales were up 22 percent to $1.168 billion, while income had risen from a loss of $196 million the previous year to a gain of $123 million in 1997. For stockholders this translated into earnings per share of $1.41 from $2.37 loss in 1996. Table 5.4 shows the trend in revenues and income of Sunbeam through 1997.

In October 1997, barely a year on the job, Dunlap announced that the turnaround was complete and that he was seeking a buyer for Sunbeam. Stockholders had much to be pleased about. From a low of $12 a share in 1996, the price had risen to

---

[2] *Ibid.*, p. 6.

[3] Joseph Weber and Paula Dwyer, "Scott Rolls Out a Risky Strategy," *Business Week* (May 22, 1995), p. 48.

[4] Joann S. Lublin and Steven Lipin, "Scott Paper's 'Rambo in Pin Stripes' Is on the Prowl for Another Company to Fix" *Wall Street Journal* (July 18, 1995), p. B1.

TABLE 5.4   Trend of Sunbeam Revenues and Income, 1991–1997

	1991	1992	1993	1994	1995	1996	1997
				(millions $)			
Revenues	886	967	1,066	1,198	1,203	964	1,168
Net Income	47.4	65.6	88.8	107	50.5	−196	123

Source: Company annual reports.

Commentary: Dunlap came on the scene in July 1996, the year that Sunbeam incurred $196 million in losses. The $123 million profit for 1997 showed a remarkable and awesome recovery, and would seemingly make Dunlap a hero with his slash-and-burn strategy. Unfortunately, a reaudit did not confirm these figures. The inaccurate figures were blamed on questionable accounting, including prebooking sales and incorrectly assigning costs to the restructuring. The auditors said the company overstated its loss for 1996, and overstated profits for 1997. The revised figures showed a loss of $6.4 million for 1997, instead of the $123 million profit. (*Sources:* Martha Brannigan, "Sunbeam Audit to Repudiate '97 Turnaround," *Wall Street Journal*, October 20 1998, p. A3; and "Audit Shows Sunbeam's Turnaround Really a Bust," *Cleveland Plain Dealer*, October 21, 1998, pp. 1-C and 2-C.)

$50. Unfortunately, this high price for Sunbeam stock took it out of the range for any potential buyer; $50 gave a market capitalization of $4.6 billion, or four times revenues, a multiple reserved for only a few of the premier companies. So, for the time being the stockholders were stuck with Dunlap.

Since he was not successful in selling the company, Dunlap went on a buying binge. He began talking about his "vision," with such words as "We have moved from constraining categories to expanding categories. Small kitchen appliances become kitchen appliances. We'll move from grills to outdoor cooking. Health care moves from just a few products to a broad range of products."[5]

So, he bought Coleman Company, Signature Brands and its Mr. Coffee, and First Alert for an aggregate of approximately $2.4 billion in cash and stock. Part of this was financed with $750 million of convertible debentures, as well as $60 million of accounts receivable that were sold to raise cash. Critics maintained he had paid too much for these, especially the $2.2 billion for money losing Coleman. The effect of these acquisitions on Sunbeam's balance sheet was sobering if any stockholders had looked closely.

When Dunlap took over Sunbeam, though it was performing poorly, it had only $200 million in debt. By 1998, Sunbeam was over $2 billion in debt, and its net worth had dropped from $500 million to a negative $600 million.[6]

THE DEBACLE OF 1998, AND THE DEMISE OF DUNLAP

The first quarter of 1998 showed a complete reversal of fortunes. Revenues were down and a first-quarter loss was posted of $44.6 million—all this far below expectations. Sunbeam's stock price plunged 50 percent, from $53 to $25. By midsummer it was to reach a low of $4.62.

Dunlap conceded that he and top executives had concentrated their attention too much on "sealing" the acquisitions of Coleman and the two smaller companies, allow-

[5] As quoted in Holman W. Jenkins, Jr., "Untalented Al? The Sorrows of a One-Trick Pony," *Wall Street Journal* (June 24, 1998), p. A19.

[6] Matthew Schifrin, "The Unkindest Cuts," *Forbes* (May 4, 1998), p. 45.

ing underlings to offer "stupid, low-margin deals" on outdoor cooking grills. He pointed to glitches with new products, a costly recall, and El Niño. "People don't think about buying outdoor grills during a storm," he said. "Faced with sluggish sales, a marketing executive offered excessive discounts," he further said. More job cuts were promised, through eliminating one-third of the jobs at the newly acquired companies.[7]

On Monday, June 15, after deliberating over the weekend, Sunbeam's board abruptly fired Al Dunlap, having "lost confidence in his ability to carry out the long-term growth potential of the company."[8] Now a legal fight ensued as to what kind of severance package, if any, Dunlap deserved as a consequence of his firing. A severance package for Mr. Dunlap would be "obscene—an obscenity on top of an obscenity, capitalism gone crazy," said Michael Cavanaugh, union leader.[9] Other comments were reported in the media; a sampling is in the following Information Box.

INFORMATION BOX

THE POPULARITY OF "CHAINSAW" AL DUNLAP

Not surprising, the slashing policy of Dunlap did not bring him a lot of friends, even though he may have been admired in some circles. The following are some comments reported in the press, immediately following his firing:

> He finally got what he's been doing to a lot of people. It was a taste of his own medicine. (union representative)
> I'm happy the son-of-a-bitch is fired. (former supervisor)
> Somebody at that company finally got some sense. (small-town mayor)
> I couldn't think of a better person to deserve it. It tickled me to death. We may need to have a rejoicing ceremony. (small-town mayor)
> I guess the house of cards came tumbling down ... when you reduce your workforce by 50 percent, you lose your ability to manage. (former plant manager)

Is there a lesson to be learned from such comments as these? Perhaps it is that the human element in organizations and communities needs to be considered.

Taking a devil's advocate position (one who takes an opposing viewpoint for the sake of argument and full discussion), defend the philosophy of Dunlap.

Sources: Thomas W. Gerdel, "Workers at Glenwillow Plant Cheer Firing of 'Chainsaw' Al," *Cleveland Plain Dealer* (June 16, 1998), 2-C; and "No Tears for a Chainsaw," *Wall Street Journal* (June 16, 1998), p. B1.

---

[7] James R. Hagerty and Martha Brannigan, "Sunbeam Plans to Cut 5,100 Jobs as CEO Promises Rebound from Dismal Quarter," *Wall Street Journal* (May 12, 1998), pp. A3 and A4.

[8] Martha Brannigan and James Hagerty, "Sunbeam, Its Prospects Looking Ever Worse, Fires CEO Dunlap," *Wall Street Journal* (June 15, 1998), pp. A1 and A14.

[9] Martha Brannigan and Joann S. Lublin, "Dunlap Faces a Fight Over His Severance Pay," *Wall Street Journal* (June 16, 1998), p. B3.

After Dunlap's departure, some accounting irregularities began coming to light. At the end of a three-month audit, the "turnaround" that Dunlap announced for 1997 apparently was tainted. Rather than a turnaround, the good results came from improper accounting moves that adversely affected 1996 and 1998 results, while making 1997, the first full year of Dunlap's leadership, seem far better than it really was. The restated numbers showed that Sunbeam actually had a small operating loss in 1997, while 1996 showed a modest profit.

The inaccurate figures came from dubious accounting, including premature booking sales in 1997 that should have been 1998, incorrectly assigning certain costs to the restructuring, as well as certain other questionable accounting irregularities. Dunlap denied any involvement or knowledge of such matters and that any accounting changes by the auditors were "judgment calls" on matters subject to interpretation.[10]

On May 15, 2001, the Securities and Exchange Commission in a suit charged that Al Dunlap and some of his executives including the company's chief accountant broke securities laws to make Sunbeam look healthier and more attractive for a buyer. Shareholders had made similar allegations in fraud suits as Sunbeam fell into bankruptcy from a $5 billion market capitalization. The troubles appear not to be over for the once high-flying Dunlap.[11]

ANALYSIS

Was Dunlap's Management Style of "Slash and Burn" Appropriate?

We see conflicting evidence in the Scott and Sunbeam cases. Without doubt, he achieved his goal to make Scott an attractive acquisition candidate, and thus reward shareholders and himself. That he did this so quickly seems a strong endorsement of his strategy for turning around sick companies—simply decimate the organization, sell off all ancillary units, cut costs to the bone, and virtually force the company into increased profitability.

The flaw with this reasoning is that it tends to boost short-term performance at the expense of the longer term. Morale and dedication of surviving employees are often devastated. Vision and innovative thinking may be impeded, since the depleted organization lacks time and commitment to deal effectively with more than day-to-day basic operations.

His strategy backfired with Sunbeam. When he couldn't sell the company after massaging the performance statistics for 1997, he was left with a longer-term management challenge, and he was by no means up to this. It is ironic that his reputation for turning around sick companies acted against him with Sunbeam. Investors were so confident of his ability to quickly turn around the company that they bid up the price so high that no one would buy it. And they were stuck with Dunlap.

---

[10] Martha Brannigan, "Sunbeam Slashes Its 1997 Earnings in Restatement," *Wall Street Journal* (October 21, 1998), p. B23.

[11] "SEC Says Sunbeam Ex-execs Fudged the Company's Books," *Wall Street Journal*, May 16, 2001, pp. 1C, 3C.

Yet, many firms have become too bureaucratic, burdened with high overhead and chained to established policies and procedures. Such organizations desperately need paring down, eliminating bloated staff and executive levels, and, not the least, curbing the red tape that destroys flexibility and creativity.

The best answer lies in moderation, cutting the dead wood, but not bone and muscle. The worst scenario is to cut with little investigation and reflection. This cost-cutting climate may degenerate to the extent that worthy operations and individuals are pruned regardless of their merit and future promise.

Dunlap's credentials describe a short-term hero, but one with no record of longer-term commitment. We are left to question his staying power, and what we saw with the handling of Sunbeam is damning.

Did the Affliction Require Such Drastic Changes?

Sales of both Scott and Sunbeam were flat, with profit performance deteriorating. Stock prices were falling counter to a bull market, and investors were disillusioned. Did such situations call for draconian measures?

Perhaps, but not necessarily. Neither company was in danger of going belly-up. True, they both were off the growth path, but their brands were still well regarded by consumers. Would less drastic actions have turned around these companies? Maybe, but an ingrained, powerful bureaucracy that is stifling efficiency often requires a complete overhaul if things are to be turned around; moderate efforts just will not do it.

Creeping Bureaucracy

As a firm experiences years of reasonable success and viability, it tends to spawn bureaucratic excesses. The following Information Box discusses the bureaucratic type of organization.

INFORMATION BOX

THE BUREAUCRATIC ORGANIZATION

The bureaucratic organization is a natural consequence of size and age. Its characteristics include the following:

A clear-cut division of labor
A strict hierarchy of authority
Staffing by technical competence
Formal rules and procedures
Impersonal approaches to decision making[12]

---

[12] This section is adapted from John R. Schermerhorn, Jr., *Management,* 6th ed. (New York: Wiley, 1999), pp. 75, 223.

(continues)

THE BUREAUCRATIC ORGANIZATION *(continued)*

Although a well-structured organization would appear to be best in many circumstances, it tends to be too rigid. It relies heavily on rules and procedures and as a result is often slow to adapt to change. Red tape usually predominates, as do many layers of hierarchy, an abundance of staff, and overspecialization. Consequently, creativity and initiative are stifled, and communication between upper management and lower operations is cumbersome and often distorted. Perhaps even more serious, a bureaucratic organization, with its entrenched administrators and staff positions, has a built-in high overhead that makes it difficult to compete against low-cost competitors.

TABLE 5.5 Contrasts of Bureaucratic and Adaptive Organizations

Organizational Aspects	Bureaucratic	Adaptive
Hierarchy of authority	Centralized	Decentralized
Rules and procedures	Many	Few
Division of labor	Precise	Open
Spans of control	Narrow	Wide
Coordination	Formal and impersonal	Informal and personal

A bureaucratic organization does not have to be inevitable as a firm attains large size and dominance, as shown in Table 5.5: a firm can still mold itself as an adaptive organization. But the temptation is otherwise.

Can you identify the type of person who tends to work best in a bureaucracy? The one who performs worst in this setup?

We can suspect that Scott fitted this mode. After all, Dunlap eliminated 71 percent of the headquarters staff. Perhaps the cuts were too deep, but maybe this was a bureaucracy grown top heavy and badly needing pruning. The natural consequence of too many administrators and staff people is a company failing to respond well to a changing environment and burdened with overhead too high to enable it to match prices of more lean and aggressive competitors. So while some may disagree with the extent of cost cutting, paring down probably was needed.

Was the same thing true with Sunbeam? Perhaps not to the same extreme, although without detailed records we cannot know for sure. We can suspect, however, that Dunlap, caught up in his success at Scott, simply transferred his strategy to Sunbeam with little consideration of their differences. Can we call this "slashing by formula"? This suggests a rigid mindset devoid of flexibility or compassion.

Paying Too Much for Acquisitions

We see in both Scott and Sunbeam the likelihood that too much was paid for acquisitions. Dunlap quickly sold off the S. D. Warren unit of Scott, and it added $1.6

billion to Scott coffers. But doesn't this mean that someone else thought it was highly attractive with good potential? Could they be right?

Luck can also play a part. Previous Scott management, for example, invested heavily in what seemed a reasonable diversification into commercial paper, only to encounter an unexpected industry downturn. How can you predict this? Was Warren worth keeping? Perhaps sufficient research would have found this out.

With Sunbeam, Dunlap made three questionable acquisitions, and burdened the firm with several billions of dollars of debt. The Coleman acquisition, in particular, caused him grave problems and led to his at least tacitly encouraging some questionable accounting practices to try to bring more revenues into 1997, the year he was hoping to convince investors to buy the company.

WHAT CAN BE LEARNED?

How to jumpstart a languid organization? Can we find any keys to stimulating an organization not performing up to potential? Or maybe even to inspire it to perform beyond its potential? The challenge is not unlike that of motivating a discouraged and downtrodden athletic team to rise up and have faith in itself and recommit itself to quality of performance.

In both athletics and business, the common notion is that personnel changes have to be made. Dunlap introduced the idea of severe downsizing. But this is controversial, and in view of Dunlap's problems with Sunbeam, almost discredited. So how much should be cut, how quickly should changes be made and how sweeping should they be, and what kind of information is most vital in making such decisions? Furthermore, there is the question of morale and its importance in any restoration.

We find more art than science in this mighty challenge of restoration. In particular, the right blend or degree of change is crucial. Let us look at some considerations:

How much do we trim? In most revival situations, some pruning of personnel and operations is necessary. But how much is too much, and how much is not enough? Is an ax always required for a successful turnaround? One would hope not. Certainly those personnel who are not willing to accept change may have to be let go. And weak persons and operations that show little probability of improvement need to be pruned, just as the athlete who can't seem to perform up to expectations may have to be let go. Still, it is often better to wait for sufficient information as to the "why" of poor performance, before assigning blame for the consequences.

How long do we wait? Mistakes can be made both in taking action before all the facts are known, and in waiting too long. If the changemaker procrastinates for weeks, an organization that at first was psychologically geared to major change might find it more traumatic and disruptive.

What role does strategic planning play? Major actions should hardly be taken without *some* research and planning, but strategic plans too often delay change implementation. They tend to be the products of a fumbling bureaucracy and of some abdication of responsibility. (Despite the popularity of strategic planning, it often is a vehicle for procrastination and blame-dilution: "I simply followed the strategy recommendations of the consultants.") Dunlap had an aversion to strategic planning, seeing this as indicative of a top-heavy bureaucratic organization. Perhaps he was right on this, when carried to an extreme. But going into an organization and heedlessly slashing positions without due regard for the individuals involved and the potential is akin to "shooting from the hip," with little regard for careful aiming. Then there is the matter of morale.

Morale considerations. Major restructuring usually is demoralizing to the organizations involved. The usual result is massive layoffs and forced retirements, complete reassignment of people, traumatic personnel and policy changes, and destruction of accustomed lines of communication and authority. This is hardly conducive to preserving stability and morale and any faint spark of teamwork. (You may want to look ahead to Chapter 9 and the Continental Air case for how Gordon Bethune achieved an amazing revitalization of employee morale.)

Moderation is usually best. Much can be said for moderation, for choosing the middle position, for example, between heavy cost-cutting and little cost-cutting. Of course, the condition of the firm is a major consideration. One on the verge of bankruptcy, unable to meet its bills, needs drastic measures promptly. But the problems both of Scott and Sunbeam were by no means so serious. More moderate action could have been taken.

It is better to view the restoration challenge as a *time for building rather than tearing down*. This focuses attention more on the longer view than on short-term results that may come back to haunt the firm, as well as the change-maker, like Dunlap.

Periodic housecleaning produces competitive health. In order to minimize the buildup of dead wood, all aspects of an organization periodically ought to be objectively appraised. Weak products and operations should be pruned, unless solid justification exists for keeping them. Such justification might include good growth prospects or complementing other products and operations or even providing a desired customer service. In particular, staff and headquarters personnel and functions should be scrutinized, perhaps every five years, with the objective of weeding out the redundant and superfluous. Most important, these "axing" evaluations should be done objectively, with decisive actions taken where needed. While some layoffs may result, they might not be necessary if suitable transfers are possible.

CONSIDER

Can you add any other learning insights?

QUESTIONS

1. "Periodic evaluations of personnel and departments aimed at pruning cause far too much harm to the organization. Such 'axing' evaluations

LATE-BREAKING NEWS

Dunlap's exploits brought turmoil to the executive-search industry. It seems major search firms checking his employment history prior to being hired by Sunbeam failed to uncover that he had been fired from two previous positions. He was terminated at Max Phillips & Sons in 1973 after only seven weeks. Three years later in 1976, he had been fired as president of Nitec Paper Corp. under circumstances of alleged fraud involving misstated profits. This was a situation not unlike his departure from Sunbeam.

While these episodes took place twenty years before the recruiting for Scott Paper and Sunbeam and were apparently overlooked because of his supposedly strong track record in recent years, still significant and pertinent omissions in Dunlap's job history were not caught by search firms supposedly conducting thorough background checks. Sunbeam has yet to decide whether it will sue the search firms.

Source: Joann S. Lublin, "Search Firms Have Red Faces in Dunlap Flap," *Wall Street Journal,* July 17, 2001, pp. B1 and B4.

should themselves be pruned." Argue this position as persuasively as you can.

2. Now marshal the most persuasive arguments for such "axing" evaluations.

3. Describe a person's various stages of morale and dedication to the company as it goes through a restructuring, with massive layoffs expected and realized, but with the person finding himself or herself one of the survivors. How, in your opinion, would this affect productivity and loyalty?

4. Is it likely that any decades-old organization will be bloated with excessive bureaucracy and overhead? Why or why not?

5. What decision guides should be used to determine which divisions and subsidiaries are to be divested or sold?

6. What arguments would you make in a time of restructuring for keeping your particular business unit? Which are likely to be most persuasive to an administration committed to a program of heavy pruning?

HANDS-ON EXERCISES

1. You are one of the nine high-ranking executives fired by Dunlap his third day on the job. Describe your feelings and your action plan at this point. (If you want to make some assumptions, state them specifically.)

2. You are one of the two high-level executives kept by Dunlap as he sweeps into office. Describe your feelings and your likely performance on the job.

3. You are one of the three outsiders brought into Scott vice-presidential jobs by Dunlap. You have worked for him before and must have impressed him. Describe your feelings and your likely performance on the job. What specific problems, if any, do you foresee?

TEAM DEBATE EXERCISE

It is early 1996. The board of Sunbeam is considering bringing in a turnaround team. One is the team of Dunlap, which argues for major and rapid change. Another team under consideration is Clarence Ripley's, who advocates more modest immediate changes. Array your arguments and present your positions as persuasively as possible. Attack the recommendations of the other side as aggressively as possible. We are talking about millions of dollars in fees and compensation at stake for the winning team.

INVITATION TO RESEARCH

What is Dunlap up to after being fired by the Sunbeam board in mid-1998? Has he gracefully retired? Is he still fighting for severance pay? Who replaced Dunlap, and how well is he doing? Are his policies much different from Dunlap's?

CHAPTER SIX

Herman Miller: Change Management for a Role Model

*H*erman Miller, Inc., an office-furniture maker based in Zeeland, Michigan, had long been a celebrated company, extolled by numerous business texts, including Tom Peters' best seller, *A Passion for Excellence,* and *The 100 Best Companies to Work For in America* by Robert Levering and Milton Moskowitz. Its furniture designs have been displayed in New York's Museum of Modern Art. It was a model of superb employee relations, and it stood in the forefront with environmentally sensitive policies. This company had been a paragon for almost seven decades.

But in the 1990s, circumstances began changing, and not for the best from Herman Miller's perspective. While sales had generally been increasing, although far from robustly, profits were seriously diminishing. Herman Miller remained the high-price, high-cost contender in an increasingly competitive market, and a market that itself was only expanding modestly. Amid these difficulties, one could wonder whether the enlightened approach to management might be turning out to be an albatross. Should it be modified or even abandoned?

BACKGROUND

D. J. DePree founded the company in 1923 in a small town in west-central Michigan. He named it Herman Miller after his father-in-law, who provided startup capital. For seven decades it was run by the DePree family, devout members of the Dutch Third Reformed Church, and they maintained a paternalistic relationship with their employees through the decades.

Employee Relations

Early on, the family sought to set a kinder, gentler tone with employees, offering profit-sharing and employee-incentive programs long before they were fashionable. Along with this, participative management almost bordering on democracy was practiced. (See the following Information Box for a discussion of participative

71

INFORMATION BOX

PARTICIPATIVE MANAGEMENT: IS IT THE BEST?

Directing or issuing instructions to subordinates as to what is to be done can take two extremes. In *participative direction*, the manager consults with the people responsible for doing the task about how best to accomplish it; the subordinates participate in the decision. *Authoritative direction* is simply issuing orders unilaterally, with no consultation with or participation by subordinates. Sometimes more extreme positions have been identified: *dictatorial* and *democratic*. The following diagram depicts the range of managerial styles:

dictatorial	authoritative	participative	democratic

$\longleftarrow$
degree of subordinate involvement
least   in planning and decision making $\longrightarrow$
most

The democratic style is similar to participative except that the subordinates get to vote, with the decision going to the most votes. In participative style, the manager may or may not go along with the ideas of subordinates.

Several advantages come from a greater use of participation. People tend to be more cooperative and enthusiastic when they have some involvement in the planning. Not uncommonly, better decisions also come with the different experiences and points of view. The executive may even become more a coordinator of ideas than a "boss." In such an atmosphere employee development is maximized.

The major drawback is time. Consultation takes time. Many decisions are too minor to be worth such discussion. Other times actions have to be taken quickly and there is little time for participation. And if employees are new and untrained, if they lack interest, or if they are not very competent, no benefit would be likely.

The best managers tend to use participation whenever they can, especially where the decision directly involves employees. But they choose their opportunities carefully. It can be used with just one or two subordinates, or with a whole group.

Do you think another objection to a participative management style is that it undermines the manager's authority? Why or why not?

---

management.) This helped create a loyal work force that turned out well-made products that could be sold at premium prices.

Through the 1960s and 1970s the company prospered with the expanding office furniture industry. D. J.'s sons, Hugh and Max, took the enterprise public but continued to nurture employees' commitment to the company. For example:

- In the 1980s, when hostile takeovers threatened many firms, the company instituted "silver parachutes" for all employees so that any who might lose their jobs would receive big checks.

- It may be the only company in the United States to have a *vice president of people.*

- In a time of escalating top executives' salaries by 1990 to as much as a hundred times the companies' lowest wages, Herman Miller limited the top salary to no more than 20 times the average wage of a line worker in the factory.   *Capts*
- Employees were organized into work teams and every six months both work-   *B*S ers and their bosses evaluated each other.
- In the middle 1980s, Max DePree, in the interest of ensuring the fullest career development of promising managers, announced that he would be the last member of the family to head up Herman Miller. Henceforth, the next generation of DePrees would not even be permitted to work at the company.

Of course, there had never been any serious efforts to unionize the workforce.

Product Development

Since 1968, the company had turned its attention to designing products for a so-called Action Office. It introduced components, such as desk consoles, cabinets, chairs, flexible panels, and the like, that could give flexibility, and some degree of privacy, to the workplace. It emphasized innovative designs, and dealt with a number of "enormously gifted but extremely high-strung designers."[1] These vaulted Herman Miller into the top ranks of the industrial design world.

The company regularly budgeted between 2 and 3 percent of sales for design research, double the industry average. Sometimes its commitment to doing what was right (rather than what was best) brought it to a new level of corporate consciousness. For example:

- In the 1970s, an enormously successful desk chair called the Ergon was introduced. Millions of these designed-for-the-body chairs were sold. Then an advanced desk chair called the Equa was proposed. It would cost about the same as the Ergon. At this point many companies would have scrapped it rather than cannibalize (take sales away from) their star. But Herman Miller introduced it nevertheless.
- In March 1990, the Eames chair, the company's signature piece, was given a routine evaluation of the materials used. This was a distinctive office chair with a rosewood exterior finish, priced at $2,277. The research manager, Bill Foley, realized that two species of trees used, rosewood and Honduran mahogany, came from vulnerable rain forests. The decision was made to ban the use of these woods once existing supplies were exhausted, even though the CEO, Richard H. Ruch, predicted that this decision would kill the chair.[2]

Environmental Sensitivity

Few firms have shown the concern for the environment that Herman Miller has. In addition to the rain forest example above, here are several other instances of such concern:

[1] Kenneth Labich, "Hot Company, Warm Culture," *Fortune* (February 27, 1989), p. 75.

[2] D. Woodruff, "Herman Miller: How Green Is My Factory?" *Business Week* (September 16, 1991), pp. 54–55.

- The firm cut the trash it hauled to landfills by 90 percent since 1982.
- It built an $11 million waste-to-energy heating and cooling plant, thus saving $750,000 per year in fuel and landfill costs.
- Herman Miller employees used 800,000 Styrofoam cups, material anathema to waste disposal. Then it distributed 5,000 mugs and banished Styrofoam. The mugs carried this admonition, "On spaceship earth there are no passengers ... only crew."[3]
- The company spent $800,000 for two incinerators that burned 98 percent of the toxic solvents coming from the staining of woods, thereby exceeding Clean Air Act requirements. CEO Ruch, under questioning from the board of directors for the costly exceeding of standards, stated that having the machines was "ethically correct."[4]

EMERGING SOBERING REALITIES

By 1995, Herman Miller was a $1 billion corporation. But given that its sales in 1989 had been almost $800 million, this was not a significant accomplishment, especially since profits had slid from over $40 million in most of the 1980s to $4.3 million in 1995. And in 1992, it recorded a net loss of $3.5 million, its first loss ever. Table 6.1 shows the trend in revenues for selected years from 1985 to 1995. Table 6.2 shows the net income disappointments during these years. Earnings by 1995 were 90 percent less, on higher sales, than in many years in the 1980s. And net income as a percent of revenues had been declining steadily from 1985, from 8.3 percent to only .4 percent in 1995.

Perhaps most indicative of the worsening performance of Herman Miller was in its "competitive battles." A close competitor, one with virtually the same size and aiming at similar markets, was Hon Industries. Table 6.3 shows the sales and net income

TABLE 6.1   Herman Miller Revenues, 1985–1995

	Millions	Percent Change
1985	$ 492	
1987	574	17.6
1989	793	38.2
1991	879	10.8
1993	856	(2.6)
1995	1,083	26.5

Source: Company public records.

Commentary: While somewhat erratic, the increase in sales should hardly in itself be a cause for alarm. But this does not tell the whole story of Herman Miller's problems. See the next table.

[3] *Ibid.*
[4] *Ibid.*

TABLE 6.2 Herman Miller's Total Net Income, and Percent of Sales, 1985–1995

	Millions	Percent of Sales
1985	$40.9	8.3
1987	33.3	5.8
1989	41.4	5.2
1991	14.1	1.6
1993	22.1	2.6
1995	4.3	.4

Source: Company public records.

Commentary: Here the trend is far more serious than in Table 6.1. The trend in total profits is steadily downward since the 1980s, despite the increase in sales during most of these years. While the results for 1995 are particularly troubling (and resulted in the chairman's "retirement"), of particular concern is the erosion of profits as a percentage of total sales. And this is not for a single year but for all of the 1990s.

of Hon during these same years. Unlike Herman Miller, Hon's profits had risen steadily, and net income as a percentage of revenues was two to three times better in the 1990s. Figures 6.1 and 6.2 show these competitive battles graphically.

Any top executive has to be concerned with the fortunes of the company's stock price, and the satisfaction of shareholders. While Hon Industries' stock had climbed fourfold in the last decade, Herman Miller's barely moved: In 1985, its

TABLE 6.3 Sales and Profit Performance of Major Competitor, Hon Industries, 1985–1994

	Revenues (millions)	Net Income (millions)	Income as Percent of Sales
1985	$473.3	$26.0	
1987	555.4	24.8	5.5
1989	602.0	27.5	4.5
1991	607.7	32.9	5.4
1993	780.3	44.6	5.7
1994	846.0	54.4	6.4

Source: Company public records.

Commentary: Hon and Herman Miller are surprisingly close in total sales. If anything, Herman has been growing slightly faster than Hon. But looking at profits tells a different story. While Herman's profits have been badly eroding. Hon's have steadily been increasing. And the improvement in profits as a percent of sales for Hon is impressive indeed, while this is the great source of Herman Miller's trepidation.

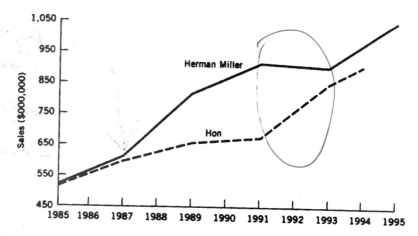

Figure 6.1 *The Competitive War:* sales comparisons, Herman Miller and Hon, 1985–1995.

over-the-counter shares sold at $24; in 1995 they were about the same—this in the midst of the greatest bull market in stock market history.

J. Kermit Campbell became the company's first outsider CEO in 1992. He had had a 32-year career at Dow Corning. In an annual report, he seemed to espouse all the best values of the DePrees: "I truly believe that there is something in human nature that wants to soar."[5]

Campbell was named chairman in May 1995 when Max DePree retired. He acted quickly to cut costs, and, in the process, to discharge several top executives. The

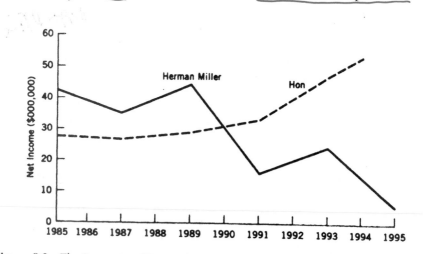

Figure 6.2 *The Competitive War:* net income comparisons, Herman Miller and Hon, 1985–1995.

[5] Justin Martin, "Broken Furniture at Herman Miller," *Fortune* (August 7, 1995), p. 32.

head of Herman Miller's biggest division, workplace systems, a 20-year veteran, was let go. Also, the company's chief financial officer was removed. Campbell's goal was to pare selling and administrative costs to 25 percent from the current 30 percent.

He wanted to cut about 200 employees from a workforce of 6,000, doing so through early retirements but also from firings. He closed plants in Texas and New Jersey, as well as several showrooms. At this point, Herman Miller was rapidly losing its reputation as one of the best companies to work for in America. But Campbell could point out that survival was more important than preserving a pristine worker relationship.

Campbell's tenure proved to be short. In mid-July, barely two months into his chairmanship, on the same day the company announced its annual results and the nearly 90 percent drop in profits from the previous year, his departure was also announced. What was not clear was whether the board was dissatisfied with Campbell's cost-cutting as being too little or too much.

In any case, the board named Michael Volkema as new chief executive. Volkema had joined Herman Miller in 1990 when it acquired cabinetmaker Meridian. He had the reputation of being driven and charismatic, and he was young—only 39. He had come to the board's attention for his cost-cutting efforts in the small Meridian operation ($100 million in sales).

Problems in the Changing Market   *THE MARKET*

The marketplace was hardly the same in the 1990s as it was in the heydays of the 1960s and 1970s. Sales of office furniture were not expected to grow at more than 5 percent, even if corporate profits remained high. A basic shift in demand was blamed for this: Computer technology required fewer layers of management, leading to general downsizing of office space needs.

Not only was total demand growing slowly, but the premium-end of the market, which had long been Herman Miller's niche, was also drying up as businesses in general chose to reduce costs by using lower-priced furniture.

In 1994, Herman Miller introduced the new Aeron chair, made from a mesh material that helped keep the body cooler. Although its design was unique and artistic, it retailed for up to $1,150, hundreds of dollars more than most other office chairs. Sales were disappointing.

Given limitations in the business market, the company turned optimistic for the home office sector. "We'll have 40 million to 50 million people working some part of their day at home," Campbell predicted. He hoped that the firm's quality image would be especially appealing to a significant part of this market.[6] So, the company introduced its first home office line, carrying a price tag of $1,799 for a desk. Early results were not promising; hundreds of OfficeMax and Office Depot stores featured fully acceptable desks for no more than $725.

Herman Miller's problem of arousing demand for its admittedly high-quality, well-designed furniture was further impeded by the company's traditional practice of

Home Office did Not Work out — little or no advertising — Distribution

[6] Marcia Berss, "Tarnished Icon," *Forbes* (July 31, 1995), p. 45.

doing very little product advertising. While such a strategy worked in decades past, was it still appropriate in the 1990s?

ANALYSIS

A central issue in the Herman Miller shift toward operational mediocrity and deterioration in recent years had to do with its enlightened management style toward both employees and the environment. Long the model for superb employee relations, Herman Miller faced a dilemma: In an age of impersonal cost-cutting and downsizing, can a company be competitive with altruistic policies that protect employees and the environment? Perhaps more to the point, were Herman Miller's problems the result of such policies being unrealistic today, or was something else wrong, something having little to do with employee relations and environmental concerns?

Let us address the crucial question: Do the best in employee relations add unacceptable costs? What employee relations are we talking about? Giving employees participation in many decisions? Giving them profit-sharing incentives? Giving them opportunities for advancement as far as their abilities will take them? Making them feel wanted and appreciated, and part of a team? Giving them a feeling of job security at a time when so many firms were downsizing and forcing many employees out, whether done under the guise of early retirement or outright forced discharges? Involving them with products they can take pride in? Do such things add to unacceptable costs against lean-and-mean competitors?

While these questions or issues could be debated at some length, perhaps the only question that really is a detriment to achieving necessary cost savings is that of job security. Some paring down might need to be done to stay competitive costwise, especially in a computer age when some middle management and staff positions can be consolidated.

Unfortunately, management and workers alike must face the grim realities of today's environment: that their skills and experience may no longer be as needed today. That they must be prepared to shift their jobs and learn new skills, or be prepared for early retirement, no matter how enlightened the firm. To compete, it must be "lean" if not "mean." Such early retirements or terminations can be done meanly or empathetically. Empathetically suggests reasonable early retirement incentives, help with finding alternative employment or with the training needed to develop new skills. Counseling can be important—and time. Time to adjust to the harsh realities and to pursue alternative employment opportunities before being cast out. All these add some costs. But an organization does not have to be mean in seeking to be competitive. Can't a firm be kind to loyal employees, even if it adds a little to its costs temporarily?

Regarding the environment, did Herman Miller lose money by not using for its chairs certain tropical hardwoods found in rain forests? Maybe some; yet substitute woods should have proven acceptable to virtually all customers. Other costs, such as going beyond 1990 Clean Air Act requirements for incinerators and building an $11 million waste-to-energy heating and cooling plant, resulted in some cost savings, although not as much as the investments made. On the other hand, substituting reusable mugs for Styrofoam cups reportedly resulted in cost savings of $1.4 million.[7] So, environmental concern and action does not have to result in major additional expenditures.

It seems, then, that indicting the altruistic policies of Herman Miller for its less-than-laudable recent operating results might be mistaken. Perhaps the blame rather lies in the aged strategy: high-quality, well-designed products, priced at the top of the market, with the major promotional reliance on word-of-mouth rather than advertising. What worked well in the 1980s and before may need to be reevaluated in the 1990s and beyond. This is more an age of austerity, with aggressive competitors and category-killer chains, such as Office Depot, offering good merchandise at prices half or less those of Herman Miller. In particular, perhaps Herman Miller should have tested the waters for medium-priced goods. It would not need—or want to—discard its quality reputation, nor abandon the high end of the market. Rather, it could have expanded its offerings downward from the very-high end.

Herman Miller also seemed to have miscalculated in the receptivity of the home-office market to its high-priced furniture. While undoubtedly a few wealthy individuals would willingly pay the steep price for a desk and other furniture of highest quality at the cutting edge of design, this market might not be very sizable.

UPDATE

Michael Volkema changed things for the better, after the painful downsizing and restructuring of Herman Miller in the industry slump of the mid-1990s. By the end of 2000, five years under Volkema, sales almost doubled to $1.938 billion and operating income went from $1.2 million to $140 million for a net income percent of revenues of 7.2 percent. Comparing with the major competitor, Hon Industries, revenues were almost the same, but Herman Miller's net income was well above Hon's of $106 million and net profit percentage of 5.2 percent.

In January 2000, *Forbes* selected Herman Miller to its "Platinum List," a list of exceptional corporations that "pass a stringent set of hurdles measuring both long- and short-term growth and profitability.[8]

Volkema had expanded the narrow high-end customer base to emerging and mid-size businesses, and homes. In three years he spent more than $200 million on computer systems and other technology, aimed at assuring speedy delivery, and another $100-million-plus on research and development for new products. To attract consumers, a website was developed, featuring office furniture specially designed for this market.

Employees are still catered to, with a new plant in Holland, Michigan, that is bright and airy, with workers assembling furniture to music by U2, the Allman Brothers, and Sting. "A sign near the front door boasts that workers there haven't been late in shipping a single order in 75 days."[9]

---

[7] Woodruff, p. 55.

[8] Brian Zajac, "The Best of the Biggest," *Forbes* (January 10, 2000), pp. 84, 85.

[9] "Reinventing Herman Miller," *Business Week* (April 3, 2000), p. EB88; and Ashlea Ebeling, "Herman Miller: Furnishing the Future," *Forbes* (January 10, 2000), pp. 94–96.

WHAT CAN BE LEARNED?

A firm has to adapt to changing competitive forces. Not many firms can afford the luxury of decades of undeviating policies and strategies. Most find that some adaptability is essential for the dynamic environment they face.

Such alertness to changing conditions is not difficult. Nor does it require constant research and investigation. Most changes do not occur suddenly and without warning. Indeed, the business press is quick to highlight innovations and changing circumstances. The rise of the super-office-equipment chains, such as OfficeMax, Staples, and Office Depot, were widely heralded and discussed, and their great growth was very visible. Before its changeover, Herman Miller made no attempt to cope with the obvious changes in the office furniture market. The company either did not grasp the significance of change, or else judged its high-end niche to be solid and not contracting.

In adversity altruistic concerns become dulled. It is perhaps only natural that when firms face hard times, their benevolent tendencies toward employees and their proactive treatment of the environment lessens, and sometimes even disappears. Where downsizing is indicated, actions toward employees, even longtime ones, sometimes become ruthless. "Voluntary" early retirement may be mandatory, and severance pay far from generous.

But survival of the company is at stake, management counters critics. In a widely quoted statement, Albert Dunlap, the merciless terminator described in the previous chapter, said, "I see no point in sacrificing 100 percent of the employees for the 35 percent who ought to leave."[10]

Objectively, one wonders how many companies have grown so fat that more than one-third of the employees should be laid off.

Shareholder discontent is unhealthy for executives. This is as it should be. Stockholders have the right to agitate for drastic shakeups when the company fortunes, as reflected in unsatisfactory stock prices, show little promise of improving, especially when competitive firms are doing much better, as Hon Industries was. Such comparisons indicate that the disappointing performance is not industry-related but reflects the failings of current and past executives.

Executives who wish to keep their jobs should be concerned with shareholder satisfaction. Of course, this is easier said than done. Sometimes a company's problems are too deepseated for easy remedies. But this leaves the current executives vulnerable to hostile takeovers by those who think the parts of the firm are worth more than the whole entity, and that it should be broken up, or that the bloated cost structure requires severe pruning by a new administration willing to wield a mean ax.

On the other hand, a complacent and management-dominated board may perpetuate incompetence far too long, and leave shareholders little recourse but to sell their stock, probably at a sizable loss.

---

[10] Kenneth Labich, "Why Companies Fail," *Fortune* (November 14, 1994), p. 53.

CONSIDER

Can you think of additional learning insights?

QUESTIONS

1. "A worker-sensitive firm is bound eventually to face a competitive disadvantage. It cannot control its labor costs." Evaluate this statement.

2. Do you see any risks in Herman Miller lowering its quality and its prices? Do you think it should have done so?

3. What do you think of the "enlightened" policy announced by Max DePree as he retired that henceforth no DePree will ever work for the firm again, in order that able people can have unimpeded career paths within the company? Discuss as many facets of this policy change as you can.

4. Evaluate the statement by Dunlap of Scott Paper that "I see no point in sacrificing 100 percent of the employees for the 35 percent who ought to leave."

5. What do you think of the decision to forgo using an attractive wood because it was taken from the rain forest, which needs to be protected?

6. What would be your prescription for a successful change manager? You might want to compare with Al Dunlap, and with Campbell who only lasted two months at Herman Miller.

HANDS-ON EXERCISES

Before

1. Operating results for fiscal year 1987 have just come out. They show that net income dropped 11.9 percent from the preceding year and 19 percent from 1985. What is even more troubling, net income as a percent of sales fell from 8.3 percent in 1985 to 5.8 percent. What do you propose at this time?

After

2. It is July 1995. Chairman Campbell has just "resigned" under pressure from the board. You have been named his successor. What do you do now? (You may have to make some assumptions, but keep them reasonable and state them specifically.) Don't be bound by what actually happened. Maybe a different strategy would have been more successful.

TEAM DEBATE EXERCISE

Debate both sides of the controversy of whether a firm with enlightened and empathetic employee relations can compete in a climate of aggressive competitors and severe downsizing.

INVITATION TO RESEARCH

What is the situation with Herman Miller today? Is Michael Volkema still chief executive? Has Herman Miller continued its turnaround? Can you find any recent information about its employee and environmental relations?

CHAPTER SEVEN

Perrier: Poor Handling of Adversity

On a Friday in early February 1990 the first news reached Perrier executive suites that traces of benzene had been found in its bottled water. Ronald Davis, president of the Perrier Group of America, ordered a sweeping recall of all bottles in North America. Just a few days later, Source Perrier S.A., the French parent, expanded the recall to the rest of the world, while the company sought to identify the source of the problem and correct it.

Although at first view such a reaction to an unexpected crisis seems zealous and the ultimate in customer concern and social responsibility, a deeper study reveals mistakes of major proportions.

BEFORE

In late 1989, Ronald Davis, 43-year-old president of Perrier's U.S. operations, had reason to be pleased. During his 10-year tenure, Perrier's U.S. sales had risen from $40 million to more than $800 million at retail, which was a significant 25 percent of the company's worldwide sales. He was also proud of his firm being depicted in a May 1989 issue of *Fortune* as one of six companies that compete best. *Fortune* captioned: "These are companies you don't want to come up against in your worst nightmare. In the businesses they're in, they amass crushing market share."[1]

A company report in 1987 described the French source, a spring in Vergeze, as follows:

> One of Perrier's identifying qualities is its low mineral (particularly sodium) content. This is because the water spends only a short time filtering through minerals. While flowing underground, the water meets gas flowing vertically through porous volcanic rocks. This is how Perrier gets its fizz ... the company assured us that production has never been limited by the source output. The company sells approximately one billion bottles of which 600 million are exported.[2]

[1] Bill Saporito, "Companies That Compete Best," *Fortune* (May 22, 1989), pp. 36ff.
[2] B. Facon, *Source Perrier—Company Report* (November 13, 1987), p. 4.

TABLE 7.1   Average Annual Growth of Beverage Sales, 1985–1989

Beverage Type	Percent of Growth
Bottled water	+ 11.1
Soft drinks	+ 3.2
Milk	+ 1.5
Tea	+ 1.2
Beer	+ 0.4
Coffee	− 0.4
Wine	− 2.0
Distilled spirits	− 2.6

Source: Beverage Marketing Corporation, as reported in *Fortune* (April 23, 1990), p. 277.

Davis recognized that he was in two businesses, albeit both involved bottled water: (1) sparkling water, in the famous green bottle, which he had been successful in positioning as an adult soft drink with a French mystique, an alternative to soft drinks or alcohol; and (2) still water, a tap-water replacement, with the product delivered to homes and offices and dispensed through watercoolers. This latter business he saw as more resembling package delivery such as UPS and Federal Express, and less akin to pushing soft drinks. Accordingly, he emphasized quality of professional service for his route drivers. While best known for the green-bottled Perrier, a mainstay of most restaurants and bars, the company owned nine other brands of bottled water, including Poland Spring, Great Bear, Calistoga, and Ozarka.

At a price of 300 to 1200 times that of tap water, bottled water was the fastest growing segment of the U.S. beverage industry (see Table 7.1). Perrier controlled 24 percent of the total U.S. bottled-water business. Of the imported-bottled-water sector, the green bottle dominated with almost 50 percent of the market, although this market share had fallen when more competitors attempted to push into the rapidly growing market. In the 1980s, more than 20 firms had taken a run at the green bottle, but without notable success; these included such behemoths as Coca-Cola, PepsiCo, and Anheuser-Busch. Now Davis was more concerned with expanding the category, and was trying to shift the brand's image from chic to healthy, so as to make the brand more acceptable to the "masses."

THE CRISIS

The North American Recall

Davis, as he prepared his five-year plan in early 1990, wrote that competing in the 1990s would require not strategic planning, but "flexibility planning."[3] In retrospect, he seemed to be prophetic.

[3] Patricia Sellers, "Perrier Plots Its Comeback," *Fortune* (April 23, 1990), p. 277.

As he was fine-tuning his plan, the first news trickled in that a lab in North Carolina had discovered traces of benzene, a carcinogen, in some of the bottles. That same day, February 9, he ordered Perrier removed from distribution in North America.

Source Perrier officials were soon to inform reporters that the company believed the contamination occurred because an employee had mistakenly used cleaning fluid containing benzene to clean the production-line machinery that fills bottles for North America. Frederik Zimmer, managing director of Source Perrier, said that the machinery in question had been cleaned and repaired over the weekend. But in another news conference, Davis announced that he expected Perrier to be off the market for two to three months.

Such a long absence was seen by some marketing observers as potentially devastating to Perrier, despite its being the front-runner of the industry. Al Ries, chairman of a consulting firm and well-known business writer, was quoted in a *Wall Street Journal* article as saying: "If I were Perrier, I would make a desperate effort to reduce that time as much as possible, even if I had to fly it in on 747s from France."[4]

Without doubt, competitors were salivating at a chance to pick up market share of the $2.2 billion annual U.S. sales. Major competitors included Evian and Saratoga, both owned by BSN of France, and San Peligrino, an Italian import. In 1989, PepsiCo had begun test marketing H_2 OH!, and in January 1990, Adolph Coors Company introduced Coors Rocky Mountain Sparkling Water. The Perrier absence was expected to accelerate their market entry.

Despite competitive glee at the misfortune of Perrier, some in the industry were concerned. They feared that consumers would forsake bottled water altogether, with its purity now being questioned. Would the public be as willing to pay a substantial premium for any bottled brand? See the following Issue Box for a discussion of the relationship between *price and quality.*

Worldwide Recall

A few days later, the other shoe fell. After reports of benzene being found in Perrier bottles in Holland and Denmark, on February 14, Source Perrier expanded its North American recall to the rest of the world, and acknowledged that all production lines for its sparkling water had been contaminated in recent months by tiny amounts of benzene.

At a news conference in Paris, company officials acknowledged for the first time that benzene occurs naturally in Perrier water, and that the current problem came about because workers failed to replace filters designed to remove it. This was a critical reversal of previous statements that the water was tainted only because an employee mistakenly used cleaning fluid containing benzene to clean machinery. Zimmer even went further, revealing that Perrier water naturally contains several gases, including benzene, that have to be filtered out.

The company insisted that its famous spring was unpolluted. But now questions were being raised about this and about contradictory statements made about the problem. For example, how widespread was the contamination? Was benzene a nat-

---

[4] Alix M. Freedman and Thomas R. King, "Perrier's Strategy in the Wake of Recall," *Wall Street Journal* (February 12, 1990), p. B1.

urally occurring phenomenon, or does it represent man-made pollution? Suspicions were tending toward the man-made origin. While benzene occurs naturally in certain foods, it is more commonly found as a petroleum-based distillate used in many manufacturing processes.

Particularly surprising was the rather nonchalant attitude of Perrier executives. Zimmer, the president, even suggested that "all this publicity helps build the brand's renown."[5]

Ronald Davis was quick to point out that the company did not have to recall its entire 70-million-bottle U.S. inventory. After all, health officials both in the U.S. and France had noted that the benzene levels found in Perrier did not pose any significant health risk. The major risk really was to the image of Perrier: it had gone to great lengths to establish its water as naturally pure. And while not particularly dangerous, it was certainly not naturally pure—as all the world was finding out from the publicity about it. Add to this the undermining of the major attraction of bottled water that it was safer than ordinary tap water, and the recall and subsequent publicity assumed more ominous proportions.

THE COMEBACK

It took until mid-July before Perrier was again widely available in the United States; this was five months rather than the expected three months. Still, Davis was confident

---

ISSUE BOX

IS QUALITY BEST JUDGED BY PRICE?

We as consumers today have difficulty in judging the quality of competing products. With their complex characteristics and hidden ingredients, we cannot rely on our own expertise to determine the best. So, what sources of information can we use? We can rely on our past experiences with the brand; we can be swayed by our friends and neighbors; we might be influenced by advertising and salespeople (but more and more we become skeptical of their claims); we can study *Consumer Reports* and other consumer information publications. But all of these sources are flawed in that the experience and information usually is dated, and is a limited sample—usually of 1—so that we can seriously question how representative the experience is.

Most people judge quality by price: the higher the price, the better the quality. But such a price/quality perception sets us up. While it may be valid, it also may not be. With the publicity about the impurity of Perrier, we are brought to the realization that paying many times the price of tap water gives us no assurance of better quality, as measured by purity.

Is a price/quality misperception mostly limited to bottled water, do you think? How about liquor? Designer clothes? Perfume?

---

[5] Alix M. Freedman and Thomas R. King, "Perrier Expands North American Recall to Rest of Globe," *Wall Street Journal* (February 15, 1990), p. B1.

that Perrier's sales would return to 85 percent of normal by the end of 1991. Actually, he was more worried about short supply than demand. He was not sure the one spring in Vergeze, France, would be able to replace the world's supply before the beginning of 1991.

Davis's confidence in the durability of the demand stemmed from his clout with retailers, where the brand does a majority of its business. He believed the brand's good reputation, coupled with the other brands marketed by Perrier that had replaced some of the supermarket space relinquished by Perrier, would bring quick renewal. To help this, he wrote letters to 550 CEOs of retail firms, pledging heavy promotional spending. The marketing budget was increased from $6 million to $25 million for 1990, with $16 million going into advertising and the rest into promotions and special events. A highly visible discount strategy was instituted, which included a buy-two, get-one-free offer. Supermarket prices had dropped, with bottles now going for $0.89 to $0.99, down from $1.09 to $1.19. To win back restaurant business, a new 52-member sales force supplemented distributor efforts. However, a setback of sorts was the Food and Drug Administration order to drop the words "naturally sparkling" from Perrier labels.

Still, a recent consumer survey indicated that 84 percent of Perrier's U.S. drinkers intended to buy the product again.[6] Davis could also take heart from the less than aggressive actions of his competitors during the hiatus. None appeared to have strongly reacted, although most improved their sales considerably. The smaller competitors proved to be short of marketing money and bottling capacity, and apparently were fearful that a beleaguered Perrier would negatively affect the overall market. Big competitors, such as PepsiCo and Coors, who were introducing other bottled waters, somehow also appeared reluctant to move in aggressively.

CONSEQUENCES

By the end of 1990, however, it was clear that Perrier was not regaining market position as quickly and completely as Davis had hoped. Now more aggressive competitors were emerging. Some, such as Saratoga, La Croix, and Quibell, had experienced major windfalls in the wake of the recall. Evian, in particular, a nonsparkling water produced by the French firm BSN S.A. was the biggest winner. Through aggressive marketing and advertising it had replaced Perrier by the end of 1990 as the top-selling imported bottled water.

Perrier's sales had only reached 60 percent of prerecall levels, and its share of the imported bottled-water market had sunk to 20.7 percent from the 44.8 percent of one year earlier. While the Perrier Group of America expected to report a sales gain for 1990 of 3.7 percent, this was largely because of the strong performance of such domestic brands as Calistoga and Poland Spring.

Particularly worrisome for Davis was the slow return of Perrier to bars and restaurants, which formerly accounted for about 35 percent of its sales. A sampling

---

[6] Sellers, "Perrier Plots," p. 278.

of comments of restaurant managers, as reported in such prestigious papers as the *Wall Street Journal* and *Washington Post*, were far from encouraging. For example:

> The manager of the notable Four Seasons restaurant in New York City said his patrons had begun to shift to San Pellegrino: "I think Perrier is finished," he said. "We can write it off."[7]

> The general manager of Spago restaurant in Los Angeles said: "Now consumers have decided that other brands are better or at least as good, so Perrier no longer holds the monopoly on water." And Spago no longer carries Perrier.[8]

> Le Pavillon restaurant in Washington, D.C., switched to Quibell during the recall, and has not gone back to Perrier. "Customers still ask for Perrier, but it's a generic term like Kleenex, and customers aren't unhappy to get a substitute.[9]

Evian

David Daniel, 34, was Evian's U.S. CEO since June 1988. He joined the company in 1987 as the first director of marketing at a time when the American subsidiary was a two-person operation. By 1990 there were 100 employees.

Daniel came from PepsiCo, and his background was marketing. He saw Evian's sphere to be portable water that is good for you, a position well situated to capitalize on the health movement. He was particularly interested in broadening the distribution of Evian, and he sought out soft-drink and beer distributors, showing them that their basic industries were only growing at 1 to 3 percent a year, while bottled water was growing at over 10 percent per year. In 1989, Evian sales doubled to 65 million, with $100 million in sight for 1990. The attractiveness of such growth to these distributors was of no small moment.

Daniel made Evian the most expensive water on the market. He saw the price as helping Evian occupy a certain slot in the consumer's mind—remember the price/quality perception discussed earlier. For example, at a fancy grocery in New York's West Village, a one liter bottle of Evian sold for $2.50; the city charges a fraction of a penny for a gallon of tap water[10]—a lot of perceived quality in that. This type of pricing along with the packaging that made Evian portable—plastic nonbreakable bottles and reusable caps—were seen as keys in the selling of bottled water.

Then, late in 1990, Evian benefited greatly from the Persian Gulf War, with free publicity from several newspapers and from all three national TV networks: GIs were shown gulping water from Evian bottles.

---

[7] Freedman and King, "Perrier's Strategy," p. B3.

[8] Alix M. Freedman, "Perrier Finds Mystique Hard to Restore," *Wall Street Journal* (December 1, 1990), p. B1.

[9] Lori Silver, "Perrier Crowd Not Taking the Waters," *Washington Post* (July 4, 1990), p. 1.

[10] Seth Lubove, "Perched Between Perrier and Tap," *Forbes,* (May 14, 1990), p. 120.

ISSUE BOX

ARE BOTTLED WATER CLAIMS BUNK?[11]

The bottled water industry came under serious attack in April 1991. As if the Perrier massive recall was not enough, now a congressional panel with wide media coverage accused the Food and Drug Administration of "inexcusably negligent and complacent oversight of the bottled-water industry." Despite its high price, the panel said, bottled water may be less safe than tap water. The panel noted that although consumers pay 300 to 1200 times more for bottled water than for tap water, 25 percent of all bottled water comes from public drinking water sources. For example:

> Lithia Springs Water Company touts its "world's finest" bottled mineral water as "naturally pure" and recommends its special Love Water as an "invigorator" before bedtime. Yet, it was found to be tainted with bacteria.
>
> Artisia Waters, Inc., promotes its "100% pure sparkling Texas Natural Water." But it comes from the same underground sources that San Antonio uses for its municipal water supply.

Furthermore, the FDA released a list of 22 bottled-water recalls because of contaminants such as kerosene and mold. For the most part, these went unnoticed by consumers, being overshadowed by the Perrier recall.

At issue: Are we being hoodwinked?

Debate two positions: (1) the bottled-water industry really is a throwback to the snake-oil charlatans of the last century; and (2) a few unscrupulous or careless bottlers are denigrating the image of the entire industry, an industry that is primarily focused on health and purity.

---

[11] Examples are taken from Bruce Ingersoll, "FDA Finds Bunk in Bottled-Water Claims," *Wall Street Journal* (April 10, 1991), p. B1.

ANALYSIS

Was the massive recall overkill, or was it a prudent necessity? Did it show a concerned corporate citizen, or rather a panicked executive? Were consumers impressed with the responsibleness of the company, or were they more focused on its carelessness? These questions are all directed at the basic impact of the recall and the subsequent actions and admissions: Was it to have favorable, neutral, or unfavorable public reactions?

Perrier did *not* have to recall its product. It was a North Carolina county laboratory that first noticed the excessive amounts of benezene in Perrier and reported its findings to the state authorities. The state agriculture and health departments did not believe that a recall was necessary, but they did insist on issuing a health advisory, warning that Perrier should not be consumed until further tests could be made. It was the state's plan to issue the health advisory that was reported to Davis on the afternoon of the critical day, February 9. He announced the recall later that same day.

We are left to wonder. Perhaps a full and complete recall was not needed. Perhaps things could have been worked out entirely satisfactorily with less drastic measures. Given that a recall meant a 3- to 5-months' absence from the marketplace, should it not have been the action of last resort?

But let us consider Davis's thought processes on that ill-fated afternoon in February. He did not know the source of the problem; he certainly had no reason to suspect that it emanated from the spring in southern France or that it was a world-wide problem. He probably considered it of less magnitude. Perhaps he thought of the total North American recall as a gesture showing the concerned thinking of the management of this product that had developed such a reputation of health and purity and, yes, status. Only with the experience after the fact do we know the error of this decision: that it was to result in an absence up to 5-months from the hotly competitive market; that it was to result in revelations of far more serious implications than a simple employee error or even a natural occurrence largely beyond the company's control.

So, perhaps Davis's drastic decision was fully justified and prudent. But it turned out to be confounded by circumstances he did not envision.

A lengthy complete absence from the marketplace is a catastrophe of rather monumental proportions—all the more so for a product that is habitually and frequently consumed, in Perrier's case, sometimes several times daily. Such an absence forces even the most loyal customers to establish new patterns of behavior, in this case switching brands. Once behavior becomes habituated, at least for some people, a change back becomes less likely. This is especially true if the competitive offerings are reasonably similar and acceptable. Anything that Perrier could have done to lessen the time away from the market would have been desirable—regardless of expense.

Perhaps the biggest problem for Perrier concerned the false impressions, and even outright deception, that the company had conveyed regarding the purity of its product. Now, in the wake of this total recall and the accompanying publicity, all was laid bare. Company officials in France had to own up that the contamination had occurred "in recent months," and not suddenly and unexpectedly on February 9.

But more than this, under intense pressure from the media to explain what caused the problem, Source Perrier ultimately conceded that its water does not bubble up pure, already carbonated and ready to drink, from its renowned spring in southern France. Instead, contrary to the image that it had spent tens of millions of dollars to promote, the company extracts the water and carbon dioxide gas separately, and must pipe the gas through charcoal filters before combining it mechanically with the water to give the fizz. Without the filters, Perrier water would contain benzene and, even worse, would taste like rotten eggs.

Finally, the public relations efforts were flawed. Source Perrier officials issued a confusing series of public statements and clarifications. Early on, the company tried to maintain the mystique of Perrier by concealing information about the cause of the contamination and by blaming it on a mistake by cleaning personnel in using an oily rag, which could have contained some benzene, to wipe equipment used for bottles to be shipped to the United States, when the spokespeople knew the problem was more fundamental than that.

An aura of nonchalance was conveyed by corporate executives and reported in the press. This was hardly in keeping with a serious problem having to do with the possible safety of customers. Furthermore, Source Perrier relied mainly on media reports to convey information to consumers. Misinformation and rumors are more likely with this approach to public relations than in a more proactive strategy of direct company advertisement and statements.

UPDATE

By the turn of the millennium, Perrier's fortunes had improved, although its market share never regained precrisis levels. Another contender than Evian had invaded this growing market and had become dominant in only a few years. Still, there was room as the bottled water market continued to grow phenomenally.

Pepsi introduced Aquafina in 1994, and in 1997, after quietly gauging consumer reaction, began its national rollout. By 1999 it had become the number-one selling bottled water in the United States. Estimates were that consumption of bottled water increased 8.3 percent in one year, 1999–2000. Of this total market, the single-serve segment with its plastic bottles showed an increase of 28 percent in 2000, recording total revenue of $5.7 billion. Aquafina had the largest share of this market, with $445 million. Perrier Group, which included Poland Spring and Arrowhead brands, was second, while Evian, Crystal Geyser, and Coca-Cola's Dasani, trailed.[12]

WHAT CAN BE LEARNED?

Exiting a market for several months or more poses critical risks, particularly for a habitually consumed product. To allow new habits to be established and new loyalties to be created not only among consumers but also dealers may be impossible to fully recover from. This is especially true if competing products are comparable, and if competitors are aggressive in seizing the proferred opportunity. Since a front-runner is a target anyway, abandoning the battlefield simply invites competitive takeover.

Deception discovered and grudgingly admitted destroys a mystique. No mystique is forever. Consumer preferences change, competitors become more skilled at countering, or perhaps a firm becomes complacent in its quality control or innovative technology. These conditions act to nibble away at a mystique and eventually destroy it. As in the case of Perrier, where long-believed images of a product, its healthfulness and purity, are suddenly revealed to be false—that the advertising was less than candid and was even deceptive—then any mystique

---

[12] Louisa Kasdon Sidell, "Taking the Plunge," *Continental* (June 2001), pp. 42–45.

comes tumbling down and is unlikely to ever be regained. This scenario can only be avoided if the publicity about the deception or misdeed is not widespread. But, with a popular product such as Perrier, publicity reaches beyond business journals to the popular press. Such is the fate of large, well-known firms.

A price/quality misperception strongly exists. Without doubt, most consumers judge quality by price: the higher the price, the higher the quality. Is a $2.50 liter of Evian better quality than a gallon of tap water costing a fraction of a cent? Perhaps. But is it a hundred times better? And yet many people embrace the misconception that price is the key indicator of quality, and are consequently taken advantage of every day.

An industry catering to health is particularly vulnerable to a few unscrupulous operators. We, the general public, are particularly vulnerable to claims for better health, beauty, and youthfulness. It is human nature to reach out, hopefully, for the false promises that can be made about such important personal concerns. We become gullible in our desire to find ways to change our condition. And so we have become victims of quacks and snake-oil charmers through the ages. Governmental agencies try to exercise strong monitoring in these areas, but budgets are limited, and all claims cannot be investigated. As recent congressional scrutiny has revealed, the bottled-water industry had long been overlooked by governmental watchdogs. Now this is changing, thanks at least partly to the Perrier recall.

Should an organization have a crisis-management team? Perrier did a poor job in its crisis management. Would a more formal organizational unit devoted to this have handled things better, instead of leaving it to top executives unskilled in handling catastrophes? The issue can hardly be answered simply and all-inclusively. Crises occur rarely; and a serious crisis may never happen to a particular organization. A crisis team then would have to be composed of executives and staff who have other primary responsibilities. And their decisions and actions under fire may be no better than a less formal arrangement. For severe crises—and Perrier's was certainly that—top executives who bear the ultimate responsibility therefore have to be the final decision makers. Some will be cooler under fire than others, but this usually cannot be fully ascertained until the crisis occurs. More desirable for most organizations would seem to be contingency plans, with plans formulated for various occurrences, including the worst scenarios. With such action plans drawn up under more normal conditions, better judgements are likely to result.

CONSIDER

Can you think of additional learning insights?

QUESTIONS

1. How could the public relations efforts of Perrier have been better handled?
2. Discuss the desirability of Perrier's price-cutting during its comeback. Was it really necessary?

3. Whom do you see as the primary customers for Perrier? For Evian? For other bottled waters? Are these customers likely to be enduring in their commitment to bottled water?

4. A devil's advocate technique is sometimes used in which planners are formally assigned to develop worst-case scenarios. Do you think that would have been helpful in this crisis? Do you see any problems in relying on devil's advocates for advanced planning?

5. What arguments would you make for drastically reducing the size of the recall?

6. Are we being hoodwinked by bottled-water claims and images?

7. "The gullibility of the American public in paying high prices for bottled water is strictly related to snob appeal, and not to any tangible quality differences." Discuss.

HANDS-ON EXERCISES

1. Put yourself in the position of Ronald Davis on the afternoon of February 9, 1990. The first report of benzene found by a Carolina lab has just come in. What would you do? Be as specific as you can, and describe the logic behind your decisions.

2. How would you attempt to build up or resurrect the mystique of Perrier after the recall? What problems do you anticipate?

TEAM DEBATE EXERCISE

Debate these two contrasting positions regarding the recall:

1. The drastic recall of Davis.

2. A much less drastic recall, both in sheer numbers of bottles recalled and in length of time withheld from the market.

INVITATION TO RESEARCH

Has the surging demand for bottled water slowed? Is PepsiCo's Aquafina still the big winner? What has been the secret of its success, and in such a short time?

CHAPTER EIGHT

The Classic Masterpiece in Crisis Management: Johnson & Johnson's Tylenol Scare

[handwritten: Industry - high R+D costs - 12-15 years to bring in New products]

[handwritten: Crises: Food Lion   Exxon   Suzuki Trooper   Firestone   Intel Pentium]

In one of the greatest examples of superb crisis management, James Burke, CEO of Johnson & Johnson, in 1982 handled a catastrophe that involved loss of life in the criminal and deadly contamination of its flagship product, Tylenol. The company exhibited what has become a model for corporate responsibility to customers, regardless of costs.

[handwritten: MODEL for good crisis mgmt]

PRELUDE

[handwritten: 1982] It was September 30, 1982. On the fifth floor of the Johnson & Johnson (J&J) headquarters in New Brunswick, New Jersey, Chairman James E. Burke was having a quiet meeting with President David R. Clair. The two liked to hold such informal meetings every two months to talk over important but nonpressing matters that they usually did not get around to in the normal course of events. That day both men had reason to feel good, for J&J's sales and earnings were up sharply and the trend of business could hardly have been more promising. They even had time to dwell on some nonbusiness matters that sunny September morning.

Their complacency and self-satisfaction did not last long. Arthur Quill, a member of the executive committee, burst into the meeting. Consternation and anguish flooded the room as he brought word of cyanide deaths in Chicago that were connected to J&J's most important and profitable product, Extra-Strength Tylenol capsules.

THE COMPANY

Johnson & Johnson manufactures and markets a broad range of health care products in many countries of the world. Table 8.1 shows the various categories of products and their percent of total corporate sales. In 1981 J&J was number 68 on the *Fortune* 500 list of the largest industrial companies in the United States, and it had sales of

$5.4 billion. It was organized into four industry categories: professional, pharmaceutical, industrial, and consumer. The professional division included products such as ligatures, sutures, surgical dressings, and other surgery-related items. The pharmaceutical division included prescription drugs, and the industrial area included textile products, industrial tapes, and fine chemicals.

The largest division was the consumer division, consisting of toiletries and hygienic products such as baby care items, first aid products, and nonprescription drugs. These products were marketed primarily to the general public and distributed through wholesalers and directly to independent and chain retail outlets.

Through the years, J&J had assiduously worked to cultivate an image of responsibility and trust. Its products were associated with gentleness and safety—for all customers, from babies to the elderly. The corporate sense of responsibility fully covered the products and actions of any firms that it acquired, such as McNeil Laboratories.

THE PRODUCT

The success of Tylenol, an acetaminophen-based analgesic, in the late 1970s and early 1980s had been sensational. It had been introduced in 1955 by McNeil Laboratories as an alternative drug to aspirin, one that avoided aspirin's side effects. In 1959 Johnson & Johnson had acquired McNeil Laboratories, and the company ran it as an independent subsidiary.

By 1974 Tylenol sales had grown to $50 million at retail, primarily achieved through heavy advertising to physicians. A national consumer advertising campaign, instituted in 1976, proved very effective. By 1979 Tylenol had become the largest selling health and beauty aid in drug and food mass merchandising, breaking the 18-year domination of Procter & Gamble's Crest toothpaste. By 1982 Tylenol had captured 35.3 percent of the over-the-counter analgesic market. This was more than the market shares of Bayer, Bufferin, and Anacin combined. Table 8.2 shows the competitive

TABLE 8.1 Contribution to Total Johnson & Johnson Sales of Product Categories, 1983

Product Classification	Sales (millions)	Percent of Total Company Sales
Surgical and First-Aid Supplies	$1,268	21%
Pharmaceuticals	1,200	20
Sanitary Napkins and Tampons	933	16
Baby Products	555	9
Diagnostic Equipment	518	9
Tylenol and Variants	460	8
Other (includes hospital supplies, dental products, contraceptives)	1,039	17
Total	$5,973	100%

Source: "After Its Recovery, New Headaches for Tylenol," *Business Week* (May 14, 1984), p. 137.

**TABLE 8.2 Market Shares of Major Brands—
Over-the-Counter Analgesic Market, 1981**

Brand	Percent of Market
Tylenol	35.3
Anacin	13
Bayer	11
Excedrin	10.1
Bufferin	9

Source: "A Death Blow for Tylenol?" *Business Week* (October 18, 1982), p. 151.

positions of Tylenol and its principal competitors in this analgesic market. Total sales of all Tylenol products went from $115 million in 1976 to $350 million in 1982, a whopping 204 percent increase in a highly competitive market. As such, Tylenol accounted for 7 percent of all J&J sales. More important, it contributed 17 percent of all profits.

Then catastrophe struck.   *7% of Sales; 17% of profits*

THE CRISIS

On a Wednesday morning in late September 1982, Adam Janus had a minor chest pain, so he purchased a bottle of Extra-Strength Tylenol capsules. He took one capsule and was dead by midafternoon. Later that same day, Stanley Janus and his wife also took capsules from the same bottle—both were dead by Friday afternoon. By the weekend four more Chicago-area residents had died under similar circumstances. The cause of death was cyanide, a deadly poison that can kill within 15 minutes by disrupting the blood's ability to carry oxygen through the body, thereby affecting the heart, lungs, and brain. The cyanide had been used to contaminate Extra-Strength Tylenol capsules. Dr. Thomas Kim, chief of the critical care unit of Northwest Community Hospital in Arlington Heights, Illinois, noted, "The victims never had a chance. Death was certain within minutes."[1]

Medical examiners retrieved bottles from the victims' homes and found another 10 capsules laced with cyanide. In each case the red half of the capsule was discolored and slightly swollen, and its usual dry white powder had been replaced with a gray substance that had an almond odor. One of the capsules had 65 mg of cyanide—a lethal does is considered to be 50 mg.

The McNeil executives learned of the poisonings from reporters calling for comment about the tragedy—calls came from all the media, and then from pharmacies, doctors, hospitals, poison control centers, and hundreds of panicky consumers. McNeil quickly gathered information on the victims, causes of deaths, lot

[1] Susan Tifft, "Poison Madness in the Midwest," *Time* (October 11, 1982), p. 18.

gather info first

numbers on the poisoned Tylenol bottles, outlets where they had been purchased, dates when they had been manufactured, and the route they had taken through the distribution system.

After the deaths were linked to Tylenol, one of the biggest consumer alerts ever took place. Johnson & Johnson recalled batches and advised consumers not to take any Extra-Strength Tylenol capsules until the mystery had been solved. Drugstores and supermarkets across the country pulled Tylenol products from their shelves; it soon became virtually impossible to obtain Tylenol anywhere.

Those tracking down the mysterious contamination quickly determined that the poisoning did not occur in manufacturing, either intentionally or accidentally. The poisoned capsules had come from lots manufactured at both McNeil plants. Therefore, the tampering had to have happened in Chicago, since poisoning at both plants at the same time would have been almost impossible. The FDA suspected that someone unconnected with the manufacturer had bought the Tylenol over the counter, inserted cyanide in some capsules, then returned the bottles to the stores. Otherwise, the contamination would have been widespread, and not only in the Chicago area.

RE- CALL

N.O.

At this point, Johnson & Johnson was virtually cleared of any wrongdoing, but the company was stuck with having one of its major products publicly associated with poison and death, no matter how innocent it was. Perhaps the task of coping with the devastating impact of the tragedy would have been easier for Johnson & Johnson if the perpetrator were conclusively identified and caught. This was not to be, despite a special task force of 100 FBI agents and Illinois investigators who chased down more than 2,000 leads and filed 57 volumes of reports.[2]

J&J is a victim too.

COMPANY REACTION *CRISIS MGMT.*

Johnson & Johnson decided to elevate the management of the crisis to the corporate level and a game plan developed that company executives hoped would ensure eventual recovery. The game plan consisted of three phases: Phase I was to figure out what had actually happened; Phase II was to assess and contain the damage; and Phase III was to try to get Tylenol back into the market.

1, 2, 3

The company that had always tried to keep a low profile now turned to the media to provide it with the most accurate and current information, as well as to help it prevent a panic. Twenty-five public relations specialists were recruited from Johnson & Johnson's other divisions to help McNeil's regular staff of 15. Advertising was suspended at first. All Tylenol capsules were recalled—31 million bottles with a retail value of more than $100 million. Through advertisements promising to exchange tablets for capsules, through 500,000 telegrams to doctors, hospitals, and distributors, and through statements to the media, J&J hoped to demystify the situation.

OPEN UP COMM

With proof that the tampering had not occurred in the manufacturing process, the company moved into Phase II. Financially it experienced immediate losses

Cause → Damage Control → recovery

[2] "Tylenol Comes Back as Case Grows Cold," *Newsweek* (April 25, 1983), p. 16.

$100 MILL LOSS!

amounting to over $100 million, the bulk coming from the expense of buying unused Tylenol bottles from retailers and consumers and shipping them to disposal points. The cost of sending the telegrams was estimated at $500,000, and the costs associated with expected product liability suits were expected to run in the millions.

BRAND HURT Of more concern to the management was the impact of the poisoning on the brand itself. Many predicted that Tylenol as a brand could no longer survive. Some suggested that Johnson & Johnson reintroduce the product under a new name to give it a fresh start and thus rid itself of the devastated brand image.

Surveys conducted by Johnson & Johnson about a month after the poisonings seemed to buttress the death of Tylenol as a brand name. In one survey 94 percent of the consumers were aware that Tylenol was involved with the poisonings. Although 87 percent of these respondents realized that the maker of Tylenol was not to blame for the deaths, 61 percent said they were not likely to buy Tylenol in the future. Even worse, 50 percent of the consumers said they would not use the Tylenol tablets either. The only promising result from the research was that 49 percent of the *frequent* users answered that they would eventually use Tylenol.[3]

DILEMMA The company found itself in a real dilemma. It wanted so much to keep the Tylenol name; after all, the acceptance had been developed by years of advertising. Now, was it all to be destroyed in a few days of adversity? On the one hand, if J&J brought Tylenol back too soon, before the hysteria had subsided, the product could *period* die on the shelves. On the other hand, if the company waited too long to bring the product back, competitors might well gain an unassailable market share lead. The marketing research results were not entirely acceptable to Johnson & Johnson executives. One manager expressed the company's doubts: "The problem with consumer research is that it reflects attitudes and not behavior. The best way to know what consumers are really going to do is put the product back on the shelves and let them vote with their hands."[4] But what was the right timing?

Johnson & Johnson decided to rebuild the brand by focusing on the frequent users and then to expand to include other consumers. It hoped that a core of loyal users would want the product in both its tablet and capsule forms. In order to regain regular user confidence, J&J ran television commercials informing the public that the company would do everything it could to regain their trust. The commercials featured *feel good ad* Dr. Thomas Gates, medical director of McNeil, urging consumers to continue to trust Tylenol: "Tylenol has had the trust of the medical profession and 100 million Americans for over 20 years. We value that trust too much to let any individual tamper with it. We want you to continue to trust Tylenol."[5]

Johnson & Johnson also tried to encourage Tylenol capsule users to switch to tablets, which are more difficult to sabotage. In an advertising campaign it offered to exchange tablets for capsules at no charge. In addition it placed 76 million coupons in Sunday newspaper ads good for $2.50 toward the purchase of Tylenol.

[3] Thomas Moore, "The Fight to Save Tylenol," *Fortune* (November 29, 1982), p. 48.

[4] *Ibid.*, p. 49.

[5] Judith B. Gardner, "When a Brand Name Gets Hit by Bad News," *U.S. News & World Report* (November 8, 1982), p. 71.

Finally, it designed a tamper-resistant package to prevent the kind of tragedy that occurred in Chicago. Extra-strength capsules were now sold only in new triple-sealed packages. The flaps of the box were glued shut and were visibly torn apart when opened. The bottle's cap and neck were covered with a tight plastic seal printed with the company name, and the mouth of the bottle was covered with an inner foil seal. Both the box and the bottle were labeled, "Do Not Use If Safety Seals Are Broken." This triple-seal package cost an additional 2.4 cents per bottle, but Johnson & Johnson hoped it would instill consumer confidence in the safety of the product and spur sales. In addition the company offered retailers higher-than-normal discounts— up to 25 percent on orders.

Consumers who said they had thrown away their Tylenol after the scare were given a toll-free number to call, and they received $2.50 in coupons too—in effect, a free bottle, since bottles of 24 capsules or 30 tablets sold for about $2.50.

Over 2,000 salespeople from all Johnson & Johnson domestic subsidiaries were mobilized to persuade doctors and pharmacists to again begin recommending Tylenol tablets to patients and customers. This was similar to the strategy initially used when the product was introduced some 25 years before.

The Outcome

Immediately after the crisis, J&J's market share plunged from 35.3 percent of the pain reliever market to below 7 percent. Competitors were quick to take advantage of the situation. Upjohn Company and American Home Products Corporation were seeking Food and Drug Administration permission to sell an over-the-counter version of ibuprofen, a popular prescription pain reliever. Upjohn also granted marketing rights for its brand, Nuprin, to Bristol-Myers Co., maker of Bufferin, Excedrin, and Datril. Upjohn's prescription brand, Motrin—a stronger formulation than Nuprin—was generating some $200 million in 1982, making Motrin the company's biggest-selling drug. And lurking in the wings was mighty Procter & Gamble Company (P&G), the world's heaviest advertiser. P&G was launching national ads for Norwich aspirin and was test-marketing a coated capsule containing aspirin granules.

Yet, there were some encouraging signs for J&J. When *Psychology Today* polled its readers regarding whether Tylenol would survive as a brand name, 92 percent thought Tylenol would survive the incident. This figure corresponded closely with the results of another survey conducted by Leo Shapiro, an independent market researcher, just two weeks after the deaths occurred, in which 91 percent said they would probably buy the product again.

Psychology Today tried to get at the roots of such loyalty and roused comments such as these:

A 23-year old woman wrote that she would continue to use Tylenol because she felt that it was "tried and true."

A 61-year old woman said that the company had been "honest and sincere."

And a young man thought Tylenol was an easy name to say.[6]

---

[6] Carin Rubenstein, "The Tylenol Tradition," *Psychology Today* (April 1983), p. 16.

8 MO. LATER

Such survey results presaged an amazing comeback: J&J's conscientious actions paid off. By May 1983 Tylenol had regained almost all the market share lost the previous September; its market share reached 35 percent, which it held until 1986, when another calamity struck.

New industry safety standards had been developed by the over-the-counter drug industry in concert with the Food and Drug Administration for tamper-resistant packaging. Marketers under law had to select a package "having an indicator or barrier to entry, which if breached or missing, can reasonably be expected to provide visible evidence to the consumer that the package has been tampered with or opened."[7] Despite toughened package standards, in February 1986, a Westchester, New York, woman died from cyanide-laced Extra-Strength Tylenol capsules. The tragedy of 3 1/2 years before was being replayed. J&J immediately removed all Tylenol capsules from the market and offered refunds for capsules consumers had already bought.

Fall '86 AGAIN

Now the company made a major decision. It decided no longer to manufacture any over-the-counter capsules because it could not guarantee their safety from criminal contamination. Henceforth, the company would market only tablets and so-called caplets, which were coated and elongated tablets that are easy to swallow. This decision was expected to cost $150 million. The president explained: "People think of this company as extraordinarily trustworthy and responsible, and we don't want to do anything to damage that."[8]

By July 1986 Tylenol had regained most of the market share lost in February, and it now stood at 32 percent.

THE INGREDIENTS OF CRISIS MANAGEMENT

Johnson & Johnson was truly a management success in its handling of the Tylenol problem. It overcame the worst kind of adversity, that in which human life was lost in using one of its products, and a major product at that. Yet, in only a few months it recouped most of its lost market share and regained its public image of corporate responsibility and trust. What accounted for the success of J&J in overcoming such adversity?

We can identify five significant factors:

KEY

1. Keeping communication channels open
2. Taking quick, corrective action
3. Keeping faith in the product
4. Protecting the public image at all costs
5. Aggressively bringing back the brand

Effective communication has seldom been better done. Rapport must be gained with the media, to enlist their support and even their sympathy. Alas, this is

---

[7] "Package Guides Studied," *Advertising Age* (October 18, 1982), p. 82.

[8] Richard W. Stevenson, "Johnson & Johnson's Recovery," *New York Times* (July 5, 1986), pp. 33–34.

not easily done, for the press is inclined to sensationalize, criticize, and take sides against the big corporation. Johnson & Johnson gained the needed rapport through corporate openness and cooperation. In the disaster's early days it sought good two-way communication, with the media furnishing information from the field while J&J gave full and honest disclosure of its internal investigation and corrective actions. Important for good rapport, company officials need to be freely available and open to the press. Unfortunately, this goes against most executives' natural bent so that a spirit of antipathy often is fostered.

(2) When product safety is in jeopardy, quick corrective action must be taken, *regardless* of the cost. This usually means immediate recall of the affected product, and this can involve millions of dollars. Even if the fault lies with only an isolated batch of products, a firm may need to recall them all since public perception of the danger likely will transfer to all units of that brand.

(3) Johnson & Johnson kept faith with its product and brand name, despite the counsel of experts who thought the Tylenol name should be abandoned because public trust could never be regained. Of course, the company was not at fault: There was no culpability, no carelessness. The cause was right. Admittedly, in keeping faith with a product there is a thin line between a positive commitment and recalcitrant stubbornness to face up to any problem and accept any blame. But J&J's faith in Tylenol was justified, and without it the company would have had no chance of resurrecting the product and its market share.

(4) Johnson & Johnson strove to protect its public image of being a socially responsible and caring firm. The following Information Box discusses *social responsiblity* and presents the J&J credo regarding this. It is interesting to note that this credo is still prominently positioned in company annual reports ten years later. If there was to be any chance for a fairly quick recovery from adversity, this public image had to be guarded, no matter how beset it was. With the plight of Tylenol well known, with corrective actions prompt and thorough, many people were thus assured that safety was restored. We should note here that for the public image to be regained under adverse circumstances, the corrective actions must be well publicized. Public relations efforts and good communication with the media are essential for this. And, again, it helps when the fault of the catastrophe is clearly not the firm's.

(5) A superb job was done in aggressively bringing back the Tylenol brand. In so doing, coordination was essential. Efforts to safeguard the public image had to be reasonably successful, the cause of the disaster needed to be conclusively established, the likelihood of the event ever happening again had to be seen as virtually impossible. Then aggressive promotional efforts could fuel the recovery.

Johnson & Johnson's efforts to come back necessarily focused on correcting the problem. Initially it designed a tamper-resistant container to prevent the kind of tragedy that had occurred in Chicago. Extra-strength capsules were now to be sold only in new triple-sealed packages. When another death occurred in 1986, the company dropped capsules entirely and offered Tylenol only in tablet form.

With the safety features in place, J&J then used heavy promotion. This included consumer advertising, with the theme of safety assurance and company social responsibility. J&J offered to exchange capsules for tablets at no charge. It

---

INFORMATION BOX

SOCIAL RESPONSIBILITY AND THE JOHNSON & JOHNSON'S CREDO REGARDING IT

We can define social responsibility as the sense of responsibility a firm has for the needs of society, over and above its commitment to maximizing profits and stockholders inter-ests. The following credo of J & J illustrates the wide circle of corporate social respon-sibility that more and more firms are beginning to accept.

Johnson & Johnson's Credo[9]

We believe our first responsibility is to the doctors, nurses, and patients, to mothers and all others who use our products and services. In meeting their needs everything we do must be of high quality. We must constantly strive to reduce our costs in order to main-tain reasonable prices. Customers' orders must be serviced promptly and accurately. Our suppliers and distributors must have an opportunity to make a fair profit.

We are responsible to our employees, the men and women who work with us throughout the world. Everyone must be considered as an individual. We must respect their dignity and recognize their merit. They must have a sense of security in their jobs. Compensation must be fair and adequate, and working conditions clean, orderly, and safe. Employees must feel free to make suggestions and complaints. There must be equal opportunity for employment, development, and advancement for those qualified. We must provide competent management, and their actions must be just and ethical.

We are responsible to the communities in which we live and work and to the world community as well. We must be good citizens—support good works and charities and bear our fair share of taxes. We must encourage civic improvements and better health and education. We must maintain in good order the property we are privileged to use, protecting the environment and natural resources.

Our final responsibility is to our stockholders. Business must make a sound profit. We must experiment with new ideas. Research must be carried on, innovative programs devel-oped, and mistakes paid for. New equipment must be purchased, new facilities provided, and new products launched. Reserves must be created to provide for adverse times. When we operate according to these principles, the stockholders should realize a fair return.

"Such statements are only pious platitudes. Social responsibility requires more than lip service." How would you answer this?

---

[9] From a company recruiting brochure and annual reports.

---

offered millions of newspaper coupons good for $2.50 toward the purchase of Tylenol. Retailers were also given incentives to back Tylenol through discounts, advertising allowances, and full refunds for recalled capsules with all handling costs paid. These efforts, directed to consumers and retailers alike, bolstered dealer confidence in the resurgence of the brand.

UPDATE

Johnson & Johnson has been an enduring growth company, with sales reaching $29 billion in 2000, and profits $4.8 billion. It ranks as the largest and most diversified health care company in the world. Its products now range from blockbuster prescription drugs, to professional products such as sutures, surgical accessories, and catheters, to a wide list of consumer products such as Tylenol, bandages, and toiletries.

With this broad product mix, how important is Tylenol to J&J today? In 1997, $1.3 billion, or almost 6 percent, came from Tylenol. (In 1982, at the time of the contamination, Tylenol contributed 8% of the $5.9 billion total company sales.) J&J heavily promoted Tylenol to maintain this prominence. In 1997, for example, the company's domestic ad budget for Tylenol was estimated at $250 million, more than Coca-Cola spent for Coke.[10]

WHAT CAN BE LEARNED?

Any company's nightmare is having its product linked to death or injury. Such a calamity invariably results in fear and loss of public confidence in the product and the firm. At worst, such disaster can kill a company, as happened with some canned-food firms whose products were contaminated with the deadly botulism toxin. The more optimistic projections would have a firm losing years of time and money it had invested in a brand, with the brand never able to regain its former robustness. In the throes of the catastrophe, J&J executives grappled with the major decision of abandoning the brand at the height of its popularity or keeping it. The decision could have gone either way. Now with hindsight, we know that the decision not to abandon was unmistakably correct, but at the time it was recklessly courageous.

Faced with a catastrophe, a brand may still be saved, but cost might be staggering. J&J successfully brought back Tylenol, but it cost hundreds of millions of dollars. The company's size at the time, over $5 billion in sales from a diversified product line, enabled it to handle the costs without jeopardy. A smaller firm would not have been able to weather this, especially without a broad product line.

Whenever product safety is an issue, the danger of lawsuits must be reckoned with. In the absence of corporate neglect, the swift constructive reaction, and the fact that the company could hardly have anticipated a madman, J&J escaped the worst scenario regarding litigation. Still, hundreds of millions of dollars in lawsuits were filed. Such suits accused J&J of failing to package Tylenol in a tamper-proof container, and the legal expenses of defending were high. The threat of litigation must be a major consideration for any firm. Even if the organization is relatively blameless, legal costs can run into the millions, and no one can predict the decisions of juries.

---

[10] Thomas Easton and Stephen Herrera, "J&J's Dirty Little Secret," *Forbes* (January 12, 1998), p. 44.

Copycat crimes are a danger. Although other firms in an industry stand to gain an advantage in a competitor's crisis, they and firms in related industries need to be alert for copycat crimes. By November, a month after the deaths, the Food and Drug Administration had received more than 270 reports of chemicals, pills, poisons, needles, pins, and razor blades in everything from food to drinks to medications. Fortunately, no deaths resulted from these incidents. But FDA Commissioner Hayes worried: "My greatest fear is that because of the notoriety of the case and the financial damage to the company, someone else will take out his or her grudges on a product and do something similar."[11] Actually, the Tylenol case was not the first time products had been deliberately contaminated. Eyedrops, nasal sprays, milk of magnesia, foods, and cosmetics have all been targets of tampering. An Oregon man was sentenced to 20 years in prison for attempting to extort diamonds from grocery chains by putting cyanide in food products on their shelves.

A firm can come back from extreme adversity with good crisis management. Certainly, one of the major things we can learn from this case is that it is possible to come back from extreme adversity. Before the Tylenol episode, most experts did not realize this. The general opinion was that severe negative publicity resulted in such an image destruction that recovery could take years. The most optimistic predictions were that Tylenol might recover to about a 20 to 21 percent market share in a year; the pessimistic predictions were that the brand would never recover and should be abandoned.[12] Actually, in eight months, Tylenol had regained almost all of its market share, to a satisfactory 35 percent. For such a recovery, a firm has to manifest unselfish concern, quick corrective action, and unsparing spending, and it must have a good public image before the catastrophe.

Contingency planning can aid crisis management. Although not all crisis possibilities can be foreseen, or even imagined, many can be identified. For example, contingency plans for worse-case scenarios can be developed for the possibility of food and medicine tampering or the loss of major executives in an accident of some sort. Sometimes in such planning, precautionary moves may become evident for minimizing the potential dangers. For example, with food and medicine tampering, different containers and sealed bottle tops might virtually eliminate the danger. And with executive accidents, many firms have a policy that key executives not fly on the same flight or ride in the same car.

CONSIDER

Can you think of other learning insights?

QUESTIONS

1. Did J&J move too far in recalling all Extra-Strength Tylenol capsules? Would not a sufficient action have been to recall only those in the Chicago area, thus saving millions of dollars? Discuss.

---

[11] "Lessons That Emerge from Tylenol Disaster," *U.S. News & World Report* (October 18, 1982), p. 68.

[12] "J&J Will Pay Dearly to Cure Tylenol," *Business Week* (November 20, 1982), p. 37.

2. How helpful do you think the marketing research results were in the decision on keeping the Tylenol name?

3. "We must assume that someone had a terrible grudge against J&J to have perpetrated such a crime." Discuss.

4. "J&J's 'recovery' has to be attributed to the fact that some evil person was to blame, and not J&J. The situation would not have worked out so well if J&J had major culpability." Discuss.

5. Assuming that J&J was at least partially to blame in not having adequate security, for example, should it have revised its crisis plan, and if so, how? Support your position.

6. Compare and contrast the handling of the Tylenol crisis with that of Perrier in the previous chapter. What learning insights can you suggest for the handling of these two crises?

HANDS-ON EXERCISES

1. Assume this scenario: It has been established that the fault of the contamination was accidental introduction of cyanide at a company plant. Now, how will you, as CEO of J&J, direct your recovery strategy? Give your rationale.

2. Assume this scenario: It has been established that the fault of the contamination was deliberate introduction of cyanide by a disgruntled employee. This person had a serious grievance about sexual harassment, and such grievances in the past had always been downplayed. The publicity about this has leaked out. Now, as CEO, what would you do?

TEAM DEBATE EXERCISE

Debate both sides of the burning issue at the height of the crisis of keeping the Tylenol name and trying to recoup it, or abandoning it. You must not use the benefit of hindsight for this exercise.

INVITATION TO RESEARCH

Can you find any instances of J&J not always having been a good citizen with superb customer concern? If so, investigate and draw conclusions about J&J's enviable position as a role model. Are there any learning insights?

GREAT COMEBACKS

CHAPTER NINE

Continental Airlines: From the Ashes

In the fourth edition of *Mistakes*, published in 1994, we described massive management blunders at Continental Airlines as a "confrontational destruction of an organization." In only a few years, in a remarkable recovery under new management, Continental became a star of the airline industry. The changemaker, CEO Gordon Bethune, wrote a best-selling book about his efforts to turn around the moribund company, titled *From Worst to First*. In this chapter we will look first at the unfolding scenario leading to the difficulties of Continental, and then examine the ingredients of the great comeback.

THE FRANK LORENZO ERA

Lorenzo was a consummate manipulator, parlaying borrowed funds and little of his own money to build an airline empire. By the end of 1986, he controlled the largest airline network in the non-Communist world: only Aeroflot, the Soviet airline, was larger. Lorenzo's network was a leveraged amalgam of Continental, People Express, Frontier, and Eastern, with $8.6 billion in sales—all this from a small investment in Texas International Airlines in 1971. In the process of building his network, Lorenzo defeated unions and shrewdly used the bankruptcy courts to further his ends. When he eventually departed, his empire was swimming in red ink, had a terrible reputation, and was burdened with colossal debt and aging planes.

The Start

After getting an MBA from Harvard, Lorenzo's first job was as a financial analyst at Trans World Airlines. In 1966, he and Robert Carney, a buddy from Harvard, formed an airline consulting firm, and in 1969 the two put up $35,000 between them to form an investment firm, Jet Capital. Through a public stock offering they were able to raise an additional $1.15 million. In 1971 Jet Capital was called in to fix ailing Texas International and wound up buying it for $1.5 million, and Lorenzo became CEO.

He restructured the debt as well as the airline's routes, found funds to upgrade the almost obsolete planes, and brought Texas International to profitability.

In 1978, acquisition-minded Lorenzo lost out to Pan Am in a bidding war for National Airlines, but he made $40 million on the National stock he had acquired. In 1980 he created nonunion New York Air and formed Texas Air as a holding company. In 1982 Texas Air bought Continental for $154 million.

Lorenzo's Treatment of Continental

In 1983 Lorenzo took Continental into bankruptcy court, filing for Chapter 11. This permitted the corporation to continue to operate but spared its obligation to meet heavy interest payments and certain other contracts while it reorganized as a more viable enterprise. The process nullified the previous union contracts, and this prompted a walkout by many union workers.

Lorenzo earned the lasting enmity of organized labor and the reputation of union-buster as he replaced strikers with nonunion workers at much lower wages. (A few years later, he reinforced this reputation when he used the same tactics with Eastern Airlines.)

In a 1986 acquisition achievement that was to backfire a few years later, Lorenzo struck deals for a weak Eastern Airlines and a failing People Express/Frontier Airlines. That same year Continental emerged out of bankruptcy. Now Continental, with its nonunion workforce making it a low-cost operator, was Lorenzo's shining jewel. The low bid accepted for Eastern reinforced Lorenzo's reputation as a visionary builder.

What kind of executive was Lorenzo? Although he was variously described as a master financier and visionary, his handling of day-to-day problems bordered on the inept.[1] One former executive was quoted as saying, "If he agreed with one thing at 12:15, it would be different by the afternoon."[2] Inconsistent planning and poor execution characterized his lack of good operational strength. Furthermore, his domineering and erratic style alienated talented executives. From 1983 to 1993, nine presidents left Continental.

But Lorenzo's treatment of his unions brought the most controversy. He became the central figure of confrontational labor-management relations, to a degree perhaps unmatched by any other person in recent years. Although he won the battle with Continental's unions and later with Eastern's, he was burdened with costly strikes and the residue of ill feeling that impeded any profitable recovery during his time at the helm.

The Demise of Eastern Airlines

In an environment of heavy losses and its own militant unions, Eastern in 1986 accepted the low offer of Lorenzo. With tough contract demands and the

---

[1] See, for example, Todd Vogel, Gail DeGeorge, Pete Engardio, and Aaron Bernstein, "Texas Air Empire in Jeopardy," *Business Week* (March 27, 1989), p. 30.

[2] Mark Ivey and Gail DeGeorge, "Lorenzo May Land a Little Short of the Runway," *Business Week* (February 5, 1990), p. 48.

stockpiling of $1 billion in cash as strike insurance, Lorenzo seemed eager to precipitate a strike that he might crush. He instituted a program of severe downsizing, and in 1989, after 15 months of fruitless talks, some 8,500 machinists and 3,800 pilots went on strike. Lorenzo countered the strike at Eastern by filing for Chapter 11 bankruptcy, and replaced many of the striking pilots and machinists within months.

At first Eastern appeared to be successfully weathering the strike, while Continental benefited with increased business. But soon revenue dropped drastically with Eastern planes flying less than half full amid rising fuel costs. Fares were slashed in order to regain business, and a liquidity crisis loomed. Then, on January 16, 1990, an Eastern jet sheared the top off a private plane in Atlanta. Even though the accident was attributed to air controller error, Eastern's name received the publicity.

Eastern creditors now despaired of Lorenzo's ability to pay them back in full and they pushed for a merger with Continental, which would expose it to the bankruptcy process. On December 3, 1990, Continental again tumbled into bankruptcy, burdened with overwhelming debt. In January 1991, Eastern finally went out of business.

CONTINENTAL'S EMERGENCE FROM BANKRUPTCY, AGAIN

Lorenzo was gone. The legacy of Eastern remained, however. Creditors claimed more than $400 million in asset transfers between Eastern and Continental, and Eastern still had $680 million in unfunded pension liabilities. The board brought in Robert Ferguson, veteran of Braniff and Eastern bankruptcies, to make changes. On April 16, 1993, the court approved a reorganization plan for Continental to emerge from bankruptcy, the first airline to have survived two bankruptcies. However, creditors got only pennies on the dollar.[3]

Still, despite its long history of travail and a terrible profit picture, Continental in 1992 was the nation's fifth largest airline, behind American, United, Delta, and Northwest, and it served 193 airports. Table 9.1 shows the revenues and net profits (or losses) of Continental and its major competitors from 1987 through 1991.

The Legacy of Lorenzo

Continental was savaged in its long tenure as a pawn in Lorenzo's dynasty-building efforts. He had saddled it with huge debts, brought it into bankruptcy twice, left it with aging equipment. Perhaps a greater detriment was a ravished corporate culture. The following Information Box discusses corporate culture.

A devastated reputation proved to be a major impediment. The reputation of a surly labor force had repercussions far beyond the organization itself. For years Continental had had a problem wooing the better-paying business travelers. Being on expense accounts, they wanted quality service rather than cut-rate prices. A

---

[3] Bridget O'Brian, "Judge Backs Continental Airlines Plan to Regroup, Emerge from Chapter 11," *Wall Street Journal* (April 19, 1993), p. A4.

TABLE 9.1 **Performance Statistics, Major Airlines, 1987–1991**

	1987	1988	1989	1990	1991	Percent 5-Year Gain
Revenues:						
(millions $)						
American	6,368	7,548	8,670	9,203	9,309	46.0%
Delta	5,638	6,684	7,780	7,697	8,268	46.6
United	6,500	7,006	7,463	7,946	7,850	20.8
Northwest	3,328	3,395	3,944	4,298	4,330	30.1
Continental	3,404	3,682	3,896	4,036	4,031	18.4
Income						
(millions $)						
American	225	450	412	(40)	(253)	
Delta	201	286	467	(119)	(216)	
United	22	426	246	73	(175)	
Continental	(304)	(310)	(56)	(1,218)	(1,550)	

Source: Company annual reports.

Commentary: Note the operating performance of Continental relative to its major competitors during this period. It ranks last in sales gain. It far and away has the worst profit performance, having massive losses during each of the years in contrast to its competitors, who, while incurring some losses, had neither the constancy nor the magnitude of losses of Continental. And the relative losses of Continental are even worse than they at first appear: Continental is the smallest of these major airlines.

reputation for good service is not easily or quickly achieved, especially when the opposite reputation is well entrenched.

On another dimension, Continental's reputation also hindered competitive parity. Surviving two bankruptcies does not engender confidence among investors, creditors, or even travel agents.

A Sick Airline Industry

Domestic airlines lost a staggering $8 billion in the years 1990 through 1992. Tense fare wars and excess planes proved to be albatrosses. Even when planes were filled, discount prices often did not cover overhead.

A lengthy recession was mostly to blame, inducing both firms and individuals to fly more sparingly. Business firms were finding teleconferencing to be a viable substitute for business travel, and consumers, facing diminished discretionary income and the threat of eventual layoffs or forced retirements, were hardly in an optimistic mood. The airlines suffered.

Part of the blame for the red ink lay directly with the airlines—they were reckless in their expansion efforts—yet they did not deserve total blame. In the late 1980s, passenger traffic climbed 10 percent per year, and in response the airlines ordered

IMPORTANCE OF A POSITIVE CORPORATE CULTURE

A corporate or organizational culture can be defined as the system of shared beliefs and values that develops within an organization and guides the behavior of its members.[4] Such a culture can be a powerful influence on performance results:

> If employees know what their company stands for, if they know what standards they are to uphold, then they are much more likely to make decisions that will support those standards. They are also more likely to feel as if they are an important part of the organization. They are motivated because life in the company has meaning for them.[5]

Lorenzo had destroyed the former organizational climate as he beat down the unions. The replacement employees had little reason to develop a positive culture or esprit de corps given the many top management changes, the low pay relative to other airline employees, and the continuous possibility of corporate bankruptcy. Employees had little to be proud of. But this was to change abruptly under new management.

Can a corporate climate be too upbeat? Discuss.

[4] Edgar H. Schein, "Organizational Culture," *American Psychologist,* vol. 45 (1990), pp. 109–119.
[5] Terrence E. Deal and Alan A. Kennedy, *Corporate Cultures: The Rites and Rituals of Corporate Life* (Reading, MA: Addison-Wesley, 1982), p. 22.

hundreds of jetliners.[6] The recession arrived just as the new planes were being delivered. The airlines greatly increased their debt structure in their expansion efforts; the big three, for example—American, United, and Delta—doubled their leverage in the four years after 1989, with debt by 1993 at 80 percent of capitalization.[7]

In such a climate, cost-cutting efforts prevailed. But how much can be cut without jeopardizing service and even safety? Some airlines found that hubs, heralded as the great strategy of the 1980s, were not as cost effective as expected. With hub cities, passengers were gathered from outlying "spokes" and then flown to final destinations. Maintaining too many hubs, however, brought costly overheads. While the concept was good, some retrenchment seemed necessary to be cost effective.

Airlines such as Continental with heavy debt and limited liquidity had two major concerns: first, how fast the country could emerge from recession; second, the risk of fuel price escalation in the coming years. Despite Continental's low operating costs, external conditions impossible to predict or control could affect viability.

THE GREAT COMEBACK UNDER GORDON BETHUNE

In February 1994, Gordon Bethune left Boeing and took the job of president and chief operating officer of Continental. He faced a daunting challenge. While it was

[6] Andrea Rothman, "Airlines: Still No Wind at Their Backs," *Business Week* (January 11, 1993), p. 96.
[7] *Ibid.*

the fifth largest airline, Continental was by far the worst among the nation's 10 biggest according to these quality indicators of the Department of Transportation:

- In on-time percentage (the percentage of flights that land within 15 minutes of their scheduled arrival)
- In number of mishandled-baggage reports filed per 1,000 passengers
- In number of complaints per 100,000 passengers
- In involuntarily denied boarding (i.e., passengers with tickets who are not allowed to board because of overbooking or other problems)[8]

In late October he became chief executive officer. Now he sat in the pilot's seat.

He made dramatic changes. In 1995, through a "renewed focus on flight schedules and incentive pay" he greatly improved on-time performance, along with lost-baggage claims, and customer complaints. Now instead of being dead last in these quality indicators of the Department of Transportation, Continental by 1996 was third best or better in all four categories.

Customers began returning, especially the higher-fare business travelers, climbing from 32.2 percent in 1994 to 42.8 percent of all customers by 1996. In May 1996, based on customer surveys Continental was awarded the J. D. Power Award as the best airline for customer satisfaction on flights of 500 miles or more. It also received the award in 1997, the first airline to win two years in a row. Other honors followed. In January 1997, it was named "Airline of the Year" by *Air Transport World,* the leading industry monthly. In January 1997, *Business Week* named Bethune one of its top managers of 1996.

Bethune had transformed the workforce into a happy one, as measured by these statistics:

- Wages up an average of 25 percent
- Sick leave down more than 29 percent
- Personnel turnover down 45 percent
- Workers compensation claims down 51 percent
- On-the-job injuries down 54 percent[9]

Perhaps nothing illustrates the improvement in employee morale as much as this: In 1995, not long after he became top executive, employees were so happy with their new boss's performance that they chipped in to buy him a $22,000 Harley-Davidson.[10]

Naturally such improvement in employee relations and customer service had major impact on revenues and profitability. See Table 9.2 for the trend since 1992.

Gordon Bethune

Bethune's father was a crop duster, and as a teenager Gordon helped him one summer and learned firsthand the challenges of responsibility: in this case, preparing a crude

---

[8] Gordon Bethune, *From Worst to First* (New York: Wiley, 1998), p. 4.

[9] *Ibid.,* pp. 7–8.

[10] *Ibid.,* frontispiece.

TABLE 9.2   Continental Sales and Profits, Before and After Bethune, 1992–1997

	Before Bethune			After Bethune		
	1992	1993	1994	1995	1996	1997
Revenues (millions $)	5,494	3,907	5,670	5,825	6,360	7,213
Net Income (millions $)	−110	−39	−612	224	325	389
Earnings per Share ($)		−1.17	−11.88	3.60	4.25	5.03

Sources: Company annual reports.

Commentary: While the revenue statistics do not show a striking improvement, the net income certainly does. Most important to investors, the earnings per share show a major improvement.

These statistics suggest the fallacy of a low-price strategy at the expense of profitability in the 1992–1994 era. At the same time, we have to realize that the early 1990s were recession years, particularly for the airline industry.

landing strip for nightime landings, with any negligence disastrous. He joined the Navy at 17, before finishing high school. He graduated second in his class at the Naval Technical School to become an aviation electronics technician, and over 19 years worked his way up to lieutenant. After leaving the Navy he joined Braniff, then Western, and later Piedmont Airlines as senior vice president of Operations. He finally left Piedmont for Boeing as VP/general manager of Customer Service. There he became licensed as a 757 and 767 pilot: "An amazing thing happened. All the Boeing pilots suddenly thought I was a great guy," he writes. "I hope I hadn't given them any reason to think otherwise of me before that, but this really got their attention."[11]

HOW DID HE DO IT?

Bethune stressed the human element in guiding the comeback of a lethargic, even bitter, organization, even by doing the simple things: "On October 24, 1994, I did a very significant thing in the executive suite of Continental Airlines. ... I opened the doors. ... [Before] the doors to the executive suite were locked, and you needed an ID to get through. Security cameras added to the feeling of relaxed charm. ... So the day I began running the company, I opened the doors. I wasn't afraid of my employees, and I wanted everybody to know it."[12] Still, he had to entice employees to the twentieth floor of headquarters, and he did this with open houses, supplying food and drink, and personal tours and chat sessions. "I'd take a group of employees into my office, open up the closet, and say, 'You see? Frank's not here.' Frank Lorenzo had left Continental years before; the legacy of cost cutting and infighting of that era was finally gone, and I wanted them to know it."[13]

Of course, the improved employee relations needed tangible elements to cement and sustain it, and to improve the morale. Bethune worked hard to instill a spirit of

[11] *Ibid.,* p. 268.
[12] *Ibid.,* p. 14.
[13] *Ibid.,* p. 32.

teamwork. He did this by giving on-time bonuses to all employees, not just pilots. He burned the employee procedure manual that bound them to rigid policies instead of being able to use their best judgment. He even gave the planes a new paint job to provide tangible evidence of a disavowal of the old and an embracing of new policies and practices. This new image impressed both employees and customers.

Better communications was also a key element in improving employee relationships and the spirit of teamwork. Information was shared with employees through newsletters, updates on bulletin boards, e-mail, voice-mail, and electronic signs over worldwide workplaces. To Bethune it was a cardinal sin for any organization if employees first heard of something affecting them through the newspaper or other media. The following Information Box contrasts the classic Theory X and Theory Y managers. Bethune was certainly a Theory Y manager, and Lorenzo Theory X.

INFORMATION BOX

THE THEORY X AND THEORY Y MANAGER

Douglas McGregor, in his famous book, *The Human Side of Enterprise*, advanced the thesis of two different types of managers, the traditional Theory X manager with rather low opinion of subordinates, and his new Theory Y manager, whom we might call a human-relations type of manager.

Schermerhorn contrasts the two styles as follows:[14]

Theory X views subordinates as

- Disliking work
- Lacking in ambition
- Irresponsible
- Resistant to change
- Preferring to be led than to lead

Theory Y sees subordinates this way:

- Willing to work
- Willing to accept responsibility
- Capable of self-direction
- Capable of self-control
- Capable of imagination, ingenuity, creativity

Which is better? With the success of Bethune in motivating his employees for strong positive change in the organization, one would think Theory Y is the only way to go. McGregor certainly thought so and predicted that giving workers more participation, freedom, and responsibility would result in high productivity.[15]

So, is there any room for a Theory X manager today? If so, under what circumstances?

[14] John R. Schermerhorn, Jr., *Management*, 6th ed. (New York: J. Wiley 1999), p. 79.

[15] Douglas McGregor, *The Human Side of Enterprise* (New York: McGraw-Hill), 1960.

Now Continental had to win back customers. Instead of the company's old focus on cost savings, efforts were directed to putting out a better product. This meant emphasis on on-time flights, better baggage handling, and the like. By giving employees bonuses for meeting these standards, the incentive was created.

Bethune sought to do a better job of designing routes with good demand, to "fly places people wanted to go." This meant, for example, cutting back on six flights a day between Greensboro, North Carolina, and Greenville, South Carolina. It meant not trying to compete with Southwest's Friends Fly Free Fares, which "essentially allowed passengers to fly anywhere within the state of Florida for $24.50.[16] The frequent flyer program was reinstated. Going a step further, the company apologized to travel agents, business partners, and customers and showed them how it planned to do better and earn their business back.

Continental queried travel agents about their biggest clients, the major firms that did the most traveling, asking how could it better serve their customers. As a result, more first-class seats were added, particular destinations were given more attention, discounts for certain volumes were instituted. Travel agents themselves were made members of the team and given special incentives beyond normal airline commissions.

This still left financial considerations. Bethune was aggressive in renegotiating loans and poor airplane lease agreements, and in getting supplier financial cooperation. Controls were set up to monitor cash flow and stop waste. Tables 9.3 and 9.4 show the results of Bethune's efforts from the dark days of 1992–1994, and how the competitive position of Continental changed. Remember, Bethune joined

TABLE 9.3 Competitive Position of Continental Before and After Bethune, 1992–1997

	Before Bethune			After Bethune		
	1992	1993	1994	1995	1996	1997
Revenues (millions $):						
AMR (American)	14,396	15,701	16,137	16,910	17,753	18,570
UAR (United)	12,890	14,511	13,950	14,943	16,362	17,378
Delta	10,837	11,997	12,359	12,194	12,455	13,590
Northwest	NA	8,649	9,143	9,085	9,881	10,226
Continental	5,494	3,907	5,670	5,825	6,360	7,213
Continental's Market Share (percent of total sales of Big Five Airlines):		7.1%	9.9%	9.9%	10.1%	10.8%

Sources: Company annual reports.

NA = information not available.

Commentary: Most significant is the gradual increase in market share of Continental over its four major rivals. This is an improving competitive position.

[16] *Ibid.,* pp. 51–52.

TABLE 9.4   Profitability Comparison of Big Five Airlines, 1992–1997

	Before Bethune			After Bethune		
	1992	1993	1994	1995	1996	1997
Net Income (millions $):						
AMR	–474	–96	228	196	1,105	985
UAL	–416	–31	77	378	600	958
Delta	–505	–414	–408	294	156	854
Northwest	NA	–114	296	342	536	606
Continental	–110	–39	–696	224	325	389

Source: Company annual reports.

NA = information not available.

Commentary: Of interest is how the good and bad times for the airlines seem to move in lockstep. Still, the smallest of the Big Five, Continental, incurred the biggest loss of any airline in 1994. Under Bethune, it has seen a steady increase in profitability, but so have the other airlines, although AMR and Delta have been more erratic

the firm in February 1994 and did not become the top executive until late October of that year.

WHAT CAN BE LEARNED?

It is possible to quickly turn around an organization. This idea flies in the face of conventional wisdom. How can a firm's bad reputation with employees, customers, creditors, stockholders, and suppliers be overcome without years of trying to prove that it has changed for the better? This conventional wisdom is usually correct: a great comeback does not often occur easily or quickly. But it sometimes does, with a streetwise leader, and a bit of luck perhaps. Gordon Bethune is proof that negative attitudes can be turned around quickly.

This possibility of a quick turnaround should be inspiring to other organizations mired in adversity.

Still, reputation should be carefully guarded. In most cases, a poor image is difficult to overcome, with trust built up only over time. The prudent firm is careful to safeguard its reputation.

Give employees a sense of pride and a caring management. Bethune proved a master at changing employees' attitudes and their sense of pride. Few top executives ever faced such a negative workforce, reflecting the Lorenzo years. But Bethune changed all this, and in such a short time. His open-door policy and open houses to encourage employees to interact with him and other top executives was such a simple gesture, but so effective, as was his opening wide the channels of communication about company plans. The incentive plans for improving performance, and the freeing up of employee initiatives by abolishing the rigidity of formal policies, were further positives. He engendered an atmosphere of teamwork and a personal image of an appreciative CEO. What is truly remarkable is how quickly such simple actions could turn around the attitudes of a workforce from adversarial with morale in the pits to pride and an eagerness to build an airline.

Contradictory and inconsistent strategies are vulnerable. Lorenzo was often described as mercurial and subject to knee-jerk planning, and poor execution.[17] Clearly focused objectives and strategies mark effective firms. They bring stability to an organization and give customers, employees, and investors confidence in undeviating commitments. Admittedly, some objectives and strategies may have to be modified occasionally to meet changing environmental and competitive conditions, but the spirit of the organization should be resolute, provided it is a positive influence and not a negative one.

The dangers of competing mostly on low price. Bethune inherited one of the lowest-cost air carriers, and it was doing badly. He says "you can make an airline so cheap nobody wants to fly it," [just as] "you can make a pizza so cheap nobody wants to eat it." "Trust me on this—we did it. ... In fact, it was making us lousy, and people didn't want to buy what we offered."[18]

We might add here that competing strictly on a price basis usually leaves any firm vulnerable. Low prices can easily be matched or countered by competitors if such low prices are attracting enough customers. On the other hand, competition based on such nonprice factors as better service, quality of product, a good public image or reputation are not so easily matched, and can be more attractive to many customers.

ISSUE BOX

SHOULD AN ORGANIZATION BE NURTURED OR CONFRONTED?

Lorenzo used a confrontational and adversarial approach to his organization and the unions. He was seemingly successful in destroying the unions and hiring nonunion replacements at lower pay scales. This resulted in Continental becoming the lowest-cost operator of the major carriers, but there were negatives: service problems, questionable morale, diminished reputation, and devastated profitability.

Bethune used the opposite tack. It is hard to argue against nurturing and supporting an existing organization, avoiding the adversarial mindset of "them or us" if at all possible. Admittedly this may sometimes be difficult—sometimes impossible, at least in the short-run—but it is worth trying. It should result in better morale, motivation, and commitment to the company's best interest. (See Chapter 17 for Southwest Airlines' approach to organizational relations.)

---

[17] For example, Ivey and DeGeorge, *op. cit.*, p. 48.

[18] Bethune, *op. cit.*, p. 50.

In Chapter 17, again with Southwest Airlines, we find a firm competing ever so successfully with a low-price strategy. But Southwest has operational efficiency unmatched in the industry.

CONSIDER

Can you add any other learning insights?

QUESTIONS

1. Could Lorenzo's confrontation with the unions of Continental have been more constructively handled? How?
2. Do you see any limitations to Bethune's employee relations, especially in the areas of discipline and acceptance of authority?
3. Compare Bethune's handling of employees with that of Kelleher of Southwest Airlines in Chapter 17. Are there commonalities? Contrasts?
4. Compare Bethune's management style with that of Lorenzo. What conclusions can you draw?
5. Bethune gave great credit to his open-door policy when he became CEO. Do you think this was a major factor in the turnaround? How about changing the paint of the planes?
6. How do you motivate employees to give a high priority to customer service?
7. Evaluate the causes and the consequences of frequent top executive changes such as Continental experienced in the days of Lorenzo?
8. How can replacement workers—in this case pilots and skilled maintenance people hired at substantially lower salaries than their unionized peers at other airlines—be sufficiently motivated to provide top-notch service and a constructive esprit de corps?

HANDS-ON EXERCISES

1. It is 1994 and Bethune has just taken over. As his staff adviser he has asked you to prepare a report on improving customer service as quickly as possible. He has also asked you to design a program to inform both business and nonbusiness potential passengers of this new commitment. Be as specific as possible in your recommendations.
2. You are the leader of the machinists' union at Eastern. It is 1986 and Lorenzo has just acquired your airline. You know full well how he broke the union at Continental, and rumors are flying that he has similar plans for Eastern. Describe your tactics under two scenarios:

    a. You decide to take a conciliatory stance.

    b. You plan to fight him every step of the way.

    How successful do you think you will be in saving your union?

TEAM DEBATE EXERCISE

In this case we have a great contrast in management styles. While the participative approach of Bethune seems the winner in this particular case, such is not always so. There are good arguments for the autocratic style, and, indeed, Lorenzo made himself a wealthy man by so doing. Debate the general issue of autocratic versus participative management from as many aspects as you can.

INVITATION TO RESEARCH

What is the situation with Continental today? Is Bethune still CEO? Whatever happened to Lorenzo?

CHAPTER TEN

Harley Davidson: At Last

In the early 1960s, a staid and unexciting market was shaken up, was rocked to its core, by the most unlikely invader. This intruder was a smallish Japanese firm that had risen out of the ashes of World War II, and was now trying to encroach on the territory of a major U.S. firm, a firm that had in the space of 60 years destroyed all of its U.S. competitors, and now had a solid 70 percent of the motorcycle market.

Yet, almost inconceivably, in half a decade this market share was to fall to 5 percent, and the total market was to expand many times over what it had been for decades. A foreign invader had furnished a textbook example of the awesome effectiveness of carefully crafted marketing efforts. In the process, this confrontation between Honda and Harley Davidson was a harbinger of the Japanese invasion of the auto industry.

Eventually, by the late 1980s, Harley was to make a comeback. But only after more than two decades of travail and mediocrity.

THE INVASION

Sales of motorcycles in the United States were around 50,000 per year during the 1950s, with Harley Davidson, Britain's Norton and Triumph, and Germany's BMW accounting for most of the market. By the turn of the decade, Honda began to penetrate the U.S. market. In 1960 less than 400,000 motorcycles were registered in the United States. While this was an increase of almost 200,000 from the end of World War II, 15 years before, it was far below the increase in other motor vehicles. But by 1964, only four years later, the number had risen to 960,000; two years later it was 1.4 million; and by 1971 it was almost 4 million.

In expanding the demand for motorcycles, Honda instituted a distinctly different strategy. The major elements of this strategy were lightweight cycles and an advertising approach directed toward a new customer. Few firms have ever experienced such a shattering of market share as did Harley Davidson in the 1960s. (Although its market share declined drastically, its total sales remained nearly constant, indicating that it was getting none of the new customers for motorcycles.)

122

Reaction of Harley Davidson to the Honda Threat

Faced with an invasion of its staid and static U.S. market, how did Harley react to the intruder? They did not react. At least not until far too late. Harley Davidson considered themselves the leader in full-size motorcycles. While the company might shudder at the image tied in with their product's usage by the leather jacket types, it took solace in the fact that almost every U.S. police department used its machines. Perhaps this is what led Harley to stand aside and complacently watch Honda make deep inroads into the American motorcycle market. The management saw no threat in Honda's thrust into the market with lightweight machines. The attitude was exemplified in this statement by William H. Davidson, the president of the company and son of the founder:

> Basically, we don't believe in the lightweight market. We believe that motorcycles are sport vehicles, not transportation vehicles. Even if a man says he bought a motorcycle for transportation, it's generally for leisure-time use. The lightweight motorcycle is only supplemental. Back around World War I, a number of companies came out with lightweight bikes. We came out with one ourselves. They never got anywhere. We've seen what happens to these small sizes.[1]

Eventually Harley recognized that the Honda phenomenon was not an aberration, and that there was a new factor in the market. The company attempted to fight back by offering an Italian-made lightweight in the mid-1960s. But it was far too late; Honda was firmly entrenched. The Italian bikes were regarded in the industry to be of lower quality than the Japanese. Honda, and toward the end of the 1960s other Japanese manufacturers, continued to dominate what had become a much larger market than ever dreamed.

AFTERMATH OF THE HONDA INVASION: 1965–1981

In 1965, Harley Davidson made its first public stock offering. Soon after, it faced a struggle for control. The contest was primarily between Bangor Punta, an Asian company, and AMF, an American company with strong interests in recreational equipment including bowling. In a bidding war, Harley Davidson's stockholders chose AMF over Bangor Punta, even though the bid was $1 less than Bangor's $23 a share offer. Stockholders were leery of Bangor's reputation of taking over a company, squeezing it dry, and then scrapping it for the remaining assets. AMF's plans for expansion of Harley Davidson seemed more compatible.

But the marriage was troubled: Harley Davidson's old equipment was not capable of the expansion envisioned by AMF. At the very time that Japanese manufacturers—Honda and others—were flooding the market with high-quality motorcycles, Harley was falling down on quality. One company official noted that "quality was going down just as fast as production was going up."[2] Indicative of the depths of the

---

[1] Tom Rowan, "Harley Sets New Drive to Boost Market Share," *Advertising Age* (January 29, 1973), pp. 34–35.

[2] Peter C. Reid, *Well Made in America—Lessons from Harley Davidson on Being the Best* (New York: McGraw-Hill, 1990), p. 10.

Q. C.

problem at a demoralized Harley Davidson, quality-control inspections failed 50–60 percent of the motorcycles produced. This compared to 5 percent of Japanese motorcycles that failed their quality-control checks.

AMF put up with an average $4.8 million operating loss for eleven years. Finally, it called quits and put the division up for sale in 1981. Vaughan Beals, vice president of motorcycle sales, still had faith in the company: he led a team that used $81.5 million in financing from Citicorp to complete a leveraged buyout. All ties with AMF were severed.

VAUGHAN BEALS

Beals was a middle-aged Ivy Leaguer, a far cry from what one might think of as a heavy motorcycle aficionado. He had graduated from MIT's Aeronautical Engineering School, and was considered a production specialist.[3] But he was far more than that. His was a true commitment to motorcycles, personally as well as professionally. Deeply concerned with AMF's declining attention to quality, he achieved *1981* the buyout from AMF.

3% The prognosis for the company was bleak. Its market share, which had domi-
M.S. nated the industry before the Honda invasion, now was 3 percent. In 1983, Harley Davidson would celebrate its eightieth birthday; some doubted it would still be around by then. Tariff protection seemed Harley's only hope. And massive lobbying paid off. In 1983, Congress passed a huge tariff increase on Japanese motorcycles.
Reagan Instead of a 4 percent tariff, now Japanese motorcycles would be subject to a 45 per-
Support cent tariff for the coming five years.

The tariff gave the company new hope, and it slowly began to rebuild market share. Key to this was restoring confidence in the quality of its products. And Beals took a leading role in this. He drove Harley Davidsons to rallies where he
New met Harley owners. There he learned of their concerns and their complaints, and
Outreach he promised changes. At these rallies a core of loyal Harley Davidson users, called HOGs (for Harley Owners Group), were to be trailblazers for the successful growth to come.
HOGS Beals had company on his odyssey, Willie G. Davidson, grandson of the company's founder, and the vice president of design. Willie was an interesting contrast to the more urbane Beals. His was the image of a middle-age hippie. He wore a Viking helmet over his long, unkempt hair, while a straggly beard hid some of his windburned face. An aged leather jacket was compatible. Beals and Davidson fit in nicely at the HOG rallies.

THE STRUGGLE BACK

In December 1986, Harley Davidson asked Congress to remove the tariff barriers, more than a year earlier than originally planned. The confidence of the company

---

[3] Rod Willis, "Harley Davidson Comes Roaring Back," *Management Review* (March 1986), pp. 20–27.

had been restored and it believed it could now compete with the Japanese head to head.[4]

Production Improvements

Shortly after the buyout, Beals and other managers visited Japanese plants both in Japan and Honda's assembly plant in Marysville, Ohio. They were impressed that they were being beaten not by "robotics, or culture, or morning calisthenics and company songs, [but by] professional managers who understood their business and paid attention to detail."[5] As a result, Japanese operating costs were as much as 30 percent lower than Harley's. *BASICS*

Beals and his managers tried to implement some of the Japanese management techniques. Each plant was divided into profit centers, with managers assigned total responsibility within their particular area. Just-in-time (JIT) inventory and materials-as-needed (MAN) systems sought to control and minimize all inventories both inside and outside the plants. Quality circles (QCs) were formed to increase employee involvement in quality goals and to improve communication between management and workers. See the following Information Box for further discussion of quality circles. Another new program called statistical operator control (SOC) gave employees the responsibility for checking the quality of their own work and making proper correcting adjustments. Efforts were made to improve labor relations by more sensitivity to employees and their problems as well as better employee assistance and benefits. Certain product improvements were also introduced, notably a new engine and mountings on rubber to reduce vibration. A well-accepted equipment innovation was to build stereo systems and intercoms into the motorcycle helmets.

The production changes between 1981 and 1988 resulted in:[6]

- Inventory reduced by 67 percent
- Productivity up by 50 percent
- Scrap and rework down two-thirds
- Defects per unit down 70 percent

81–'88

In the 1970s, the joke among industry experts was, "If you're buying a Harley, you'd better buy two—one for spare parts."[7] Now this had obviously changed, but the change still had to be communicated to consumers, and believed.

Marketing Moves

Despite its bad times and its poor quality, Harley had a cadre of loyal customers almost unparalleled. Company research maintained that 92 percent of its customers remained

---

[4] "Harley Back in High Gear," *Forbes* (April 20, 1987), p. 8.

[5] Dexter Hutchins, "Having a Hard Time with Just-in-Time," *Fortune* (June 19, 1986), p. 65.

[6] Hutchins, *op. cit.* p. 66.

[7] *Ibid.*

INFORMATION BOX

QUALITY CIRCLES

Quality circles were adopted by Japan in an effort to rid its industries of poor quality control and junkiness after World War II. Quality circles are worker–management committees that meet regularly, usually weekly, to talk about production problems, plan ways to improve productivity and quality, and resolve job-related gripes on both sides. They have been described as "the single most significant explanation for the truly outstanding quality of goods and services produced in Japan."[8] For example, Mazda had 2,147 circles with more than 16,000 employees involved. They usually consisted of seven to eight volunteer members who met on their own time to discuss and solve the issues they were concerned with. In addition to making major contributions to increased productivity and quality, they provided employees an opportunity to participate and gain a sense of accomplishment.[9]

The idea—like so many ideas adopted by the Japanese—did not originate with them: it came from two American personnel consultants. The Japanese refined the idea and ran with it. Now, American industry had rediscovered quality circles. Some firms have found them a desirable way to promote teamwork and good feelings, and to avoid at least some of the adversarial relations stemming from collective bargaining and union grievances that must be negotiated.

Despite sterling claims for quality circles, they have not always worked out well. Some workers claim they smack of "tokenism," and are more a facade than anything practical. Questions are also raised as to how much lasting benefits such circles have, once the novelty has worn off. Others doubt that the time invested in quality circles by management and workers is that productive. And few U.S. workers accept the idea of participating in quality circles on their own time.

How would you feel about devoting an hour or more to quality circle meetings every week or so, on your own time? If your answer is, "No way," do you think this is a fair attitude on your part? Why or why not?

---

[8] "A Partnership to Build the New Workplace," *Business Week* (June 30, 1980), p. 101.

[9] As described in a Mazda ad in *Forbes* (May 24, 1982), p. 5.

---

with Harley.[10] Despite such hard-core loyalists, the company had always had a serious public image problem. It was linked to an image of the pot-smoking, beer-drinking, woman-chasing, tattoo-covered, leather-clad biker: "When your company's logo is the number-one requested in tattoo parlors, it's time to get a licensing program that will return your reputation to the ranks of baseball, hot dogs, and apple pie."[11]

Part of Harley's problem had been with bootleggers ruining the name by placing it on unlicensed goods of poor quality. Now the company began to use warrants and federal marshalls to crack down on unauthorized uses of its logo at motorcycle conventions. And it began licensing its name and logo on a wide variety of products,

[10] Mark Marvel, "The Gentrified HOG," *Esquire* (July 1989), p. 25.

[11] "Thunder Road," *Forbes* (July 18, 1983), p. 32.

Brand Loyalty VS. Image

from leather jackets to cologne to jewelry—even to pajamas, sheets, and towels. Suddenly retailers realized that these licensed goods were popular, and were even being bought by a new customer segment, undreamed of until now: bankers, doctors, lawyers, and entertainers. This new breed of customers soon expanded their horizons to include the Harley Davidson bikes themselves. They joined the HOGs, only now they became known as Rubbies—the rich urban bikers. And high prices for bikes did not bother them in the least.

RUBBIES

Beals was quick to capitalize on this new market with an expanded product line with expensive heavyweights. In 1989 the largest motocycle was introduced, the Fat Boy, with 80 cubic inches of V-twin engine and capable of a top speed of 150 mph. By 1991, Harley had 20 models, ranging in price from $4,500 to $15,000.

The Rubbies brought Harley back to a leading position in the industry by 1989, with almost 60 percent of the super-heavyweight motorcycle market; by the first quarter of 1993, this had become 63 percent. See Figure 10.1. The importance of this customer to Harley could be seen in the demographic statistics supplied by the *Wall Street Journal* in 1990: "One in three of today's Harley Davidson buyers are professionals or managers. About 60 percent have attended college, up from only 45 percent in 1984. Their median age is 35, and their median household income has risen sharply to $45,000 from $36,000 five years earlier."[12]

profile of customer

In 1989, Beals stepped down as CEO, turning the company over to Richard Teerlink, who was chief operating officer of the Motorcycle Division. Beals, however, retained his position as chairman of the board. The legacy of Beals in the renaissance of Harley led management writer John Schermerhorn to call him a visionary leader.[13] The Information Box discusses visionary leadership.

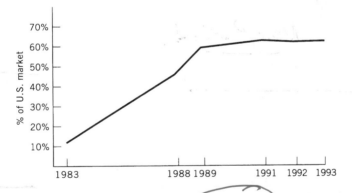

Figure 10.1. Harley Davidson's share of the U.S. heavyweight motorcycle market, selected years, 1983–1993.

Sources: Company reports; R. L. Polk & Company; Gary Slutsker, "Hog Wild," *Forbes* (May 24, 1993), pp. 45–46.

[12] Robert L. Rose, "Vrooming Back," *Wall Street Journal* (August 31, 1990), p. 1.

[13] John R. Schermerhorn, Jr., *Management for Productivity,* 4th ed. (New York: Wiley, 1993), pp. 410–411.

INFORMATION BOX

VISIONARY LEADERSHIP

Vision has been identified as an essential ingredient of effective leadership. Having vision characterizes someone who has a clear sense of the future environment and the actions needed to thrive in it.

Undoubtedly, a visionary leader is an asset in a dynamic environment. Such a leader can help a firm grasp opportunities ahead of competitors, revitalize itself, pull itself up from adversity. Schermerhorn states that a visionary begins with a clear vision, communicates that vision to all concerned, and motivates and inspires people in pursuit of that vision. He proposes these five principles of visionary leadership:

1. **Challenge the process.** Be a pioneer—encourage innovation and people with ideas.
2. **Be enthusiastic.** Inspire others through personal example to share in a common vision.
3. **Help others to act.** Be a team player, and support the efforts and talents of others.
4. **Set the example.** Provide a consistent model of how others should act.
5. **Celebrate achievements.** Bring emotion into the workplace and rally "hearts" as well as "minds."[14]

Can you name any visionary leaders? What makes you think they were visionary? Could some of our acclaimed visionary leaders have been merely lucky rather than prophetic?

---

[14] John R. Schermerhorn, Jr., *Management*, 6th ed. (New York: Wiley, 1999) pp. 262–263.

SUCCESS

By 1993 Harley Davidson had a new problem, one born of success. Now it could not even come close to meeting demand. Customers faced empty showrooms, except perhaps for rusty trade-ins or antiques. Waiting time for a new bike could be six months or longer, unless the customer was willing to pay a 10 percent or higher premium to some gray marketer advertising in biker magazines.

Some of the 600 independent U.S. dealers worried that these empty showrooms and long waiting lists would induce their customers to turn to foreign imports, much as they had several decades before. But other dealers recognized that somehow Beals and company had engendered a brand loyalty unique in this industry, and perhaps in all industries. Assuaging the lack of big bike business, dealers were finding other sources of revenues. Harley's branded line of merchandise, available only at Harley dealers and promoted through glossy catalogs, had really taken off. Harley black leather jackets were bought eagerly at $500; fringed leather bras went for $65; even shot glasses brought $12—all it seemed to take was the Harley name and logo. So substantial was this ancillary business, that in 1992 non-cycle business generated $155.7 million in sales, up from $130.3 million in 1991.

Production

In one sense, Harley's production situation was enviable: it had far more demand than production capability. More than this, it had such a loyal body of customers that delays in product gratification were not likely to turn many away to competitors. The problem, of course, was that full potential was not being realized. *[handwritten: Opportunity loss]*

Richard Teerlink, the successor of Beals, expressed the corporate philosophy to expanding quantity to meet the demand: "Quantity isn't the issue, quality is the issue. We learned in the early 1980s you do not solve problems by throwing money at them."[15]

The company increased output slowly. In early 1992 it was making 280 bikes a day; by 1993, this had risen to 345 a day. With increased capital spending, goals were to produce 420 bikes a day, but not until 1996. *[handwritten: 280 - 345 - 420/day]*

Export Potential

Some contrary concerns with the conservative expansion plans of Teerlink surfaced regarding international operations. The European export market beckoned. Harleys had become very popular in Europe. But the company had promised its domestic dealers that exports would not go beyond 30 percent of total production, until the North American market was fully satisfied. Suddenly the European big-bike market grew by an astounding 33 percent between 1990 and 1992. Yet, because of its production constraints, Harley could only maintain a 9 to 10 percent share of this market. In other words, it was giving away business to foreign competitors. *[handwritten: Exports vs Domestic]*

To enhance its presence in Europe, Harley opened a branch office of its HOG club in Frankfurt, Germany, for its European fans.

Specifics of the Resurgence of Harley Davidson

Table 10.1 shows the trend in revenues and net income of Harley since 1982. The growth in sales and profits did not go unnoticed by the investment community. In 1990, Harley Davidson stock sold for $7; in January of 1993, it hit $39. Its market share of heavyweight motorcycles (751 cubic centimeters displacement and larger) had soared from 12.5 percent in 1983, to 63 percent by 1993. Let the Japanese have the lightweight bike market! Harley would dominate the heavyweights.

Harley acquired Holiday Rambler in 1986. As a wholly owned subsidiary, this manufacturer of recreational and commerical vehicles was judged by Harley management to be compatible with the existing motorcycle business as well as moderating some of the seasonality of the motorcycle business. The diversification proved rather mediocre. In 1992, it accounted for 26 percent of total corporate sales, but only 2 percent of profits.[16]

Big motorcycles, made in America by the only U.S. manufacturer, continued the rage. Harley's ninetieth anniversary was celebrated in Milwaukee on June 12, 1993. As many as 100,000 people, including 18,000 HOGS, were there to celebrate.

---

[15] Gary Slutsker, "Hog Wild," *Forbes* (May 24, 1993), p. 46.

[16] Company annual reports.

TABLE 10.1 **Harley Davidson's Growth in Revenue and Income 1983–1994 (millions of $)**

Year	Revenue	Net Income
1982	$ 210	def. $25.1
1983	254	1.0
1984	294	2.9
1985	287	2.6
1986	295	4.3
1987	685	17.7
1988	757	27.2
1989	791	32.6
1990	865	38.3
1991	940	37.0
1992	1,100	54.0
1993	1,210	68.0
1994	1,537	83.0

Source: Company annual reports.

Commentary: The steady climb in sales and profits, except for a pause in 1985, is noteworthy. The total gain in revenues over these years was 631.9%, while income rose more than eightyfold since 1983.

Hotel rooms were sold out for a 60-mile radius. Harley Davidson was up and doing real well.

1993–1998

The 1990s continued to be kind to Harley. Demand continued to grow, with the mystique as strong as ever. The company significantly increased its motorcycle production capacity with a new engine plant in Milwaukee completed in 1997 and a new assembly plant in Kansas City in 1998. It expected that demand in the United States would still exceed the supply of Harley bikes.

ANALYSIS

One of Vaughan Beals's first moves after the 1981 leveraged buyout was to improve production efficiency and quality control. This became the foundation for the strategic regeneration moves to come. In this quest, he borrowed heavily from the Japanese, in particular in cultivating employee involvement.

The cultivation of a new customer segment for the big bikes had to be a major factor in the company's resurgence. To some, that more affluent consumers embraced the big, flashy Harley motorcycles was a surprise of no small moment. After all, how could you have two more incompatible groups than the stereotyped black-jacketed cyclists and the Rubbies? Perhaps part of the change was due to high-profile people such as Beals and some of his executives frequently participating at motorcycle rallies and charity rides. Technological and comfort improvements in motorcycles and their equipment added to the new attractiveness. Dealers were also coaxed to make their stores more inviting.

Along with this, expanding the product mix not only made such Harley-branded merchandise a windfall for company and dealers alike, but also piqued the interest of upscale customers in motorcycles themselves. The company was commendably aggressive in running with the growing popularity of the ancillary merchandise, and making this well over a $100 million revenue booster.

Some questions remained. How durable was this popularity, both of the big bikes and the complementary merchandise, with this affluent customer segment? Would it prove to be only a passing fad? If so, then Harley needed to seek diversifications as quickly as possible, even though the Holiday Rambler Corporation had brought no notable success by 1992. Diversifications often bring disappointed earnings compared with a firm's core business.

Another question concerned Harley's slowness in expanding production capability. Faced with a burgeoning demand, was it better to go slowly, to be carefully protective of quality, and to refrain from heavy debt commitments? This had been Harley's most recent strategy, but it raised the risk of permitting competitors to gain market share in the United States and especially in Europe. The following Issue Box discusses aggressive versus conservative planning.

ISSUE BOX

SHOULD WE BE AGGRESSIVE OR CONSERVATIVE IN OUR PLANNING?

The sales forecast—the estimate of sales for the periods ahead—serves a crucial role because it is the starting point for all detailed planning and budgeting. A volatile situation presents some high-risk alternatives: Should we be optimistic or conservative?

On one hand, with conservative planning in a growing market, a firm risks underestimating demand and being unable to expand its resources sufficiently to handle the potential. It may lack the manufacturing capability and sales staff to handle growth potential, and it may have to abdicate a good share of the growing business to competitors who are willing and able to expand their capability to meet the demands of the market.

On the other hand, a firm facing burgeoning demand should consider whether the growth is likely to be a short-term fad or a more permanent situation. A firm can easily become overextended in the buoyancy of booming business, only to see the collapse of such business jeopardizing its viability.

Harley's conservative decision was undoubtedly influenced by concerns about expanding beyond the limits of good quality control. The decision was probably also influenced by management's belief that Harley Davidson had a loyal body of customers who would not switch despite the wait.

Do you think Harley Davidson made the right decision to expand conservatively? Why or why not? Defend your position.

The following numbers show how motorcycle shipments increased from 1993 to 1997, both domestically and export, in thousands of units:

	U.S.	Exports
1997	96.2	36.1
1993	57.2	24.5

Despite continuous increases in production, U.S. consumers still had to wait to purchase a new Harley Davidson bike, but the waits only added to the mystique. The following shows the growth in revenues and income from 1993 to 1997:

(Millions $)	Revenues	Net Income
1997	1,763	174.0
1993	1,217	18.4

Indicative of the popularity of the Harley Davidson logo, Wolverine World Wide, maker originally of Hush Puppies, but now the largest manufacturer of footwear in the United States, entered into a licensing agreement with Harley to use its "sexy" name for a line of boots and fashion shoes.[17]

WHAT CAN BE LEARNED?

Again, a firm can come back from adversity. The resurrection of Harley Davidson almost from the point of extinction proves that adversity can be overcome. It need not be fatal or forever. This should be encouraging to all firms facing difficulties, and to their investors. Noteworthy, however, in comparing Harley with the previous case of Continental Air, is the great difference in time these two firms took to turn around. Continental under Bethune achieved spectacular results in only months; it took Harley decades before a Vaughan Beals came on the scene as changemaker. We will find another changemaker in the next case, IBM.

What does a turnaround require? Above all, it takes a leader who has the vision and confidence that things can be changed for the better. The change may not necessitate anything particularly innovative. It may involve only a rededication to basics, such as better quality control or an improved commitment to customer service brought about by a new positive attitude of employees. But such a return to basics requires that a demoralized or apathetic organization be rejuvenated and remotivated. This calls for leadership of a high order. If the core business has still been maintained, it at least provides a base to work from.

Preserve the core business at all costs. Every viable firm has a basic core or distinctive position—sometimes called an "ecological niche"—in its business environment. This unique position may be due to its particular location, or to a certain product. It may come from somewhat different operating methods or from the

---

[17] Carleen Hawn, "What's in a Name? Whatever You Make It," *Forbes* (July 27, 1998), p. 88.

customers served. Here, a firm is better than its competitors. This strong point is the basic core of a company's survival. Though it may diversify and expand far beyond this area, the firm should not abandon its main bastion of strength.

Harley almost did this. Its core—and indeed, only—business was its heavyweight bikes sold to a limited and loyal, thought not at the time particularly savory, customer segment. Harley almost lost this core business by abandoning reasonable quality control to the point that its motorcycles became the butt of jokes. To his credit, upon assuming leadership Beals acted quickly to correct the production and employee motivation problems. By preserving the core, Beals could pursue other avenues of expansion.

The power of a mystique. Few products are able to gain a mystique or cult following. Coors beer did in the 1960s and early 1970s, when it became the brew of celebrities and the emblem of the purity and freshness of the West. In the cigarette industry, Marlboro rose to become the top seller from a somewhat similar advertising and image thrust: the Marlboro man. The Ford Mustang had a mystique at one time. Somehow the big bikes of Harley Davidson developed a mystique. Harleys appealed to the HOGS and to the Rubbies: two disparate customer segments, but both loyal to their Harleys. The mystique led to "logo magic": Simply put the Harley Davidson name and logo on all kinds of merchandise, and watch the sales take off.

How does a firm develop (or acquire) a mystique? There is no simple answer, no guarantee. Certainly a product has to be unique, but though most firms strive for this differentiation, few achieve a mystique. Image-building advertising, focusing on the target buyer, may help. Perhaps even better is image-building advertising that highlights the people customers might wish to emulate. But what about the black-leather-jacketed, perhaps bearded, cyclist?

Perhaps in the final analysis, acquiring a mystique is a more accidental and fortuitous success than something that can be deliberately orchestrated. Two lessons, however, can be learned about mystiques. First, they do not last forever. Second, firms should run with them as long as possible and try to expand the reach of the name or logo to other goods, even unrelated ones, through licensing.

LATE-BREAKING NEWS

In its January 7, 2002 issue, *Forbes* declared Harley to be its "Company of the Year," a truly prestigious honor. In supporting its decision, *Forbes* noted that:

> In a disastrous year for hundreds of companies, Harley's estimated 2001 sales grew 15 percent to $3.3 billion and earnings grew 26 percent to $435 million. Its shares were up 40 percent in 2001, while the S&P stock average dropped 15 percent. Since Harley went public in 1986, its shares have risen an incredible 15,000 percent. Since 1986, GE generally considered the paragon of American business, had risen only 1,056 percent.

(continues)

LATE-BREAKING NEWS *(continued)*

Jeffrey Bleustein, a 26-year company veteran now CEO, was diversifying into small, cheaper bikes to attract younger riders as well as women who had shunned the big lumbering machines and who represented only 9 percent of Harley riders. The cult image was stronger than ever. Half of the company's 8,000 employees rode Harleys and many of them appeared at rallies around the country for pleasure and to promote the company. There were now 640,000 owners, the parts-and-accessories catalog numbered 720 pages, and the Harley Davidson name was on everything from blue jeans to pickup trucks. Harley would celebrate its 100th birthday in 2002, and some 250,000 riders were expected at the rally in Milwaukee.

Source: Jonathan Fahey, "Love Into Money," *Forbes*, January 7, 2002, pp. 60–65.

CONSIDER

What additional learning insights can you see coming from this Harley Davidson resurgence?

QUESTIONS

1. Do you think Beals's rejuvenation strategy for Harley Davidson was the best policy? Discuss and evaluate other strategies that he might have pursued.

2. How durable do you think the Rubbies' infatuation with the heavyweight Harleys will be? What leads you to this conclusion?

3. A Harley Davidson stockholder criticizes present management: "It is a mistake of the greatest magnitude that we abdicate a decent share of the European motorcycle market to foreign competitors, simply because we do not gear up our production to meet the demand." Discuss.

4. Given the resurgence of Harley Davidson in the 1990s, would you invest money in the company? Discuss, considering as many factors bearing on this decision as you can.

5. "Harley Davidson's resurgence is only the purest luck. Who could have predicted, or influenced, the new popularity of big bikes with the affluent?" Discuss.

6. "The tariff increase on Japanese motorcycles in 1983 gave Harley Davidson badly needed breathing room. In the final analysis, politics is more important than management in competing with foreign firms." What are your thoughts?

HANDS-ON EXERCISES

1. As a representative of a mutual fund with a major investment in Harley Davidson, you are particularly critical of Vaughn Beals's visible presence at

motorcycle rallies and his hobnobbing with black-jacketed cycle gangs. He maintains this is a fruitful way to maintain a loyal core of customers. Playing the devil's advocate (a person who opposes a position to establish its merits and validity), argue against Beals's practices.

2. As a vice president at Harley Davidson, you believe the recovery efforts should have gone well beyond the heavyweight bikes into lightweights. What arguments would you present for this change in strategy, and what specific recommendations would you make for such a new course of action? What contrary arguments would you expect? How would you counter them?

3. As a staff assistant to Vaughan Beals, you have been charged to design a strategy to bring a mystique to the Harley Davidson name. How would you propose to do this? Be as specific as you can, and defend your reasoning.

TEAM DEBATE EXERCISE

A major schism has arisen in the executive ranks of Harley Davidson. Many executives believe that a monumental mistake is being made not to gear up production to match the burgeoning worldwide demand for Harleys. The other side believes the present go-slow approach to increasing production is more prudent. Persuasively support your position and attack the opposing view.

INVITATION TO RESEARCH

What is the situation with Harley Davidson today? Has the diversification into lower-priced bikes done well and attracted more women bikers? Is the Harley cult as strong as ever? Are any new competitors or threats emerging?

both in Minnesota !

Victory by Polaris

Excelsior Henderson

CHAPTER ELEVEN

IBM: A Recovered Giant

*I*BM exhibited similar rollercoaster fortunes as did Continental Air and Harley Davidson, with the major difference that it was so much bigger and had so many years of industry domination. The common notion is that the bigger the firm, the more difficult it is to turn it around, just as the grand ship needs far more room to maneuver to avoid catastrophe than a smaller vessel.

THE REALITY AND THE FLAWED ILLUSION

On January 19, 1993, International Business Machines Corporation reported a record $5.46 billion loss for the fourth quarter of 1992, and a deficit for the entire year of $4.97 billion, the biggest annual loss in American corporate history. (General Motors recorded a 1991 loss of $4.45 billion, after huge charges for cutbacks and plant closings. And Ford Motor Company reported a net loss of more than $6 billion for 1992, but that was a noncash charge to account for the future costs for retiree benefits.) The cost in human lives, as far as employment was concerned, was also consequential, as some 42,900 had been laid off during 1992, with an additional 25,000 planned to go in 1993. In its fifth restructuring, seemingly endless rounds of job cuts and firings had eliminated 100,000 jobs since 1985. Not surprisingly, IBM's share price, which was above $100 in the summer of 1992, closed at an 11-year low of $48.375. And yet IBM had long been the ultimate blue-chip company, reigning supreme in the computer industry. How could its problems have surfaced so suddenly and so violently?

THE ROAD TO INDUSTRY DOMINANCE

"They hired my father to make a go of this company in 1914, the year I was born," said Thomas J. Watson, Jr. "To some degree I've been a part of IBM ever since."[1] Watson took over his father's medium-sized company in 1956 and built it into a technological giant. Retired for almost 19 years by 1992, he was now witnessing the company in the throes of its greatest adversity.

---

[1] Michael W. Miller, "IBM's Watson Offers Personal View of the Company's Recent Difficulties," *Wall Street Journal* (December 21, 1992), p. A3.

IBM had become the largest computer maker in the world. With its evergrowing revenues, since 1946 it had become the bluest of blue-chip companies. It had 350,000 employees worldwide and was one of the largest U.S.-based employers. Its 1991 revenues had approached $67 billion, and while profits had dropped some from the peak of $6.5 billion in 1984, its common stock still commanded a price/earnings ratio of over 100, making it a darling of investors. In 1989, it ranked first among all U.S. firms in market value (the total capitalization of common stock, based on the stock price and the number of shares outstanding), fourth in total sales, and fourth in net profits.[2]

During the days of the younger Watson, IBM was known for its centralized decision making. Decisions affecting product lines were made at the highest levels of management. Even IBM's culture was centralized and standardized, with strict behavioral and dress codes. For example, a blue suit, white shirt, and dark tie was the public uniform, and IBM became widely known as "Big Blue."

One of IBM's greatest assets was its research laboratories, by far the largest and costliest of their kind in the world, with staffs that included three Nobel Prize winners. IBM treated its research and development (R&D) function with loving care, regularly budgeting 10 percent of sales for this forward-looking activity: In 1991, for example, the R&D budget was $6.6 billion.

The past success of IBM and the future expectations for the company, with a seeming stranglehold over the technology of the future, made it a favorite of consultants, analysts, and market researchers. Management theorists from Peter Drucker to Tom Peters (of *In Search of Excellence* fame) lined up to analyze what made IBM so good. And the business press regularly produced articles in praise and awe of IBM.

Alas, the adulation was to change abruptly by 1992. Somehow, insidiously, IBM had gotten fat and complacent over the years. (In Chapter 10, the case on Harley Davidson, we encounter a similar situation of complacency stemming from long-standing market dominance.) IBM's problems, however, went deeper, as we will explore in the next section.

CHANGING FORTUNES

Perhaps the causes of the great IBM debacle of 1992 started in the early 1980s with a questionable management decision. Perhaps the problems were more deep-rooted than any single decision; perhaps they were a consequence of the bureaucracy that often typifies giant organizations (Sears and General Motors faced somewhat similar problems), growing layers of policies, and entrenched interests.

In the early 1980s, two little firms, Intel and Microsoft, were upstarts, just emerging in the industry dominated by IBM. Their success by the 1990s can be attributed largely to their nurturing by IBM. Each got a major break when it was "anointed" as a key supplier for IBM's new personal computer (PC). Intel was signed on to make the chips, and Microsoft, the software. The aggressive youngsters set standards for successive PC generations and in the process wrested from IBM control

---

[2] "Ranking the Forbes 500s," *Forbes* (April 30, 1990), p. 306.

over the PC's future. And the PC was to become the product of the future, shouldering aside the giant mainframe that was IBM's strength.

As IBM began losing ground in one market after another, Intel and Microsoft were gaining dominance. In 1982, the combined market value of Intel's and Microsoft's stock amounted to about one-tenth of IBM's. By October 1992, their combined stock value surpassed IBM's; by the end of the year, they topped IBM's market value by almost 50 percent. See Table 11.1 for comparative operating statistics of IBM, Intel, and Microsoft. Table 11.2 shows the market valuation of IBM, Intel, and Microsoft from 1989 to 1992, the years before and during the collapse of investor esteem.

Defensive Reactions of IBM

As the problems of IBM became more visible to the investment community, chairman John Akers sought to institute reforms to turn the behemoth around. His problem—and need—was to uproot a corporate structure and culture that had developed when IBM had no serious competition.

A cumbersome bureaucracy stymied the company from being innovative in a fast-moving industry. Major commitments still went to high-margin mainframes, but these were no longer necessary in many situations, given the computing power of desktop PCs. IBM had problems getting to market quickly with the technological innovations that were revolutionizing the industry. In 1991 Akers warned an unbelieving group of IBM managers of the coming difficulties. "The business is in

TABLE 11.1 Growth of IBM and the Upstarts, Microsoft and Intel 1983–1992 (in millions)

	1983	1985	1987	1989	1991	1992
IBM						
Revenues	$40,180	$50,056	$54,217	$62,710	$64,792	$67,045
Net income	5,485	6,555	5,258	3,758	(2,827)	(2,784)
% of revenue	13.6%	13.1%	9.7%	6.0%	—	—
Microsoft						
Revenues	$50	$140	$346	$804	$1,843	$2,759
Net income	6	24	72	171	463	708
% of revenue	12.0%	17.1%	20.8%	21.3%	25.1%	25.7%
Intel						
Revenues	$1,122	$1,365	$1,907	$3,127	$4,779	$5,192
Net income	116	2	176	391	819	827
% of revenue	10.3%	0.1%	9.2%	12.5%	17.1%	15.9%

Sources: Company annual statements. Figures from 1992 are estimates from "Annual Report of American Industry" *Forbes* (January 4, 1993), pp. 115–116.

Commentary: Note the great growth of the "upstarts" both in revenues and in profits, compared with IBM. Also note the performance of Microsoft and Intel in profit as a percent of revenues.

TABLE 11.2   Market Value and Rank of IBM, Microsoft, and Intel Among All U.S. Companies, 1989 and 1992

	Rank		Market Value ($ millions)	
	1989	1992	1989	1992
IBM	1	13	$60,345	$30,715
Microsoft	92	25	6,018	23,608
Intel	65	22	7,842	24,735

Source: "The Forbes Market Value 500," *Forbes* Annual Directory Issue (April 13, 1990), pp. 258–259; and *Forbes* (April 26, 1993), p. 242.

The market value is the per-share price multiplied by the number of shares outstanding for all classes of common stock.

Commentary: The market valuation reflects the stature of the firms in the eyes of investors. Obviously, IBM has declined during this period, while Microsoft and Intel have more than tripled their market valuation, almost approaching that of IBM. Yet IBM's sales were $65.5 billion in 1992, against sales of $3.3 for Microsoft and $5.8 for Intel.

crisis."[3] He attempted to push power downward, to decentralize some of the decision making that for decades had resided at the top. His more radical proposal was to break up IBM, to divide it into 13 divisions and give each division more autonomy. He sought to expand the services business and make the company more responsive to customer needs. And, perhaps most important, he saw a crucial need to pare costs by cutting the fat from the organization.

The need for cost-cutting was evident to all but the entrenched bureaucracy. IBM's total costs grew 12 percent a year in the mid-1980s, but revenues were not keeping up with this growth.[4] Part of the plan for reducing costs involved cutting employees, which violated a cherished tradition dating back to Thomas Watson's father and the beginning of IBM: a promise never to lay off IBM workers for economic reasons.[5] (Most of the downsizing was indeed accomplished by voluntary retirements and attractive severance packages, but eventually outright layoffs became necessary.)

The changes decreed by Akers would leave the unified sales division untouched, but each of the new product group divisions would act as a separate operating unit, with financial reports broken down accordingly. Particularly troubling to Akers was the recent performance of the personal computer (PC) business. At a time when demand, as well as competition, was burgeoning for PCs, this division was languishing. Early in 1992 Akers tapped James Cannavino to head the $11 billion Personal Systems Division, which also included workstations and software.

IBM PCs

PCs had been the rising star of the company, despite the fact that mainframes still accounted for about $20 billion in revenues. But in 1990, market share dropped dras-

---

[3] David Kirkpatrick, "Breaking up IBM," *Fortune* (July 27, 1992), p. 44.

[4] *Ibid.,* p. 53.

[5] Miller, *op. cit.,* p. A4.

tically as new competitors offered PCs at much lower prices than IBM; many experts even claimed that these clones were at least equal to IBM's PCs in quality. Throughout 1992, IBM had been losing market share in an industry price war. Even after it attempted to counter Compaq's price cuts in June, IBM's prices still remained as much as one-third higher than its competitor's prices. Even worse, IBM had announced new fall models, and this development curbed sales of current models. At the upper end of the PC market, firms such as Sun Microsystems and Hewlett Packard were bringing out more powerful workstations that tied PCs together with mini- and mainframe computers. James Cannavino faced a major challenge in reviving the PC.

Cannavino planned to streamline operations by slicing off a new unit to focus exclusively on developing and manufacturing PC hardware. By doing so, he would cut PCs loose from the rest of Personal Systems and the workstations and software. This, he believed, would create a streamlined organization that could cut prices often, roll out new products several times a year, sell through any kind of store, and provide customers with whatever software they wanted, even if it was not IBM's.[6] Such autonomy was deemed necessary in order to respond quickly to competitors and opportunities, without having to deal with the IBM bureaucracy.

THE CRISIS

On January 25, 1993, John Akers announced that he was stepping down as IBM's chairman and chief executive. He had lost the confidence of the board of directors. Until mid-January, Akers seemed determined to see IBM through its crisis, at least until he would reach IBM's customary retirement of age 60, which would be December 1994. But the horrendous $4.97 billion loss in 1992 changed that, and investor and public pressure mounted for a top management change. The fourth quarter of 1992 was particularly shocking, brought on by weak European sales and a steep decline in sales of minicomputers and mainframes. Now IBM's stock sank to a 17-year low, below $46.

Other aspects of the operation also accentuated IBM's fall from grace: most notably, the decline of the jewel of its operation, IBM's mainframe processors and storage systems.

For 25 years IBM had dominated the $50 billion worldwide mainframe industry. In 1992, overall sales of such equipment grew at only 2 percent, but IBM experienced a 10 to 15 percent drop in revenue. At the same time, its major mainframe rivals, Amdahl Corporation and Unisys Corporation had respective sales gains of 48 percent and 10 percent.[7]

IBM was clearly lagging in developing new computers that could out-perform the old ones, such as IBM's old system/390. Competitors' models exceeded IBM's old computers not only in absolute power but in prices, selling at prices of a tenth or less of IBM's price per unit of computing. For example, with IBM's mainframe

[6] "Stand Back, Big Blue—And Wish Me Luck," *Business Week* (August 17, 1992), p. 99.

[7] John Verity, "Guess What: IBM Is Losing Out in Mainframes, Too," *Business Week* (February 8, 1993), p. 106.

computers, customers paid approximately $100,000 for each MIPS, or the capacity to execute 1 million instructions per second, this being the rough gauge of computing power. Hewlett Packard offered similar capability at a cost of only $12,000 per MIPS, and AT&T's NCR unit could sell a machine for $12.5 million that outperformed IBM's $20 million ES/9000 processor complex.[8]

In a series of full-page advertisements appearing in such business publications as the *Wall Street Journal*, IBM defended the mainframe and attacked the focus on MIPS:

> One issue surrounding mainframes is their cost. It's often compared using dollars per MIPS with the cost of microprocessors systems, and on that basis mainframes lose. But … dollars per MIPS alone is a superficial measurement. The real issue is function. Today's appetite for information demands serious network and systems management, around-the-clock availability, efficient mass storage and genuine data security. MIPS alone provides none of these, but IBM mainframes have them built in, and more fully developed than anything available on microprocessors.[9]

On March 24, 1993, 51-year-old Louis V. Gerstner, Jr., was named the new chief executive of IBM. The two-month search for a replacement for Akers had captivated the media, with speculation ranging widely. The choice of an outsider caught many by surprise: Gerstner was chairman and CEO of RJR Nabisco, a food and tobacco giant, but Nabisco was a far cry from a computer company. And IBM had always prided itself on promoting from within—for example, John Akers—with most IBM executives being lifelong IBM employees. Not all analysts supported the selection of Gerstner. While most did not criticize the board for going outside IBM to find a replacement for Akers, some questioned going outside the computer industry or other high-tech industries. Geoff Lewis, senior editor of *Business Week*, fully supported the choice. He had suggested the desirability of bringing in some outside managers to Akers in 1988.

> Akers seemed shocked—maybe even offended—by my question. After a moment, he answered: "IBM had the best recruitment system anywhere and spends more than anybody training. Sometimes it might help to seek outsiders with unusual skills, but the company already had the best people in the world."[10]

See the following Issue Box for a discussion of promotion from within.

ANALYSIS

In examining the major contributors to IBM's fall from grace, we will analyze the predisposing or underlying factors, resultants, and controversies.

---

[8] *Ibid.*

[9] Taken from advertisement, *Wall Street Journal* (March 5, 1993), p. B8.

[10] Geoff Lewis, "One Fresh Face at IBM May Not Be Enough," *Business Week* (April 12, 1993), p. 33.

ISSUE BOX

SHOULD WE PROMOTE FROM WITHIN?

A heavy commitment to promoting from within, as had long characterized IBM, is sometimes derisively called "inbreeding." The traditional argument against this stand maintains that an organization with such a policy is not alert to needed changes, that it is enamored with the status quo, "the way we have always done it." Proponents of promotion from within talk about the motivation and great loyalty it engenders, with every employee knowing that he or she has a chance of becoming a high-level executive.

However, the opposite course of action—that is, heavy commitment to placing outsiders in important executive positions—plays havoc with morale of trainees and lower-level executives and destroys the sense of continuity and loyalty. A middle ground seems preferable: filling many executive positions from within, promoting this idea to encourage both the achievement of current executives and the recruiting of trainees, and at the same time bringing the strengths and experiences of outsiders into the organization.

Do you think there are particular circumstances in which one extreme or the other regarding promotion policy might be best? Discuss.

Predisposing Factors

Cumbersome Organization

As IBM grew with its success, it became more and more bureaucratic. One author described it as big and bloated. Another called it "inward-looking culture that kept them from waking up on time."[11] Regardless of phraseology, by the late 1980s IBM could not bring new machines quickly into the market, nor was it able to make the fast pricing and other strategic decisions of its smaller competitors. Too many layers of management, too many vested interests, a tradition-ridden mentality, and a gradually emerging contentment with the status quo shackled it—this in an industry that some thought to be mature, but which in reality was gripped by burgeoning change in important sectors. As a huge ship requires considerable time and distance to turn or to stop, so the giant IBM found itself at a competitive disadvantage compared with smaller, hungrier, more aggressive, and above all, more nimble firms. And impeding all efforts to make major changes effective was the typical burden facing all large and mature organizations: resistance to change. The accompanying Information Box discusses this phenomenon.

Overly Centralized Management Structure

Often related to a cumbersome bureaucratic organization is rigid centralization of authority and decision making. Certain negative consequences may result when all

---

[11] Jennifer Reese, "The Big and the Bloated: It's Tough Being No. 1," *Fortune* (July 27, 1992), p. 49.

INFORMATION BOX

RESISTANCE TO CHANGE

People as well as organizations have a natural reluctance to embrace change. Change is disruptive. It can destroy accepted ways of doing things and familiar authority–responsibility relationships. It makes people uneasy because their routines will likely be disrupted; their interpersonal relationships with subordinates, coworkers, and superiors may well be modified. Positions that were deemed important before the change may be downgraded. And persons who view themselves as highly competent in a particular job may be forced to assume unfamiliar duties.

Resistance to change can be combatted by good communication with participants about forthcoming changes. Without such communication, rumors and fears can assume monumental proportions. Acceptance of change can be facilitated if managers involve employees as fully as possible in planning the changes, solicit and welcome their participation, and assure them that their positions will not be impaired, only changed. Gradual rather than abrupt changes also make a transition smoother, as participants can be initially exposed to the changes without drastic upheavals.

In the final analysis, however, needed changes should not be delayed or canceled because of their possible negative repercussions on the organization. If change is necessary, it should be initiated. Individuals and organizations can adapt to change, although it may take some time.

The worst change an employee may face is layoff. And when no one knows when the next layoff will occur or who will be affected, morale and productivity may both be devastated. Discuss how managers might best handle the necessity of upcoming layoffs.

major decisions have to be made at corporate headquarters rather than down the line. Decision making is necessarily slowed, since executives believe they must investigate fully all aspects, and not being personally involved with the recommendation, they may be not only skeptical but critical of new projects and initiatives. More than this, the enthusiasm and creativity of lower level executives may be curbed by the typical conservatism of a higher management team divorced from the intimacy of the problem or the opportunity. The motivation and morale needed for a climate of innovation and creativity is stifled under the twin bureaucratic attitudes "Don't take a chance" and "Don't rock the boat."

The Three C's Mindset of Vulnerability

Firms that have been well entrenched in their industry and that have dominated it for years tend to fall into a particular mindset that leaves them vulnerable to aggressive and innovative competitors.

The following "three C's" are detrimental to a frontrunner's continued success:

Complacency

Conservatism

Conceit

Complacency is smugness—a complacent firm is self-satisfied, content with the status quo, no longer hungry and eager for growth. *Conservatism* when excessive characterizes a management that is wedded to the past, to the traditional, to the way things have always been done. Conservative managers see no need to change because they believe nothing is different today (e.g., "Mainframe computers are the models of the industry and will always be"). Finally, *conceit* further reinforces the myopia of the mindset: conceit for current and potential competitors. The beliefs that "we are the best" and "no one else can touch us" can easily permeate an organization that has enjoyed success for years.

The three C's leave no incentive to undertake aggressive and innovative actions, causing growing disinterest in such important facets of the business as customer relations, service, and even quality control. Furthermore, they inhibit interest in developing innovative new products that may cannibalize—that is, take business away from—existing products or disrupt entrenched interests. (We will discuss cannibalization in more detail in the following Information Box.)

INFORMATION BOX

CANNIBALIZATION—AGAIN

Cannibalization occurs when a company's new product takes some business away from an existing product. The new product's success consequently does not contribute its full measure to company revenues since some sales will be shifted from older products. The amount of cannibalization can range from virtually none to almost total. In the latter case, the new product simply replaces the older product, with no real sales gain achieved. If the new product is less profitable than the older one, the impact and the fear of cannibalization become all the greater.

For IBM, the PCs and the other equipment smaller than mainframes would not come close to replacing the bigger units. Still, some cannibalization was likely. And the profits on the lower-priced computers were many times less than those of mainframes.

The argument can justifiably be made that if a company does not bring out new products then competitors will, and that it is better to compete with one's own products. Still, the threat of cannibalization can cause a hesitation, a blink, in a full-scale effort to rush to market an internally competing product. This reluctance and hesitation need to be guarded against, lest the firm find itself no longer in the vanguard of innovation.

Assume the role of a vocal and critical stockholder at the annual meeting. What arguments would you introduce for a crash program to rush the PC to market, despite possible cannibalization? What contrary arguments would you expect, and how would you counter them?

Resultants

Overdependence on High-Margin Mainframes

The mainframe computers had long been the greatest source of market power and profits for IBM. But the conservative and tradition-minded IBM bureaucracy could not accept the reality that computer power was becoming a desktop commodity. Although a market still existed for the massive mainframes, it was limited and had little growth potential; the future belonged to desktop computers and workstations. And thus IBM, in a lapse of monumental proportions, relinquished its dominance. The minicomputers first opened up a whole new industry, one with scores of hungry competitors. But the cycle of industry creation and decline started anew by the early 1980s as personal computers began to replace minicomputers in defining new markets and fostering new competitors. The mainframe was not replaced, but its markets became more limited, and cannibalization became the fear.

Neglect of Software and Service

At a time when software and service had become ever more important, IBM still had a fixation on hardware. In 1992 services made up only 9 percent of IBM's revenue. Criticisms flowed:

> Technology is becoming a commodity, and the difference between winning and losing comes in how you deliver that technology. Service will be the differentiator.
>
> As a customer, I want a supplier who's going to make all my stuff work together.
>
> The job is to understand the customer's needs in detail.[12]

In the process of losing touch with customers, the sales force had become reluctant to sell low-margin open systems if it could push proprietary mainframes or minicomputers.

Bloated Costs

As indications of the fat that had insidiously grown in the organization, some 42,900 jobs were cut in 1992, thankfully all through early retirement programs. An additional 25,000 people were expected to be laid off in 1993, some without the benefit of early retirement packages. Health benefits for employees were also scaled down. Manufacturing capacity was reduced 25 percent, and two of three mainframe development labs were closed. But perhaps the greatest bloat was R&D.

The Diminishing Payoff of Massive R&D Expenditures

As noted earlier, IBM spent heavily on research and development, often as much as 10 percent of sales (see Table 11.3). Its research labs were by far the largest and costliest of their kind in the world.

And IBM labs were capable of inventing amazing things. For example, they developed the world's smallest transistor, 1/75,000th the width of a human hair.

---

[12] Kirkpatrick, *op. cit.*, pp. 49, 52.

TABLE 11.3 IBM Research and Development Expenditures as a Percent of Revenues, 1987–1991

	1987	1988	1989	1990	1991
Revenues ($ millions)	$54,217	$59,681	$62,710	$64,792	$67,045
Research, development and engineering costs	5,434	5,925	6,827	6,554	6,644
Percent of revenues	10.0%	9.9%	10.9%	10.1%	9.9%

Source: Company annual reports.

Commentary: Where has been the significant contribution from such heavy investment in R&D?

Somehow, with all these R&D resources and expenditures, IBM lagged in transferring its innovations to the marketplace. The organization lacked the ability to quickly translate laboratory prototypes into commercial triumphs. Commercial R&D is wasted without this translation.

Controversies

Questionable Decisions

No executive has a perfect batting average of good decisions. Indeed, most executives do well to bat more than 500—that is, to have more good decisions than bad decisions. But, alas, decisions are all relative. Much depends on the importance, the consequences, of these decisions.

IBM made a decision of monumental long-term consequences in the early 1980s. At that time IBM designated two upstart West Coast companies to be the key suppliers for its new personal computer. Thus, it gave away its chances to control the personal computer industry. Over the next 10 years, each of the two firms would develop a near-monopoly—Intel in microprocessors and Microsoft in operating-systems software—by setting standards for successive PC generations. Instead of keeping such developments proprietary (that is, within its own organization) IBM, in an urge to save developmental time, gave these two small firms a golden opportunity, which both grasped to the fullest. By 1992, Intel and Microsoft had emerged as the computer industry's most dominant firms.

The decision still is controversial. It saved IBM badly needed time in bringing its PC to market, and as computer technology becomes ever more complex, not even an IBM can be expected to have the ability and resources to go it alone. Linking up with competitors offers better products and services and a faster flow of technology today, and it seems to be the way of the future.

Former IBM CEO Thomas Watson, Jr., has criticized his successors Frank Cary and John Opel for phasing out rentals and selling the massive mainframe computer outright. Originally, purchasers could only lease the machines, thus giving IBM a dependable cushion of cash each year ("my golden goose," Mr. Watson called it.)[13]

---

[13] Miller, *op. cit.*, p. A4.

Doing away with renting left IBM, and John Akers, a newly volatile business, just as the industry position began worsening. Akers, newly installed as CEO, was thus left with a hostile environment without the cushion or support of steady revenues from such rentals, according to Watson's argument. But the counterposition holds that selling brought needed cash quickly into company coffers. Furthermore, opponents say it is unlikely, given the competitive climate that was emerging in the 1980s, that big customers would continue to tolerate the leasing arrangement when they could buy their machines, if not from IBM, then from another supplier whose machines were just as good or better.

Breaking Up IBM

The general consensus of management experts was to support Akers's reforms to break up Big Blue into 13 divisions and give them increasing autonomy—even to the point that shares of some of these new Baby Blues might be distributed to stockholders. The idea is not unlike that of Japan's *keiretsu,* in which alliances of companies with common objectives but with substantial independence seek and develop business individually.

The assumption in favor of such breaking up is that the sum of the parts is greater than the whole, that the autonomy and motivation will bring more total revenues and profits. But these hypothesized benefits are not guaranteed. At issue is whether the good of the whole would be better served by suboptimizing some business units—that is, by reducing the profit maximizing of some units in order to have the highest degree of coordination and cooperation. Giving disparate units of an organization goals of individual profit maximization lays the seeds for intense intramural competition, with cannibalization and infighting likely. IBM has embarked on a program of decentralization and internal competition. But will gross profit margins deteriorate even more with such competition? Is the whole better served by a less intensely competitive internal environment?

Intrapreneurship reinforced by *skunkworks* is an approach that some firms have found valuable in bringing an aura of entrepreneurship to large organizations, beset as they are with tendencies toward rigidity and bureaucratic malaise. The following Information Box describes this plan for fostering innovation in large firms.

THE COMEBACK UNDER GERSTNER

Louis Gerstner took command in March 1993. The company, as we have seen, was reeling. In a reversal of major proportions, he brought IBM back to record profitability. Table 11.4 shows the statistics of what appears to be a sensational turnaround. In 1994, the company earned $3 billion, its first profitable year since 1990. Perhaps of greater significance, compared with the previous year this represented a profit swing of $11 billion. And revenue grew for the first time since 1990. Annual expenses were reduced by $3.5 billion, about 15 percent. And 1994 finished with financial strength: IBM had more than $10 billion in cash; basic debt was reduced by $3.3 billion. Of greater importance to stockholders, IBM stock nearly tripled in price, racing from a 1993 low of 40 to a high of 114 on August 17, 1995.

INFORMATION BOX

INTRAPRENEURSHIP AND SKUNKWORKS—PURSUING INNOVATION

Intrapreneurship is the term used to describe the encouragement of entrepreneurial behavior within the large organization. Such a spirit of entrepreneurship—usually only the domain of smaller enterprises—is more conducive to innovative thinking, calculated risk-taking, and quick actions, qualities that are crucial as organizations grow to cumbersome size.

Skunkworks refers to the creation of smaller subunits within the larger corporate structure "where groups of people are allowed to work together in a setting that is highly creative and free of many of the restrictions of large organizations."[14]

As an example of the skunkworks concept, Ford Motor Company in late 1989 considered overhauling the Mustang, once a legend but by the 1980s only a fading star. "Team Mustang," a group of about 400 people, scrambled to save this beloved car "on a skinflint budget." In the process they broke rules that previously had governed product development in the rigidly disciplined corporation. They upset the status quo as they vigorously pursued their redesign goal. The result: The Mustang was redone in three years for about $700 million, 25 percent faster and for 30 percent less money than for any comparable new car program in recent years.[15]

In similar fashion, a small group of enthusiastic Apple Computer employees were given separate facilities and permitted to operate free from Apple's normal product development bureaucracy: They set their own norms, and worked without outside interference. They even raised a "jolly roger" over their building as a symbol of their independence. The result? The Macintosh Computer.[16]

Would intrapreneurship or confederations of entrepreneurs within IBM be a viable alternative to breaking up the company into a number of smaller divisions? Do you see any problems with skunkworks?

[14] John R. Schermerhorn, Jr., *Management*, 6th ed. (New York: Wiley, 1999), p. 175.

[15] Joseph B. White and Oscar Suris, "How a 'Skunkworks' Keeps Mustang Alive—On a Tight Budget," *Wall Street Journal* (September 21, 1993), pp. Al, Al2.

[16] For further information, see Apple Computer *Annual Report*, 1991.

By all such performance statistics, Gerstner had done an outstanding job of turning the giant around. Yet, there were still doubters. For the most part, their skepticism was rooted in the notion that Gerstner was not aggressive enough.

Gerstner did not tamper mightily with the organizational structure of IBM. Before he took over, IBM was moving toward a breakup into 13 independent units: one for mainframes, one for PCs, one for disk drives, and so on. But he saw IBM's competitive advantage to be offering customers a complete package, a one-stop shopping to all those seeking help in solving technological problems: a unified IBM—somehow, an IBM with a single, efficient team.

TABLE 11.4   IBM's Resurgence Under Gerstner, 1993–1994

	1993	1994
	(millions of dollars)	
Revenue	$62,716	$64,052
Net earnings (loss)	(8,101)	3,021
Net earnings (loss) per share of common stock	(14.22)	5.02
Working capital	6,052	12,112
Total debt	27,342	22,118
Number of employees	256,207	219,839

Source: Company annual reports.

Commentary: In virtually all measures of performance, IBM has made a significant turnaround from 1993 to 1994. Note in particular the decrease in debt, the decrease in number of employees, and the great profit turnaround.

The critics persisted. *Fortune* questioned, "Is He Too Cautious to Save IBM?" The article said, "After running IBM for more than a year and a half, CEO Lou Gerstner has revealed himself to be something other than the revolutionary whom the directors of this battered and demoralized enterprise once seemed to want … he seems to be attempting a conventional turnaround: deep-cleaning and redecorating the house rather than gutting and renovating it."[17] The article admitted the "surprisingly good" results, but attributed this to luck: "Unexpectedly high demand for mainframe computers has given the company temporary respite from the inevitable shift to less lucrative products."[18]

So, what do we have here? A turnaround of monumental proportions, or a dud? Is Gerstner a hero or a flop? Whatever, we do not have sensationalism here, nor a ransacking of the company in the process.

The Quiet Revolution

The critics inclined toward revolutionary measures had to be disappointed. "Transforming IBM is not something we can do in one or two years," Gerstner had stated. "The better we are at fixing some of the short-term things, the more time we have to deal with the long-term issues."[19] His efforts were contrasted with those of Albert Dunlap, who overhauled Scott Paper at about the same time. Dunlap replaced 9 of the 11 top executives in the first few days and laid off one-third of the total workforce. Gerstner brought in only 8 top executives from outside IBM to sit on the 37-person Worldwide Management Council.

[17] Allison Rogers, "Is He Too Cautious to Save IBM?" *Fortune* (October 3, 1994), p. 78.

[18] *Ibid.*

[19] *Ibid.*, p. 78.

A nontechnical man, Gerstner's strengths were in selling: cookies and cigarettes at RJR, travel services during an 11-year career at American Express Company. Weeks after taking over, he talked to IBM's top 100 customers at a retreat in Chantilly, Virginia. He asked them what IBM was doing right and wrong. They were surprised and delighted: This was the first time the chairman of the 72-year-old company had ever polled its customers. The input was revealing:

> The customers told him IBM was difficult to work with and unresponsive to customers' needs. For example, customers who needed IBM's famed mainframe computers were being told that the machines were dinosaurs and that the company would have to consider getting out of the business.[20]

Gerstner told these customers that IBM was in mainframes to stay, and would aggressively cut prices and focus on helping them set up, manage, and link the systems. And IBM's hardware sales turned around also, rising from $30.6 billion in 1993 to $35.6 billion in 1995.

Perhaps the most obvious change Gerstner instituted was the elimination of a dress code that once kept IBM salespeople in blue suits and white shirts.

By the spring of 1997, *Fortune* magazine highlighted Gerstner on its cover with the feature article, "The Holy Terror Who's Saving IBM."[21] Total company sales for 1996 were $75.947 billion, up 5.6 percent from the previous year, and net profits gained 30 percent over 1995, to $5.429 billion.

The growth continued. Revenues in 1997 were $78.508 and net income $6.093. The first three quarters of 1998 showed surprisingly robust sales growth, with practically all the portfolios of businesses contributing to the sparkling performance. For example, third-quarter earnings were up 10 percent, on an unexpectedly healthy sales growth of 8 percent. For the year, IBM shares were one of the leading gainers among the companies that make up the Dow Jones Industrial Average.[22] Gerstner's turnaround was no fluke.

UPDATE

By mid-2001, Louis Gerstner was talking retirement, with expected successor Samuel Palmisano, 49, an IBM lifer, named president in September 2000. During his reign, Gerstner transformed the company from the big-box mainframes that made it famous to services and high-tech parts. Without acquisitions, IBM's global services business became the world's largest, in 2000 generating $33.1 billion of total company revenues of $88.4 billion, this being more than 70 percent greater than the nearest competitor. Such services included sales-force automation and operation of websites and hosting and servicing customers' computer operations. Strategic alliances became key to

---

[20] "IBM Focuses on Sales," *Cleveland Plain Dealer* (September 10, 1996), p. 6C.

[21] Betsy Morris, "He's Saving Big Blue," *Fortune* (April 14, 1997), pp. 68–81.

[22] *1998 Annual Report;* and Raju Narisetti, "IBM Profit Rose 10% in 3rd Period, Topping Estimates, Amid Robust Sales," *Wall Street Journal* (October 21, 1998), p. A3.

growth, and were a win/win situation for both IBM and its partners: "Partners get access to IBM's 177,000-person global sales force and service providers, while IBM gets the partners' promise to adapt their software to IBM's mainframe and middleware platforms." Such strategic software alliances totaled over 100 partners by the end of 2001.[23]

WHAT CAN BE LEARNED?

Beware of cannibalization phobia. We have just set the parameters of the issue of cannibalization—that is, how far a firm should go in developing products and encouraging intramural competition that will take sales away from other products and other units of the business. The issue is particularly troubling when the part of business that is likely to suffer is the most profitable in the company. And yet cannibalization should not even be an issue. At stake is the forward-leaning of the company, its embracing of innovation and improved technology, and its competitive stance. Unless a firm has an assured monopoly position, it can expect competitors to introduce advances in technology and new efficiencies in productivity and customer service.

In general we can conclude that no firm should rest on its laurels, that firms must introduce improvements and change as soon as possible, hopefully ahead of competition—all without regard to any possible impairment of sales and profits of existing products and units.

Remember the need to be lean and mean (sometimes called "acting small"). The marketplace is uncertain, especially in high-tech industries. In such environments a larger firm needs to keep the responsiveness and flexibility of smaller firms. It must avoid layers of management, delimiting policies, and a tradition-bound mindset. Otherwise a big firm is like the enormous vessel that is unable to stop or change course without losing precious time and distance. But how can a big firm keep the maneuverability and innovative thinking of a small firm? How can it remain lean and mean with increasing size?

We can identify certain conditions, or factors, of lean and mean firms:

1. They have simple organizations. Typically, they are decentralized, with decision making moved lower in the organization. This decentralization discourages the buildup of cumbersome bureaucracy and staff, which tend to add both increasing overhead expenses and the red tape that stultifies fast reaction time.

---

[23] Matthew Schifrin, "Partner or Perish," *Forbes* (May 21, 2001), p. 28; also, William M. Bulkeley, "IBM's Next CEO May Be the One to Bring Change," *Wall Street Journal* (May 21, 2001), pp. B1 and B4; William M. Bulkeley, "These Days Big Blue Is About Big Services, Not Just Big Boxes," *Wall Street Journal* (July 11, 2001), pp. A1, A10. For an article criticizing Gerstner just before the early 2001 high-tech meltdown, see Daniel Lyons, "Baby Blues," *Forbes* (November 27, 2000), pp. 56–58.

With a simple organization comes a relatively flat structure, with fewer levels of management than comparable firms. This tendency also has certain desirable consequences. Overhead is greatly reduced, with fewer executives and their expensive staffs. But communications is also improved, because higher executives are more accessible, and directions and feedback are less distorted because of more direct communications channels. Even morale is improved because of the better communications and accessibility to leaders of the organization.

2. They encourage new ideas. A major factor in the inertia of large firms is the vested interests of those who see their power threatened by new ideas and innovative directions. Consequently, real creativity is stymied by going unappreciated; often it is even discouraged.

   A firm that wishes to be lean and mean must seek new ideas. To do so requires rewards and recognition for creativity but, even more, acting upon the worthwhile ideas. Few things thwart creativity in an organization more than pigeonholing good ideas of eager employees.

3. Participation in planning is moved as low in the organization as possible. Important employees and lower-level managers are involved in decisions concerning their responsibilities, and their ideas receive reasonable weight in final decisions. Performance goals and rewards should be moved to the lowest possible level in the organization. Such an organizational climate encourages innovation, improves motivation and morale, and can lead to the fast reaction time that characterizes small organizations and often eludes the large.

4. A characteristic of some highly successful, proactive large organizations, as well as small firms, is minimum frills—even austerity at the corporate level. Two of our most successful firms today, Wal-Mart and Southwest Airlines, evince this philosophy to the utmost. A nofrills management philosophy is the greatest corporate model for curbing frivolous costs throughout an organization.

5. A final factor is the regular use of periodic evaluations and housecleaning of products, operations, and staff. Those deemed to be contributing little now, or to be unlikely in the future to contribute, should be objectively phased out or reassigned.

Beware the "king-of-the-hill" three-C's mindset. As a firm gains dominance and maturity, it must guard against a natural mindset evolution toward conservatism, complacency, and conceit. Usually the C's insidiously move in at the highest levels and eagerly filter down to the rest of the organization. As discussed earlier, this mindset leaves a firm highly vulnerable to competitors who are smaller, hungrier, and anxious to topple the king of the hill.

Although top management usually initiates such a mindset, top management can also lead in inhibiting it. The lean and mean organization is anathema to the three-C's mindset. If managers can curb bureaucratic buildup, then the seeds are thwarted. Keys to preventing this mindset are encouragement of innovative thinking throughout the organization and introduction of fresh talent from outside the organization to fill some internal positions. A strict adherence to promotion from within is inhibiting.

The power of greater commitment to customers. One of the bigger contributions Gerstner may have made to the turnaround of IBM was his customer focus: putting the needs of customers first and relying on his in-house experts for the technology; asking, not merely talking—finding out what customers wanted, and seeing what could be done to best meet these needs as quickly as possible; at the same time, toning down the arrogance of an "elite" staff of sales representatives. Perhaps the style change from blue suits and white shirts was the visible sign of a change in culture and attitudes.

Many firms profess a great commitment to customers and service. So common are such statements that one wonders how much is mere lip service. It is so easy to say this, and then not really follow up. In so doing, the opportunity to develop a trusting relationship is lost.

We can overcome adversity! We saw this with Continental Air and Harley Davidson, and now with IBM. Such examples should be motivating and inspiring for any organization and the executives trying to turn them around. Firms and their managers should be capable of learning from mistakes. As such, mistakes should be valuable learning experiences, leading the way to better performance and decisions in the future.

CONSIDER

What additional learning insights do you see emerging from the IBM case?

QUESTIONS

1. Assess the pro and con arguments for the 1982 decision to offer Microsoft and Intel a foothold in software and operating systems. (Keep your perspective to that of the early 1980s; don't be biased with the benefit of hindsight.)

2. Do you see any way that IBM could have maintained its nimbleness and technological edge as it grew to a $60 billion company? Reflect on this, and be as creative as you can.

3. "Tradition has no place in corporate thinking today." Discuss this statement.

4. Playing devil's advocate (one who takes an opposing position for the sake of argument), can you defend the position that the problems besetting IBM were not its fault, that they were beyond its control?

5. Giant organizations are often plagued with cumbersome bureaucracies. Discuss how this tendency could be prevented as an organization grows to large size over many years.

6. Which of the three C's do you think was most to blame for IBM's problems? Why do you conclude this?

HANDS-ON EXERCISES

1. You are a management consultant reporting to the CEO in the late 1980s. IBM is still racking up revenue and profit gains. But you detect serious emerging weaknesses. What do you advise management to do at this time? (Make any assumptions you feel necessary, but state them clearly.) Persuasively explain your rationale.

2. You are the executive assistant to Gerstner. It is 2001 and the great growth in revenues and profits of the last seven years has slowed. The critics are again demanding a drastic overhaul. Gerstner still stoutly maintains that customer service is the key, and that this has somehow slipped. He charges you to come up with concrete recommendations for improving the effectiveness of customer service. Be as specific as you can.

TEAM DEBATE EXERCISES

1. At issue: whether to break up the company into 10 to 15 semiautonomous units, or to keep basically the same organization. Debate the opposing views as persuasively as possible.

2. Debate the pros and cons of strategic partnering or alliances. Are the potential gains worth the sharing of technological expertise, as well as authority and responsibility?

INVITATION TO RESEARCH

What is the current situation of IBM? Have any new problems arisen? Has Palmisano instituted any major changes? Is the company still as enthusiastic with strategic alliances as it was under Gerstner?

PLANNING BLUNDERS
AND SUCCESSES

CHAPTER TWELVE

Euro Disney: Bungling a Successful Format

With high expectations Euro Disney opened just outside Paris in April 1992. Success seemed ensured. After all, the Disneylands in Florida, California, and, most recently, Japan were all spectacular successes. But somehow all the rosy expectations became a delusion. The opening results cast even the future continuance of Euro Disney into doubt. How could what seemed so right be so wrong? What mistakes were made?

PRELUDE

Optimism

Perhaps a few early omens should have raised some cautions. Between 1987 and 1991, three $150 million amusement parks had opened in France with great fanfare. All had fallen flat, and by 1991 two were in bankruptcy. Now Walt Disney Company was finalizing its plans to open Europe's first Disneyland early in 1992. This would turn out to be a $4.4 billion enterprise sprawling over 5,000 acres 20 miles east of Paris. Initially it would have six hotels and 5,200 rooms, more rooms than the entire city of Cannes, and lodging was expected to triple in a few years as Disney opened a second theme park to keep visitors at the resort longer.

Disney also expected to develop a growing office complex, one only slightly smaller than France's biggest, La Defense, in Paris. Plans also called for shopping malls, apartments, golf courses, and vacation homes. Euro Disney would tightly control all this ancillary development, designing and building nearly everything itself, and eventually selling off the commercial properties at a huge profit.

Disney executives had no qualms about the huge enterprise, which would cover an area one-fifth the size of Paris itself. They were more worried that the park might not be big enough to handle the crowds:

My biggest fear is that we will be too successful.

157

I don't think it can miss. They are masters of marketing. When the place opens it will be perfect. And they know how to make people smile—even the French.[1]

[handwritten: forecast] Company executives initially predicted that 11 million Europeans would visit the extravaganza in the first year alone. After all, Europeans accounted for 2.7 million visits to the U.S. Disney parks and spent $1.6 billion on Disney merchandise. Surely a park in closer proximity would draw many thousands more. As Disney executives thought more about it, the forecast of 11 million seemed most conservative. They reasoned that since Disney parks in the United States (population of 250 million) attract 41 million visitors a year, then if Euro Disney attracted visitors in the same proportion, attendance could reach 60 million with Western Europe's 370 million people. *[handwritten: Too simple?]* Table 12.1 shows the 1990 attendance at the two U.S. Disney parks and the newest Japanese Disneyland, as well as the attendance/population ratios.

[handwritten: ?] Adding fuel to the optimism was the fact that Europeans typically have more vacation time than do U.S. workers. For example, five-week vacations are commonplace for French and German employees, compared with two to three weeks for U.S. workers.

The failure of the three earlier French parks was seen as irrelevant. Robert Fitzpatrick, Euro Disneyland's chairman, stated, "We are spending 22 billion French francs before we open the door, while the other places spent 700 million. This means we can pay infinitely more attention to details—to costumes, hotels, shops, trash baskets—to create a fantastic place. There's just too great a response to Disney for us to fail."[2]

[handwritten: Cocky/Can't fail attitude. Blinded by past success]

TABLE 12.1   Attendance and Attendance/Population Ratios, Disney Parks, 1990

	Visitors	Population	Ratio
	(millions)		
United States			
Disneyland (Southern California)	12.9	250	5.2%
Disney World/Epcot Center (Florida)	28.5	250	11.4%
Total United States	41.4		16.6%
Japan			
Tokyo Disneyland	16.0	124	13.5%
Euro Disney	?	310[a]	?

Source: Euro Disney, *Amusement Business Magazine.*

[a] Within a two-hour flight.

Commentary: Even if the attendance/population ratio for Euro Disney is only 10 percent, which is far below that of some other theme parks, still 31 million visitors could be expected. Euro Disney "conservatively" predicted 11 million the first year.

[1] Steven Greenhouse, "Playing Disney in the Parisian Fields," *New York Times* (February 17, 1991), Section 3, 1, 6.

[2] Greenhouse, "Playing Disney," 6.

Nonetheless, a few scattered signs indicated that not everyone was happy with the coming of Disney. Leftist demonstrators at Euro Disney's stock offering greeted company executives with eggs, ketchup, and "Mickey Go Home" signs. Some French intellectuals decried the pollution of the country's cultural ambiance with the coming of Mickey Mouse and company: They called the park an American cultural abomination. The mainstream press also seemed contrary, describing every Disney setback "with glee." And French officials in negotiating with Disney sought less American and more European culture at France's Magic Kingdom. Still, such protests and bad press seemed contrived, unrepresentative, and certainly not predictive. Company officials dismissed the early criticism as "the ravings of an insignificant elite."[3]

The Location Decision   *DENIAL! CULTURE CLASH! RED FLAGS!*

In the search for a site for Euro Disney, Disney executives examined 200 locations in Europe. The other finalist was Barcelona, Spain. Its major attraction was warmer weather, but its transportation system was not as good as that around Paris, and it lacked level tracts of land of sufficient size. The clincher for the Paris decision was its more central location. Table 12.2 shows the number of people within 2 to 6 hours of the Paris site.

The beet fields of the Marne-la-Vallee area were the choice. Being near Paris seemed a major advantage, since Paris was Europe's biggest tourist draw. And France was eager to win the project to help lower its jobless rate and also to enhance its role as the center of tourist activity in Europe. The French government expected the project to create at least 30,000 jobs and to contribute $1 billion a year from foreign visitors.

To entice the project, the French government allowed Disney to buy up huge tracts of land at 1971 prices. It provided $750 million in loans at below-market rates, and it spent hundreds of millions of dollars on subway and other capital improvements for the park. For example, Paris's express subway was extended out to the park; a 35-minute ride from downtown cost about $2.50. A new railroad station for the

TABLE 12.2   Number of People Within 2–6 Hours of the Paris Site

Within a 2-hour drive	17 million people
Within a 4-hour drive	41 million people
Within a 6-hour drive	109 million people
Within a 2-hour flight	310 million people

Source: Euro Disney, *Amusement Business* magazine.

Commentary: The much more densely populated and geographically compact European continent makes access to Euro Disney much more convenient than it is in the United States.

[3] Peter Gumbel and Richard Turner, "Fans Like Euro Disney But Its Parent's Goofs Weigh the Park Down," *Wall Street Journal* (March 10, 1994), p. A12.

high-speed Train a Grande Vitesse was built only 150 yards from the entrance gate. This enabled visitors from Brussels to arrive in only 90 minutes. And when the English Channel tunnel opened in 1994, even London was only 3 hours and 10 minutes away. Actually, Euro Disney was the second largest construction project in Europe, second only to construction of the English Channel tunnel.

Financing

$4.4 BILL

Euro Disney cost $4.4 billion. Table 12.3 shows the sources of financing, in percentages. The Disney Company had a 49 percent stake in the project, which was the most that the French government would allow. For this stake it invested $160 million, while other investors contributed $1.2 billion in equity. The rest was financed by loans from the government, banks, and special partnerships formed to buy properties and lease them back.

less risk

The payoff for Disney began after the park opened. The company receives 10 percent of Euro Disney's admission fees and 5 percent of the food and merchandise revenues. This is the same arrangement as Disney has with the Japanese park. But in the Tokyo Disneyland, the company took no ownership interest, opting instead only for the licensing fees and a percentage of the revenues. The reason for the conservative position with Tokyo Disneyland was that Disney money was heavily committed to building the Epcot Center in Florida. Furthermore, Disney had some concerns about the Tokyo enterprise. This was the first non-American and the first cold-weather Disneyland. It seemed prudent to minimize the risks. But this turned out to be a significant blunder of conservatism, because Tokyo became a huge success, as the following Information Box discusses in more detail.

money felt they had been too conservative.

Special Modifications

With the experiences of the previous theme parks, and particularly that of the first cold-weather park in Tokyo, Disney construction executives were able to bring state-of-the-art refinements to Euro Disney. Exacting demands were placed on French

TABLE 12.3   Sources of Financing for Euro Disney (percent)

Total to Finance: $4.4 billion	100%
Shareholders equity, including $160 million from Walt Disney Company	32
Loan from French government	22
Loan from group of 45 banks	21
Bank loans to Disney hotels	16
Real estate partnerships	9

Source: Euro Disney.

Commentary: The full flavor of the leverage is shown here, with equity comprising only 32 percent of the total expenditure.

INFORMATION BOX

THE TOKYO DISNEYLAND SUCCESS

Tokyo Disneyland opened in 1983 on 201 acres in the eastern suburb of Urazasu. It was arranged that an ownership group, Oriental Land, would build, own, and operate the theme park with advice from Disney. The owners borrowed most of the $650 million needed to bring the project to fruition. Disney invested no money but receives 10 percent of the revenues from admission and rides and 5 percent of sales of food, drink, and souvenirs.

Although the start was slow, Japanese soon began flocking to the park in great numbers. By 1990 some 16 million a year passed through the turnstiles, about one-fourth more than visited Disneyland in California. In fiscal year 1990, revenues reached $988 million with profits of $150 million. Indicative of the Japanese preoccupation with things American, the park serves almost no Japanese food, and the live entertainers are mostly American. Japanese management even apologizes for the presence of a single Japanese restaurant inside the park: "A lot of elderly Japanese came here from outlying parts of Japan, and they were not very familiar with hog dogs and hamburgers."[4]

Disney executives were soon to realize the great mistake they made in not taking substantial ownership in Tokyo Disneyland. They did not want to make the same mistake with Euro Disney.

Would you expect the acceptance of the genuine American experience in Tokyo to be indicative of the reaction of the French and Europeans? Why or why not?

---

[4] James Sterngold, "Cinderella Hits Her Stride in Tokyo," *New York Times* (February 17, 1991), p. 6.

---

construction companies, and a higher level of performance and compliance resulted than many thought possible to achieve. The result was a major project on time, if not completely on budget. In contrast, the Channel tunnel was plagued by delays and severe cost overruns.

One of the things learned from the cold-weather project in Japan was that more needed to be done to protect visitors from such weather problems as wind, rain, and cold. Consequently, Euro Disney's ticket booths were protected from the elements, as were the lines waiting for attractions and even the moving sidewalk from the 12,000-car parking area.

Certain French accents—and British, German, and Italian accents as well—were added to the American flavor. The park has two official languages, English and French, but multilingual guides are available for Dutch, Spanish, German, and Italian visitors. Discoveryland, based on the science fiction of France's Jules Verne, is a new attraction. A theater with a full 360-degree screen acquaints visitors with a sweep of European history. And, not the least modification for cultural diversity, Snow White speaks German, and the Belle Notte Pizzeria and Pasticceria are right next to Pinocchio.

Disney had foreseen that it might encounter some cultural problems. This was one of the reasons for choosing Robert Fitzpatrick as Euro Disney's president. He is American but speaks French, knows Europe well, and has a French wife. However, he was unable to establish the rapport needed and was replaced in 1993 by a French native. Still, some of his admonitions that France should not be approached as if it were Florida fell on deaf ears.

RESULTS

As the April 1992 opening approached, the company launched a massive communications blitz aimed at publicizing the fact that the fabled Disney experience was now accessible to all Europeans. Some 2,500 people from various print and broadcast media were lavishly entertained while being introduced to the new facilities. Most media people were positively impressed with the inauguration and with the enthusiastic spirit of the staffers. These public relations efforts, however, were criticized by some for being heavy-handed and for not providing access to Disney executives.

As 1992 wound down after the opening, it became clear that revenue projections were, unbelievably, not being met. But the opening turned out to be in the middle of a severe recession in Europe. European visitors, perhaps as a consequence, were far more frugal than their American counterparts. Many packed their own lunches and shunned the Disney hotels. For example, a visitor named Corine from southern France typified the "no spend" attitude of many: "it's a bottomless pit," she said as she, her husband, and their three children toured Euro Disney on a three-day visit. "Every time we turn around, one of the kids wants to buy something."[5] Perhaps investor expectations, despite the logic and rationale, were simply unrealistic.

Indeed, Disney had initially priced the park and the hotels to meet revenue targets and had assumed demand was there, at any price. Park admission was $42.25 for adults—higher than at the American parks. A room at the flagship Disneyland Hotel at the park's entrance cost about $340 a night, the equivalent of a top hotel in Paris. It was soon averaging only a 50 percent occupancy. Guests were not staying as long or spending as much on the fairly high-priced food and merchandise. We can label the initial pricing strategy at Euro Disney as *skimming pricing*. The following Information Box discusses skimming and its opposite, penetration pricing.

Disney executives soon realized they had made a major miscalculation. Whereas visitors to Florida's Disney World often stayed more than 4 days, Euro Disney—with one theme park compared to Florida's three—was proving to be a two-day experience at best. Many visitors arrived early in the morning, rushed to the park, staying late at night, then checked out of the hotel the next morning before heading back to the park for one final exploration.

The problems of Euro Disney were not public acceptance (despite the earlier critics). Europeans loved the place. Since the opening it attracted just under 1 million visitors a month, thus easily achieving the original projections. Such patronage made it Europe's biggest paid tourist attraction. But the large numbers of frugal

[5] "Ailing Euro Disney May Face Closure," *Cleveland Plain Dealer* (January 1, 1994), E1.

INFORMATION BOX

SKIMMING AND PENETRATION PRICING

A firm with a new product or service may be in a temporary monopolistic situation. If there is little or no present and potential competition, more latitude in pricing is possible. In such a situation (and, of course, Euro Disney was in this situation), one of two basic and opposite approaches may be taken in the pricing strategy: skimming or penetration.

Skimming is a relatively high-price strategy. It is the most tempting where the product or service is highly differentiated because it yields high per-unit profits. It is compatible with a quality image. But it has limitations. It assumes a rather inelastic demand curve, in which sales will not be appreciably affected by price. And if the product or service is easily imitated (which was hardly the case with Euro Disney), then competitors are encouraged because of the high profit margins.

The penetration strategy of low prices assumes an elastic demand curve, with sales increasing substantially if prices can be lowered. It is compatible with economies of scale, and it discourages competitive entry. The classic example of penetration pricing was the Model T Ford. Henry Ford lowered his prices to make the car within the means of the general public, expanded production into the millions, and in so doing realized new horizons of economies of scale.

Euro Disney correctly saw itself in a monopoly position; it correctly judged that it had a relatively inelastic demand curve with customers flocking to the park regardless of rather high prices. What it did not reckon with was the shrewdness of European visitors: Because of the high prices they shortened their stay, avoided the hotels, brought their own food and drink, and bought only sparingly the Disney merchandise.

What advantages would a lower price penetration strategy have offered Euro Disney? Do you see any drawbacks?

patrons did not come close to enabling Disney to meet revenue and profit projections and cover a bloated overhead.

Other operational errors and miscalculations, most of these cultural, hurt the enterprise. A policy of serving no alcohol in the park caused consternation in a country where wine is customary for lunch and dinner. (This policy has since been reversed.) Disney thought Monday would be a light day and Friday a heavy one and allocated staff accordingly, but the reverse was true. It found great peaks and valleys in attendance: The number of visitors per day in the high season could be ten times the number in slack times. The need to lay off employees during quiet periods came up against France's inflexible labor schedules.

One unpleasant surprise concerned breakfast. "We were told that Europeans don't take breakfast, so we downsized the restaurants," recalled one executive. "And guess what? Everybody showed up for breakfast. We were trying to serve 2,500 breakfasts at 350-seat restaurants. The lines were horrendous."[6]

[6] Gumbel and Turner, "Fans Like Euro Disney," A12.

Disney failed to anticipate another demand, this time from tour bus drivers. Restrooms were built for 50 drivers, but on peak days 2,000 drivers were seeking the facilities. "From impatient drivers to grumbling bankers, Disney stepped on toe after European toe."[7]

For the fiscal year ending September 30, 1993, the amusement park had lost $960 million, and the future of the park was in doubt (as of December 31, 1993, the cumulative loss was 6.04 billion francs, or $1.03 billion). Walt Disney made $175 million available to tide Euro Disney over until the next spring. Adding to the problems of the struggling park were heavy interest costs. As depicted in Table 12.3, against a total cost of $4.4 billion, only 32 percent of the project was financed by equity investment. Some $2.9 billion was borrowed primarily from 60 creditor banks, at interest rates running as high as 11 percent. Thus, the enterprise began heavily leveraged, and the hefty interest charges greatly increased the overhead to be covered from operations. Serious negotiations began with the banks to restructure and refinance.

ATTEMPTS TO RECOVER

The $921 million lost in the first fiscal year represented a shortfall of more than $2.5 million a day. The situation was not quite as dire as these statistics would seem to indicate. Actually, the park was generating an operating profit, but nonoperating costs were bringing it deeply into the red.

Still, operations were far from satisfactory, although they were becoming better. It had taken 20 months to smooth out the wrinkles and adjust to the miscalculations about demand for hotel rooms and the willingness of Europeans to pay substantial prices for lodging, meals, and merchandise. Operational efficiencies were slowly improving.

By the beginning of 1994, Euro Disney had been made more affordable. Prices of some hotel rooms were cut—for example, at the low end, from $76 per night to $51. Expensive jewelry was replaced by $10 T-shirts and $5 crayon sets. Luxury sit-down restaurants were converted to self-service. Off-season admission prices were reduced from $38 to $30. And operating costs were reduced 7 percent by streamlining operations and eliminating over 900 jobs.

Efficiency and economy became the new watchwords. Merchandise in stores was pared from 30,000 items to 17,000, with more of the remaining goods being pure U.S. Disney products. (The company had thought that European tastes might prefer more subtle items than the garish Mickey and Minnie souvenirs, but this was found not so.) The number of different food items offered by park services was reduced more than 50 percent. New training programs were designed to remotivate the 9,000 full-time permanent employees, to make them more responsive to customers and more flexible in their job assignments. Employees in contact with the public were given crash courses in German and Spanish.

Still, as we have seen, the problem had not been attendance, although the recession and the high prices had reduced it. Some 18 million people passed through the

[7] *Ibid.*

turnstiles in the first 20 months of operation. But they were not spending money as people did in the U.S. parks. Furthermore, Disney had alienated some European tour operators with its high prices, and it diligently sought to win them back.

Management had hoped to reduce the heavy interest overhead by selling the hotels to private investors. But the hotels had an occupancy rate of only 55%, making them unattractive to investors. Although the recession was a factor in such low occupancy rates, a significant part of the problem lay in the calculation of lodging demands. With the park just 35 minutes from the center of Paris, many visitors stayed in town. About the same time as the opening, the real estate market in France collapsed, making the hotels unsalable in the short term. This added to the overhead burden and confounded the business plan forecasts.

While some analysts were relegating Euro Disney to the cemetery, few remembered that Orlando's Disney World showed early symptoms of being a disappointment. Costs were heavier than expected, and attendance was below expectations. But Orlando's Disney World turned out to be one of the most profitable resorts in North America.

PROGNOSIS *Looking better . . .*

Euro Disney had many things going for it, despite the disastrous early results. In May 1994 a station on the high-speed rail running from southern to northern France opened within walking distance of Euro Disney. This should help fill many of the hotel rooms too ambitiously built. The summer of 1994, the 50th anniversary of the Normandy invasion, brought many people to France. Another favorable sign for Euro Disney was the English Channel tunnel's opening in 1994, which potentially could bring a flood of British tourists.

Furthermore, the recession in Europe was bound to end, and with it should come renewed interest in travel. As real estate prices become more favorable, hotels can be sold and real estate development around the park spurred.

Even as Disney Chairman Michael Eisner threatened to close the park unless lenders restructured the debt, Disney increased its French presence, opening a Disney store on the Champs Elysees. The likelihood of a Disney pullout seemed remote, despite the posturing of Eisner, since royalty fees could be a sizable source of revenues even if the park only breaks even after servicing its debt. With only a 3.5 percent increase in revenues in 1995 and a 5 percent increase in 1996, these could yield $46 million in royalties for the parent company. "You can't ask, 'What does Euro Disney mean in 1995?' You have to ask, 'What does it mean in 1998?'"[8]

ANALYSIS

Euro Disney, as we have seen, fell far short of expectations in the first 20 months of its operation, so far short that its continued existence was even questioned. What went wrong?

[8] Lisa Gubernick, "Mickey N'est pas Fini," *Forbes* (February 14, 1994), p. 43.

External Factors

A serious economic recession that affected all of Europe undoubtedly was a major impediment to meeting expectations. As noted before, it adversely affected attendance—although still not all that much—but drastically affected spending patterns. Frugality was the order of the day for many visitors. The recessions also affected real estate demand and prices, thus saddling Disney with hotels it had hoped to sell at profitable prices to eager investors to take the strain off its hefty interest payments.

The company assumed that European visitors would not be greatly different from those visitors, foreign and domestic, of U.S. Disney parks. Yet, at least in the first few years of operation, visitors were much more price conscious. This suggested that those within a two- to four-hour drive of Euro Disney were considerably different from the ones who traveled overseas, at least in spending ability and willingness.

Internal Factors

Despite the decades of experience with the U.S. Disney parks and the successful experience with the new Japan park, Disney still made serious blunders in its operational planning, such as the demand for breakfasts, the insistence on wine at meals, the severe peaks and valleys in scheduling, and even such mundane things as sufficient restrooms for tour bus drivers. It had problems in motivating and training its French employees in efficiency and customer orientation. Did all these mistakes reflect an intractable French mindset or a deficiency of Disney management? Perhaps both. But Disney management should have researched all cultural differences more thoroughly. Further, the park needed major streamlining of inventories and operations after the opening. The mistakes suggested an arrogant mindset by Disney management: "We were arrogant," concedes one executive. "It was like 'We're building the Taj Mahal and people will come—on our terms.'"[9]

The miscalculations in hotel rooms and in pricing of many products, including food services, showed an insensitivity to the harsh economic conditions. But the greatest mistake was taking on too much debt for the park. The highly leveraged situation burdened Euro Disney with such hefty interest payments and overhead that the breakeven point was impossibly high, and it even threatened the viability of the enterprise. See the following Information Box for a discussion of the important inputs and implications affecting breakeven, and how these should play a role in strategic planning.

Were such mistakes and miscalculations beyond what we would expect of reasonable executives? Probably not, with the probable exception of the crushing burden of debt. Any new venture is susceptible to surprises and the need to streamline and weed out its inefficiencies. While we would have expected such to have been done faster and more effectively from a well-tried Disney operation, European, and particularly French and Parisian, consumers and employees showed different behavior and attitude patterns than expected.

The worst sin that Disney management and investors could make would be to give up on Euro Disney and not to look ahead two to five years. A hint of the future

---

[9] Gumbel and Turner, "Fans Like Euro Disney," A12.

INFORMATION BOX

THE BREAKEVEN POINT

A breakeven analysis is a vital tool in making go/no go decisions about new ventures and alternative business strategies. This can be shown graphically as follows:

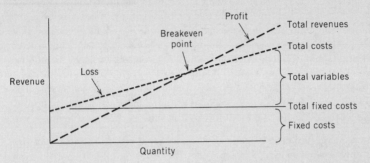

Below the breakeven point, the venture suffers losses; above it, the venture becomes profitable.

Let us make a hypothetical comparison of Euro Disney with its $1.6 billion in high interest loans (some of these as high as 11 percent) from the banks, and what the situation might be with more equity and less borrowed funds.

For this example, let us assume that other fixed costs are $240 million, that the average interest rate on the debt is 10 percent, and that average profit margin (contribution to overhead) from each visitor is $32. Now let us consider two scenarios: (a) the $1.6 billion of debt; and (b) only $0.5 billion of debt.

The number of visitors needed to break even are determined as follows:

$$\text{Breakeven} = \frac{\text{Total fixed costs}}{\text{Contribution to overhead}}$$

Scenario (a): Interest = 10% ($1,600,000,000) = $160,000,000
Fixed costs = Interest + $240,000,000
= 160,000,000 + 240,000,000
= $400,000,000

$$\text{Breakeven} = \frac{\$400,000,000}{\$32} = 12,500,000 \text{ visitors needed to breakeven}$$

Scenario (b) Interest = 10% (500,000,000) = $50,000,000
Fixed costs = 50,000,000 + 240,000,000
= $290,000,000

$$\text{Breakeven} = \frac{\$290,000,000}{\$32} = 9,062,500 \text{ visitors needed to breakeven}$$

(continues)

THE BREAKEVEN POINT (continued)

Because Euro Disney expected 11 million visitors the first year, it obviously was not going to break even while servicing $1.6 billion in debt with $160 million in interest charges per year. The average visitor would have to be induced to spend more, thereby increasing the average profit or contribution to overhead.

In making go/no go decisions, many costs can be estimated quite closely. What cannot be determined as surely are the sales figures. Certain things can be done to affect the breakeven point. Obviously it can be lowered if the overhead is reduced, as we saw in scenario b. Higher prices also result in a lower breakeven because of greater per customer profits (but would probably affect total sales quite adversely). Promotion expenses can be either increased or decreased and affect the breakeven point, but they probably also have an impact on sales. Some costs of operation can be reduced, thus lowering the breakeven. But the hefty interest charges act as a lodestone over an enterprise, greatly increasing the overhead and requiring what may be an unattainable breakeven point.

Does a new venture have to break even or make a profit the first year to be worth going into? Why or why not?

promise was Christmas week of 1993. Despite the first year's $920 million in red ink, some 35,000 packed the park most days. A week later on a cold January day, some of the rides still had 40-minute waits.

POSTSCRIPT

On March 15, 1994, an agreement was struck aimed at making Euro Disney profitable by September 30, 1995. The European banks would fund another $500 million and make concessions such as forgiving 18 months' interest and deferring all principal payments for three years. In return, Walt Disney Company agreed to spend about $750 million to bail out its Euro Disney affiliate. Thus, the debt would be halved, with interest payments greatly reduced. Disney also agreed to eliminate for five years the lucrative management fees and royalties it received on the sale of tickets and merchandise.[10]

The problems of Euro Disney were not resolved by mid-1994. The theme park and resort near Paris remained troubled. However, a new source for financing had emerged: A member of the Saudi Arabian royal family had agreed to invest up to $500 million for a 24 percent stake in Euro Disney. Prince Alwaleed had shown considerable sophistication in investing in troubled enterprises in the past. Now, his commitment to Euro Disney showed a belief in the ultimate success of the resort.[11]

Finally, in the third quarter of 1995, Euro Disney posted its first profit, some $35 million for the period. This compared with a year earlier loss of $113 million. By now,

[10] Brian Coleman and Thomas R. King, "Euro Disney Rescue Package Wins Approval," *Wall Street Journal* (March 15, 1994), pp. A3, A5.

[11] Richard Turner and Brian Coleman, "Saudi to Buy as Much as 24% of Euro Disney," *Wall Street Journal* (June 2, 1994), p. A3.

Euro Disney was only 39 percent owned by Disney. It attributed the turnaround partly to a new marketing strategy in which prices were slashed both at the gate and within the theme park in an effort to boost attendance, and also to shed the nagging image of being overpriced. A further attraction was the new "Space Mountain" ride that mimicked a trip to the moon.

However, some analysts questioned the staying power of such a movement into the black. In particular, they saw most of the gain coming from financial restructuring in which the debt-ridden Euro Disney struck a deal with its creditors to temporarily suspend debt and royalty payments. A second theme park and further property development were seen as essential in the longer term, as the payments would eventually resume.[12]

In August 1995 news broke of Walt Disney Company's proposed $10 billion acquisition of Capital Cities/ABC Inc. Experts said this would be an entertainment behemoth into the next century. Although many growth avenues were now possible, including great international growth in television programming and distribution such as ESPN and the Disney Channel, theme parks were considered very promising. Disney Chairman Michael Eisner announced possibilities of new theme parks in South America, possibly Brazil, as well as in Asia. He noted that Disney executives were scouring the globe looking for potential sites and partners in countries from Spain to China.[13]

In November 1997, *Forbes* magazine updated the situation with Euro Disney— although it had been renamed Disneyland Paris—under the provocative title, "Mickey's Last Laugh (Once Struggling Euro Disney Has Become a Favorite Tourist Destination in Europe)." The article noted that it had 11.7 million visitors in 1996, up from 8.8 million three years before. Cash flow margins had tripled since 1993, and even exceeded those of Tokyo Disneyland, the world's most popular park. The turnaround was credited to lower prices, the big new Space Mountain ride, and the 1994 restructuring that included the cash infusion from Prince Alwaleed.[14]

To the delight of the French government, plans were announced in 1999 to build a movie theme park, Disney Studios, next to the Magic Kingdom, to open in 2002. It was estimated that this expansion would attract an additional 4.2 million visitors annually, drawing people from farther afield in Europe. In 1998, Disneyland Paris had 12.5 visitors, being France's number-one tourist attraction, beating out Notre Dame.

Also late in 1999, Disney and Hong Kong agreed to build a major Disney theme park there, with Disney investing $314 million for 43 percent ownership while Hong Kong contributed nearly $3 billion. Hong Kong's leaders expected the new park would generate 16,000 jobs when it opened in 2005, certainly a motivation for the unequal investment contributions.[15]

---

[12] Brian Coleman, "Euro Disney Posts Its First Profit, $35.3 Million for Its Third Quarter," *Wall Street Journal* (July 26, 1995), p. A9.

[13] Lisa Bannon, "Expanded Disney to Look Overseas for Fastest Growth," *Wall Street Journal* (August 2, 1995), p. A3.

[14] "Mickey's Last Laugh," *Forbes* (November 3, 1997), p. 16.

[15] "Hong Kong Betting $3 billion on Success of New Disneyland," *Cleveland Plain Dealer* (November 3, 1999), p. 2C; Charles Fleming, "Euro Disney to Build Movie Theme Park Outside Paris," *Wall Street Journal* (September 30, 1999), pp. A18, A21.

WHAT CAN BE LEARNED

Beware the arrogant mindset, especially when dealing with new situations and new cultures. French sensitivities were offended by Disney corporate executives who often turned out to be brash, insensitive, and overbearing. A contentious attitude by Disney personnel alienated people and aggravated planning and operational difficulties. "The answer to doubts or suggestions invariably was, 'Do as we say, because we know best.'"[16]

Such a mindset is a natural concomitant to success. It is said that success breeds arrogance, but this inclination must be fought against by those who would spurn the ideas and concerns of others. For a proud and touchy people, the French, this almost contemptuous attitude by the Americans fueled resentment and glee at Disney miscues. It did not foster cooperation, understanding, or the willingness to smooth the process. One might almost speculate that had not the potential economic benefits to France been so great, the Euro Disney project might never have been approved.

Great success may be ephemeral. We often find that great successes are not lasting, that they have no staying power. Somehow the success pattern gets lost or forgotten or is not well rounded. Other times an operation grows beyond the capability of the originators. Hungry competitors are always in the wings, ready to take advantage of any lapse. As we saw with Euro Disney, having a closed mind to new ideas or to needed revisions of an old success pattern—the arrogance of success—makes expansion into different environments more difficult and even risky.

While corporate Disney has continued to have strong success with its other theme parks and its diversifications, competitors are moving in with their own theme parks in the United States and elsewhere. We may question whether this industry is approaching saturation, and we may wonder whether Disney has learned from its mistakes in Europe.

Highly leveraged situations are extremely vulnerable. During most of the 1980s, many managers, including corporate raiders, pursued a strategy of debt financing in contrast to equity (stock ownership) financing. Funds for such borrowing were usually readily available, heavy debt had income tax advantages, and profits could be distributed among fewer shares so that return on equity was enhanced. During this time a few voices decried the overleveraged situations of many companies. They predicted that when the eventual economic downturn came, such firms would find themselves unable to meet the heavy interest burden. Most lenders paid little heed to such lonesome voices and encouraged greater borrowing.

The widely publicized problems of some of the raiders in the late 1980s, such as Robert Campeau, who had acquired major department store corporations only to find himself overextended and unable to continue, suddenly changed some expansionist lending sentiments. The hard reality dawned that these arrangements were often fragile indeed, especially when they rested on

---

[16] Gumbel and Turner, "Fans Like Euro Disney," p. A1.

optimistic projections for asset sales, for revenues, and for cost savings to cover the interest payments. An economic slowdown hastened the demise of some of these ill-advised speculations.

Disney was guilty of the same speculative excesses with Euro Disney, relying far too much on borrowed funds and assuming that assets, such as hotels, could be easily sold off at higher prices to other investors. As we saw in the breakeven box, hefty interest charges from such overleveraged conditions can jeopardize the viability of the enterprise if revenue and profit projections fail to meet the rosy expectations.

Be judicious with the skimming price strategy. Euro Disney faced the classical situation favorable for a skimming price strategy. It was in a monopoly position, with no equivalent competitors likely. It faced a somewhat inelastic demand curve, which indicated that people would come almost regardless of price. So why not price to maximize per-unit profits? Unfortunately for Disney, the wily Europeans circumvented the high prices by frugality. Of course, a severe recession exacerbated the situation.

The learning insight from this example is that a skimming price assumes that customers are willing and able to pay the higher prices and have no lower-priced competitive alternatives. It is a faulty strategy when many customers are unable, or else unwilling, to pay the high prices and can find a way to experience the product or service in a modest way.

CONSIDER

Can you think of other learning insights from this case?

QUESTIONS

1. How could the company have erred so badly in its estimates of the spending patterns of European customers?
2. How could a better reading of the impact of cultural differences on revenues have been achieved?
3. What suggestions do you have for fostering a climate of sensitivity and goodwill in corporate dealings with the French?
4. How do you account for the great success of Tokyo Disneyland and the problems of Euro Disney? What are the key contributory differences?
5. Do you believe that Euro Disney might have done better if located elsewhere in Europe rather than just outside Paris? Why or why not?
6. "Mickey Mouse and the Disney park are an American cultural abomination." Evaluate this critical statement.
7. A deficiency in the planning was neglecting to win over European travel people, such as travel agents, tour guides, even bus drivers. How might this be corrected now?

HANDS-ON EXERCISES

Before

1. It is three months before the grand opening. As a staff assistant to the president of Euro Disney, you sense that the plans for high prices and luxury accommodations are ill-advised. What arguments would you marshal to persuade the company to offer lower prices and more moderate accommodations? Be as persuasive as you can.

After

2. It is six months after opening. Revenues are not meeting target, and a number of problems have surfaced and are being worked on. The major problem remains, however, that the venture needs more visitors and/or higher expenditures per visitor. Develop plans to improve the situation.

TEAM DEBATE EXERCISE

It is two years after the opening. Euro Disney is a monumental mistake, profitwise. Two schools of thought are emerging for improving the situation. One is to pour more money into the project, build one or two more theme parks, and really make this another Disney World. The other camp believes more investment would be wasted at this time, that the need is to pare expenses to the bone and wait for an eventual upturn. Debate the two positions.

INVITATION TO RESEARCH

Has the recent profitability of Euro Disney continued? Are expansion plans going ahead? Have other theme parks been announced?

CHAPTER THIRTEEN

28 % V7. S. Soda
$62 Bill Category
Coke 44%
Pepsi 32%

- teens
- innovation in package & product
- demographics
- need to diversify to keep customers

Coca-Cola's Classic Planning Miscalculation

*I*n this classic case we see a vivid example of the challenges, and risks, of management decision making. Despite careful planning and seemingly ample research, the decision was a strikeout. Fortunately for Coca-Cola, the consequences were more an acute embarrassment than an operational disaster.

On April 23, 1985, Roberto C. Goizueta, chairman of Coca-Cola, made a momentous announcement. It was to lead to more discussion, debate, and intense feelings than perhaps ever before encountered from one business decision.

"The best has been made even better," he proclaimed. After 99 years, the Coca-Cola Company had decided to abandon its original formula in favor of a sweeter variation, presumably an improved taste, which was named "New Coke."

Less than three months later, public pressure brought the company to admit that it had made a mistake and that it was bringing back the old Coke under the name "Coca-Cola Classic." It was July 11, 1985. Despite $4 million and two years of research, the company had made a major planning miscalculation in its estimation of customer acceptance of a product change. How could this have happened with such an astute and successful firm? The story is intriguing and provides a number of sobering insights, as well as a happy ending for Coca-Cola.

THE HISTORY OF COCA-COLA

Pemberton 1886
Candler 1892
Woodruff 1919

Early Days

Coca-Cola was invented by a pharmacist who rose to cavalry general for the Confederates during the Civil War. John Styth Pemberton settled in Atlanta after the war and began putting out patent medicines such as Triplex Liver Pills and Globe of Flower Cough Syrup. In 1885 he registered a trademark for French Wine Coca, "an Ideal Nerve and Tonic Stimulant." In 1886, Pemberton unveiled a modification of French Wine Coca, which he called Coca-Cola, and began distributing it to soda fountains in used beer bottles. He looked on the concoction less as a refreshment than as a headache cure, especially for people who had overindulged in food or drink.

173

By chance, one druggist discovered that the syrup tasted better when mixed with carbonated water.

As his health failed and Coca-Cola failed to bring in sufficient money to meet his financial obligations, Pemberton sold the rights to Coca-Cola to a 39-year-old pharmacist, Asa Griggs Candler, for a paltry $2,300. The destitute Pemberton died in 1888 and was buried in a grave that went unmarked for the next 70 years.

Candler, a small-town Georgia man born in 1851, had planned to become a physician but changed his mind after observing that druggists made more money than doctors. He struggled for almost 40 years until he bought Coca-Cola, but then his fortunes changed profoundly. In 1892 he organized the Coca-Cola Company; a few years later he downplayed the therapeutic qualities of the beverage and began emphasizing the pleasure-giving qualities. At the same time, he developed a bottling system that still exists, and for 25 years he almost single-handedly guided the drink's destiny.

Robert Woodruff and the Maturing of the Coca-Cola Company

In 1916 Candler left Coca-Cola to run for mayor of Atlanta. He left the company in the hands of his relatives, who, after only three years, sold it to a group of Atlanta businessmen for $25 million. Asa was not consulted, and he was deeply distraught. The company was then netting $5 million. By the time of his death in 1929, annual profits were approaching the $25 million sale price. The group who bought Coca-Cola was headed by Ernest Woodruff, an Atlanta banker. Coke today still remains in the hands of the Woodruff family. Under the direction of the son, Robert Winship Woodruff, Coca-Cola became not only a household word within the United States but one of the most recognized symbols the world over.

Robert Woodruff grew up in affluence but believed in the virtues of personal achievement and effort. As a young man, he ignored his father's orders to return to Emory College to complete the remaining years of his education. He wanted to earn his keep in the real world and not "waste" three years in school. Eventually in 1911 he joined one of his father's firms, the newly organized Atlantic Ice & Coal Company, as a salesman and buyer. But he and his father violently disagreed again, this time over Robert's purchases of trucks from White Motors to replace the horse-drawn carts and drays of the day. Ernest fired his son and told him never to return home. Robert promptly joined White Motors. At the age of 33, he had become the nation's top truck salesman and was earning $85,000 a year. But then he heeded his father's call to come home.

By 1920 the Coca-Cola Company was threatened by bankruptcy. An untimely purchase of sugar just before prices plummeted had resulted in a staggering amount of borrowing to keep the company afloat. Bottler relations were at an all-time low because the company had wanted to raise the price of syrup, thus violating the original franchise contracts in which the price had been permanently fixed. In April 1923 Robert was named president, and he cemented dealer relationships, stressing his conviction that he wanted everyone connected with Coca-Cola to make money. He instituted a quality control program and greatly expanded distribution: By 1930 Coca-Cola had 64 bottlers in 28 countries.

IMAGE

During World War II, Coke went with the GIs. Woodruff saw to it that every man in uniform could get a bottle of Coca-Cola for a nickel whenever he wanted, no matter what the cost to the company. Throughout the 1950s, 1960s, and early 1970s, Coca-Cola ruled the soft drink market, despite strong challenges by Pepsi. It outsold Pepsi two to one. But this was to change. *Outselling Pepsi 2:1*

BACKGROUND OF THE DECISION

Inroads of Pepsi, 1970s and 1980s

By the mid-1970s the Coca-Cola Company was a lumbering giant, and performance reflected this. Between 1976 and 1979, the growth rate of Coca-Cola soft drinks dropped from 13 percent annually to a meager 2 percent. As the giant stumbled, Pepsi Cola was finding heady triumphs. First came the "Pepsi Generation." This advertising campaign captured the imagination of the baby boomers with its idealism and youth. Pepsi's association with youth and vitality greatly enhanced its image and firmly associated it with the largest consumer market for soft drinks. *76–'79 youth mkt*

Then came another management coup, the "Pepsi Challenge," in which comparative taste tests with consumers showed a clear preference for Pepsi. This campaign led to a rapid increase in Pepsi's market share, from 6 to 14 percent of total U.S. soft-drink sales. *Pepsi gains*

Coca-Cola, in reaction, conducted its own taste tests. Alas, these tests had the same result—people liked the taste of Pepsi better, and market share changes reflected this. As Table 13.1 shows, by 1979 Pepsi had closed the gap on Coca-Cola, having 17.9 percent of the soft-drink market to Coke's 23.9 percent. By the end of 1984, Coke had only a 2.9 percent lead, and in the grocery store market it was now trailing 1.7 percent. Further indication of Coke's diminishing position relative to Pepsi was a study done by Coca-Cola's own marketing research department. This study showed that in 1972, 18 percent of soft-drink users drank Coke exclusively, whereas only 4 percent drank only Pepsi. In 10 years the picture had changed greatly: Only 12 percent now claimed loyalty to Coke, and the number of exclusive Pepsi drinkers almost matched, with 11 percent. Figure 13.1 shows this graphically. *mkt sh.*

The fact that Coca-Cola was outspending Pepsi in advertising by $100 million made Coke's deteriorating competitive performance all the more worrisome and

TABLE 13.1   Coke and Pepsi Shares of Total Soft-Drink Market 1950s–1984

	Mid-1950s Lead	1975 % of Market	Lead	1979 % of Market	Lead	1984 % of Market	Lead
Coke	Better than 2 to 1	24.2	6.8	23.9	6.0	21.7	2.9
Pepsi		17.4		17.9		18.8	

Source: Thomas Oliver, *The Real Coke, The Real Story* (New York: Random House, 1986), pp. 21, 50; "Two Cokes Really Are Better Than One—For Now," *Business Week* (September 9, 1985), p. 38.

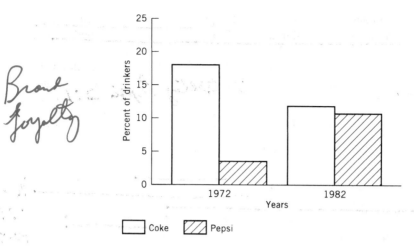

Brand loyalty [handwritten]

Figure 13.1 Coke versus Pepsi: comparison of exclusive drinkers.

Coke has much better distribution [handwritten]

frustrating. Coca-Cola had twice as many vending machines, dominated fountains, had more shelf space, and was competitively priced. Why was it still losing market share?

The Changing of the Guard *Goizueta years* [handwritten]

J. Paul Austin, the chairman of Coca-Cola, was nearing retirement in 1980. Donald Keough, the president for Coca-Cola's American group, was expected to succeed him. But a new name, Roberto Goizueta, suddenly emerged.

Goizueta's background was far different from that of the typical Coca-Cola executive. He was not from Georgia, was not even Southern. Rather, he was the son of a wealthy Havana sugar plantation owner. He came to the United States at age 16 to enter an exclusive Connecticut preparatory school, Cheshire Academy. He spoke virtually no English when he arrived, but he quickly learned the language by using the dictionary and watching movies—and became the class valedictorian.

Goizueta graduated from Yale in 1955 with a degree in chemical engineering and returned to Cuba. Spurning his father's business, he went to work in Coke's Cuban research labs.

Goizueta's complacent life was to change in 1959 when Fidel Castro seized power and expropriated foreign facilities. He fled to the United States with his wife and their three children, arriving with $20. With Coca-Cola he soon became known as a brilliant administrator, and in 1968 he was brought to company headquarters. In 1980 Goizueta and six other executives were made vice chairpersons and began battling for top spots in the company.

Chief executive officer J. Paul Austin, soon to retire because of Alzheimer's disease, favored an operations man to become the next CEO. But he was overruled by Robert Woodruff, the 90-year-old patriarch. In April 1980 the board of directors approved the recommendation of Goizueta for the president. When Goizueta moved on to become chairman of the board in March 1981, Donald Keough succeeded him as president.

Shortly after his promotion, Goizueta called a worldwide manager's conference in which he announced that nothing was sacred to the company anymore, that change was imminent, and that managers had to accept that situation. He also announced ambitious plans to diversify beyond the soft-drink industry.

In a new era of change announced by a new administration, the sacredness of the commitment to the original Coke formula became tenuous, and the ground was laid for the first flavor change in 99 years.

Marketing Research

With the market share erosion of the late 1970s and early 1980s, despite strong advertising and superior distribution, the company began to look at the product itself. Evidence was increasingly suggesting that taste was the single most important cause of Coke's decline. Perhaps the original secret formula needed to be scrapped. And so Project Kansas began.

Under Project Kansas in 1982 some 2,000 interviews in 10 major markets were conducted to investigate customers' willingness to accept a different Coke. People were shown storyboards and comic strip-style mock commercials and were asked series of questions. One storyboard, for example, said that Coke had added a new ingredient and tasted smoother; another said the same about Pepsi. Then consumers were asked about their reactions to the "change concept" (for example, "Would you be upset?" and "Would you try the new drink?"). Researchers estimated from the responses that 10 to 12 percent of Coke drinkers would be upset and that one-half of these would get over it, but one-half would not.

Although interviews showed a willingness to try a new Coke, other tests disclosed the opposite. Small consumer panels, or focus groups, revealed strong favorable and unfavorable sentiments. But the technical division persisted in trying to develop a new, more pleasing flavor. By September 1984 the division thought it had done so. The new version was a sweeter, less fizzy cola with a soft, sticky taste due to a higher sugar content from the exclusive use of corn syrup sweetener, which is sweeter than sucrose. This cola was introduced in blind taste tests in which consumers were not told what brand they were drinking. These tests were highly encouraging: The new flavor substantially outperformed Pepsi, whereas in previous blind taste tests Pepsi had always beaten Coke.

As a result researchers estimated that the new formula would boost Coke's share of the soft-drink market by one percentage point. This point would be worth $200 million in sales.

Before adopting the new flavor, Coca-Cola invested $4 million in the biggest taste test ever. Some 191,000 people in more than 13 cities participated in a comparison of unmarked various Coke formulations. The use of unmarked colas was intended to eliminate any bias toward brand names. Fifty-five percent of the participants favored New Coke over the original formula, and New Coke also beat Pepsi. The research results seemed to be conclusive in favor of the new formula.

The Go Decision

Even when the decision was made to introduce the new flavor, a number of ancillary decisions had to be made. For example, should the new flavor be added to the product line, or should it replace the old Coke? Executives thought that bottlers would be opposed to adding another cola. After considerable soul searching, top executives unanimously decided to change the taste of Coke and take the old Coke off the market.

In January 1985 the task of introducing the new Coke was given to the McCann-Erickson advertising agency. Bill Cosby was to be the spokesperson for the nationwide introduction of the new Coke, scheduled for April. All departments of this company were gearing their efforts for a coordinated introduction.

On April 23, 1985, Goizueta and Keough held a press conference at Lincoln Center in New York City in order to introduce the new Coke. Invitations had been sent to the media from all over the United States, and some 200 newspaper, magazine, and TV reporters attended the press conference. However, many of them came away unconvinced of the merits of the new Coke, and their stories were generally negative. In the days ahead, the news media's skepticism would exacerbate the public rejection of the new Coke.

The word spread quickly. Within 24 hours, 81 percent of the U.S. population knew of the change, and this was more people than were aware in July 1969 that Neil Armstrong had walked on the moon.[1] Early results looked good; 150 million people tried the new Coke—more people than had ever before tried a new product. Most comments were favorable. Shipments to bottlers rose to the highest percent in five years. The decision looked unassailable. But not for long.

AFTERMATH OF THE DECISION

The situation changed rapidly. Although some objections were expected, the protests quickly mushroomed. In the first four hours, the company received about 650 calls. By mid-May, calls were coming in at a rate of 5,000 a day, in addition to a barrage of angry letters. The company added 83 WATS lines and hired new staff to handle the responses. People were speaking of Coke as an American symbol and as a longtime friend that had suddenly betrayed them. Some threatened to switch to tea or water. Here is a sampling of the responses:[2]

> The sorrow I feel knowing not only won't I ever enjoy real Coke, but my children and grandchildren won't either… I guess my children will have to take my word for it.

> It is absolutely TERRIBLE! You should be ashamed to put the Coke label on it. … This new stuff tastes worse than Pepsi.

> It was nice knowing you. You were a friend for most of my 35 years. Yesterday I had my first taste of new Coke, and to tell the truth, if I would have wanted Pepsi, I would have ordered a Pepsi not a Coke.

---

[1] John S. Demott, "Fiddling with the Real Thing," *Time* (May 6, 1985), p. 55.
[2] Thomas Oliver, *The Real Coke, The Real Story* (New York: Random House, 1986), pp. 155–156.

In all, more than 40,000 such letters were received that spring and summer. In Seattle strident loyalists calling themselves Old Coke Drinkers of America laid plans to file a class action suit against Coca-Cola. People began stockpiling the old Coke. Some sold it at scalper's prices. When sales in June did not pick up as the company had expected, bottlers demanded the return of old Coke.

The company's research also confirmed an increasing negative sentiment. Before May 30, 53 percent of consumers said they liked the new Coke. In June the vote began to change: More than one-half of all people surveyed said they did not like the new Coke. By July only 30 percent of the people surveyed each week said that they liked the new Coke.

Anger spread across the country, fueled by media publicity. Fiddling with the formula for the 99-year-old beverage became an affront to patriotic pride. As Robert Antonio, a University of Kansas sociologist, stated, "Some felt that a sacred symbol had been tampered with."[3] Even Goizueta's father spoke out against the switch when it was announced. He told his son the move was a bad one and jokingly threatened to disown him. By now company executives began to worry about a consumer boycott.

Coca-Cola Cries "Uncle"

Company executives now began seriously thinking about how to recoup the fading prospects of Coke. In an executive meeting, the managers decided to take no action until after the Fourth of July weekend, when the sales results for this holiday weekend were in. Results were unimpressive. They decided to reintroduce Coca-Cola under the trademark of Coca-Cola Classic. The company would keep the new flavor and call it New Coke. Top executives announced the decision to the public on July 11, walking onto the stage in front of the Coca-Cola logo to make an apology to the public. They never admitted that New Coke had been a total mistake.

This presentation delivered two messages to American consumers. First, to those who were drinking New Coke and enjoying it, the company conveyed its thanks. To those who wanted the original Coke, the message was, "We heard you—the original taste of Coke is back."

The news spread fast. ABC interrupted its soap opera *General Hospital* on Wednesday afternoon to break the news. In the kind of saturation coverage normally reserved for disasters or diplomatic crises, the decision to bring back old Coke was prominently reported on every evening network news broadcast. The general feeling of soft-drink fans was joy. Democratic Senator David Pryor of Arkansas expressed his jubilation on the Senate floor: "A very meaningful moment in the history of America, this shows that some national institutions cannot be changed."[4] Even Wall Street was happy. Old Coke's comeback drove Coca-Cola stock to its highest level in 12 years.

On the other hand, Roger Enrico, president of Pepsi-Cola USA, said, "Clearly this is the Edsel of the '80s. This was a terrible mistake. Coke's got a lemon on its

[3] John Greenwald, "Coca-Cola's Big Fizzle," *Time* (July 22, 1985), p. 48.
[4] *Ibid.*

hands and now they're trying to make lemonade."[5] Other critics labeled this decision to change Coke "the blunder of the decade."[6]

WHAT WENT WRONG?

The most convenient scapegoat, according to consensus opinion, was the marketing research that preceded the decision. Yet Coca-Cola spent about $4 million and devoted two years to the marketing research. About 200,000 consumers were contacted during this time. The error in judgment was surely not from want of trying. But when we dig deeper into the research efforts, some flaws become apparent.

Flawed Marketing Research   *Problems with Research*

The major design of the marketing research involved taste tests by representative consumers. After all, the decision point involved a different-flavored Coke, so what could be more logical than to conduct blind taste tests to determine the acceptability of the new flavor, not only versus the old Coke but also versus Pepsi? And these results were significantly positive for the new formula, even among Pepsi drinkers. A "go" signal seemed clear.

But with the benefit of hindsight, some deficiencies in the research design were more apparent and should have caused concern at the time. The research participants were not told that by picking one cola, they would lose the other. This turned out to be a significant distortion: Any addition to the product line would naturally be far more acceptable to a loyal Coke user than would be a complete substitution, which meant the elimination of the traditional product.

While three to four new tastes were tested with almost 200,000 people, only 30,000 to 40,000 of these tests involved the specific formula for the new Coke. The research was geared more to the idea of a new, sweeter cola than to the final formula. In general a sweeter flavor tends to be preferred in blind taste tests. This is particularly true with youth, the largest drinkers of sugared colas, and the group that had been drinking more Pepsi in recent years. Furthermore, preferences for sweeter tasting products tend to diminish with use.[7]

Consumers were asked whether they favored change as a concept and whether they would likely drink more, less, or the same amount of Coke if there were a change. But such questions could hardly probe the depth of feelings and emotional ties to the product, and the decisions and plans based on the flawed research were themselves vulnerable.   *= Product Gestalt*

Symbolic Value

The symbolic value of Coke was the sleeper. Perhaps this should have been foreseen. Perhaps the marketing research should have considered this possibility and designed

[5] *Ibid.* p. 49.

[6] James E. Ellis and Paul B. Brown, "Coke's Man on the Spot," *Business Week* (July 29, 1985), p. 56.

[7] "New Coke Wins Round 1, But Can It Go the Distance?" *Business Week* (June 24, 1985), p. 48.

the research to map it and determine the strength and durability of these values—that is, whether they would have a major effect on any substitution of a new flavor.

Admittedly, when we get into symbolic value and emotional involvement, any researcher is dealing with vague and nebulous attitudes. But various attitudinal measures have been developed to measure the strength or degree of emotional involvement, such as the *semantic differential*, described in the following Information Box.

Traditional Values

Herd Instinct

A natural human phenomenon asserted itself in this case—the herd instinct, the tendency of people to follow an idea, slogan, or concept and to "jump on the bandwagon." At first, acceptance of the new Coke appeared to be reasonably satisfactory.

INFORMATION BOX

MEASURING ATTITUDES—THE SEMANTIC DIFFERENTIAL

An important tool in attitudinal research, image studies, and planning decisions is the *semantic differential.* It was originally developed to measure the meaning that a concept—perhaps a political issue, a person, or a work of art, or in marketing a brand, product, or company—might have for people in terms of various dimensions. As first presented, the instrument consisted of pairs of polar adjectives with a seven-interval scale separating the opposite members of each pair. For example:

Good — — — — — — Bad

The various intervals from left to right would then represent degrees of feeling or belief ranging from extremely good to neither good nor bad to extremely bad.

This instrument has been refined to obtain greater sensitivity through the use of descriptive phrases. The following are examples of such bipolar phrases for determining the image of a particular brand of beer:

Something special — — — — — — Just another drink

American flavor — — — — — — Foreign flavor

Really peps you up — — — — — — Somehow doesn't pep you up

The number of word pairs varies considerably, but there may be as many as 50 or more. Flexibility and appropriateness to a particular study are achieved by constructing tailor-made word and phrase lists.

Semantic differential scales have been used to compare images of particular products, brands, firms, and stores against competing ones. The answers of all respondents can be averaged and then plotted to provide a "profile," as shown below for three competing beers on four scales (actually, a firm would probably use 20 or more scales in such a study).

(continues)

MEASURING ATTITUDES—THE SEMANTIC DIFFERENTIAL *(continued)*

In this profile, brand A shows the dominant image over its competing brands in three of the four categories; however, the negative reaction to its price should alert the company to review pricing practices. Brand C shows a negative image, especially regarding the reliability of its product. The old-fashioned image may or may not be desirable, depending on the type of customer being sought; at least the profile indicates that brand C is perceived as being distinctive from the other two brands. Probably the weakest image of all is that of brand B; respondents viewed this brand as having no distinctive image, neither good nor bad. A serious image-building campaign is desperately needed if brand B is to compete successfully; otherwise, the price may have to be dropped to gain some advantage.

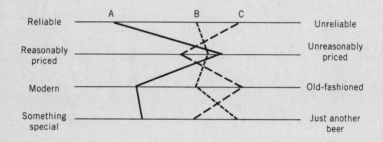

Easy to administer and simple to analyze, the semantic differential is useful in identifying where there might be opportunities in areas presently not well covered by competitors. It is also useful to a well-established firm—such as Coca-Cola—to determine the strength and the various dimensions of attitudes toward its product. Semantic differential scales are also valuable in evaluating the effectiveness of planning changes, such as a change in advertising theme. Here the semantic differential can be administered before and after the campaign, and any changes in perceptions can be pinpointed.

In the example of the three beers, how would you attempt to build up the brand image of beer B? How successful would you expect to be?

But as more and more outcries were raised—fanned by the press—about the betrayal of the old tradition (somehow Coke became identified with motherhood, apple pie, and the flag), public attitudes shifted vigorously against this perceived unworthy substitute. The bandwagon syndrome was fully activated. It is doubtful that by July 1985 Coca-Cola could have done anything to reverse the unfavorable tide. To wait for it to die down was fraught with danger, for who would be brave enough to predict the durability and possible heights of such a protest movement?

INFORMATION BOX

CONTINGENCY PLANS

Planning involves resource deployment through the use of budgets. Resources to be deployed include both work force and facilities: the number of people to be involved in the particular aspect of the operation, and the amount of money and facilities required to meet planned goals and expectations. Such resource deployment depends on certain assumptions made about both the external and internal environment. When plans are made for major projects, such as new Coke, and resources are committed, the success of the commitment depends greatly on the accuracy of the assumptions that are made. When, as events unfold, it becomes clear that certain assumptions were either overly optimistic or overly pessimistic, then plans and resource deployments need to be revised.

Contingency plans are well used when dealing with a new product or project. Different plans may thereby be developed for the different contingencies, or sets of conditions that may occur. For example, Plan A may assume a certain level of acceptance; Plan B may be developed for better-than-expected circumstances; Plan C may be ready to put to use if early results are discouraging. When such plans are drawn up in advance, a firm is better able to cope with varied outcomes and can either marshal additional resources or cut back to more realistic expectations.

With such contingency plans developed, Coca-Cola would have been better prepared to react to the surprising resistance to its new product. For example, it could have developed plans for different levels of customer acceptance, including the worse scenario that was actually encountered: nonacceptance and public agitation. Although in this case, the decision making under crisis conditions apparently worked out satisfactorily, in another instance it might not have. Carefully thought-out alternative actions generally have a better payoff than decisions made quickly in a crisis situation.

Do you think any contingency plan of Coca-Cola would have anticipated the extent of public agitation? Even if such a worst-case scenario were considered, is it likely that reactions would have been improved? Why or why not?

Could such a tide have been predicted? Perhaps not, at least not the full strength of the movement. Coca-Cola expected some resentment, but perhaps it should have been more cautious and considered a worst-case scenario in addition to what seemed the more probable. Coca-Cola would then have been prepared to react to such a *contingency*.   *WIBAI*

WHAT CAN BE LEARNED?

Planning and research do not guarantee the best decision. Most decision making occurs under conditions of uncertainty: the environment ever changing, actions of competitors not always predictable, consumers fickle and illogical. Prudent executives try to decrease the uncertainty by careful planning and diligent research. But this case illustrates that bad decisions can still result. Who could have predicted the belated attachment of consumers to the idea of tradition, or the power of the media in fanning this emotional mindset? With the benefit of hindsight we can see how planning and research efforts could have been improved. But even then the decision might have been faulty.

So, while careful planning and research does not guarantee a correct decision, or the best one, it does improve the "batting average," that is, the probability of making a good decision—sometimes a lot, sometimes only a little. But this is the best we can expect in decision making under uncertainty, that more good decisions than bad decisions will be made.

Taste is an unreliable preference factor. Taste tests are commonly used in marketing research, but some marketers remain skeptical of their validity. Take beer, for example. Do you know of anybody—despite strenuous claims—who can in blind taste tests unerringly identify which is which among three or four disguised brands of beer? We know that people tend to favor the sweeter in taste tests. But does this mean that such a sweeter flavor will always win out? Hardly. Something else is operating with consumer preference other than the fleeting essence of a taste—unless the flavor difference is extreme. Research and decisions that rely primarily on taste tests tend to be more vulnerable to mistakes.

Brand image is usually a powerful sales stimulant. Advertisers have consistently been more successful by cultivating a desirable image or personality for their brands or the types of people who use them than by standing by such vague statements as "better tasting."

Beware of tampering with the traditional image. Not many firms have a 100-year-old tradition to be concerned with, or even 25, or even 10. Most products have much shorter life cycles. No other product has been so widely used and so deeply entrenched in societal values and culture as Coke.

The psychological components of the great Coke protest make interesting speculation. Perhaps in an era of rapid change, many people wish to hang on to the one symbol of security or constancy in their lives—even if this is only the traditional Coke flavor. Perhaps many people found this protest to be an interesting way to escape the humdrum, by making waves in a rather harmless fashion, and in so doing see if a big corporation might be forced to cry "uncle."

One wonders how many consumers would even have been aware of any change in flavor had the new formula been quietly introduced. But, of course, the advertising siren call of "New!" would have been muted.

So, do we dare tamper with tradition? In Coke's case the answer is probably not, unless it is done very quietly; but, then, Coke is unique.

Tampering with a major product still in high demand may be risky indeed. Conventional wisdom advocates that changes are best made in response to problems, that when things are going smoothly the success pattern or strategy should not be tampered with. This may or may not be a good rule of thumb.

Actually, things were not going all that well for Coke by early 1985. Competitive position had steadily been declining to Pepsi for some years. Vigorous promotional efforts by Pepsi featuring Michael Jackson had increased market share of regular Pepsi by 1.5 percent in 1984, while regular Coke was dropping 1 percent. Moreover, regular Coke had steadily been losing competitive position in supermarkets, dropping almost 4 percent between 1981 and 1985. And foreign business, accounting for 62 percent of total soft-drink volume for Coca-Cola, was showing a disappointing growth rate.[8]

So there was certainly motivation for considering a change. And the obvious change was to introduce a somewhat different flavor, one more congruent with the preference of younger people who were the prime market for soft drinks. We do not subscribe to the philosophy of "Don't rock the boat" or "Don't change anything until forced to." However, Coca-Cola had another option.

Major changes often are better introduced without immediately discarding the present. The obvious alternative was to introduce the new Coke but still keep the old one. The lesson here is, "Don't burn your bridges." Of course, in July Roberto Goizueta brought back the old Coke after some months of turmoil and considerable corporate embarrassment and competitive glee—which soon turned to dismay. The obvious drawback for having two Cokes was dealer resentment at having to stock an additional product in the same limited space and bottler concern at having a more complicated production run. Furthermore, there was the real possibility that Pepsi would emerge as the number one soft drink because of two competing Cokes—and this would be an acute embarrassment for Coca-Cola.

Sheer advertising expenditures does not guarantee effectiveness. Coca-Cola was outspending Pepsi for advertising by $100 million, but its competitive position in the 1970s and early 1980s continued to erode in comparison to Pepsi's. Pepsi's campaign featured the theme of the "Pepsi Generation" and the "Pepsi Challenge." The use of a superstar such as Michael Jackson also proved to be more effective with the youth market for soft drinks than Bill Cosby for Coca-Cola. Any executive has to be left with the sobering realization that the sheer number of dollars spent on advertising does not guarantee competitive success. A smaller firm can still outdo a larger rival.

The power of the media needs to be considered in decisions that are likely to generate widespread interest. The press and broadcast media can be powerful influences of public opinion. With the new Coke, the media undoubtedly exacerbated the herd instinct by publicizing the protests to the fullest. After all, this was news. And news seems to be spiciest when an institution or person can be criticized or found wanting. The power of the press should also be sobering to an executive and ought to be one of the factors she or he considers with certain decisions that may affect the public image of the organization.

CONSIDER

What additional learning insights do you see emerging from the Coca-Cola case?

---

[8] "Pepsi's High-Priced Sell Is Paying Off," *Business Week* (March 4, 1985), pp. 34–35; "Is Coke Fixing a Coke That Isn't Broken?" *Business Week* (May 6, 1985), p. 47.

186 • *Chapter 13: Coca-Cola's Classic Planning Miscalculation*

CONSEQUENCES

Forced by public opinion into a two-cola strategy, the company found the results to be reassuring. By October 1985 Coke Classic was outselling New Coke by better than 2 to 1 nationwide and by 9 to 1 in some markets. Restaurant chains such as McDonald's, Hardees, Roy Rogers, and Red Lobster had switched back to Coke Classic.

For the full year of 1985, sales from all operations rose 10 percent and profits, 9 percent. In the United States, Coca-Cola soft-drink volume increased 9 percent; internationally it rose 10 percent. Profitability from soft drinks decreased slightly, representing heavier advertising expenses for introducing New Coke and then reintroducing old Coke.

Coca-Cola's fortunes continued to improve steadily, if not spectacularly. By 1988 it was producing 5 of the 10 top-selling soft drinks in the country and had 40 percent of the domestic market to Pepsi's 31 percent.[9]

Because the soft-drink business was generating about $1 billion in cash each year, Roberto Goizueta had made a number of major acquisitions, such as Columbia Pictures and the Taylor Wine Company. However, these did not meet his expectations and were disposed of. Still, by 1988 Coca-Cola had a hoard of $5 billion in new cash and debt capacity, and the enticing problem now was how to spend it.

The most successful diversifications were in the soft-drink area. As recently as 1981 there had been only one Coke, and not too many years before, only one container, the $6^{1}/_{2}$-ounce glass bottle. By 1987 only one-tenth of 1 percent of all Coke was sold in that bottle.[10] Classic Coke was the best-selling soft drink in the United States, and Diet Coke was the third-largest selling. New Coke was now

Table 13.2   1986 Family of Cokes

Kinds	Millions of Cases
Total of one cola, 1980	1,310.5
1986	
Coca-Cola Classic	1,294.3
Diet Coke	490.8
Coke	185.1
Cherry Coke	115.6
Caffeine-Free Diet Coke	85.6
Caffeine-Free Coke	19.0
Diet Cherry Coke	15.0

Source: "He Put the Kick Back into Coke," *Fortune* (October 26, 1987), p. 48.

[9] John H. Taylor, "Some Things Don't Go Better with Coke," *Forbes* (March 21, 1988), pp. 34–35.
[10] Thomas Moore, "He Put the Kick Back into Coke," *Fortune* (October 26, 1987), pp. 47–56.

being outsold by Classic about 7 to 1. Table 13.2 shows the total sales volume of the Coke family for 1986.

Coca-Cola's future looked bright. Per-capita soft-drink consumption in the United States had been rising significantly in the 1980s, as shown in the following table:

	Per Capita Consumption	Percent Increase
1980	34.5 gal	
1986	42 gal	22%

Source: Pepsico 1986 Annual Report, p. 13.

The international potential was also great. Per-capita consumption outside the United States was only four gallons—yet 95 percent of the world's population lives outside the United States.

CONCLUSION

Some called new Coke a misstep, others a blink. At the time of the fiasco some called it a monumental blunder, the mistake of the century. But it hardly turned out to be that. As sales surged, some competitors accused Coca-Cola of engineering the whole scenario in order to get an abundance of free publicity. Coke executives stoutly denied this and admitted their error in judgment. For who could foresee, as *Fortune* noted, that the episode would "reawaken deep-seated American loyalty to Coca-Cola"?[11]

And who could have foreseen that the widely publicized "mistake" of Coca-Cola would have other positive repercussions? The company would now be viewed as more human and more responsive to the wishes of consumers.

QUESTIONS

1. How could Coca-Cola's marketing research have been improved? Be as specific as you can.
2. When a firm is facing a negative press, as Coca-Cola was with the new Coke, what recourse does the firm have? Support your conclusions.
3. Do you think Coca-Cola would have been as successful if it had introduced the new Coke as an addition to the line and not as a substitute for the old Coke? Why or why not?
4. "If it's not broken, don't fix it!" Evaluate this statement.
5. Do you think Coca-Cola engineered the whole scenario with the new Coke, including fanning initial protests, in order to get a bonanza of free publicity? Defend your position.

[11] *Ibid.*, p. 48.

6. Would you, as a top executive at Coca-Cola, have "caved in" as quickly to the protests? Would you have "toughed it out" instead?

HANDS-ON EXERCISES

1. You are the public relations director of Coca-Cola. It is early June 1985, and you have been ordered to "do something" to blunt the negative publicity. What ideas can you offer that might counter or replace the negatives with positive publicity?

2. Assume that you are Robert Goizueta and that you are facing increasing pressure in early July 1985 to abandon the new Coke and bring back the old formula. However, your latest marketing research suggests that only a small group of agitators are making all the fuss about the new cola. Evaluate your options and support your recommendations to the board.

TEAM DEBATE EXERCISE

The decision to go with the new Coke has not been made yet. One group at headquarters is dead set against any change: "if it's not broke, don't fix it." The other group firmly believes that change is not only necessary but long overdue. Debate the two positions as comprehensively and persuasively as you can. (Be sure that you confine your arguments to what was known in early 1985. You cannot use the benefit of hindsight.)

INVITATION TO RESEARCH

What is the current situation with Coca-Cola? Is Coke Classic still the big winner? Is New Coke still being produced? Is Coca-Cola winning the battle with Pepsi? How are the two companies doing in the international arena? What is the status regarding recent diversifications of Coca-Cola?

CHAPTER FOURTEEN

Vanguard: Success in Taking the Road Less Traveled

Vanguard Group has become the largest mutual fund family in the world, besting Fidelity Investments. While Fidelity had been increasing its fund assets about 20 percent a year, Vanguard was growing at 33 percent. Fidelity advertised heavily, while Vanguard did practically no advertising, spending a bare $8 million for a few ads to get people to ask for prospectuses. The Kaufmann Fund, one-hundredth Vanguard's size, spent that much for advertising, and General Mills spent twice as much just to introduce a new cereal, Sunrise.[1]

What is Vanguard's secret? How wise is it with such a consumer product to spurn advertising? The answer lies in the vision and steadfastness of John C. Bogle, the founder and now retired chairman.

JOHN BOGLE AND THE CREATION OF VANGUARD

In 1950, as a junior at Princeton, Bogle was groping for a topic for his senior thesis. He wanted a topic that no one had written about in any serious academic paper. In December 1949 he read an article in *Fortune* on mutual funds. At that time, all mutual funds were sold with sales commissions often 8 percent of the amount invested, and this was taken off the top as a front-end load. (This meant that if you invested $1,000, only $920 would be earning you money. Today we find no funds with a front-end load more than 6.5 percent, so there has been some improvement.) In addition, these funds had high yearly overheads or expense ratios. As Bogle thought about this, he wondered why funds couldn't be bought without salespeople or brokers and their steep commissions, and if growth could not be maximized by keeping overhead down.

Right after graduation he joined a tiny mutual fund, Wellington Management Company, and moved up rapidly. In 1965, at age 35, he became the chief executive. Unwisely, he decided to merge with another firm, but the new partners turned out to be active managers (buying and selling with a vengeance), generating high overhead costs. The relationship was incompatible with Bogle's beliefs and in 1974 he was fired as chief executive.

[1] Thomas Easton, "The Gospel According to Vanguard," *Forbes* (February 8, 1999), p. 115.

TABLE 14.1 Relative Growth Comparisons of the Two
Largest Mutual Funds

| | Assets (millions $) | | 5-Year Gain |
	6/30/94	6/30/99	(percent)
Fidelity Magellan	$33,179	$97,594	194.2%
Vanguard 500 Index	8,443	92,644	997.3

Source: Company reports.

Commentary: Especially notable is the tremendous growth of Vanguard's 500 Index Fund in the last five years, growing from $8 billion in assets to over $92 billion.

He decided to go his own way and change the "very structure under which mutual funds operated" into a fund distribution company mutually owned by shareholders. The idea came from his Princeton thesis, and included such heresies as "reduction of sales loads and management fees," and "giving investors a fair shake" as the rock on which the new enterprise would be built. He chose the name "Vanguard" for his new company after the great victory of Lord Nelson over Napoleon's fleet with his flagship, HMS Vanguard. Bogle launched the Vanguard Group of Investment Companies on September 26, 1974, and he hoped "that just as Nelson's fleet had come to dominate the seas during the Napoleonic wars, our new flagship would come to dominate the mutual fund sea."[2]

But success was long in coming. Bogle brought out the first index fund the next year, a fund based on the Standard & Poor's 500 Stock Price Index, and named it Vanguard 500 Index Fund. It was designed to mirror the market averages, and thus required minimal management decisions and costs. It flopped initially. Analysts publicly derided the idea, arguing that astute management could beat the averages every time, though they ignored the costs of high-priced money managers and frequent trading.

At the millennium, twenty-five years later, this Vanguard flagship fund that tracks the 500 stocks on the Standard & Poor's Index had more than $75 billion in assets and had beat 86 percent of all actively managed stock funds in 1998, and an even higher percentage over the past decade. By early 2000 it overtook Fidelity's famed Magellan Fund as the largest mutual fund of all. The relative growth between Magellan and Vanguard's 500 Index is shown in Table 14.1.

The Vanguard family of funds had become the world's largest *no-load* mutual fund group, with 12 million shareholders and $442 billion in assets as of the beginning of 1999. Fidelity, *partly load and partly no-load,* had nearly $700 billion, but the gap was closing fast.

Bogle, the Messiah

A feature article in the February 8, 1999 issue of *Forbes* had this headline:

[2] John C. Bogle, *Common Sense on Mutual Funds* (New York: Wiley, 1999), pp. 402–403.

The Gospel According to Vanguard—How do you account for the explosive success of that strange business called Vanguard? Maybe it isn't really a business at all. It's a religion.[3]

Bogle's religion was low-cost investing and service to customers. He believed in funds being bought and not sold, thus, no loads or commissions to salespeople or brokers. Customers had to seek out and deal directly with Vanguard. The engine was frugality with the investor-owner's best interests paramount. This was not advertised, not pasted on billboards, but the gospel was preached in thousands of letters to shareholders, editors, Securities and Exchange Commission members, and congressmen. Bogle made many speeches, comments to the news media, and appearances on such TV channels as CNBC, and wrote two best-selling books. With his gaunt face and raspy voice, he became the zealot for low-cost investing, and the major critic of money managers who trade frenetically, in the process running up costs and tax burdens for their investors. As the legions of loyal and enthusiastic clients grew, word-of-mouth from past experiences, and favorable mentions in business and consumer periodicals such as *Forbes,* the *Wall Street Journal, Money,* and numerous daily newspapers, as well as TV stations, brought a groundswell of new and repeat business to Vanguard.

Bogle turned 70 in May 1999, and was forced to retire from Vanguard's board. The new chairman, John J. Brennan, 44, seemed imbued with the Bogle philosophy, and with vision. He said, "We're a small company, and we haven't begun to explore our opportunities, yet." He noted that there's Europe and Asia, to say nothing of the trillions of dollars held in non-Vanguard funds. "It's humbling."[4]

GREAT APPEAL OF VANGUARD

Performance

Each year *Forbes* presents "Mutual Funds Ratings" and "Best Buys." The Ratings list the hundreds of mutual funds that are open end, that is, can be bought and sold at current net asset prices.[5] The Best Buys are those select few that *Forbes* analysts judged to "invest wisely, spend frugally, and you get what you pay for," and that perform best in shareholder returns over both up and down markets. Vanguard equity and bond funds dominate *Forbes's* Best Buys:

Of 43 U.S. *equity* funds listed in the various categories, 12 are Vanguard funds.

Of 70 *bond* funds, 27 are Vanguard.[6]

Forbes explains that "the preponderance of Vanguard funds in our Best Buy Tables is a testament to the firm's cost controls ... Higher expenses, for most other fund families, are like lead weights. Why carry them?"[7] Table 14.2 shows

---

[3] Easton, p. 115.

[4] Easton, p. 117.

[5] A far smaller number of mutuals are closed-end funds that have a fixed number of shares and are traded like stocks. These generally have higher annual expenses, yet sell at a discount from net asset value. We will disregard these in this case.

[6] *Forbes* (August 23, 1999), pp. 128, 136–137.

[7] *Ibid.,* p. 136.

TABLE 14.2   **Comparative Expense Ratios of Representative Mutual Funds**

	Annual Expenses per $100
Balanced Equity Funds:	
Vanguard Wellington Fund	0.31
Columbia Balanced Fund	0.67
Janus Balanced Fund	0.93
Ranier Balanced Portfolio	1.19
Index Equity Funds:	
Vanguard 500 Index	.18
T. Rowe Price Equity Index 500	.40
Dreyfus S&P 500 Index	.50
Gateway Fund	1.02
Municipal Long-Term Bonds:	
Vanguard High Yield Tax Exempt	.20
Dreyfus Basic Muni Bond	.45
Strong High Yield Muni Bond	.66
High-Yield Corporate Bonds:	
Vanguard High Yield Corp.	.29
Fidelity High Income	.75
Value Line Aggressive Income	.81
Ivesco High Yield	.86

Source: Company records as reported in *Forbes Mutual Fund Guide,* August 23, 1999.
Commentary: The great cost advantage of Vanguard shows up very strikingly here. It is not a slightly lower expense ratio, but one that is usually three or four times lower than similar funds. Take, for example, the category of Index Equity Funds, where the goal is to simply track the Index averages, which suggests passive management rather than free-wheeling buying and selling. Yet, Vanguard's costs are far below the other funds; in one case, the Gateway fund is five times higher.

representative examples of the substantially lower expenses of Vanguard funds relative to others on the Best Buy list.[8]

Looking at total averages, the typical mutual fund has an expense ratio of 1.24 percent of assets annually. The ratio for Vanguard's 101 funds is .28 percent, almost a full percentage point lower.[9]

How does Vanguard achieve such a low expense ratio? We noted before the reluctance to advertise at all; nor does it have any mass sales force. Its commitment has been to pare costs to the absolute minimum. But there have been other economies.

Fidelity and Charles Schwab have opened numerous walk-in sales outposts. Certainly these bring more sales exposure to prospective customers. But are such

[8] *Ibid.,* pp. 128, 137.
[9] Easton, p. 116.

sales promotion efforts worth the cost? Vanguard decided not. It had one sales outpost in Philadelphia, but closed it to save money.

Vanguard discouraged day traders and other market timers from in-and-out trading of its funds. It even prohibited telephone switching on the Vanguard 500 Index; redemption orders had to come by mail. Why such market timing discouragement? Frequent redemptions run up transaction costs, and a flurry of sell orders might impose trading costs that would have to be borne by other shareholders as some holdings might have to be sold.

Not the least of the economies is what Bogle calls passive investing, tracking the market rather than trying to actively manage the funds by trying to beat the market. The funds with the highest expense ratios are hedge funds and these usually are the most active traders, with heavy buying and selling. Yet, they seldom beat the market but squander a lot of money in the effort and burden shareholders with sizable capital gains taxes because of the flurry of transactions. Still, the common notion prevails that more is better, that the more expensive car or service must be better than its less expensive alternative. See the following Information Box for another discussion of the price-quality perception.

INFORMATION BOX

THE PRICE-QUALITY PERCEPTION REVISITED

We had a similar box in Chapter 7 on Perrier, and will have again in Chapter 22. But the topic is worth further discussion. In the Perrier case, we considered whether high-priced bottled water was that much better than regular tap water or lower-priced bottled water, and concluded that it usually was not. The same thing applies to perfume, to beer and liquor, and to many other consumer products. "You get what you pay for" is a common perception, and its corollary is that you judge quality by price: The higher the price, the higher the quality. But this notion leads many consumers to be taken advantage of, and for top-of-the-line brands and products to command a higher profit margin than lower-priced alternatives. Admittedly, sometimes we are led to the more expensive brand or item for the prestige factor.

When it comes to money management, by no means do high fees mean better quality; the reverse is usually true. And prestige should hardly be a factor since we are not inclined to show off our investments like we might a new car. Does a high-overhead index fund deliver better performance than a cheap one, than Vanguard? Not at all. And hedge funds as we noted before seldom even beat the averages despite running up some of the highest expenses in the mutual fund industry. Looking at Table 14.2, which shows typical expense ratios of Vanguard and its competitors, are the other funds doing a better job than Vanguard with their expenses three to five times higher? No, because their high expense ratios take away from any performance advantage, even if frequent trading resulted in somewhat better gains, and that seldom is achieved.

If Vanguard advertised its great expense advantage aggressively to really get the word out, do you think it would win many more customers? Why or why not?

Another factor also contributes to the great cost advantage of Vanguard. It is a mutual firm, organized as a nonprofit owned by its customers. Almost all other financial institutions, except TIAA-CREF (and we will discuss this shortly), have stock ownership with its heavy allegiance to profit maximization.

Customer Service

Many firms espouse a commitment to customer service. It is the popular thing to do, rather like motherhood, apple pie, and the flag. Unfortunately, pious platitudes do not always match reality. Vanguard's commitment to service seems to be more tangible.

Service to customers is often composed of the simple things, such as just answering the phone promptly and courteously, or responding to mail quickly and completely, or giving complete and unbiased information. Vanguard's 2,000 phone reps are ready to answer the phone by the fourth ring. During a market panic or on April 15 when the tax deadline stimulates many inquiries, CEO John Brennan brings a brigade of executives with him to help man the phones. Vanguard works to make its monthly statements to investors as complete and easy-to-understand as possible, and it leads the industry in this.

The philosophy of a customer-service commitment was espoused by Bogle. "Our primary goal: to serve, to the best of our ability, the human beings who are our clients. To serve them with candor, with integrity, and with fair dealing. To be the stewards of the assets they have entrusted to us. To treat them as we would like the stewards of our own assets to treat us."

Bogle described a talk he gave to Harvard Business School in December 1997 on how "our focus on human beings had enabled Vanguard to become what at Harvard is called a 'service breakthrough company.' I challenged the students to find the term *human beings* in any book they had read on corporate strategy. As far as I know, none could meet the challenge. But 'human beingness' has been one of the keys to our development."[10]

Not the least of the consumer best interests has been a commitment to holding down taxable transactions for shareholders. Vanguard has led the industry with tax-managed funds aimed at minimizing the capital gains that confront most mutual fund investors to their dismay at the end of the year.

COMPETITION

Why is Vanguard's low-expense approach not matched by competitors? All the other fund giants that sell primarily to the general public are for-profit companies. Are they willing to sacrifice profits to win back Vanguard converts? Hardly likely. Are they willing to reduce their hefty marketing and advertising expenditures? Again, hardly likely. Why? Because advertising, not word-of-mouth, is vital to their visibility and to seeking out customers.

---

[10] Bogle, pp. 423, 424.

TIAA-CREF

One potential competitor looms, another low-cost fund contender. TIAA-CREF, which manages retirement money for teachers and researchers, in 1997 launched six no-load mutual funds that are now open to all investors. The funds' annual expenses range from 0.29 percent to 0.49 percent, comparable with Vanguard's. A significant potential attraction over Vanguard is that each fund's investment minimum is just $250, compared with Vanguard's usual minimum of $3,000. As of late August 1999, the combined assets of the six TIAA-CREF funds was $1.5 billion, far less, of course, than the near-$500 billion of Vanguard.

TIAA-CREF is also run solely for the benefit of its shareholders, being another mutual, with the long-term aim of providing fund-management services at cost. Still, there is some doubt that expense ratios can be kept low, should the new funds fail to attract enough investors.

Is this a gnat against the giant Vanguard? Perhaps; however, the low investment requirement of only $250 should certainly attract cost-conscious investors who cannot come up with the $3,000 that Vanguard requires on most of its funds. Still, six fund choices versus the more than 100 of Vanguard is not very attractive yet. Efforts to be as tax-efficient as Vanguard are also unknown.

ANALYSIS

The success of Vanguard with its disavowal of most traditional business strategies flies in the face of all that we have come to believe. It suggests that heavy advertising expenditures may at least be questioned as not always desirable—and what a heresy this is. It suggests that relying on word-of-mouth and whatever free publicity can be garnered may sometimes be preferable to advertising. All you need is a superior product or service. It supports the statement that textbooks like to shoot down: "If you build a better mousetrap, people will come." Conventional wisdom maintains that without advertising to get the message out, this better mousetrap will fade away from lack of buyer knowledge and interest. But the planning of Bogle and Vanguard to tread a different path and not be dissuaded despite the critics illustrates a remarkable and enduring commitment first formulated almost three decades ago.

How do we reconcile Vanguard with the commonly accepted notion that communication is essential to get products and services to customers (except perhaps when selling solely to the government or to a single customer)?

Maybe we should not try to fit Vanguard into such traditional beliefs. Maybe it is the exception, the anomaly, in its seeming repudiation of them. Still, let us not be too hasty in this judgment.

I do not believe that Vanguard contradicts traditional principles of marketing and business strategy. Rather, it has revealed another approach to the communication component: the effective use of word-of-mouth publicity. If we have a distinctive product that can be *tangibly demonstrated* as superior in relative cost advantages to competitors, then demand may be stimulated without mass advertising. Word-of-mouth, enhanced or developed through formal publicity—from media, public appearances, and publications—can replace massive advertising expenditures of competitors. But is there a downside to all this?

Let us examine the role of word-of-mouth in more detail in the following Information Box.

Vanguard illustrates a commendable application of an important marketing principle: the desirability of uniqueness or product differentiation. It differentiated itself from competitors in two respects: (1) its resolve and ability to bring out a low-priced product and at the same time one of good quality, and (2) its achievement of good customer service despite the low price.

INFORMATION BOX

THE POTENTIAL OF WORD-OF-MOUTH AND UNPAID PUBLICITY

Word-of-mouth advertising, by itself, is almost always frowned on by the experts. It is the sign of the marginal firm, one without sufficient resources, so they say, to do what is needed to get established. Such a firm is bound to succumb to competitors who are better managed and better resourced. The best they can say for word-of-mouth advertising is that if the firm can survive for an unknown number of years, and if it *really* has a superior product or service, then it might finally attain some modest success.

Compared to spending for advertising, word-of-mouth takes far longer to have any impact, and firms seldom have the staying power to wait years, so the belief holds. The best strategy would be to have both, with healthy doses of advertising to jumpstart the enterprise, and let favorable word-of-mouth reinforce the advertising.

As we have seen, Bogle and his Vanguard repudiated the accepted strategy, yet became highly successful. Still, it took time, even decades. As shown in Table 14.1, in 1994 after 16 years the flagship Index 500 fund had reached $8 billion in assets; not bad, but far below the heavily advertised Magellan fund of Fidelity. The growth of the Index 500 fund has accelerated only in recent years. Would more advertising have shortened the period?

Bogle would maintain that such advertising would have destroyed the uniqueness of Vanguard by making its expenses like other funds. He would also likely contend that the favorable publicity enhanced the word-of-mouth influence of satisfied shareholders, and thus there was no need for expensive advertising. But in the early years of Vanguard it did not have much favorable publicity. On the contrary, it took experts a long time to admit that a low-expense fund with passive management could do as well or better than aggressively managed funds with a lot of buying and selling and big trading and marketing expenses.

So the success of Vanguard without much formal advertising attests to the success of word-of-mouth heavily seasoned by favorable free publicity. But was it too conservative, especially in the early years?

Do you think Vanguard should have advertised more, especially in its early days? Why or why not? If yes, how much more do you think it should have spent?

Even today, after several decades of competitors seeing this highly effective strategy, Vanguard still is virtually unmatched in its uniqueness, except for one newcomer that is hardly a contender but could be a factor should Vanguard let down its guard and be tempted to seek more profits.

Prognosis—Can Vanguard Continue As Is?

Is it likely Vanguard can continue its success pattern without increasing advertising and other costs and becoming more like its competitors? Why should it change? It has become a giant with its low-cost strategy. The last decade saw a growing momentum created by favorable word-of-mouth and publicity that made the need for heavy advertising and selling efforts far less than in the early years. It took bravery, or audacity, in those early years not to succumb to the Lorelei beguilement that advertising and commission selling was the only viable strategy. Something would be lost if Vanguard were to change its strategy and uniqueness and become a higher-cost imitation of its competitors.

If Vanguard is so good, why are so many investors still doing business with the higher-cost competitors? We can identify four groups of consumers who are noncustomers of Vanguard:

1. Those who have not studied the statistics and editorials of publications like *Forbes* and the *Wall Street Journal,* and are not aware of the Vanguard advantage.
2. Those who are naive in investing and content to let someone else—brokers or bankers—advise them and reap the commissions.
3. Those who are swayed by the massive advertisements of firms like Fidelity, Dreyfus, T. Rowe Price, and others.
4. Those who put their faith in the price-quality perception: the higher the price the higher the quality, with quality guaranteeing higher investor returns.

In addition to continued investments of its ardent customers, Vanguard should find potential in the gradual eroding of the commitment of these four consumer groups. Of course, the overseas markets also offer a huge and virtually untapped potential for Vanguard.

WHAT CAN BE LEARNED?

Marketing can be overdone. The success of Vanguard shows that marketing can be overdone. Too much can be spent for advertising, without realizing congruent benefits. Sales expenses and branch office overhead may get out of line. Yet, few firms think they dare reduce such costs lest they be competitively disadvantaged. For example, it is the brave executive who reduces advertising in the face of increases by competitors, though the results of the advertising may be impossible to measure with any accuracy.

Still, despite the success of Vanguard in downplaying advertising, one has to wonder how much faster the growth might have been by budgeting more dollars for selling, at least in the early years.

Can word-of-mouth do the job of advertising by itself? In Vanguard's case, word-of-mouth combined with favorable unpaid publicity from the media brought it to the largest mutual fund family in the industry. However, the time it took for word-of-mouth, even eventually with good publicity, to build demand has to be a negative. Without such favorable publicity, it would have taken far longer.

The benefits of frugality. There is far too much waste in most institutions, business and nonbusiness. Some waste comes from undercontrolled costs and such extravagances as lavish expense accounts and entertainment, and expenditures that do little to benefit the bottom line. Other factors may be a top-heavy bureaucratic organization saddled with layers of staff personnel, and/or too many debt payments due to heavy investments in plant and equipment or mergers. Heavy use of advertising may not always pay off enough to justify the expenditures, as we saw in Chapter 13 when Coca-Cola was outspending Pepsi by $100 million, but was still losing market share. In money management, trading costs may get far out of line.

Vanguard shows the benefit of austerity in greatly reduced expense ratios for its funds compared to competitors. At last, more and more astute investors are recognizing this unique cost advantage that gives not only a better return on their investment dollars but some of the best customer service in the industry.

The power of differentiation. Firms seek to differentiate themselves, to come up with products or ways of doing business that are unique in some respect compared with competitors. This is a paramount quest of business strategy and accounts for the massive expenditures for advertising. Too often such attempts to find uniqueness are fragile, not very substantial, and easily lost or countered by competitors. Sometimes, though, they can be rather enduring, as, for example, the quality-image perception perpetrated by advertisements featuring the lonely Maytag repairman, described in Chapter 4. If a firm can effectively differentiate itself from competitors, it gains a powerful advantage and may even be able to charge premium prices.

While Vanguard seemingly disregarded marketing, John Bogle found a powerful and enduring way to differentiate through low-cost quality products and superb customer service. For decades no competitor has been able to match this attractive uniqueness.

Beware placing too much faith in the price-quality relationship. We are drawn to judge quality by a product's price relative to other choices. Often this is justified, although the better quality may not always match the higher price. In other words, the luxury item may not be worth the much higher price, except for the significant psychological value that some people see in the prestige of a fine brand name. Unfortunately, there are some products and services where the higher price does not really reflect higher quality, better workmanship, better service, and the like. Then we are taken advantage of with this price-quality perception. Beware of always judging quality by price.

CONSIDER

Can you think of additional learning insights?

QUESTIONS

1. "The success of Vanguard is due to media exploitation of what would otherwise be a very ordinary firm." Discuss.
2. Why do you think people continue to buy front-end load mutual funds with 5–6 percent commission fees when there are numerous no-load funds to be had?
3. Do you think Bogle's shunning advertising was really a success, or was it a mistake?
4. Was Vanguard's failure to open walk-in sales outposts a mistake and an example of misplaced frugality? Why or why not?
5. What are the differences in passive and active fund managment? How significant are these?
6. "Vanguard seems too good. There must be a downside." Discuss.
7. What is a service breakthrough company?
8. Can publicity ever take the place of massive advertising expenditures?

HANDS-ON EXERCISES

1. You are an executive assistant to John Brennan, the new CEO of Vanguard now that Bogle has retired. Brennan is thinking of judiciously adding some marketing and advertising expenditures to the paucity that Bogle had insisted on. He has directed you to draw up a position paper on the merits of adding some advertising and even some walk-in sales outposts such as other big competitors have already done.
2. You are John Brennan, CEO. It is 2005, and TIAA-CREF is turning out to be a formidable competitor, and is gaining fast on your first-place position in the industry. What actions would you take, and why? Discuss all ramifications of these actions that you can think of.

TEAM DEBATE EXERCISES

1. You are a member of the board of directors of Vanguard. John Bogle is approaching the retirement age as set forth in the company policies.

However, he wants to continue as chairman of the board, even though he is willing to let Brennan assume active management. Debate the issue of whether to force Bogle to step down or bow to his wishes.

2. Debate the no-advertising policy of Bogle.

INVITATION TO RESEARCH

Is Vanguard still number one in the mutual fund industry? Has it increased its advertising expenditures? Has Brennan made any substantial changes?

LEADERSHIP AND
STRATEGY EXECUTION

When Will They Ever Learn?—High-Tech Excesses Reminiscent of S&Ls Barely a Decade Earlier

*O*nly months after the beginning of the new millennium, the rosy optimism for Internet and telecom companies, and indeed the whole high-tech industry, was shattered. Hundreds of firms, victims of their own frenzied expansion and operational spending, were going out of business or into bankruptcy, creating fallout for employees, creditors, and stockholders alike. What made this crash particularly sobering was that, barely a decade earlier, the savings and loan (S&L) industry suffered a similar meltdown for many of the same reasons. One wonders at the lack of learning insights from past mistakes. But then many of the dot.com entrepreneurs were too young and uncaring for the problems of a bygone decade. Perhaps the learning experience from all this is: Beware of greed, wild spending, and absurd expectations.

TURMOIL IN THE INTERNET INDUSTRY

Bankruptcies among Internet service providers and telecommunications companies were indicative of the turmoil in this high-tech world. By midsummer 2001, nearly 500 Internet firms had gone under in just 18 months.[1] Some of these were large companies, such as:

	Assets (billion)
Winstar Communications	$4.975
PSInet	4.492
Viatel	2.124
Teligent	1.210

[1] Ann Grimes, "The Lawyer," *Wall Street Journal* (July 16, 2001), p. R8.

It now became clear that many of these had overreached, misjudged demand, and/or executed badly. More than 110,000 people had been laid off, and losses to investors were approaching $150 billion, a trauma on a level with the S&L crisis of the late 1980s. In less than five years, visions of wealth and global transformation that had lulled entrepreneurs and venture capitalists had collapsed.

Bankruptcies of Internet and telecom firms were particularly devastating to creditors and investors since such companies have little to liquidate beyond office equipment and "intellectual property" that anchored money-losing business plans. While telecom firms had phone lines, real estate, and networks, with the glut of such properties and equipment from all the bankruptcies fire-sale prices predominated.

HOW DID THIS HAPPEN?

Nearly 400 telecom companies had raised almost $500 billion from the stock market and had taken on an additional $400 billion in debt. The Internet was booming, and technology evangelists were preaching that the gold rush was just beginning. In this euphoria, forecasters predicted that the amount of data traveling over the Net would double every three months, and firms hastened to build up for this demand. In this atmosphere of unlimited growth potential many lost all restraint when it came to spending, even though they were not realizing any profits at all. But the stock market seemed unconcerned about profitability of such firms, and cared only for their great long-term growth potential. As an example of the extravagance, consider PSINet, one of the biggest firms to go into bankruptcy.

This Virginia-based firm went on an acquisition spree, buying companies like Metamor, a consulting company that had little to do with PSINet's goal of connecting businesses to the Net. PSINet's CEO, William Schrader, spent freely for other things, including $105 million for naming rights to Baltimore's new football stadium. (It managed to pay only $26 million before going bankrupt.)

Long-distance pioneer MCI provided the guide: Build a costly infrastructure financed by risky junk bonds and pay it back later with revenue. Wall Street enthusiastically supported this reasoning as it reveled in the fees. But when the Nasdaq crashed in 2000, financiers suddenly realized that not all of these highly leveraged upstarts could possibly succeed. Suddenly the cash spigot was turned off, and many such firms tumbled into bankruptcy.

Anatomy of a Turnaround, Kind Of

ValueAmerica.com promoted itself as "the Wal-Mart of the Internet," selling a miscellany of products from $6,000 watches to cough medicine. It did not carry any inventory itself, but passed orders to suppliers who then mailed products directly to purchasers. This resulted, however, in a consumer who ordered a variety of items having to wait for numerous different shipments from this single order—hardly conducive to customer satisfaction.

A charismatic entrepreneur, Craig Winn, founded ValueAmerica in 1996. His plan was to eliminate a layer of costs by bypassing the high retail markups of stores in the shipping process.

He and his disciples thought this idea would revolutionize the retail industry. Millions poured into the company and these investors included such big names as Paul Allen, co-founder of Microsoft. More than 450 vendors joined the stable, giving a formidable roster of products for the website. Sales rocketed from $134,000 in 1997 to $42.3 million in 1998. Winn took the company public in April 1999, a time of investor web frenzy, for $55 a share, giving a market capitalization of almost $3.2 billion. This was predicated on previous year's sales of $42 million and zero profits; still, this stratospheric stock market valuation was not unique, but rather representative of the mania sweeping the investment community at the time.

Reality soon reared a particularly ugly head. Problems emerged in implementing the ambitious retail plan, and customers might wait weeks for some simple product that could be purchased at the neighborhood grocery or drugstore. The company inaugurated a massive advertising campaign for its website, but this only added to the losses. A further problem was an inability to manage returned goods from customers. In November 1999, the board ousted Winn.

In a major retrenchment, 47 percent of the workforce was laid off, and product lines were drastically reduced. But none of this helped enough. By July 2000, the company was losing $13 million a month, and cash was drying up. As a last resort to increase revenue, the company introduced ValueDollars, giving customers a 50 percent cut in the cost of purchases. The only problem was that ValueAmerica lost money on practically every sale. High time to call in a turnaround expert, and this was Marti Kopacz, an accounting executive at PricewaterhouseCoopers.

Her first major challenge was to determine if the company was even salvageable. It had $17 million in the bank, which put it above most of the struggling dot.coms that were out of money before they sought a turnaround specialist. She also saw another plus in ValueAmerica's computer network, which was designed to handle one billion orders a year. She quickly put a clamp on spending, which still was installing dozens of custom-built mahogany desks.

The retail operation was killed because of margins so low the company could never make money as an e-tailer. She had the company file for bankruptcy, and creditors wound up being paid between 50 cents and 65 cents on the dollar for their claims, a princely sum for most dot.com settlements. ValueAmerica's computer system was sold for $2.5 million, and 46 employees were retained to run the system.[2]

The trauma was of course worse for those firms with few tangible assets, and there were many.

OUTLOOK

Can Internet and other high-tech firms make a comeback? Of course some can, and this may well have happened by the time this book comes out. Any new and easy-to-enter industry spawns a host of innovators and eager entrepreneurs, many of whose enterprises will turn out to be marginal at best. What made the excesses of the high-

---

[2] For more details, see the excellent article by Brooks Barnes, "The Turnaround Expert," *Wall Street Journal* (July 16, 2001), p. R18.

tech world so extreme was the sheer exuberance of investors in pouring money into startup firms and ones whose profitability would be years away; this resulted in stock prices so extreme that the market valuations for some would be more than entire old-line industries.

Now let us look at the father of greed running amuck, the savings and loan industry in the 1980s and early 1990s.

THE SAVINGS AND LOAN DISASTER

What made the S&L disaster worse than the dot.com meltdown was that it involved the savings of ordinary people, and not wild investors, and the long-term consequences were borne by all taxpayers. The savings and loan industry, the source of home ownership for millions of Americans, was on the verge of total collapse, and the government bailout would be the costliest in history. Yet, there were S&Ls that survived and prospered during this time. What can we learn from all this?

A SAMPLING OF FIASCOS

Sunbelt Savings

Edwin T. McBirney III was 29 years old when be began his run to a vast fortune in the savings and loan business. The year was 1981. While still in college he had shown unusual business acumen, starting his own business leasing refrigerators to college students. Upon graduation he turned to real estate, becoming a broker and investor in the booming Dallas market.

In December 1981, McBirney formed an investment group that began buying small S&Ls. One of these was Sunbelt Savings, an obscure S&L in Stephenville, Texas. McBirney was to merge these holdings into one large S&L, which he named Sunbelt Savings Association. In less than four years, Sunbelt was the nucleus of a $3.2 billion financial empire. Its growth came mostly from commercial real-estate loans that were so risky that Sunbelt gained the nickname "Gunbelt" for its shoot-from-the-hip lending policies. As one example, Sunbelt lent $125 million (secured only by raw land) to an inexperienced Dallas developer in his twenties who went on to lose $80 million.)[3] In its heyday, Sunbelt owned mortgage and development service companies, had a commercial-banking division, and made real-estate loans to developers from California to Florida.

McBirney and his executives were soon covering Texas in the company's fleet of seven aircraft. McBirney liked to throw sumptuous parties, serving lion and antelope to hundreds of guests at his palatial Dallas home. In 1984 and 1985, Sunbelt paid $1.3 million for Halloween and Christmas galas, including a $32,000 fee to McBirney's wife for organizing the parties. No end seemed to be in sight for these Texas big spenders, but it was just around the corner.

In 1984 the Empire Savings and Loan of Mesquite, Texas, collapsed after funding massive high-risk investments. Its demise raised troubling questions about the

---

[3] F. Howard Rudnitsky and John R. Hayes, "Gunbelt S&L," *Forbes* (September 19, 1988), p. 120.

entire industry. Edwin Gray, chairman of the Federal Home Loan Bank Board, a regulator of S&Ls, became fearful of a disaster and slammed on the brakes. He forced reappraisals based on current market values, increased capital requirements, limited direct appraisals, and hired hundreds of new examiners and supervisory agents. Appraisers found that the collateral backing billions of dollars of loans had been overvalued by up to 30 percent. Many thrifts had to lower the book value of their loans, reducing their already weak capital positions. Then real estate values plummeted as Texas' economy began collapsing, led by declining oil prices. The domino effect took over as a rash of loan delinquencies led to one foreclosure after another.

Now the excesses of McBirney's heyday came to roost. Hundreds of examiners descended on the Dallas home loan office in the spring of 1986, and the bulk of the Sunbelt S&Ls were declared insolvent. While Sunbelt itself was spared temporarily, McBirney was forced to resign as chairman by June. Of the foreclosed real estate on Sunbelt's books, only a few million out of its $6 billion portfolio of troubled assets could be sold off. By late 1988 the Federal Home Loan Bank Board estimated that it would cost as much as $5.5 billion just to keep Sunbelt alive over the next 10 years.[4]

To add to the insult, a lawsuit filed against McBirney and other insider shareholders charged that nearly $13 million in common and preferred dividends had been taken out in 1985 and 1986, at a time when Sunbelt's capital was rapidly evaporating because of wild expenditures and devaluation of assets.

Shamrock Federal Savings Bank

In Shamrock, Texas, the little savings and loan on the corner went belly up. The collapse of the Shamrock Federal Savings Bank left a bitter pill for this town of 3,000 in the Texas panhandle. It was a common story for many Texas communities: a small-town thrift taken over by an outsider; fast growth followed by sudden insolvency; a trail of incompetent management and soured high-risk ventures in places far beyond the limits of the town. "We made a mistake selling it. We should have kept it under local control, making loans in our community," declared one of the original directors of the town's only savings and loan.

Back in 1977 Phil Cates, a state representative and head of the local Chamber of Commerce, had a vision of a financial institution that would serve Shamrock and other small towns near the Oklahoma line. He started pushing townsfolk to start their own savings and loan association in view of the oil and gas boom that was bringing hundreds of people into the town. Shamrock's two family-owned banks shunned long-term home mortgages and refused to pay competitive interest rates. Cates sold the idea of a local S&L to hundreds of local residents. When the Red River Savings and Loan Association opened in 1979, it had more than 350 stockholders in a town of 2,834. Community pride ran high.

These were the days of S&L deregulation, and small-town thrifts like Red River were hot properties, targets of opportunity for promoters and speculators. One speculator, Jerry D. Lane, offered owners $21 a share, more than double the original

---

[4] For more detail, see "Why Our S&Ls Are in Trouble," *Reader's Digest* (July 1989), pp. 70–74.

price. The townspeople jumped at the opportunity. Lane changed the name to Shamrock Savings Association, and in three years deposits rocketed from $11.6 million to $111.3 million. The thrift's focus shifted far beyond the small town of Shamrock, with offices as far away as Amarillo and Colorado Springs, Colorado. Lane also began buying some of other thrifts' outstanding loans.

Disaster struck in 1987 when the Federal Savings and Loan Insurance Corporation filed a $150 million racketeering suit against Lane and others after the 1985 failure of State Savings of Lubbock, Texas. Lane had been chief executive officer there. Federal regulators had found a pattern common to the S&L industry and would soon find it at Shamrock: making fraudulent loans to developers, concentrating an "unsafe" amount of credit with one client, basing loans on inflated property appraisals, and making them without proper credit documentation. "Loans were made over lunch with a handshake."

Federal regulators closed Shamrock in November 1987; it owed $16.6 million more than it was worth. But its betrayal of the local community occurred before that. The S&L had been conceived to make loans locally for homes and other projects that could help the community, but with its buyout and the shift of emphasis far beyond the local community, its managers had little interest in providing less lucrative but less risky local loans.

Shamrock characterized a large segment of S&Ls, especially in the heady days of the oil boom when Texas and other southwestern states thought there was no stopping the runaway building boom built on the belief that oil prices could only go up. But prices dropped to $14 a barrel in the early 1980s, destroying the cash supports from under commerical real estate projects all across the Southwest.[5]

Lincoln Savings and Loan: Political Scandal

Charles Keating was the former owner of California's Lincoln Savings and Loan. He purchased Lincoln in 1984 and switched it from investing in safe, single-family mortgages to raw land speculation, junk bonds, and huge development projects like the $900-a-night Phoenician Resort in Scottsdale, Arizona.

Keating was a heavy campaign contributor, giving to five prominent U.S. senators: John Glenn, Alan Cranston, John McCain, Donald Reigle, and Dennis De Concini. In total, these influential politicians received $1.3 million from Keating. As his failing S&L came under the scrutiny of the Federal Home Loan Bank Board, which found enough bad loans and shaky business practices to shut it down, he sought help from these senators, and with their help delayed action for two years. During this time the federally guaranteed cost of paying back Lincoln's depositors went up $1.3 billion to $2.5 billion, making this one of the costliest thrift failures.[6]

Keating was eventually convicted of racketeering, fraud, and conspiracy in using the institution's funds and was sent to prison. The senators were reprimanded for their complicity.

---

[5] Adapted from "Small Town's Dreams Vanish," *Cleveland Plain Dealer* (August 13, 1989), p. 3C.

[6] Margaret Carlson, "$1 Billion Worth of Influence," *Time* (November 6, 1989), pp. 27–28.

So we see in this sampling of S&L blunders a repudiation of any concern for shareholders and employees—high-dollar deals made on the spur of the moment, without investigation, heedless of risks and probable consequences. In other words, a wild gambling mentality prevailed with many S&L top executives. Can the responsibility and accountability of the managers be repudiated? The following Information Box explores the responsibilities of managers.

THE FULL FLAVOR OF THE S&L DEBACLE

By 1988, 503 of the nation's 3178 so-called thrift institutions were insolvent. Another 629 had less capital on their books than regulators usually require. In

---

INFORMATION BOX

WHAT IS THE RESPONSIBILITY OF MANAGERS?

Managers are well paid. Isn't responsibility for protecting assets a condition of management, even if these assets are somewhat protected by the government? Is there not also a responsibility to the enterprise, that it continue and not be destroyed by gross negligence or reckless abandon or illegal activities? Are not managers custodians of shareholders' trust?

Does a high-roller gambler in pin-stripes fit this responsibility mode? The stakeholders of a typical savings and loan are far different from those of many corporations. They typically are people of moderate means and unsophisticated financial acumen; many are retirees. The preservation of customers' savings, and employees' jobs, are particularly important. Can we really accept the repudiation of such managers' responsibilities in their heedless quest for extravagance and high-risk endeavors? Should such managers guilty of gross misconduct face stiffer penalties than simply ouster from a well-paying job with most of their assets intact?

These are some of the troubling questions that arise when management has been completely oblivious to the greater good of the corporation and its shareholders (and depositors). *USA Today* opened a "hot line" for the public's response to the S&L mess. Here is a sampling of responses:[7]

> I don't see how they could have squandered this money and not get prosecuted.

> When I mishandle my money, I have nobody to go bail me out. If (S&Ls) are incapable of handling the trust that was placed in them, maybe they should go belly up.

> The guilty parties to this fraud should be paying off these banks, If a guy owns a $2 million home, it should be auctioned off, and he should be put in jail.

> They've got to take responsibility for their actions.

As the manager of a failed S&L, your defense is that you acted in the best interest of your investors. While your high-risk real estate ventures defaulted, how could you have foreseen this? Discuss the acceptability of this defense.

---

[7] Denise Kalette, "Callers Want S&L Cheats Punished," *USA Today* (February 15, 1989), p. B1.

TABLE 15.1   S&Ls on the "Deathwatch" as of September 30, 1988[a]

State	Thrift	Negative Net Worth (millions)
Texas	Gill Savings, Hondo	($542.7)
	Meridian Savings, Arlington	($387.7)
New Mexico	Sandia Federal, Albuquerque	($482.6)
Arizona	Security S&L, Scottsdale	($351.6)
Arkansas	Savers Federal, Little Rock	($286.5)
California	Westwood S&L, Los Angeles	($222.7)
	Pacific Savings, Costa Mesa	($206.6)
Florida	Freedom S&L, Tampa	($231.6)

Source: SNL Securities, Inc., and *Fortune* (January 30, 1989), p. 9.
[a] This is only a sampling.

1987, 630 thrifts had lost an estimated $7.5 billion, half again as much as the earnings of all the rest combined.[8] Most of the "terminal" S&Ls got into trouble making risky loans. But fraud also contributed to the failures of nearly 50.[9] More than one-half the troubled thrifts were to be found in Texas, but other sunbelt thrifts were also crashing: Beverly Hills Savings & Loan in California, which had much of its $2.9 billion in assets invested in dicey real estate ventures and junk bonds, closed in 1985; Sunrise Savings & Loan of Florida, with $1.5 billion in assets, was liquidated in 1986; First South Federal Savings & Loan in Arkansas closed in 1986 after 64 percent of its $1.4 billion in loans were found to be speculative. (See Table 15.1 for a sampling of S&Ls on the "deathwatch" as of September 30, 1988.) Still, the worst excesses occurred in Texas, and there were suspicions that some of the insolvent Texas S&Ls were shuffling bum loans from one to another a step ahead of the bank examiners.

Undeniably part of the motivation for taking wild risks with deposits was that individual accounts were insured up to $100,000 by the Federal Savings and Loan Insurance Corporation (FSLIC). But even the resources of this government agency were insufficient to cope with the problem without massive congressional appropriations in the billions of dollars.

The lurking danger, of course, was the domino effect. Depositor panic could create a devastating run on the nation's $932 billion in thrift deposits and bring down scores of S&Ls; this would threaten the $14 billion of capital in the 12 regional Federal Home Loan Banks, which would have to supply emergency funds to the thrifts; and emergency funds could potentially swamp the FSLIC. The most simple solution would be to write off the insolvent thrifts and pay off their depositors, but this would exceed the original resources of the FSLIC and could cost more than $200 billion. Taxpayers eventually would foot the bill.

[8] John Paul Newport, Jr., "Why We Should Save the S&Ls," *Fortune* (April 11, 1986), p. 81.
[9] Robert E. Norton, "Deep in the Hole in Texas," *Fortune* (May 11, 1987), p. 61.

HISTORY OF THE SAVINGS AND LOAN INDUSTRY

At first they were called building and loans, and they filled a real need. Before the Great Depression, many commercial banks would not lend on middle-class residential property. Working class people were eventually forced to band together to form cooperative associations to take their deposits and lend those funds out as home mortgages. The Depression saw the failure of thousands of banks and building and loans, and the Roosevelt administration created the two deposit-insurance funds we know today, the FSLIC for S&Ls and the Federal Deposit Insurance Corporation (FDIC), which insures commercial bank deposits.

In the late 1960s, the S&Ls began experiencing some troubles. By law the federally regulated S&Ls were required to make long-term loans with home mortgages, but they borrowed short-term with most of their lendable funds coming from passbook savings accounts. This situation of long-term loans and short-term lendable resources posed no problem at first—until inflation. With this scenario the value of the S&L portfolios, like that of all fixed-rate long-term debt, fell. In 1971 the S&L industry had a negative net worth of $17 billion. When the inflation rate in the 1970s worsened, the industry faced ever larger losses on its loan portfolios.

The environment was changing in other ways as well. In particular, money market mutual funds came on the scene, aided by computer technology. These money market funds accumulated high-yielding financial instruments such as jumbo certificates of deposit (CDs), commercial paper and government notes, and they allowed the small investor to own a piece of the high-yielding package. Technology enabled customers to write checks on these money funds while still receiving high interest. Computers made possible extremely complex bookkeeping for such transactions.

The effect on banks and S&Ls was substantial. Money flowed out of them and into money market funds by the hundreds of billions of dollars. This combined with the double-digit inflation of the late 1970s brought the industry, with its long-term loans at low-interest rates, seemingly to the point of disaster. By 1981, 80 percent of the thrifts were losing money, and fully 20 percent were below the minimum capital requirements set by regulators.[10] (See Table 15.2 for a summary of the worsening S&L situation during the 1980s.)

In order to save the thrift industry from a potentially devastating outflow of funds, in 1980 Congress, in the Depository Institutions Deregulation and Monetary Control Act, gradually phased out interest rate ceilings on deposits and allowed S&Ls to make various kinds of consumer loans. Congress also raised the Federal Savings and Loan Insurance Corporation's insurance coverage from $40,000 to $100,000—essentially, the government deregulated the industry. But now a rate war developed among the thrifts, with some paying depositors double-digit interest rates.

Congress acted again in 1982 to remedy the situation, only the remedy led to worse abuses. The Garn-St. Germain Act of 1982 further loosened the restraints on S&Ls, giving them lending powers to write acquisition, development, and construction loans to form development subsidiaries and to make direct investments. If properly handled,

---

[10] John J. Curran, "Does Deregulation Make Sense?" *Fortune* (June 5, 1989), pp. 184, 188, 194.

TABLE 15.2 **Summary of the Worsening S&L Situation During the 1980s**

1980–1982: Congress begins phasing out interest-rate limits. Banks and S&Ls are allowed to offer new savings accounts that compete with market interest rates. Federal deposit insurance is boosted from $40,000 to $100,000 per account. Money that flowed out of S&Ls in 1980, when deposit rates were capped at 5.5%, begins flowing back. But the new deposits cost more than S&Ls can earn on the old fixed-rate mortgages made in the 1960s and 1970s at rates as low as 6% or lower. Now S&Ls are losing billions of dollars, and hundreds fail. The Garn-St. Germain bill is passed in 1982, allowing S&Ls new lending and investment freedom.

Mid-1980s: A lending spree develops, with billions of dollars loaned for apartments, office buildings, and other projects, especially in the booming southwest. Many S&Ls seek high-profit investments to make up for the low rates on old mortgages. In a climate of drastically loosened controls, wild speculation and outright fraud characterize the operations of hundreds of thrifts.

1986: Oil prices plunge, and the Texas economy collapses. The overbuilding is evident as developer loans are defaulted and the properties foreclosed are worth only fractions of building costs. More S&Ls are brought to insolvency. The Federal Savings and Loan Insurance Corporation finds its capital depleted by earlier S&L failures and needs massive infusions of capital. Prospective acquirers are attracted to take over the dead and dying thrifts under most favorable terms.

1988–1989: A massive government bailout is prepared and enacted.

the new freedom should have enabled S&Ls to better match assets and liabilities and find a sounder footing. Now they could begin lessening their dependence on mortgage lending and instead seek higher yielding investments. Figure 15.1 shows the decline in mortgage lending by S&Ls over the past 20 years.

By 1982, with constraints of regulation mostly unraveled and a new business environment in place, S&Ls needed to reassess their strategies. More important, they needed to reevaluate their company mission, discussed in the following Information Box.

The deregulatory "solution" to S&L problems did not reckon with the unbridled greed that was soon to take place with this greater freedom. It was particularly invit-

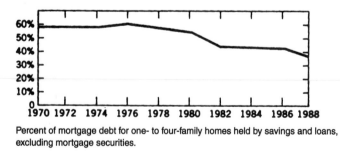

Percent of mortgage debt for one- to four-family homes held by savings and loans, excluding mortgage securities.

Figure 15.1 Decline in mortgage lending by S&Ls over the last 20 years.

Source: Federal Reserve.

INFORMATION BOX

WHAT SHOULD OUR MISSION BE?

A company's mission involves a decision: "What business should we seek to be in?" Such a determination should involve the following factors:

1. Assessing the environment and how it is changing or is expected to change.
2. Appraising competitive factors and how these may be changing.
3. Weighing the particular strengths and weaknesses of the company—what it does best and where it has been deficient.

Mission statements can be too broad—for example, "to make a profit"—or too narrow, focusing on a particular product or service that may become obsolete as technology and customer requirements change. Narrow definitions restrict perspectives and the grasping of different opportunities, just as too broad a definition is useless as a guide for definitive action. An example of a definitive and useful mission statement of a manufacturer is the following:

> The mission is to serve the industry and government with quality instruments used for the primary measurement, analysis, and local control of fluid flow, level, pressure, temperature, and fluid properties ... Markets served include instrumentation for oil and gas production, gas transportation, chemical and petro-chemical processing, cryogenics, power generation, aerospace, Government and marine, as well as other instrument and equipment manufacturers.[11]

A company's mission, whether formally stated or merely held in the top executive's mind, can be distorted to a reckless abandonment of former successful and durable practices. It can repudiate community best interest and trust, as we saw with Shamrock and with Sunbelt. Government deregulation in the early 1980s provided S&Ls with a vastly expanded arena for doing business. Far too many managers saw their mission now to be one of wild growth, unrestrained by cost considerations and risk potential. Leadership now became opportunistic, rash, showy, and completely oblivious to stakeholder long-term best interests.

Critique this position: "Mission statements are a waste of time. Our executives are going to try to make the most profit they can. That is all investors need be concerned with."

---

[11] John A. Pearce II, "The Company Mission as a Strategic Tool," *Sloan Management Review* (Spring 1982), p. 17.

ing for schemers and eager speculators in Texas. Previously, Texas regulations had limited lending power of S&Ls to the lesser of the purchase price or the appraised value of any project. But the new federal regulations overrode this requirement, permitting S&Ls to lend 100 percent of appraised value, even if the actual purchase price was much lower. And it was not difficult to find appraisers who would greatly inflate the value of property.

At this point, using federal deposit insurance, the developers got low-rate debt to put into their housing and shopping center developments. If the projects were successful, they made fortunes. If unsuccessful, the Federal Home Loan Bank Board and the Federal Savings and Loan Insurance Corporation absorbed the loss. As Art Soter, a bank analyst at the Morgan Stanley investment banking firm, noted: "What regulators failed to see is that the current system of deposit insurance increases the propensity to take risks."[12]

A further error of deregulation occurred: Equity capital standards were lowered. For years thrifts had to have capital equal to at least 6 percent of their deposits. Then as industrywide losses caused capital to deteriorate—in only two years, 1980 to 1982, the value of capital in the industry fell from $32 billion to less than $21 billion—thrifts were allowed to expand by taking as many deposits as they could.

Brokered deposits soon moved in. These are funds collected by stockbrokers and sent in large amounts to the highest yielding thrifts. With this, there was nothing to slow the growth of the reckless S&L operators. Phenomenal growth was possible, as described in the following example:

> American Diversified Savings was a small thrift in a rural town, Lodi, California. In June 1983, it had $11 million in assets. In only 18 months its assets totaled $792 million, mostly from brokered deposits attracted by its high yielding certificates of deposit. The owner, Ranhir Sahni, a former commercial pilot, put the money into his favorite projects: geothermal plants, wind-driven electric generators, as well as a venture to supply local manure to a fertilizer business. In 1988, the government had to find $1.1 billion to pay off the depositors and liquidate the thrift.[13]

The seeds for disaster were laid. Washington aggravated the problem and the potential for disaster by failing to hire adequate regulatory staff or to replenish the reserves of the Bank Board or FSLIC. And all this time S&Ls in the southwest continued to slide into bankruptcy.

THE GOVERNMENT BAILOUT

Thus we had a situation of thrifts with billions of dollars of losses, while governmental agencies responsible for them had not nearly the resources to bail out the insolvents. In August 1989 Congress enacted a costly bailout measure and the president signed it. Upward of $166 billion was expected to have to be spent to close or sell hundreds of insolvent S&Ls over the next decade.

An obvious solution was to attract would-be acquirers to take over the dead and dying thrifts and rejuvenate them, so Congress allowed acquirers to use the great bulk of the accumulated tax losses of the previous owners. This decision reduced federal income and other taxes; taxpayers absorbed the losses through a higher deficit, reduced government services, and new taxes. The Federal Home Loan Bank Board made the deal even better: not only would it guarantee the losses on the nonperforming portfolios, but it also would guarantee the performing portfolios against losses. For example, should interest rates move adversely and lower the value of the

---

[12] Curran, *op. cit.*, p. 188.

[13] Curran, *op. cit.*

performing assets (i.e., those assets still viable and paying interest), the Bank Board would make up the loss if the S&L later found itself not to be liquid. This was a gold mine for acquirers. As *Barron's* noted.

> From the moment an acquirer signed the papers, he would be able to deduct already acquired losses of, say, $1 billion. Against a combined corporate tax rate of about 40%, he would be saving about $400 million in year one. For his out-of-pocket outlay of $50 million, he would have made a return of eight times.[14]

In December 1988 Robert Bass, a 40-year-old Texas billionaire, took over the crippled American Savings and Loan of Stockton, California. This represents perhaps the consummate gilt-edged deal to one of America's richest men.

American Savings was once the largest thrift in the United States, but it got into the same trouble as many others, with brokered deposits and high-risk loans. The Bank Board seized American in 1984 and installed fresh management, but the new team gambled and failed, and the Bank Board eventually granted exclusive bargaining rights to Bass.

In the deal American Savings was split into two entities: a healthy S&L with $15.4 billion of good assets and a "bad" one that would liquidate $14.4 billion in sour loans. For a total investment of only $500 million, the Bass Group got 70 percent ownership of the good thrift, a huge, healthy S&L with 186 branches. As another sure thing, more than one-half of this thrift's assets consisted of a $7.8 billion loan to the "bad" S&L that was fully guaranteed by FSLIC to pay a handsome 2 percent more than the cost of the funds. Also as part of the deal, Bass was rewarded with some $300 million in tax benefits.

Taking all this into account, Bass stood to make $400 to $500 million in straight profits over the next four years over his original investment of $500 million.[15]

WAS THE S&L ENVIRONMENT IN THE 1980S IMPOSSIBLE TO MANAGE?

As we have seen, more than one-third of the nation's S&Ls were either insolvent or on the verge of insolvency by 1988. In 1987 the losses were so prodigious for 630 thrifts—$7.5 billion—that these were one-half again as much as the meager earnings of the other 2500.

In such a catastrophic environment, can we find any success stories, any S&Ls that had effectively bucked the trend? The answer is a resounding yes.

Suncoast Savings and Loan Association

Suncoast S&L of Hollywood, Florida, is one of the largest originators and servicers of mortgages in the Southeast. Its strategy has been to reduce the interest rate risk inherent in rate fluctuations. As we have seen before, many of the devastated S&Ls

---

[14] Described in Benjamin J. Stein, "Steal of the Century?" *Barron's* (February 20, 1989), p. 7.

[15] Described in S. C. Gwynne, "Help Your Country and Help Yourself," *Time* (February 20, 1989), p. 72.

blamed their demise on rising interest rates in which the costs of funds increased while the return remained low because of long-term mortgage commitments.

How did Suncoast reduce such risks? By the purchase and resale of mortgages complemented by its loan servicing capability. Suncoast and its subsidiaries purchase and originate mortgage loans for resale into the secondary market. In the process of reselling, however, Suncoast retains servicing rights on these mortgages, and these fees comprise a major part of its income. These two activities—purchase and resale of mortgages and loan-servicing capability—are complementary. For example, in declining interest rates, mortgage lending increases as more people buy property during such favorable conditions. But when interest rates rise and loan volume decreases, loan servicing increases in importance as more borrowers hold on to their existing mortgages.

Suncoast gains further risk reduction by contracts in which major Wall Street investment banks purchase mortgage-backed securities on specific dates at agreed on interest rates and discounts. While this conservative approach is costly, the risk protection from higher interest rates is deemed worth it. The conservative operating strategy caused assets to more than double between 1987 and 1988, with net income rising from 60 cents per share in fiscal 1987 to 98 cents a share one year later. By December 31, 1988, $2.7 billion was serviced in mortgage loans versus $1.1 billion a year earlier. And the return on equity was 14 percent in 1988.[16]

The Boston Bancorp

Boston Bancorp Management consciously decided not to pursue diversification into nontraditional activities, reasoning that the historical focus on retail deposit accounts and home mortgages could be profitable if costs were kept low.

And this Boston Bancorp has done. It limited investment in "brick and mortar," having only four branches serving middle-income communities in metropolitan Boston. A long-established bank-by-mail program eliminated the need for an extensive branch system. Use of funds is primarily in single-family mortgages, commercial mortgages in apartment buildings, and high-quality government obligations and corporate stock—far from risky. With this approach, Boston Bancorp's return on equity has exceeded 18 percent, and it has grown to $1.4 billion in assets.[17]

Austerity has also paid off for other S&Ls—for example, TCF Banking and Savings. When new management took over during the turbulent mid-1980s, the first thing to go was a luxurious suite of executive offices as well as 35 of the association's top brass.[18]

USA Today, in a feature story, described a number of thrifts that bucked the trend and were successful during a time of turmoil in the industry. The common

---

[16] Robert Chaut, "The Well-Managed Thrift: Five Success Stories," *The Bankers Magazine* (July–August 1989), pp. 35, 38.

[17] *Ibid.*

[18] Harlan Byrne, "Practicing Thrift, Austerity Pays Off for a Midwestern S&L," *Barron's* (September 21, 1987), p. 15.

INFORMATION BOX

DISCIPLINED LEADERSHIP

Leadership is vulnerable to abuses—abuses in overreaching, in not carefully assessing rewards versus risks in proposals, in operating beyond reasonable means, in simply not keeping a tight rein on costs, and, most important, not guiding the organization with the best interests of the stakeholders in mind. Such abuses are especially tempting in times of wild optimism, such as was occurring in the Southwest during the oil and land booms.

Discipline needs to be imposed when the inclination is to run amuck. Discipline implies controlled behavior, careful evaluation of actions and opportunities, not growing beyond resources and management capabilities. In the quest for the fine line between disciplined and undisciplined growth, the executive faces the dual risk of being too conservative or too aggressive. The first risk may be of missed opportunities and giving competitors an advantage, but this generally is less risky than jeopardizing the company with too much high-stakes leadership. Continued viability has to receive top priority. Gambling the company is hardly acceptable stakes, even in Las Vegas.

Discuss how disciplined leadership can be imposed on a top executive with wilder leanings.

---

denominator for all of these was *careful growth*, dedicated commitment to pursuing home mortgages rather than commercial deals and brokeraged deposits, and creativity in improving customer service.[19] The Information Box above discusses disciplined leadership and strategy execution.

WHERE THE BLAME LIES

The S&L industry in the 1980s represents the greatest industry debacle since the Great Depression of the 1930s. The pervasiveness of the disaster engulfed hundreds of savings and loans in all types of communities, from the very small rural towns to the largest cities, from areas of depression to those of the greatest growth. The taxpayers' bill to salvage what can be salvaged will be in the hundreds of billions of dollars.

How could this have happened? Could it have been avoided? What, if anything, can we learn from all this that might be transferable to other situations and other times, that in effect may lessen the probability of such happenings occurring again?

Some have attributed the blame to external circumstances that S&L executives could not control. They were simply victims, these people would lead us to believe. Others blame the government, claiming that in its desire to help the industry during a time of high and increasing interest rates, it relaxed equity restraints and promoted

---

[19] David Elbert and Harriet Johnson Brackey, "Slow Growth Was the Key to Survival," *USA Today* (February 15, 1989), pp. B1, B2.

dangerous deregulation, permitting S&Ls wide latitude to invest their funds far beyond the traditional home mortgage lending. No one could foresee that ballooning oil prices and land values would so abruptly be deflated.

Yet such "excuses" for the debacle rest on unsubstantial foundations. While hundreds of S&Ls failed, more hundreds maintained viability and even showed strength and growth. The common denominator of uncontrollable environmental factors does not hold the valid answer of who or what to blame and how disaster could have been avoided. Furthermore, it was the height of imprudence to expect boom conditions to last.

Where, then, lies the blame? As with most mistakes, management cannot escape primary responsibility. In this case, the fault lay with a management that violated the integrity of the planning function. The violation occurred in two respects: (1) injudicious failure to rein in expenses during a time when the profitable spread of traditional mortgage business was narrowing and (2) a wild spree to highly risky undertakings and investments once the constraints of governmental regulation were loosened. To these one must add a good dash of outright fraud, asset-stripping, and corruption—white-collar crimes. (Of course, the inability of government inspectors to monitor closely enough permitted some of the worst excesses. But we are concerned here with *management* mistakes, not government mistakes.)

WHAT CAN BE LEARNED?

We can draw significant insights from the planning blunders of the sick and dying thrifts and from comparisons of sick and prospering ones.

Adversity creates opportunities. We are left with the growing recognition that adversity—in this case, a supposedly inhospitable environment—can also create opportunities for those who would adjust, adapt, and plan creatively in this environment, even embrace it with gusto—but without reckless abandon. The S&L situation created great opportunities for firms and individuals who had the resources and skill to "rescue" the troubled thrifts, with substantial government largess. And for the healthy competitors, new growth opportunities were also created, albeit the bad image of the failures cast all S&Ls in suspicious light.

The fallacy of aggressive and conservative extremes. Many of the failed thrifts were victims of their own aggressiveness, carried to the extreme of recklessness. If real estate prices and a building boom had continued in the high-growth areas of the south and west, then some of the reckless speculations would have brought above-average payoffs. Unfortunately, a wild house-of-cards philosophy eventually collapses. Excesses can only be tolerated so long in the normal course of events, as has been proven time and again over many centuries. The dangers of a speculative frenzy date back to at least 1634 in Holland, when individual tulip bulbs were bid up to fantastic prices in wild but doomed speculation.

The extremes of conservatism have dangers, too. As we examine in the next learning insight, the environment is in flux; it is constantly changing. Failing to take even minor risks regardless of potential opportunities or to make needed adjustments to a changing business clime can hardly be praised. The extreme example here is the buggy whip manufacturer unwilling to adapt to the new environment of horseless carriages. In general, a middle ground between extreme aggressiveness and ultraconservatism will usually lead to the most durable success.

Any business firm faces a dynamic environment; nothing can be expected to remain constant. This requires some degree of adaptability. A useful perspective of reactions to a changing environment can be gained by considering a continuum of behavior:

Degree of Responsiveness to Environmental Change

Inflexible Unchanging	Adaptive	Innovative

Thus, a firm can be viewed as occupying a certain point along this continuum: the more conservative and rigid firm toward the left, the more progressive firm that is constantly developing new ideas toward the right.

The terms *adaptive* and *innovative* are somewhat different, although related. We will consider them as different degrees of responsive behavior on the same dimension. *Innovative* may be defined as originating significant changes, implying improvement. *Adaptive* implies a better coping with changing circumstances, but a response somewhat less significant than an innovative reaction.

In a sense the failed thrifts were adaptive to a changed environment, that of greater deregulation. They adapted by forsaking any plans of judicious expansion in favor of a free-wheeling strategy of high risks and opportunism. Then they found themselves unable to cope with the suddenly menacing environment of drastically falling real estate prices and a newly concerned regulatory climate.

Austerity wins out over high living. Nowhere is the contrast of high living and lack of cost constraints compared with relative austerity more evident than here. Reckless spending is a trap. Admittedly, when things are going well, when prospects seem boundless, the temptation is to open the flood-gates of spending, at both the corporate and the personal level.

On the one hand, many of the failed thrifts were guilty of wild spending. Conspicuous examples of this were lavish entertainment, grand facilities, fleets of airplanes, even expensive art collections.[20]

On the other hand, we have examples of firms that owe their viability to their austerity. They kept themselves lean, controlled costs, and were able to survive and prosper and even be in position to take over their extravagant competitors.

Whereas some would argue that lavish spending created a public image of great success and prosperity, thus winning new business, a more sober appraisal would be one of foolish waste. Lack of cost restraints is incompatible with effective management and should not be tolerated by shareholders or creditors.

---

[20] For example, see Martha Brannigan and Alexandra Peers, "S&L's Art Collection, Ordered to be Sold, Faces Skeptical Market," *Wall Street Journal* (October 18, 1989), pp. 1, A12.

A government "crutch" is a destructive delusion. The knowledge that depositors' accounts were insured up to $100,000 by the Federal Savings and Loan Insurance Corporation undoubtedly motivated some of the reckless investments and other dealings of the failed thrifts. That the government would foot the cost of any speculations that turn sour and would bail out depositors seemed a siren call for some executives. But those who felt entirely shielded by this governmental crutch were to learn to their dismay that while depositors were protected—at great cost to the government and taxpayers—they, the management, faced ouster and even the possibility of legal prosecution.

The shifting tides of politics and the effects on legislation and regulation bring a threat of being "blindsided" to those who rely too much on government support and protection. And the government has no great history of sound legislation: Witness the S&L legislation of the early 1980s that was designed to save the S&Ls but that in reality presented temptation for doom that many found impossible to resist.

CONSIDER

Can you find any additional learning insights for either the dot.coms or the S&Ls, or both?

QUESTIONS

1. Do you think all of these learning insights, except the government "crutch," apply as much to Internet firms as they do to thrifts? If not, which ones would not apply and why?

2. Do you think the government should consider bailing out high-tech and Internet firms as it did the savings and loans? Why or why not?

3. What are the major differences between the Internet and high-tech problems and the savings and loans problems?

4. How would you respond to an S&L executive who carefully pointed out to you that if land and oil prices had not collapsed without warning his portfolio of high-interest loans would have brought great profitability to the firm?

5. A thin line seems to exist between aggressive opportunism and outright fraud. Where do you think the line should be drawn? Or are both to be criminally condemned?

6. Would you conclude that Edward McBirney's greatest flaw was that he liked ostentatious high living? Why or why not?

7. After the examples described in the case, would you conclude that an "edifice complex" (i.e., an inclination to build prestigious physical facilities) is ill-advised and even, from the viewpoint of an investor, something to encourage divestment?

HANDS-ON EXERCISES

1. You are the controller of a medium-size S&L in the mid-1980s. Your CEO is a flamboyant individual who has just announced his intention of building a new home office on a rather lavish scale. He claims this is necessary to convey the desired image of the firm. Develop a systematic analysis to disprove his idea.

2. Put yourself in the mind of the founder of a failed dot.com firm. The stock has fallen from over $100 a share to barely $1, and your net worth from hundreds of millions to maybe little or nothing depending on what can be salvaged from the detritus of your firm. Describe your feelings, your future expectations (e.g., is entrepreneurship still to be sought?), and the adjustments you will need to make.

TEAM DEBATE EXERCISES

1. Debate this issue: The aggressive growth of lending and promoting development would have been the greatest service ever rendered to many parts of the country, except for the collapse of real estate prices. And who could have foreseen that?

2. Debate this issue: There is always risk in new ventures at the cutting edge of technology. But we must not be timid in embracing innovation and expanding to grasp it.

INVITATION TO RESEARCH

What is the state of the S&L industry today? Are high-tech stock prices resurging, and is the climate becoming favorable for a new wave of entrepreneurs?

CHAPTER SIXTEEN

Boeing Can't Handle Success

Cyclical

The commercial-jet business had long been subject to booms and busts: major demand for new aircraft and then years of little demand. By the second half of the 1990s, demand burgeoned as never before. Boeing, the world's leading producer of commercial airplanes, seemed in the catbird seat amid the worldwide surge of orders. This was an unexpected windfall, spurred by markets greatly expanding in Asia and Latin America at the same time as domestic demand, helped by deregulation and prosperity, boomed. In the midst of this seeming prosperity, Boeing in 1997 incurred its first loss in 50 years, with longer-term prospects questionable. How could this have happened? How could it have been prevented? How can the situation be corrected?

BACKGROUND OF THE COMPANY

Boeing's was a fabled past, being a major factor in the World War II war effort, and in the late 1950s leading the way in producing innovative, state-of-the-art commercial aircraft. It introduced the 707, the world's first commercially viable jetliner. In the late 1960s, it almost bankrupted itself to build a jetliner twice the size of any other then in service, as critics predicted it could never fly profitably. But the 747 dramatically lowered costs and airfares and brought passenger comfort previously undreamed of in flying. In the mid-1990s, it introduced the high technology 777, the first commercial aircraft designed entirely with the use of computers.

In efforts to reduce the feast-to-famine cycles of the commercial aircraft business, Boeing acquired Rockwell International's defense business in 1996, and in 1997 purchased McDonnell Douglas for $16.3 billion. *M&A*

In 1997, Boeing's commercial aircraft segment contributed 57 percent of total revenues. This segment ranged from 125-passenger 737s to giant 500-seat 747s. In 1997, Boeing delivered 374 aircraft, up from 269 in 1996. The potential seemed enormous: over the next twenty years, air passenger traffic worldwide was projected to rise 4.9 percent a year, and airlines were predicted to order 16,160 aircraft to expand their fleets and replace aging planes.[1] As the industry leader, Boeing had 60 percent of this market in recent years. At the end of 1997, its order backlog was $94 billion.

[1] *Boeing 1997 Annual Report.* *60% Share*

Defense and space operations constituted 41 percent of 1997 revenues. This included Airborne Warning and Control Systems (AWACS), helicopters, B-2 bomber subcontract work, and the F-22 fighter, among other products and systems.

PROBLEMS WITH THE COMMERCIAL AIRCRAFT BUSINESS SEGMENT

Production Problems

Boeing proved to be poorly positioned to meet the surge in aircraft orders. Part of this resulted from drastic layoffs it had made of experienced workers during the industry's last slump, in the early 1990s. Though it hired 32,000 new workers over 18 months starting in 1995, the experience gap upped the risk of costly mistakes. Boeing had also cut back its suppliers in strenuous efforts to slash parts inventories and increase cost efficiency.

But Boeing had other problems. Its production systems were a mess. It had somehow evolved some 400 separate computer systems, and these were not linked. Its design system was labor intensive and paper dependent, and very expensive as it tried to cater to customer choices. A $1 billion program had been launched in 1996 to modernize and computerize the production process. But this was too late: the onslaught of orders had already started. (It is something of an anomaly that a firm that had the sophistication to design the 777 entirely by computers was so antiquated in its use of computers otherwise.)

Demands for increased production were further aggravated by unreasonable production goals and too many plane models. Problems first hit with the 747 Jumbo, and then with a new version of the top-selling 737, the so-called next-generation 737NG. Before long, every program was affected: also the 757, 767, and 777. In 1997, while Boeing released over 320 planes to customers for a 50 percent increase over 1996, this was far short of the planned completion rate. For example, by early 1998 a dozen 737NGs had been delivered to airlines, but this was less than one-third of the 40 supposed to have been delivered by then. Yet, the company maintained through September 1997 that everything was going well, that there was only a month's delay in the delivery of some planes.

Soon it became apparent that problems were much greater. In October, the 747 and 737 assembly lines were shut down for nearly a month to allow workers to catch up and ease part shortages. The *Wall Street Journal* reported horror stories of parts being rushed in by taxicab, of executives spending weekends trying to chase down needed parts, of parts needed for new planes being shipped out to replace defective parts on an in-service plane. Overtime pay brought some assembly-line workers incomes over $100,000, while rookie workers muddled by on the line.[2]

Despite its huge order backlog, Boeing took a loss for 1997, the first in over 50 years. See Table 16.1 for the trend in revenues and net income over the last ten years.

The loss came mostly from two massive writedowns. One, for $1.4 billion, arose from the McDonnell Douglas acquisition and in particular from its ailing commercial

---

[2] Frederic M. Biddle and John Helyar, "Behind Boeing's Woes: Clunky Assembly Line, Price War with Airbus," *Wall Street Journal* (April 24, 1998), p. A16.

TABLE 16.1 Boeing's Trend of Revenues and Income, 1988–1997

	Revenue	Net Income
	(million $)	
1988	16,962	614
1989	20,276	675
1990	27,595	1,385
1991	29,314	1,567
1992	30,184	1,554
1993	25,438	1,244
1994	21,924	856
1995	19,515	393
1996	22,681	1,095
1997	45,800	–177

Source: Boeing Annual Reports.

Commentary: Note the severity of the decline in revenues and profits during the industry downturn in 1993, 1994, and 1995. It is little wonder that Boeing was so ill-prepared for the deluge of orders starting in 1995. Then in an unbelievable anomaly, the tremendous increase in revenues in 1997, to the highest ever, resulted in a huge loss.

aircraft operation at Long Beach, California. The bigger writeoff, $1.6 billion, reflected production problems, particularly on the new 737NG. Production delays continued, with more writedowns likely.

As Boeing moved into 1998, analysts wondered how much longer it would take to clear up the production snafus. This would be longer than anyone had been led to expect. Now a new problem arose for Boeing. Disastrous economic conditions in Asia brought major order cancellations.

Customer Relations

Not surprisingly, Boeing's production problems resulting in delayed shipments seriously impacted customer relations. For example, Southwest Airlines had to temporarily cancel adding service to another city because ordered planes were not ready. Boeing paid Southwest millions of dollars of compensation for the delayed deliveries. Continental also had to wait for five overdue 737s.

Other customers switched to Boeing's only major competitor, Airbus Industrie, of Toulouse, France.

Airbus   *Only Competitor*

Airbus Industrie had to salivate at Boeing's troubles. It was a distant second in market share to the 60 percent of Boeing. Now this was changing and it could see achieving a sustainable 50 percent market share. See the following Information Box for a discussion of market share.

Airbus was positioned to supply planes to airlines whose needs Boeing couldn't meet near term. Some thought it was even producing better planes than Boeing.

United Airlines chose Airbus's A320 twinjets over Boeing's 737s, saying passengers preferred the Airbus product. Several South American carriers also chose A320s over the 737, placing a $4 billion order with Airbus. For 1997, Airbus hacked out a 45 percent market share, the first time Boeing's 60 percent market share had eroded.

The situation worsened drastically in 1998. US Air, which had previously ordered 400 Airbus jets, announced in July that it would buy 30 more. But the biggest defection came in August when British Airlines announced plans to buy 59 Airbus jetliners and take options for 200 more. This broke its long record as a Boeing-loyal customer. The order would be worth as much as $11 billion, the biggest victory of Airbus over Boeing.[3]

Beyond the production delays of Boeing, Airbus had other competitive strengths. While it had less total production capability than Boeing (235 planes vs. Boeing's

Defection to Airbus

INFORMATION BOX

IMPORTANCE OF MARKET SHARE

The desire to surpass a competitor is a common human tendency, whether in sports or business. A measurement of performance relative to competitors encourages this and can be highly motivating for management and employees alike. Furthermore, market share performance is a key indicator in ascertaining how well a firm is doing and in spotting emerging problems, as well as sometimes allaying blame. As an example of the latter, declining sales over the preceding year, along with a constant and improving market share, can suggest that the firm is doing a good job, even though certain factors adversely affected the whole industry.

Market share is usually measured by (1) share of overall sales, and/or (2) share relative to certain competitors, usually the top one or several in the industry. Of particular importance is trend data: Are things getting better or worse? If worse, why is this, and what needs to be done to improve the situation?

Since Boeing and Airbus were the only real competitors in this major industry relative market shares became critical. The perceived importance of gaining, or not losing, market share led to severe price competition that cut into the profits of both firms, as will be discussed later.

How would you respond to the objection that market share data is not all that useful, since "it doesn't tell us what the problem really is"?

Can emphasizing market share be counterproductive? If so, why?

---

[3] "British to Order Airbus Airliners," *Cleveland Plain Dealer* (August 25, 1998), p. 6-C.

550), its production line was efficient and it had done a better job of trimming its costs. This meant it could go head-to-head with Boeing on price. And price seemed to be the name of the game in the late 1990s. This contrasted with earlier days when Boeing rose to world leadership with performance, delivery, and technology more important than cost. "They [the customers] do not care what it costs us to make the planes," Boeing chairman and chief executive Philip Condit admitted. With airline design plateaued, he saw the airlines buying planes today as chiefly interested in how much carrying capacity they can buy for a buck.[4]

WHO CAN WE BLAME FOR BOEING'S TROUBLES?

Was It CEO Philip Condit?

Philip Condit became chief executive in 1996, just in time for the massive emerging problems. He had hardly assumed office before he was deeply involved in the defense industry's merger mania, first buying Rockwell's aerospace operation and then McDonnell Douglas. He later admitted that he probably spent too much time on these acquisitions, and not enough time on watching the commercial part of the operation.[5]

Condit's credentials were good. His association with Boeing began in 1965 when he joined the firm as an aerodynamics engineer. The same year, he obtained a design patent for a flexible wing called the sailwing. Moving through the company's engineering and managerial ranks, he was named CEO in 1996 and chairman in 1997. Along the way, he earned a master's degree in management from the Massachusetts Institute of Technology in 1975, and in 1997 a doctorate in engineering from Science University of Tokyo, where he was the first westerner to earn such a degree.

Was Condit's pursuit of the Rockwell and McDonnell Douglas mergers a major blunder? While analysts do not agree on this, prevailing opinion is more positive than negative, mostly because these businesses could smooth the cyclical nature of the commercial sector.

Interestingly, in the face of severe adversity, no heads have rolled, as they might have in other firms. See the following Issue Box for a discussion of management climate during adversity.

Were the Problems Mostly Due to Internal Factors?

The unexpected buying binge by airlines that was brought about by worldwide prosperity fueling air travel maybe should have been anticipated. However, probably even the most prescient decision maker would have missed the full extent of this boom. For example, orders jumped from 124 in 1994 to 754 in 1996. With hindsight we know that Boeing made a grievous management mistake in trying to bite off too much, by promising expanded production and deliveries that were

---

[4] Howard Banks, "Slow Learner," *Forbes* (May 4, 1998), p. 54.
[5] *Ibid.*, p. 56.

ISSUE BOX

MANAGEMENT CLIMATE DURING ADVERSITY: WHAT IS BEST FOR MAXIMUM EFFECTIVENESS?

Management shakeups during adversity can range from practically none to widespread head-rolling. In the first scenario, a cooperative board is usually necessary, and it helps if the top executive(s) controls a lot of stock. But the company's problems will probably continue. In the second scenario, we earlier saw an avowed turnaround expert, Albert Dunlap, come in wielding a mean ax, and indeed seemed to turn around the faltering Scott Paper in a short time. But excessive management changes can destroy a company. And Dunlap's success with Scott did not carry over to Sunbeam. On the other hand, Gordon Bethune turned around Continental Air without wielding a mean ax. So, can we make any conclusions from a sample of cases?

In general, neither extreme—complacency or upheaval—is good. A sick company usually needs drastic changes, but not necessarily widespread bloodletting that leaves the entire organization cringing and sending out resumes. But we need to further define *sick*. At what point is a company so bad off it needs a drastic overhaul? Was Boeing such a sick company? Would a drastic overhaul have quickly changed things? Certainly Boeing management had made some miscalculations, mostly in the area of too much optimism and too much complacency, but these were finally recognized. Major executive changes and resignations might not have helped at all with Boeing.

How do you personally feel about the continuity of management at Boeing during these difficult times? Should some heads have rolled? What criteria would you use in your judgment of whether to roll heads or not?

wholly unrealistic. We know what triggered such extravagant promises: trying to keep ahead of arch-rival Airbus.

Huge layoffs in the early 1990s contributed to the problems of gearing up for new business. An early-retirement plan had been taken up by 9,000 of 13,000 eligible people. This was twice as many as Boeing expected, and it removed a core of production-line workers and managers who had kept a dilapidated system working. New people could not be trained or assimilated quickly enough to match those lost.

Boeing had begun switching to the Japanese practice of lean inventory management that delivers parts and tools to workers precisely as needed so that production costs could be reduced. Partly because of this and also because of the downturn in the early 1990s, Boeing's supplier base changed significantly. Some suppliers quit the aviation business; others had suffered so badly in the slump that their credit was affected and they were unable to boost capacity for the suddenly increased business. The result was serious parts shortages.

Complicating production problems was Boeing's long-standing practice of customizing, thereby permitting customers to choose from a host of options, to fine tune not only for every airline but for every order. For example, it offered the 747's customers 38 different pilot clipboards, and 109 shades of the color white.[6] Such tailoring added significantly to costs and production time. This perhaps was acceptable when these costs could be easily passed on to customers in a more leisurely production cycle, but it was far from maximizing efficiency. Deregulation fare wars made extreme customizing archaic. Boeing apparently got the message with the wide-bodied 777, designed entirely by computers. Here, choices of parts were narrowed to standard options, such as carmakers offer in their transmissions, engines, and comfort packages.

Cut-rate pricing between Boeing and Airbus epitomized the situation by the mid-1990s. Now, costs became critical if a firm was to be profitable. In this climate, Boeing was so obsessed with maintaining its 60 percent market share that it fought for each order with whatever price it took. Commercial airline production had somehow become a commodity business, with neither Boeing nor Airbus having products all that unique to sell. Innovation seemed disregarded, with price the only factor in getting an order. So, every order became a battleground, and prices might be slashed 20 percent off list in order to grab all the business possible.[7] And Boeing did not have the low-cost advantage over Airbus.

Such price competition worked to the advantage of the airlines, and they grew skillful at gaining big discounts from Boeing and Airbus by holding out huge contracts and negotiating hard.

The cumbersome production systems of Boeing—cost inefficient—became a burden in this cost-conscious environment. While some of the problems could be attributed to computer technology not well applied to the assembly process, others involved organizational myopia regarding even such simple things as a streamlined organization and common parts. For example, before recent changes the commercial group had five wing-design groups, one for each aircraft program. Finally it has one. Another example cited in *Forbes* tells of different tools needed in the various plane models to open their wing access hatches.[8] Why not the same tool?

We see a paradox in Boeing's dilemma. Its 777 was the epitome of high technology and computer design, as well as efficient production planning. Yet, much of the other production was mired in a morass with supplies, parts management, and production inefficiency.

Harry Stonecipher, former CEO of McDonnell Douglas before the acquisition and now president and chief operating officer of Boeing, cited arrogance as the mindset behind Boeing's problems. He saw this as coming from a belief that the company could do no wrong, that all its problems came from outside, and that business-as-usual will solve them.[9]

---

[6] John Greenwald, "Is Boeing Out of Its Spin?," *Time* (July 13, 1998), p. 68.

[7] "Behind Boeing's Woes…," pp. A1, A16.

[8] Banks, *op. cit.*, p. 60.

[9] Bill Sweetman, "Stonecipher's Boeing Shakeup," *Interavia Business & Technology* (September 1998), p. 15.

The Role of External Factors

Adding to the production and cost-containment difficulties of Boeing was increased regulatory demands. These came not only from the U.S. Federal Aviation Administration, but also from the European Joint Airworthiness Authority (a loose grouping of regulators from more than 20 European countries). The first major consequence of this increased regulatory climate concerned the new 730NG. Boeing apparently thought it could use the same over-the-wings emergency exits as it had on the older 737. But Europe wanted a redesign. They were concerned that the older type of emergency exits would not permit passengers in the larger version of the plane to evacuate quickly enough. So Boeing had to design two new over-the-wing exits on each side. This was no simple modification since it involved rebuilding the most crucial aspect of the plane. The costly refitting accounted for a major part of the $1.6 billion writedown Boeing took in 1997.

Europe's Airbus Industrie had made no secret of its desire to achieve parity with Boeing and have 50 percent of the international market for commercial jets. This mindset led to the severe price competition of the latter 1990s as Boeing stubbornly tried to maintain its 60 percent market share even at the expense of profits. While its total production capacity was somewhat below that of Boeing, Airbus had already overhauled its manufacturing process, and was better positioned to compete on price. Airbus's competitive advantage seemed stronger with single-aisle planes, those in the 120–200 seat category, mostly 737s of Boeing and A320s of Airbus. But this accounted for 43 percent of the $40 billion expected to be spent on airliners in 1998.[10]

The future was something else. Airbus placed high stakes on a superjumbo successor to the 747, with seating capacity well beyond the 568 people that the 747 carried. Such a huge plane would hold up to a thousand people and operate from hub airports such as New York City's JFK. Airbus was spending $9 billion to develop what it called the A3XX to be debuted by 2004. Meantime, Boeing staked its future on its own 767s and 777s, which could connect smaller cities around the world without the need for passenger concentration at a few hubs.

Have you ever heard of a firm complaining of too much business? Probably not, were it not for Boeing's immersion in red ink trying to cope with too many orders. However, indications began surfacing that Boeing's feast of too much business had abruptly ended. Financial problems in Asia brought cancellations and postponements of orders and deliveries.

In October 1998, Boeing disclosed that 36 completed aircraft were sitting in company storage areas in the desert, largely because of canceled orders. This compared with only 8 such aircraft at the end of 1997 and 19 at the end of the second quarter of 1998.

By December 1998, Boeing warned that its operations may be hurt by the Asian situation for as long as five years, and it announced an additional 20,000 jobs would be eliminated and production cut 25 percent.[11] Of course, it didn't help that Airbus

---

[10] Banks, *op. cit.*, p. 60.

[11] Frederick M. Biddle and Andy Pasztor, "Boeing May Be Hurt Up to 5 Years by Asia," *Wall Street Journal* (December 3, 1998), p. A3.

was capitalizing on the production difficulties of Boeing to wrest orders from the stable of Boeing's long-term customers and planned a 30 percent production increase for 1999.

UPDATE

By 2001 the competition between Airbus and Boeing continued unabated. Airbus had gone ahead with its superjumbo A-380, the world's largest passenger jet, with delivery to start in 2006 for a list price of $230 million. In its standard configuration, it would carry 555 passengers between airport "hubs." With delivery still five years away, Airbus already had orders for 72 of the jumbos, and expected to reach the 100 milestone early in 2002. It would break even with 250 of the wide-bodies.

In March 2001, Boeing scrapped plans for an updated but still smaller 747-X project. Instead it announced plans for a revolutionary delta-winged "Sonic Cruiser," carrying 150 to 250 passengers higher and faster than conventional planes: The savings in time would amount to 50 minutes from New York City to London, and almost 2 hours between Singapore and London. Further savings in time would come from the plane flying to point-to-point destinations, bypassing layovers at such congested hubs as London and Hong Kong. Delivery was expected in 2007 or 2008.

Both companies had undergone major organizational changes. As of January 1, 2001, Airbus was no longer a four-nation consortium, but now an integrated company with centralized purchasing and management systems. Operations were streamlined toward bottom-line responsibilities.

Boeing had previously diversified itself away from so much dependence on commercial aircraft through its acquisitions of Rockwell's aerospace and defense business, McDonnell Douglas, Hughes Space & Communications, and several smaller companies. It was expected that within five years more than half the revenues would come from new business lines, including financing aircraft sales, providing high-speed Internet access, and managing air-traffic problems.[12]

WHAT CAN BE LEARNED?

Beware the 3 C's syndrome, again. So many times this mindset rears up and humbles the frontrunner. We saw it earlier with Harley Davidson and IBM. But the firms succumbing are far more than these.

Stonecipher, former CEO of McDonnell Douglas and then president of Boeing, admitted to company self-confidence bordering on arrogance. But it is

---

[12] Compiled from such sources as: David J. Lynch, "Airbus Comes of Age With A-380," *USA Today* (June 21, 2001), pp. 1B, 2B; J. Lynn Lunsford, Daniel Michaels, and Any Pasztor, "At Paris Air Show, Boeing-Airbus Duel Has New Twist," *Wall Street Journal* (June 15, 2001), p. B4; and Bruce Stanley, Associated Press, as reported in "Airbus' Aircraft Sales Taking Off," *Cleveland Plain Dealer*, June 19, 2001, p. 4C.

more than this, this plague that infects successful firms. To review, the 3 C's are <u>conservatism, complacency, and conceit</u>. Complacency is smugness, contentment, self satisfaction. Conservatism is wedded to the past, to tradition. Conceit is disdain for competitors. The current problems of Boeing should have destroyed any vestiges of the 3 C's mindset. But the former "king of the hill" position may be lost.

Growth must be manageable. Boeing certainly showed the fallacy of attempting growth beyond immediate capabilities in a growth-at-any-cost mindset. The rationale for embracing great growth is that we "need to run with the ball" if we ever get that rare opportunity to suddenly double or triple sales. But there are times when a slower, more controlled growth is prudent.

Risks lie on both sides as we reach for these opportunities. When a market begins to boom and a firm is unable to keep up with demand without greatly increasing capacity and resources, it faces a dilemma: (1) Stay conservative in fear that the opportunity will be short-lived, but thereby abdicate some of the growing market to competitors, or (2) expand vigorously to take full advantage of the opportunity, but risk being overextended and vulnerable should the potential suddenly fade. Regardless of the commitment to a vision of great growth, a firm must develop an organization and systems and controls to handle it, or find itself in the morass of Boeing, with quality control problems, inability to meet production targets, alienated customers, and costs far out of line. And not the least, having its stock price savaged by Wall Street investors, while its market share tumbles. Growth must not be beyond the ability of the firm to manage it.

Perils of downsizing. Boeing presents a sobering example of the risks of downsizing in this era when downsizing is so much in fashion. With incredibly bad timing, it encouraged many of its most experienced and skilled workers and supervisors to take early retirement, just a few years before the boom began. Boeing found out the hard way that it could replace bodies, but not the skills needed to produce the highly complex planes under severe time pressure for output. It would have been better off to have maintained a core of experienced workers during the downturn, rather than lose them forever. It would have been better to have suffered with higher labor costs during the lean times, disregarding management's typical attitude of paring costs to the bone during such times. Yet, when we look at Table 16.1 and see the severe decreases of revenues and income in 1993, 1994, and lasting well into 1995, we can appreciate the dilemma of Boeing's management.

Problems of competing mostly on price. Price competition almost invariably leads to price cutting and even price wars to win market share. In such an environment, the lowest-cost, most-efficient producer wins.

More often, all firms in an industry have rather similar cost structures, and severe price competition hurts the profits of all competitors without bringing much additional business. Any initial pricing advantage is quickly matched by competitors unwilling to lose market share. In this situation, competing on nonprice bases has much to recommend it. Nonprice competition emphasizes uniqueness, perhaps in some aspects of product features and quality, perhaps through service and quicker deliveries or maybe better quality control. A firm's reputation, if good, is a powerful nonprice advantage.

Usually new and rapidly growing industries face price competition as marginal firms are weeded out and more economies of operation are developed. The more mature an industry, the greater likelihood of nonprice competition since cutthroat pricing causes too much hardship to all competitors.

Certainly the commercial aircraft production industry is mature, and much has been made of airlines being chiefly interested in how much passenger-carrying capacity they can buy for the same buck, and of their pitting Airbus and Boeing against each other in bidding wars.[13] Nonprice competition badly needs to be reinstated in this industry.

The synergy of mergers and acquisitions is suspect. The concept of synergy says that a new whole is better than the sum of its parts. In other words, a well-planned merger or acquisition should result in a better enterprise than the two separate entities. Theoretically, this would seem possible since operations can be streamlined for more efficiency and since greater management and staff competence can be brought to bear as greater financial and other resources can be tapped; or in Boeing's case, since the peaks and valleys of commercial demand could be countered by defense and space business.

Unfortunately, such synergy often is absent, at least in the short and intermediate term. More often such concentrations incur severe digestive problems—problems with people, systems, and procedures—that take time to resolve. Furthermore, greater size does not always beget economies of scale. The opposite may in fact occur: an unwieldy organization, slow to act, and vulnerable to more aggressive, innovative, and agile smaller competitors. The siren call of synergy is often an illusion.

The acquisitions of McDonnell Douglas and Rockwell may yet work out well for Boeing. But their assimilation came at a most troubling time for Boeing. The Long Beach plant of McDonnell Douglas alone led to a massive $1.4 billion write-off and contributed significantly to the losses of 1997. Less easily calculated, but certainly a factor, was the management time involved in coping with these new entities.

CONSIDER

Can you think of additional learning insights?

QUESTIONS

1. Do you think Boeing should have anticipated the impact of Asian economic difficulties long before it did?

2. If it had anticipated sooner the drying up of the Asian market for planes, would this have prevented most of the problems later confronting Boeing? Discuss.

3. Do you think top management at Boeing should have been fired after the disastrous miscalculations in the late 1990s? Why or why not?

---

[13] For example, Banks, *op. cit.,* p. 54.

4. A major stockholder grumbles, "Management worries too much about Airbus, and to hell with the stockholders." Evaluate this statement. Do you think it is valid?

5. Take an optimistic stance. What do you see for Boeing three to five years down the road?

6. Do you think it likely that Boeing will have to contend with new competitors over the next ten years? Why or why not?

7. Discuss synergy in mergers. Why does it so many times seem to be lacking despite expectations?

8. You are a skilled machinist for Boeing, and had always been quite proud of participating in the building of giant planes. You have just received notice of another lengthy layoff, the second in five years. Discuss your likely attitudes and actions.

HANDS-ON EXERCISES

Before

1. You are a management consultant advising top management at Boeing. It is 1993 and the airline industry is in a slump, but early indications are that things will improve greatly in a few years. What would you advise that might have prevented the problems Boeing faced a few years later? Be as specific as you can, and support your recommendations as to practicality and probable effectiveness.

After

2. It is late 1998, and Boeing has had to announce drastic cutbacks, with little improvement likely before five years, and Boeing's stock has collapsed and Airbus is charging ahead. What do you recommend now? (You may need to make some assumptions; if so, state them clearly and keep them reasonable.)

TEAM DEBATE EXERCISE

A business columnist writes: Boeing could "have told customers 'no thanks' to more orders than its factories could handle. ... It "could have done itself a huge favor by simply building fewer planes and charging more for them."[14] Debate the merits of this suggestion.

INVITATION TO RESEARCH

What is the situation with Boeing today? Has it recovered its profitability? How is the competitive position with Airbus?

[14] Holman W. Jenkins Jr., "Boeing's Trouble: Not Enough Monopolistic Arrogance," *Wall Street Journal* (December 16, 1998), p. A23.

CHAPTER SEVENTEEN

Southwest Airlines Finds Success with a Strategic Niche That Seems Unassailable

In 1992 the airlines lost a combined $2 billion, matching a dismal 1991, and bringing their three-year red ink total to a disastrous $8 billion. Three carriers—TWA, Continental, and America West—were operating under Chapter 11 bankruptcy, and others were lining up to join them. But one airline, Southwest, was profitable as well as rapidly growing, with a 25 percent sales increase in 1992 alone. Interestingly enough, this was a low-price, bare-bones operation run by a flamboyant CEO, Herb Kelleher. Kelleher had found a niche, a strategic window of opportunity, and oh, how he milked it! See the following Information Box for further discussion of a strategic window of opportunity and its desirable accompaniment, a SWOT analysis.

HERBERT D. KELLEHER

Herb Kelleher impresses people as an eccentric. He likes to tell stories, himself often the butt, and many involve practical jokes. He admits he is sometimes a little scatterbrained. In his cluttered office, he displays a dozen ceramic wild turkeys as a testimonial to his favorite brand of whiskey. He regularly smokes five packs of cigarettes a day. As an example of his zaniness, he painted one of his 737s to look like a killer whale to celebrate the opening of Sea World in San Antonio. Another time, during a flight he had flight attendants dress up as reindeer and elves while the pilot sang Christmas carols over the loudspeaker as he gently rocked the plane. Kelleher is a "real maniac," said Thomas J. Volz, vice president of marketing at Braniff Airlines. "But who can argue with his success?"[1]

---

[1] Kevin Kelly, "Southwest Airlines: Flying High with 'Uncle Herb,'" *Business Week* (July 3, 1989), p. 53.

INFORMATION BOX

STRATEGIC WINDOW OF OPPORTUNITY AND SWOT ANALYSIS

A strategic window is an opportunity in the marketplace, one that is currently neglected by competitors and one that fits well with the firm's competencies. Strategic windows often last for only a short time (although Southwest's strategic window has been much more durable) before they are filled by alert competitors.

Strategic windows are usually found by systematically analyzing the environment, examining the threats and opportunities it holds. The competencies of the firm, its physical and financial resources, and, not the least, its people resources—management and employees and their strengths and weaknesses—should also be assessed. The objective is to determine what actions might be appropriate for that particular enterprise and its orientation. This is commonly known as a SWOT analysis: analyzing strengths and weaknesses of the firm and opportunities and threats in the environment.

Although SWOT analysis may be a formal part of the planning process, it may also be informal and even intuitive. We suspect that Herb Kelleher instinctively sensed a strategic window in short hauls and low prices. While he must have recognized the danger that his bigger competitors would try to match his prices, he believed that with his simplicity of operation he would be able to make a profit while bigger airlines were racking up losses.

Why do you think the major airlines overlooked the possibilities in short hauls at low prices? *—low per unit profits — conflict with image — drastic streamlining of operations — not part of their core companies*

The son of a Campbell Soup Company executive, Kelleher grew up in Haddon Heights, New Jersey. He graduated from Wesleyan University and New York University Law School. In 1961 he moved to San Antonio, where his father-in-law helped him set up a law firm, and in 1968, he and a group of investors' put up $560,000 to found Southwest. Of this amount, Kelleher contributed $20,000.

In the early years Kelleher was the general counsel and a director of the fledgling enterprise. But in 1978 he was named chairman, although he had no managerial experience, and in 1981 he became CEO. His flamboyance soon made him the most visible aspect of the airline, and he starred in most of its TV commercials. A rival airline, America West, charged in ads that Southwest passengers should be embarrassed to fly such a no-frills airline, whereupon Kelleher appeared in a TV spot with a bag over his head. He offered the bag to anyone ashamed to fly Southwest, suggesting it could be used to hold "all the money you'll save flying us."[2]

Kelleher knew many of his employees by name, and they called him "Uncle Herb" or "Herbie." He held weekly parties for employees at corporate headquarters, and he encouraged such antics by his flight attendants as organizing trivia contests,

[2] *Ibid.*

delivering instructions in rap, and awarding prizes for the passengers with the largest holes in their socks. But such wackiness had a shrewd purpose: to generate a gungho spirit to boost productivity. "Herb's fun is infectious," said Kay Wallace, president of the Flight Attendants Union Local 556. "Everyone enjoys what they're doing and realizes they've got to make an extra effort."[3]

THE BEGINNINGS

Southwest was conceived in 1967 on a napkin, according to folklore. Rollin King, a client of Kelleher, then a lawyer, had an idea for a low-fare, no-frills airline to fly between major Texas cities. He doodled a triangle on the napkin, labeling the points Dallas, Houston, and San Antonio.

The two tried to go ahead with their plans but were stymied for more than three years by litigation, battling Braniff, Texas International, and Continental over the right to fly. In 1971 Southwest won, and it went public in 1975. At that time it had four planes flying between the three cities. Lamar Muse was president and CEO from 1971 until he was fired by Southwest's board in 1978. At that point the board of directors tapped Kelleher.

At first Southwest was in the throes of life and death low-fare skirmishes with its giant competitors. Kelleher liked to recount how he came home one day "beat, tired, and worn out. So I'm just kind of sagging around the house when my youngest daughter comes up and asks what's wrong. I tell her, 'Well, Ruthie, it's these damned fare wars.' And she cuts me right off and says, 'Oh, Daddy, stop complaining. After all, you started 'em.'"[4]

For most small firms, competing on a price basis with much larger, well-endowed competitors is tantamount to disaster. The small firm simply cannot match the resources and staying power of such competitors. Yet Southwest somehow survived. Not only did it initiate the cut-throat price competition, but it achieved cost savings in its operation that the larger airlines could not. How long would the big carriers be content to maintain their money-losing operations and match the low prices of Southwest?

In its early years, Southwest faced other legal battles, such as Dallas and Love Field. The original airport, Love Field, is close to downtown Dallas, but it could not geographically expand although air traffic was increasing mightily. A major new facility, Dallas/Fort Worth International Airport, consequently replaced it in 1974. This airport boasted state-of-the-art facilities and enough room for foreseeable demand, but it had one major drawback: It was 30 minutes further from downtown Dallas. Southwest was able to avoid a forced move to the new airport and to continue at Love, but in 1978, competitors pressured Congress to bar flights from Love Field to anywhere outside Texas. Southwest was able to negotiate a compromise, now known as the Wright Amendment, that allowed flights from Love Field to the four states contiguous to Texas. In retrospect, the Wright

---

[3] Richard Woodbury, "Prince of Midair," *Time* (January 25, 1993), p. 55.

[4] Charles A. Jaffe, "Moving Fast by Standing Still," *Nation's Business* (October 1991), p. 58.

Amendment forced onto Southwest a key ingredient of its later success: the strategy of short flights.[5]

GROWTH

Southwest grew steadily but not spectacularly through the 1970s. It dominated the Texas market by appealing to passengers who valued price and frequent departures. Its one-way fare between Dallas and Houston, for example, was $59 in 1987 versus $79 for unrestricted coach flights on other airlines.

In the 1980s Southwest's annual passenger traffic count tripled. At the end of 1989, its operating costs per revenue mile—the industry's standard measure of cost-effectiveness—was just under 10 cents, about 5 cents per mile below the industry average.[6] Although revenues and profits were rising steadily, especially compared with the other airlines, Kelleher took a conservative approach to expansion, financing it mostly from internal funds rather than debt. *EQUITY, not DEBT*

Perhaps the caution stemmed from an ill-fated acquisition in 1986. Kelleher bought a failing long-haul carrier, Muse Air Corporation, for $68 million and renamed it TransStar. (This firm had been founded by Lamar Muse after he left Southwest.) But by 1987 TransStar was losing $2 million a month, and Kelleher shut down the operation. *A FAILURE*

By 1993 Southwest had spread to 34 cities in 15 states. It had 141 planes, and each made 11 trips per day. It used only fuel-thrifty 737s and still concentrated on flying large numbers of passengers on high-frequency, one-hour hops at bargain fares (average $58). Southwest shunned the hub-and-spoke systems of its larger rivals and took its passengers directly from city to city, often to smaller satellite airfields rather than congested major metropolitan fields. With rock-bottom prices and no amenities, it quickly dominated most new markets it entered. *SUCCESS FORMULA*

As an example of the company's impact on a new market, Southwest came to Cleveland, Ohio, in February 1992, and by the end of the year was offering 11 daily flights. In 1992 Cleveland Hopkins Airport posted record passenger levels, up 9.74 percent from 1991. "A lot of the gain was traffic that Southwest Airlines generated," noted John Osmond, air trade development manager.[7]

In some markets Southwest found itself growing much faster than projected, as competitors either folded or else abandoned directly competing routes. For example, in Phoenix, Arizona, America West Airlines cut back service in order to conserve cash after a Chapter 11 bankruptcy filing. Southwest picked up the slack, as it did in Chicago when Midway Airlines folded in November 1992. And in California, Southwest's arrival led several large competitors to abandon the Los Angeles–San Francisco route, unable to meet Southwest's $59 one-way fare. Before Southwest fares had been as high as $186 one way.[8]

---

[5] Bridget O'Brian, "Southwest Airlines Is a Rare Air Carrier: It Still Makes Money," *Wall Street Journal* (October 28, 1992), p. A7.

[6] Jaffe, *op. cit.*, p. 58.

[7] "Passenger Flights Set Hopkins Record," *Cleveland Plain Dealer* (January 30, 1993), p. 3D.

[8] O'Brian, *op. cit.*, p. A7.

Demand heats up!

Now cities that Southwest did not serve were petitioning for service. For example, Sacramento sent two county commissioners, the president of the chamber of commerce and the airport director, to Dallas to petition for service. Kelleher consented a few months later. In 1991 the company received 51 similar requests.[9]

A unique situation was developing. On many routes Southwest's fares were so low that they competed with buses and even with private cars. By 1991 Kelleher did not even see other airlines as his principal competitors: "We're competing with the automobile, not the airlines. We're pricing ourselves against Ford, Chrysler, GM, Toyota, and Nissan. The traffic is already there, but it's on the ground. We take it off the highway and put it on the airplane."[10]

Tables 17.1, 17.2, and 17.3 and Figure 17.1 depict various aspects of Southwest's growth and increasingly favorable competitive position. Although total revenues of Southwest were still far less than the four major airlines in the industry (five if we count Continental, which has emerged from two bankruptcies), its growth pattern presages a major presence, and its profitability is second to none.

Tapping California

The formidable competitive power of Southwest was perhaps never better epitomized than in its 1990 invasion of populous California. By 1992 it had become the

TABLE 17.1 Growth of Southwest Airlines: Various Operating Statistics, 1982–1991

Year	Operating Revenues (000,000)	Net Income (000,000)	Passengers Carried (000)	Passenger Load Factor
1991	$1,314	$26.9	22,670	61.1%
1990	1,187	47.1	19,831	60.7
1989	1,015	71.6	17,958	62.7
1988	880	58.0	14,877	57.7
1987	778	20.2	13,503	58.4
1986	769	50.0	13,638	58.8
1985	680	47.3	12,651	60.4
1984	535	49.7	10,698	58.5
1983	448	40.9	9,511	61.6
1982	331	34.0	7,966	61.6

Source: Company annual reports.

Commentary: Note the steady increase in revenues and in numbers of passengers carried. Although the net income and load factor statistics show no appreciable improvement, these statistics are still in the vanguard of an industry that has suffered badly in recent years. See Table 17.2 for a comparison of revenues and income with the major airlines.

[9] *Ibid.*

[10] Subrata N. Chakravarty, "Hit 'Em Hardest with the Mostest," *Forbes* (September 16, 1991), p. 49.

TABLE 17.2   Comparison of Southwest's Growth in Revenues and Net Income with Major Competitors, 1987–1991

	1991	1990	1989	1988	1987	% 5-yr gain
Operating Revenue Comparisons ($ millions)						
American	$9,309	$9,203	$8,670	$7,548	$6,369	46.0
Delta	8,268	7,697	7,780	6,684	5,638	46.6
United	7,850	7,946	7,463	7,006	6,500	20.8
Northwest	4,330	4,298	3,944	3,395	3,328	30.1
Southwest	1,314	1,187	1,015	860	778	68.9
Net Income Comparisons ($ millions)						
American	(253)	(40)	412	450	225	
Delta	(216)	(119)	467	286	201	
United	(175)	73	246	426	22	
Northwest	10	(27)	116	49	64	
Southwest	27	47	72	58	20	

Source: Company annual reports.

Commentary: Southwest's revenue gains over these five years outstripped those of its largest competitors. Although the percentage gains in profitability are hardly useful because of the erratic nature of airline profits during these years, Southwest stands out starkly as the only airline to be profitable each year.

second largest player, after United, with 23 percent of intrastate traffic. Southwest achieved this position by pushing fares down as much as 60 percent on some routes. The big carriers, which had tended to surrender the short-haul niche to Southwest in other markets, suddenly faced a real quandary in competing in this "Golden State." Some described Southwest as a "500-pound cockroach, too big to stamp out."[11]

The California market was indeed enticing. Some 8 million passengers each year fly between the five airports in metropolitan Los Angeles and the three in the

TABLE 17.3   Market Share Comparison of Southwest and Its Four Major Competitors, 1987–1991 (in $ billions)

	1991	1990	1989	1988	1987
Total Revenues:					
American, Delta, United, Northwest	$29,757	$29,144	$27,857	$24,633	$21,835
Southwest Revenues	$1,314	$1,187	$1,015	$860	$778
Percent of big four	4.4	4.1	3.6	3.5	3.6

Increase in Southwest's market share, 1987–1991: 22%

Source: Company annual reports.

[11] Wendy Zellner, "Striking Gold in the California Skies," *Business Week* (March 30, 1992), p. 48.

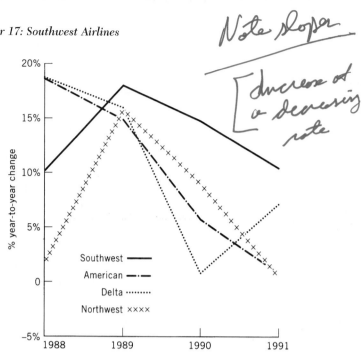

Figure 17.1 Year-to-year percentage changes in revenues, Southwest and three major competitors, 1988–1991.

San Francisco Bay area, this being the busiest corridor in the United States. It was also one of the more expensive, because the low fares of AirCal and Pacific Southwest Airlines had been eliminated when these two airlines were acquired by American and US Air.

Southwest charged into this situation with low fares and frequent flights. While airfares dropped, total air traffic soared 123 percent in the quarter Southwest entered the market. Competitors suffered: American lost nearly $80 million at its San Jose hub, and US Air lost money even though it cut service drastically. United, the market leader, quit flying the San Diego–Sacramento and Ontario–Oakland routes where Southwest had rapidly built up service. The quandary of the major airlines was compounded because this critical market fed traffic into the rest of their systems, especially the lucrative transcontinental and trans-Pacific routes. The competitors could hardly abdicate California to Southwest. American, for one, considered creating its own no-frills shuttle for certain routes.[12] Could anyone stop Southwest, with its formula of lowest prices and lowest costs and frequent schedules? And, oh yes, its good service and fun?

INGREDIENTS OF SUCCESS

Southwest's operation under Kelleher had numerous distinctive characteristics contributing to its success pattern and its seizing of a strategic window of opportunity,

[12] *Ibid.*

but the key factors appear to be cost containment, employee commitment, and conservative growth.

Cost Containment

Southwest had been the lowest cost carrier in its markets. Even when its larger competitors tried to match its cut-rate prices, they could not do so without incurring sizable losses, unlike Southwest. Nor did they seem able to trim their costs to match Southwest. For example, in the first quarter of 1991, Southwest's operating costs per available seat mile (i.e., the number of seats multiplied by the distance flown) were 15 percent lower than America West's costs, 29 percent lower than Delta's, 32 percent lower than United's, and 39 percent lower than US Air's.[13]

Many aspects of the operation contributed to these lower costs. Because all its planes were a single aircraft type, Boeing 737s, Southwest had low costs of training, maintenance, and inventory. And since a plane earns revenues only when flying, Southwest worked to achieve a faster turnaround time on the ground than any other airline. While competitors take more than an hour to load and unload passengers and to clean and service the planes, about 70 percent of Southwest's flights have a turnaround time of 15 minutes, and 10 percent have even pared the turnaround time to 10 minutes.

In areas of customer service, Southwest curbed costs as well. It offered peanuts and drinks, but no meals. Boarding passes were reusable plastic cards. Boarding time was saved because no seats were assigned. Southwest subscribed to no centralized reservation service. It did not even transfer baggage to other carriers; that was the passengers' responsibility. Admittedly, such customer service frugalities would be less acceptable on longer flights—and this helped to account for the difficulty competing airlines had in cutting their costs to match Southwest's. Still, if the price is right, many passengers might also opt for no frills on longer flights.

Employee Commitment

Kelleher was able to achieve an esprit de corps unmatched by other airlines despite the fact that Southwest employees were unionized. Unlike the adversarial relationship between unions and, for example, Frank Lorenzo at Eastern and Continental Airlines, Southwest was able to negotiate flexible work rules, with flight attendants and even pilots helping with plane cleanup. Employee productivity continued very high, permitting the airline to carry a lean staff. Kelleher resisted the inclination to hire extravagantly when times were good, necessitating layoffs during leaner times, a policy that contributed to employee feelings of security and loyalty. And the low-key attitude and sense of fun that Kelleher engendered helped, perhaps more than anyone could have foreseen. As Kelleher declared, "Fun is a stimulant to people. They enjoy their work more and work more productively."[14]

---

[13] Chakravarty, *op. cit.*, p. 50.
[14] *Ibid.*

Conservative Growth

Not the least of the ingredients of success was the conservative approach to growth that Kelleher maintained. He resisted the temptation to expand vigorously (for example, to seek to fly to Europe or get into head-to-head competition with larger airlines with long-distance routes). Even in the company's geographical expansion, conservatism prevailed. The philosophy of expansion was to do so only when enough resources could be committed to go into a city with 10 to 12 flights a day, rather than just 1 or 2. Kelleher called this "guerrilla warfare," concentrating efforts against stronger opponents in only a few areas rather than dissipating strength by trying to compete everywhere. *shows discipline*

The conservative approach to expansion resulted in a debt-to-equity ratio of 49 percent, the lowest in the industry. Southwest also had the airline industry's highest Standard & Poor's credit rating, A minus.

GALLOPING TOWARD THE NEW MILLENNIUM

In its May 2, 1994 edition, prestigious *Fortune* magazine devoted its cover story to Herb Kelleher and Southwest Airlines. It raised an intriguing question: "Is Herb Kelleher America's best CEO?" It called him a "peoplewise manager who wins where others can't."[15] The operational effectiveness of Southwest continued to surpass all rivals, for example, in such productivity ratios as cost per available seat mile, passengers per employee, and employees per aircraft. Only Southwest remained consistently profitable among the big airlines, by the end of 1998 having been profitable for 26 consecutive years. Operating revenue had grown to $4.2 billion (it was $1.3 billion in 1991—see Table 17.2), and net income was $433 million, up from $27 million in 1991. In 1999, Herb Kelleher was named CEO of the Year by *Chief Executive* magazine.

Geographical Expansion

Late in October 1996, Southwest launched a carefully planned battle for East Coast passengers that would drive down air fares and pressure competitors to back away from some lucrative markets. It chose Providence, Rhode Island, just 60 miles from Boston's Logan Airport, thus tapping the Boston–Washington corridor. The Providence airport escaped the congested New York and Boston air-traffic-control areas, and from the Boston suburbs was hardly a longer trip than to Logan Airport. Experience had shown that air travelers would drive a considerable distance to fly with Southwest's cheaper fares.

As Southwest entered new markets, most competitors refused any longer to try to compete pricewise: They simply could not cut costs enough to compete. Their alternative then was either to pull out of these short-haul markets, or be content to let Southwest have its market share while they tried to hold onto other customers by stressing first-class seating, frequent-flyer programs, and other in-flight amenities.

---

[15] Kenneth Labich, "Is Herb Kelleher America's Best CEO?," *Fortune* (May 2, 1994), pp. 45–52.

In April 1997, Southwest quietly entered the transcontinental market. From its major connecting point of Nashville, Tennessee, it began nonstops both to Oakland, California and to Los Angeles. With Nashville's direct connections with Chicago, Detroit, Cleveland, Providence, and Baltimore–Washington, as well as points south, this afforded *one-stop,* coast-to-coast service, with fares about half as much as the other major airlines.

Two other significant moves were announced in late 1998. One was an experiment. On Thanksgiving Day, a Southwest 737–700 flew *nonstop* from Oakland, California to the Baltimore–Washington Airport, and back again. It provided its customary no-frills service, but a $99 one-way fare, the lowest in the business. The test *Text* was designed to see how pilots, flight attendants, and passengers would feel about spending five hours on a 737, with only peanuts and drinks served in-flight. The older 737s lacked the fuel capacity to fly coast-to-coast nonstop, but with Boeing's new 737–700 series this was no problem. The Thanksgiving Day test was a precursor of more nonstop flights as Southwest had firm orders for 129 of the new planes to be delivered over the next seven years. This would enable it to compete with the major carriers on their moneymaking transcontinental flights.

In November 1998, plans were also announced for starting service to MacArthur Airport at Islip, Long Island, which would enable Southwest to tap into the New York City market. By the end of the old millennium, Southwest had added 10 new nonstop flights, three one-stop flights, and several special Saturday-only nonstop flights, all of these nonstops with introductory fares of $99 or less. It was flying to 55 cities in 29 states.

Manchester N.H.

WHAT CAN BE LEARNED?

The power of low prices and simplicity of operation. If a firm can maintain prices below those of its competitors, and do so profitably and without sacrificing expected quality of service, then it has a powerful advantage. We noted in Chapter 14 the great advantage Vanguard had with its lowest expense ratio in the mutual fund industry. Here, Southwest also achieved this with its simplicity of operation and no-frills, but dependable service. Competition on the basis of price is seldom used in most mature industries (although the airline industry has been an exception), primarily because competitors can quickly match prices with no lasting advantage to anyone. As profits are destroyed, only customers benefit, and then only in the short run before the industry realizes the futility of price competition. (With new and rapidly changing industries, price competition is effective as productivity and technology improve and marginal competitors are driven from the market.)

The effectiveness of the cost controls of Southwest, however, shows the true competitive importance of low prices. Customers love the lowest price if the provider does not sacrifice too much quality, comfort, and service. While there was some sacrifice of service and amenities with Southwest, most customers found this acceptable because of the short-haul situation; friendly, dependable and reasonable service was still maintained. Apparently the same no-frills service was found acceptable on longer flights too, as Southwest expanded these to meet demand.

An intriguing factor regarding the relationship of customer satisfaction and price is explored in the following Information Box.

The power of a niche strategy. Directing efforts toward a particular customer segment or niche can provide a powerful competitive advantage. Especially is this true if no competitor is catering directly to such a niche, and if it is fairly sizable. Such an untapped niche then becomes a strategic window of opportunity.

Kelleher revealed the niche strategy of Southwest: while other airlines set up hub-and-spoke systems in which passengers are shunted to a few major hubs from which they are transferred to other planes going to their destination, "we wound up with a unique market niche: we are the world's only short-haul, high-frequency, low-fare, point-to-point carrier.... We wound up with a market segment that is peculiarly ours, and everything about the airline has been adapted to serving that market segment in the most efficient and economical way possible."[17] The follow-

---

INFORMATION BOX

THE KEY TO CUSTOMER SATISFACTION: MEETING CUSTOMER EXPECTATIONS

Southwest consistently earns high ratings for its customer satisfaction, higher than those of its giant competitors. Yet, these major airlines all offer more than Southwest's food service; they also provide advance seat assignments, in-flight entertainment on longer flights, the opportunity to upgrade, and a comprehensive frequent-flyer program. Yet Southwest gets the highest points for customer satisfaction.

Could something else be involved here?

Let's call it *expectations.* If a customer has high expectations, perhaps because of a high price and/or the advertising promising high-quality, luxury accommodations, dependable service or whatever, then if product or service does not live up to these expectations, customer satisfaction dives. Turning to the airlines, customers are not disappointed in the service of Southwest because they don't expect luxury; Southwest does not advertise this. They expect no frills, but pleasant and courteous treatment by employees, dependable and safe flights, and the low price. On the other hand, expectations are higher for the bigger carriers with their higher prices. This is well and good for first- or business-class service. But for the many who fly coach...?[16]

Do you think there is a point where a low-price/no-frills strategy would be detrimental to customer satisfaction? What might it depend on?

---

[16] This idea of expectations affecting customer satisfaction was suggested by Ed Perkins for Tribune Media Services and reported in "Hotels Must Live Up to Promises," *Cleveland Plain Dealer* (November 1, 1998), p. 11K.

---

[17] Jaffe, p. 58.

ing Information Box discusses the criteria needed for a successful niche or segmentation strategy.

Southwest has been unrelenting in its defense of its niche. While others have tried to copy, none have fully duplicated it. Southwest remains the nation's only high-frequency, short-distance, low-fare airline. As an example of its virtually unassailable position, Southwest accounts for more than two-thirds of the passengers flying within Texas, and Texas is the second-largest market outside the West Coast. When Southwest invaded California, some San José residents

---

INFORMATION BOX

CRITERIA FOR SELECTING NICHES OR SEGMENTS

In deciding what specific niches to seek, these criteria should be considered:

1. **Identifiability.** Is the particular niche identifiable so that those persons who constitute it can be isolated and recognized? It was not difficult to identify the short-route travelers, and while their numbers may not have been readily estimated initially, this was soon to change as demand burgeoned for Southwest's short-haul services.

2. **Size.** The segment must be of sufficient size to be worth the efforts to tap. And again, the size factor proved to be significant, with Southwest soon offering 83 flights daily between Dallas and Houston.

3. **Accessibility.** For a niche strategy to be practical, the segment(s) chosen must be such that promotional media can be used to reach it without much wasted coverage. Southwest had little difficulty in reaching its target market through billboards, newspapers, and other media.

4. **Growth potential.** A niche is more attractive if it shows some growth characteristics. The growth potential of short-haul flyers proved to be considerably greater than that for airline customers in general. Partly the growth reflected customers won from other higher cost and less convenient airlines. And some of the emerging growth reflected customers choice of giving up their cars to take a flight that was almost as economical and certainly more comfortable.

5. **Absence of vulnerability to competition.** Competition, both present and potential, must certainly be considered in making specific niche decisions. By quickly becoming the low-cost operator in its early routes, and gradually expanding without diluting its cost advantage, Southwest became virtually unassailable in its niche. The bigger airlines, with their greater overhead and less-flexible operations, could not match Southwest prices without going deeply into the red. And the more Southwest became entrenched in its markets, the more difficult it was to pry it loose.

Assume you are to give a lecture to your class on the desirability of a niche strategy, and you cite Southwest as a classic example. But suppose a classmate asks, "If a niche strategy is so great, why didn't the other airlines practice it?" How do you respond?

drove an hour north to board Southwest's Oakland flights, skipping the local airport where American had a hub. In Georgia, so many people were bypassing Delta's huge hub in Atlanta and driving 150 miles to Birmingham, Alabama to fly Southwest that an entrepreneur started a van service between the two airports.[18]

Unlike many firms, Southwest did not permit success to dislodge its niche strategy. It has not attempted to fly to Europe or South America, or match the big carriers in offering amenities in coast-to-coast flights. In curbing such temptations it has not had to sacrifice growth potential: Its strategy still has many U.S. cities to embrace.

Seek dedicate employees. Stimulating employees to move beyond their individual concerns to a higher level of performance, a true team approach, was by no means the least of Kelleher's accomplishments. Such esprit de corps enabled planes to be turned around in 15 minutes instead of the hour or more of competitors; it brought a dedication to service far beyond what could ever have been expected of a bare-bones, cut-price operation; it brought a contagious excitement to the job obvious to customers and employees alike.

The nurturing of such dedicated employees was not due solely to Kelleher's extraverted, zany, and down-home personality—although this certainly helped. So did a legendary ability to remember employee names and company parties, and a sincere interest in the employees. Flying in the face of conventional wisdom, which says an adversarial relationship between management and labor is inevitable with the presence of a union, Southwest achieved its great teamwork while being 90 percent unionized. It helped that Kelleher started the first profit-sharing plan in the U.S. airline industry in 1974. Now, employees own 13 percent of the company stock.

Whether such worker dedication can pass the test of time, and the test of increasing size, is uncertain. Kelleher himself was 68 in 1999. A successor will be a different personality. Yet here is a model for an organization growing to large size and still maintaining employee commitment.

The attainment of dedicated employees is partly a product of the firm itself, and how it is growing. A rapidly growing firm—especially when such growth starts from humble beginnings, with the firm as an underdog—promotes a contagious excitement. Opportunities and advancements depend on growth. Where employees can acquire stock in the company and see the value of their shares rising, potential financial rewards seem almost infinite. Success tends to creat a momentum that generates continued success.

CONSIDER

Can you identify additional learning insights that could be applicable to other firms in other situations?

---

[18] O'Brian, "Rare Air Carrier," p. A7.

QUESTIONS

1. In what ways might airline customers be segmented? Which segments or niches would you consider to be Southwest's prime targets? Which segments probably would not be?

2. Do you think the employee dedication to Southwest will quickly fade when Kelleher leaves? Why or why not?

3. Discuss the pros and cons for expansion of Southwest beyond short hauls. Which arguments do you see as most compelling?

4. Evaluate the effectiveness of Southwest's unions.

5. On August 18, 1993, a fare war erupted. To initiate its new service between Cleveland and Baltimore, Southwest announced a $49 fare (a sizable reduction from the then-standard rate of $300). Its rivals, Continental and USAir, retaliated. Before long the price was $19, not much more than the tank of gas it would take to drive between the two cities—and the airlines also supplied a free soft-drink. Evaluate the implications of such a price war for the three airlines.

6. A price cut is the most easily matched strategy, and it usually provides no lasting advantage to any competitor. Identify the circumstances when you see it as desirable to initiate a price cut and a potential price war.

7. Do you think it likely that Southwest's position will continue to remain unassailable by competitors? Why or why not?

8. In Chapter 9 we described another airline, Continental, and its employee-oriented leader, Gordon Bethune. Compare Bethune and Kelleher on as many traits as you can. Which do you think is the greater leader, and why?

HANDS-ON EXERCISES

1. Herb Kelleher has just retired, and you are his successor. Unfortunately, your personality is far different from his. You are an introvert and far from flamboyant, and your memory for names is not good. What is your course of action to try to preserve the great employee dedication of the Kelleher era? How successful do you think you will be? Did the board make a mistake in choosing you?

2. Herb Kelleher has not retired. He is going to continue beyond age 70. Somehow, his appetite for growth has increased as he has grown older, and he has charged you with developing plans for expanding into longer hauls—maybe to South and Central America, maybe even to Europe. Be as specific as you can in developing such expansion plans.

   Kelleher has also asked for your evaluation of these plans. Be as persuasive as you can in presenting this evaluation.

3. How would you personally feel about a 5-hour transcontinental flight with only a few peanuts, and no other food or movies? Would you be willing to pay quite a bit more to have more amenities?

TEAM DEBATE EXERCISE

The Thanksgiving Day nonstop transcontinental experiment went fairly well, although customers and even flight attendants expressed some concern about the long 5-hour flight with no food and no entertainment. No one complained about the price.

Debate the two alternatives of going ahead slowly with the transcontinental plan with no frills, or adding a few amenities, such as some food, reading material, or whatever else might make the flight less tedious. You might even want to debate a third alternative of dropping this idea entirely at this time.

INVITATION TO RESEARCH

What is Southwest's current situation? What is its market share in the airline industry? Is it still maintaining a high growth rate? Has the decision been made to expand the nonstop transcontinental service, and have any changes been made in the no-frills service for this? How about international? Has Kelleher retired, and if so, what sort of person has succeeded him?

CONTROL WEAKNESSES AND STRENGTHS

CHAPTER EIGHTEEN

United Way: Where Were the Controls?

*T*he United Way, the preeminent charitable organization in the United States, celebrated its 100-year anniversary in 1987. It had evolved from local community chests, and its strategy for fund-raising had proven highly effective: funding local charities through payroll deductions. The good it did seemed unassailable.

Abruptly in 1992, the persona of honesty and integrity that United Way had built was jeopardized by investigative reporters' revelations of free-spending practices and other questionable deeds of its greatest builder and president, William Aramony. A major point of public concern was Aramony's salary and uncontrolled perks in a lifestyle that seemed inappropriate for the head of a charitable organization that depended mostly on contributions from working people.

In 1993 another paragon of not-for-profit social enhancement organizations came under fire: the venerable Girl Scouts. Contentions were that multimillion-dollar profits of Girl Scout cookies were found to be used mostly to support bureaucracy instead of the Girl Scout troops that provided the labor in the first place. (This is discussed in an Information Box later in the chapter.)

We are left to question the operations and lack of controls of our major charitable and not-for-profit entities. Business firms have to report to shareholders and creditors, but not-for-profit organizations have been permitted to operate largely without the checks and balances that characterize most other organizations.

THE STATURE AND ACCOMPLISHMENTS OF THE UNITED WAY

For its 100th anniversary, then-President Ronald Reagan summed up what the United Way stood for:

December 10, 1986

United Way Centennial, 1887–1987
By The President Of The United States Of America
A Proclamation

Since earliest times, we Americans have joined together to help each other and to strengthen our communities. Our deep-roots spirit of caring, of neighbor helping neighbor, has become an American trademark—and an American way of life. Over the years, our generous and inventive people have created an ingenious network of voluntary organizations to help give help where help is needed.

United Way gives that help very well indeed, and truly exemplifies our spirit of voluntarism. United Way has been a helping force in America right from the first community-wide fund raising campaign in Denver, Colorado, in 1887. Today, more than 2,200 local United Ways across the land raise funds for more than 37,000 voluntary groups that assist millions of people.

The United Way of caring allows volunteers from all walks of life to effectively meet critical needs and solve community problems. At the centennial of the founding of this indispensable voluntary group, it is most fitting that we Americans recognize and commend all the good United Way has done and continues to do.

The Congress, by Public Law 99–612, has expressed gratitude to United Way, congratulated it, and applauded and encouraged its fine work and its goals.

NOW, THEREFORE, I RONALD REAGAN, President of the United States of America, by virtue of the authority vested in me by the Constitution and laws of the United States, do hereby proclaim heartfelt thanks to a century of Americans who have shaped and supported United Way, and encourage the continuation of its efforts.

IN WITNESS WHEREOF, I have hereunto set my hand this tenth day of December, in the year of our Lord nineteen hundred and eighty-six, and of the Independence of the United States of America the two hundred and eleventh.

Ronald Reagan

Organizing the United Way as the umbrella charity to fund other local charities through payroll deduction established an effective means of fund-raising. It became the recipient of 90 percent of all charitable donations. Employers sometimes used extreme pressure to achieve 100 percent participation of employees, which led to organizational bonuses. The United Way achieved further cooperation of business organizations by involving their executives as leaders of annual campaigns, amid widespread publicity. It would consequently cause such an executive acute loss of face if his or her own organization did not go "over the top" in meeting campaign goals. A local United Way executive admitted that "if participation is 100 percent, it means someone has been coerced."[1]

For many years, outside of some tight-lipped gripes of corporate employees, the organization moved smoothly along, with local contributions generally increasing every year and with the needs for charitable contributions invariably increasing even faster.

The national organization, United Way of America (UWA), is a separate corporation and has no direct control over the approximately 2,200 local United Way offices. Most of the locals voluntarily contributed one cent on the dollar of all funds they collected, however, and in return, the national organization provided training and promoted local United Way agencies through advertising and other marketing efforts.

Much of the success of the United Way movement in becoming the largest and most respected charity in the United States was due to the 22 years of William Aramony's leadership of the national organization. When he first took over, the United Ways were not operating under a common name. He built a nationwide network of agencies, all operating under the same name and using the same logo of outstretched hands, which became nationally recognized as the symbol of charitable giving. Unfortunately in 1992 an exposé of Aramony's lavish lifestyle and questionable dealings led to his downfall and burdened local United Ways with serious difficulties in fund-raising.

WILLIAM ARAMONY

During Aramony's tenure United Way contributions increased from $787 million in 1970 to $3 billion in 1990. Aramony built up the headquarters staff to 275 employees and increased his headquarters budget from less than $3 million to $29 million in 1991. Of this amount, $24 million came from the local United Ways, with the rest coming from corporate grants, investment income, and consulting.[2] Figure 18.1 shows the organizational chart as of 1987.

Aramony moved comfortably among the most influential people in our society. He attracted a prestigious board of governors, including many top executives from America's largest corporations, but only 3 of the 37 came from not-for-profit organizations. The board was chaired by John Akers, chairman and CEO of IBM. Other board members included Edward A. Brennan, CEO of Sears; James D. Robinson III, CEO of American Express; and Paul J. Tagliabue, commissioner of the National Football League. The presence of such top executives on the board brought United Way prestige and spurred contributions from some of the largest and most visible organizations in the United States.

[1] Susan Garland, "Keeping a Sharper Eye on Those Who Pass the Hat," *Business Week* (March 16, 1992), p. 39.

[2] Charles E. Shepard, "Perks, Privileges and Power in a Nonprofit World," *Washington Post* (February 16, 1992), p. A38.

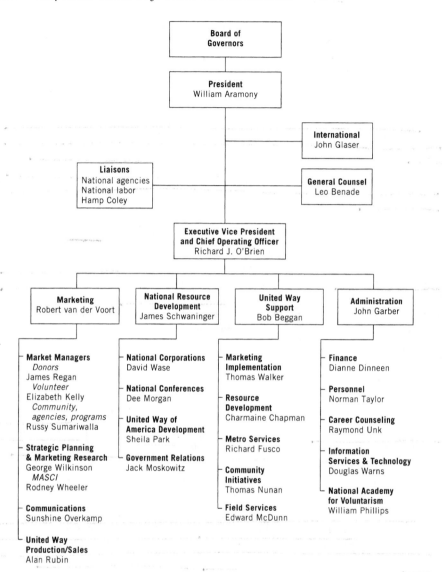

Figure 18.1

Aramony was the highest paid executive in the charity field. In 1992 his compensation package was $463,000, nearly double that of the next highest paid executive in the industry, Dudley H. Hafner of the American Heart Association.[3] The board fully supported Aramony, regularly giving him 6 percent annual raises.[4]

[3] Shepard, "Perks, Privileges, and Power," A38; and Charles E. Shepard, "United Way of America President Is Urged to Resign," *Washington Post* (February 27, 1992), p. A1.

[4] Joseph Finder, "Charity Case," *New Republic* (May 4, 1992), p. 11.

Investigative Disclosures *Reporters*

The *Washington Post* began investigating Aramony's tenure as president of United Way of America in 1991, raising questions about his high salary, travel habits, possible cronyism, and dubious relations with five spin-off companies. In February 1992 it released the following information on Aramony's expense charges.[5]

- Aramony had charged $92,265 in limousine expenses to the charity during the previous five years.
- He had charged $40,762 on airfare for the supersonic Concorde.
- He had charged more than $72,000 on international airfare that included first-class seats for himself, his wife, and others.
- He had charged thousands more for personal trips, gifts, and luxuries.
- He had made 29 trips to Las Vegas between 1988 and 1991.
- He had expensed 49 journeys to Gainesville, Florida, the home of his daughter and a woman with whom he had had a relationship.
- He had allegedly approved a $2 million loan to a firm run by his chief financial officer.
- He had approved the diversion of donors' money to questionable spin-off organizations run by long-time aides and provided benefits to family members as well.
- He had passed tens of thousands of dollars in consulting contracts from the UWA to friends and associates.

United Way of America's corporate policy prohibited the hiring of family members within the actual organization, but Aramony skirted the direct violation by hiring friends and relatives as consultants and within the spin-off companies. He paid hundreds of thousands of dollars in consulting fees, for example, to two aides in vaguely documented and even undocumented business transactions.

The use of spin-off companies provided flexible maneuvering. One of the spin-off companies Aramony created to provide travel and bulk purchasing for United Way chapters purchased a $430,000 condominium in Manhattan and a $125,000 apartment in Coral Gables, Florida, for Aramony's use. Another of the spin-off companies hired Aramony's son, Robert Aramony, as its president. Loans and money transfers between the spin-off companies and the national organization raised questions. No records showed that the board of directors had been given the opportunity to approve such loans and transfers.[6]

[5] Shepard, "Perks, Privileges, and Power"; Shepard, "President Is Urged to Resign"; Kathleen Telstch, "United Way Awaits Inquiry on its President's Practices," *New York Times* (February 24, 1992), p. A12 (L); Charles E. Shepard, "United Way Report Criticizes Ex-Leader's Lifestyle," *Washington Post* (April 4, 1992), p. A1.

[6] Shepard, "Perks, Privileges, and Power," p. A38.

CONSEQUENCES

When the information about Aramony's salary and expenses became public, reaction was severe. Stanley C. Gault, chairman of Goodyear Tire & Rubber Co., asked, "Where was the board? The outside auditors?"[7] Robert O. Bothwell, executive director of the National Committee for Responsive Philanthropy, said, "I think it is obscene that he is making that kind of salary and asking people who are making $10,000 a year to give 5 percent of their income."[8] At this point let us examine the issue of executive compensation. Are many executives overpaid? The following Issue Box addresses this controversial topic.

ISSUE BOX

EXECUTIVE COMPENSATION: IS IT TOO MUCH?

A controversy is mounting over multimillion-dollar annual compensations of corporate executives. In 1992, for example, the average annual pay of CEOs was $3,842,247; the 20 highest salaries ranged from over $11 million to a mind-boggling $127 million (for Thomas F. Frist, Jr., of Hospital Corporation of America).[9]

Activist shareholders, including some large mutual and pension funds, began protesting pay practices, especially for top executives of firms that were not doing well financially. New disclosure rules imposed in 1993 by the Securities and Exchange Commission (SEC) spotlighted questionable executive pay practices. In the past, complacent board members, themselves well paid and often closely aligned with the top executives of the organization, condoned liberal compensations, but this may be changing. The major argument supporting high executive compensations is that compared with salaries of some entertainers and athletes, they are modest. And are not their responsibilities far greater than those of any entertainer or athlete?

In light of the for-profit executive compensations, Aramony's salary was modest. And results were on his side: He made $369,000 in basic salary while raising $3 billion; Lee Iacocca, on the other hand, made $3 million while Chrysler lost $795 million. Where is the justice?

Undoubtedly Aramony, as head of a large for-profit corporation could have earned several zeros more in compensation and perks, with no raised eyebrows. But is the situation different for a not-for-profit organization, when revenues are derived from donations of millions of people of modest means? This is a real controversy. On one side, shouldn't a charity be willing to pay for the professional competence to run the organization as effectively as possible? But on the other side, how do revelations of high compensation affect the public image and fund-raising ability of such not-for-profit organizations?

What is your position regarding Aramony's compensation and perks, relative to the many times greater compensation of for-profit executives?

---

[7] Susan Garland, p. 39.

[8] Felicity Barringer, "United Way Head Is Forced Out in a Furor Over His Lavish Style," *New York Times* (February 28, 1992), p. A1.

[9] John A. Byrne, "Executive Pay: The Party Ain't Over Yet," *Business Week* (April 26, 1993), pp. 56–64.

②As a major consequence of the scandal, some United Way locals withheld their funds, at least pending a thorough investigation of the allegations. John Akers, chairman of the board, noted that by March 7, 1992, dues payments were running 20 percent behind the previous year, saying "I don't think this process that the United Way of America is going through, or Mr. Aramony is going through, is a process that's bestowing a lot of honor."[10]

In addition to the decrease in dues payments, UWA was in danger of having its ③ not-for-profit status revoked by the Internal Revenue Service due to the relationship of loans made to the spin-off companies. For example, it loaned $2 million to a spin-off corporation of which the chief financial officer of UWA was also a director, which is a violation of not-for-profit corporate law. UWA also guaranteed a bank loan taken out by one of the spin-offs, another violation of not-for-profit corporate law.[11]

The adverse publicity benefited competing charities, such as Earth Share, an envi-④ ronmental group. United Way, at one time the only major organization to receive contributions through payroll deductions, now found itself losing donations to other charities able to garner contributions in the same manner. All the building that William Aramony had done for the United Way as the primary player in the American charitable industry was now in danger of disintegration because of his uncontrolled excesses.

On February 28, amid mounting pressure from local chapters threatening to withhold their annual dues, Aramony resigned. In August 1992 the United Way board of directors hired Elaine Chao, the Peace Corps director, to replace Aramony.

Elaine Chao

Chao's story is one of great achievement for one aged only 39. She is the oldest of six daughters in a family that came to California from Taiwan when Elaine was 8 years old. She did not know a word of English. The family prospered through hard work. "Despite the difficulties ... we had tremendous optimism in the basic goodness of this country, that people are decent here, that we would be given a fair opportunity to demonstrate our abilities," she told an interviewer.[12] Chao's parents instilled in their six daughters the conviction that they could do anything they set their minds to, and all the daughters went to prestigious universities.

Elaine Chao earned an economics degree from Mount Holyoke College in 1975, then went on for a Harvard MBA. She was a White House fellow, an international banker, chair of the Federal Maritime Commission, deputy secretary of the U.S. Transportation Department, and director of the Peace Corps before accepting the presidency of the United Way of America.

Her salary is $195,000, less than one-half of Aramony's. She has cut budgets and staffs: no transatlantic flights on the Concorde, no limousine service, no plush condominiums. The board of governors has been expanded to include more local

---

[10] Felicity Barringer, "United Way Head Tries to Restore Trust," *New York Times* (March 7, 1992), p. 8L.

[11] Shepard, "Perks, Privileges, and Power"; Charles E. Shepard, "United Way Chief Says He Will Retire," *Washington Post* (February 28, 1992), p. A1.

[12] "United Way Chief Dedicated," *Cleveland Plain Dealer* (March 28, 1993), p. 24-A.

representatives and has established committees on ethics and finance. Still, Chao has no illusions about her job: "Trust and confidence once damaged will take a great deal of effort and time to heal."[13]

Local United Way's Concerns

In April 1993, for the second time in a year, United Way of Greater Lorain County (Ohio) withdrew from the United Way of America. The board of the local chapter was still concerned about the financial stability and accountability of the national agency. In particular, it was concerned about Aramony's retirement settlement. The national board and Aramony were negotiating a significant "golden parachute" retirement package in the neighborhood of $4 million.

News of this triggered the Lorain County board's decision to again withdraw from UWA. There were other reasons as well for this decision. The national agency was falling far short of its projected budget because only 890 of the 1,400 affiliates that had paid membership dues two years before were still paying. Roy Church, president of the Lorain agency, explained the board's decision: "Since February ... it has become clear that United Way of America's financial stability and ability to assist locals has been put in question. The benefit of being a United Way of America member isn't there at this time for Lorain's United Way."[14]

Elaine Chao's task of resurrecting United Way of America would not be easy.

See the following Information Box for a discussion of a related example of non-profit callousness to its parties.

ANALYSIS

Executives' lack of accountability of expenditures was a major contributor to the UWA's problems. This lack of controls encouraged questionable practices, since there was no one to approve or disapprove, and it made executives, especially Aramony, vulnerable to great shock and criticism when their practices became known. The fact that voluntary donations were the principal source of revenues made the lack of accountability all the more scandalous.

Where controls and financial reporting are deficient, and where a system of checks and balances is lacking, two consequences tend to prevail, neither one desirable or totally acceptable. The worst-case scenario is outright "white-collar theft." when unscrupulous people find it an opportunity for personal gain. The absence of sufficient controls and accountability can make even normally honest persons succumb to some temptation. Second, insufficient controls tend to promote a mindset of arrogance and allow people to play fast-and-loose with the system. Aramony seemed to fall into this category with his spending extravagances, cronyism, and other conflict-of-interest activities. (Some of the Girl Scout Councils, too, perceived

---

[13]*Ibid.*

[14] Karen Henderson, "Lorain Agency Cuts Ties with National United Way," *Cleveland Plain Dealer* (April 16, 1993), p. 7C.

INFORMATION BOX

ANOTHER CONTROVERSTY: GIRL SCOUTS AND THEIR COOKIES

The main funding source for the nation's 2.6 million Girl Scouts is the annual cookie sale, estimated to generate $400 million in revenue.[15] The practice goes back some 70 years, although in the 1920s the girls sold homemade cookies. Now each regional council negotiates with one of two bakeries that produce the cookies, sets the price per box, which ranges from $2 to $3, and divides the proceeds as it sees fit. Typically, the Girl Scout troops get 10 to 15 percent, the council takes more than 50 percent, and the rest goes to the manufacturer.

Criticisms have emerged and received public attention regarding the dictatorial handling of these funds by the councils. There are 332 regional councils in the United States, each having an office and a paid staff overseen by a volunteer board. Some councils have dozens of employees, with most serving mainly as policy enforcers and supervisors. At the troop level, volunteer leaders, often women with daughters in the troop, guide their units in the true tradition of scouting, giving their time tirelessly. For the cookie drives, the girls are an unpaid sales force—child labor, as critics assail—that supports a huge bureaucratic structure. Little of the cookie revenue comes back to the local troops.

The bureaucracy does not tolerate dissent well. The *Wall Street Journal* cites the case of a West Haven, Connecticut, troop leader, Beth Denton, who protested both the way the Connecticut Trails council apportioned revenue and the $1.6 million in salaries and benefits paid to 42 council employees. After she complained to the state attorney general, the council dismissed her as leader.[16]

Admittedly, the individual salaries in the bureaucracy were not high by corporate standards or even by not-for-profit standards. Council administrators' salaries ranged up to about $90,000. Perhaps more disturbing was that volunteer leaders saw no annual financial statements of their council's expenditures and activities.[17]

Evaluate the council's position that annual financial records of their council's activities should be entirely confidential to full-time staff.

---

[15] Ellen Graham, "Sprawling Bureaucracy Eats Up Most Profits of Girl Scout Cookies," *Wall Street Journal* (May 13, 1992), p. A1.

[16] *Ibid.*, p. A4.

[17] *Ibid.*

themselves as aloof from the dedicated volunteer troop leaders, tolerating no criticism or questioning, dictating and enforcing all policies without consultation or participation, and preventing scrutiny of their own operation.)

The UWA theoretically had an overseer: the boards, similar to the board of directors of business corporations. But when such boards act as rubber stamps, where they are closely in the camp of the chief executives, they are not really exercising control.

Board Failure

This appeared to be the case with United Way of America during the "reign" of Aramony; similarly, as discussed in the preceding box, with the regional councils of the Girl Scouts, many of the volunteer boards appear to have exercised little or no control.

Certainly a board's failure to fulfill its responsibility is not unique to not-for-profits. Corporate boards have often been notorious for promoting the interests of the incumbent executives. Although this is changing today, it still prevails. See the following Issue Box for a discussion of the role of boards of directors.

ISSUE BOX

WHAT SHOULD BE THE ROLE OF THE BOARD OF DIRECTORS?

In the past, most boards of directors have tended to be closely allied with top executives and even composed mostly of corporate officials. In some organizations today this is changing, mostly in response to critics concerned about board tendencies to support the status quo and perpetuate the "establishment."

More and more, opinion is shifting to the idea that boards must assume an active role:

> The board can no longer play a passive role in corporate governance. Today, more than ever, the board must assume an activist role—a role that is protective of shareholder rights, sensitive to communities in which the company operates, responsive to the needs of company vendors and customers, and fair to its employees.[18]

Incentives for more active boards have been the increasing risks of liability for board decisions as well as liability insurance costs. Although the board of directors has long been seen as responsible for establishing corporate objectives, developing broad policies, and selecting top executives, these duties are no longer viewed as sufficient. Boards must also review management's performance—acting as a control mechanism—to ensure that the company is well run and that stockholders' interests are furthered. And, today, they must ensure that society's best interests are not disregarded.

But the issue remains: To whom should the board owe its greatest allegiance—the entrenched bureaucracy or the external publics? Without having board members representative of the many special interests affected by the organization, the inclination is to support the interests of the establishment.

Do you think a more representative and activist board will prevent a similar scenario from damaging United Way in the future? Why or why not?

---

[18] Lester B. Korn and Richard M. Ferry, *Board of Directors Thirteenth Annual Study* (New York: Korn/Ferry International, February 1986), pp. 1–2.

UPDATE

William Aramony was convicted of defrauding the United Way out of $1 million. He was sentenced to seven years in prison for using the charity's money to finance a lavish lifestyle.

Despite this, a federal judge ruled in late 1998 that the charity must pay its former president more than $2 million in retirement benefits. "A felon, no matter how despised, does not lose his right to enforce a contract," U.S. District Judge Shira Scheindlin in New York ruled.[19]

WHAT CAN BE LEARNED?

Beware the arrogant mindset. A leader's attitude that he or she is superior to subordinates and even to concerned outsiders is a formula for disaster, both for an organization and even for a society. Such an attitude promotes dictatorship, intolerance of contrary opinions, and an attitude that "we need answer to no one." We have seen the consequences with William Aramony: moving over the edge of what is deemed by most as acceptable and ethical conduct, assuming the role of the final authority who brooks no questions or criticisms. The absence of real or imagined controls or reviews seems to bring out the worst in people. We seem to need periodic scrutiny to avoid falling into the trap of arrogant decision making devoid of responsiveness to other concerns. The Girl Scout bureaucracy's dealings with its volunteers suggest the inclination toward arrogance and dictatorship in the absence of sufficient real controls.

Checks and balances—controls—are even more important in not-for-profit and governmental bodies than in corporate entities. For-profit organizations have "bottom-line" performance (i.e., profit and loss performance) as the ultimate control and standard. Not-for-profit and governmental organizations do not have this control, so they have no ultimate measure of their effectiveness.

Consequently, not-for-profit organizations should be subject to the utmost scrutiny of objective outsiders. Otherwise, abuses seem to be encouraged and perpetuated. Often these not-for-profit organizations are sheltered from competition, which usually also demands greater efficiency. Thus without objective and energetic controls, not-for-profit organizations have a tendency to be out of hand, to be run as little dynasties unencumbered by the constraints that face most businesses. Fortunately, investigative reporting and increasing litigation by allegedly abused parties today act as the needed controls for such organizations. In view of the revelations of investigative reporters, we are left to wonder how many other abusive and reprehensible activities have not as yet been detected.

Nonprofits are particularly vulnerable to bad press. Nonprofits depend on donations for the bulk of their revenues. Unlike most businesses, they depend on people to give without receiving anything tangible in return. Consequently, any

---

[19] Reported in *Cleveland Plain Dealer* (October 25, 1998), p. 24-A.

hint or semblance of waste or misdealings with donated money can quickly dry up contributions or cause them to be shunted to other charities.

With governmental bodies, of course, their perpetuation is hardly at stake with bad publicity, but the administrators can be recalled, impeached, or not reelected with enough adverse publicity.

CONSIDER *• Ethics Audits • Open Book Mgmt.*

Can you add to these learning insights?

QUESTIONS

1. How do you feel, as a potential or actual giver to United Way campaigns, about the "high living" of Aramony? Would these allegations affect your gift giving? Why or why not?

2. What prescriptions do you have for thwarting arrogance in nonprofit and/or governmental organizations? Be as specific as you can, and support your recommendations.

3. How do you personally feel about the coercion that some organizations exert for their employees to contribute substantially to the United Way? What implications, if any, do you see as emerging from your attitudes about this?

4. Given the information supplied about the dictatorial relationships between Girl Scout councils and the local volunteers—and recognizing that such anecdotal information may not be truly representative—what do you see as the pros and cons of Girl Scout cookie drives? On balance, is this marketing fund-raising effort still desirable, or might other alternatives be better?

5. "Since there is no bottom-line evaluation for performance, nonprofits have no incentives to control costs and prudently evaluate expenditures." Discuss.

6. How would you feel, as a large contributor to a charity, about its spending $10 million for advertising? Discuss your rationale for this attitude.

7. Do you think the action taken by UWA after Aramony was the best way to salvage the public image? Why or why not? What else might have been done?

HANDS-ON EXERCISES

1. You are an advisor to Elaine Chao, who has taken over the scandal-ridden United Way. What advice would you give her for as quickly as possible restoring the confidence of the American public in the integrity and worthiness of this preeminent national charity organization?

2. You are a member of the board of governors of United Way. Allegations have surfaced about the lavish life style of the highly regarded Aramony. Most of

the board, being corporate executives, see nothing at all wrong with his perks and privileges. You, however, feel otherwise. How would you convince the other members of the board of the error of condoning Aramony's activities? Be as persuasive as you can in supporting your position.

3. You are the parent of a Girl Scout, who has assiduously worked to sell hundreds of boxes of cookies. You now realize that the efforts of your daughter and thousands of other girls are primarily supporting a bloated central and regional bureaucracy, and not the local troops. You feel strongly that this situation is an unacceptable use of child labor. Describe your proposed efforts to institute change.

TEAM DEBATE EXERCISE

Debate this issue: Should top executives of large charitable organizations be compensated comparable to corporate executives responsible for similar-size organizations?

INVITATION TO RESEARCH

What is the situation with United Way today? Are local agencies contributing to the national? Have donations matched or exceeded previous levels? Was Elaine Chao able to restore confidence? Is she still with United Way, or has she gone on to other challenges?

CHAPTER NINETEEN

Met Life: Deceptive Sales Tactics—Condoned or Poorly Controlled?

*I*n August 1993, the state of Florida blew the whistle on giant Metropolitan Life, a company dating back to 1868, and the country's second largest insurance firm. Met Life agents based in Tampa, Florida, were alleged to have duped customers out of some $11 million. Thousands of these customers were nurses, lured by the sales pitch to learn more about "something new, one of the most widely discussed retirement plans in the investment world today."[1] In reality, this was a life-insurance policy in disguise, and what clients were led to think were savings deposits were actually insurance premiums.

As we will see, the growing scandal rocked Met Life, and brought it millions of dollars in fines and restitutions. What was not clear was the full culpability of the company: Was it guilty only of not monitoring agent performance sufficiently to detect unethical and illegal activities, or was it the great encourager of such practices?

RICK URSO: THE VILLAIN?

The first premonitory rumble that something bad was about to happen came to Rick Urso on Christmas Eve 1993. Home with his family, he received an unexpected call from his boss, the regional sales manager. In disbelief he heard there was a rumor going around the executive suites that he was about to be fired. Now, Urso had known that the State of Florida had been investigating, and that company auditors had also been looking into sales practices. And on September 17, two corporate vice-presidents had even shown up to conduct the fourth audit that year, but on leaving they had given him the impression that he was complying with company guidelines.

Urso often reveled in his good fortune and attributed it to his sheer dedication to his work and the company. He had grown up in a working-class neighborhood, the son of an electrician. He had started college, but dropped out before graduating.

---

[1] Suzanne Woolley and Gail DeGeorge, "Policies of Deception?" *Business Week* (January 17, 1994), p. 24.

264

His sales career started at a John Hancock agency in Tampa, in 1978. Four years later, he was promoted to manager. He was credited with building up the agency to number two in the whole company.

He left John Hancock in 1983 for Met Life's Tampa agency. His first job was as trainer. Only three months later he was promoted to branch manager. Now his long hours and overwhelming commitment were beginning to pay off. In a success story truly inspiring, his dedication and his talent as a motivator of people swept the branch from a one-rep office to one of Met Life's largest and most profitable. In 1990 and 1991, Urso's office won the company's Sales Office of the Year award. By 1993 the agency employed 120 reps, seven sales managers, and 30 administrative employees. And Urso had risen to become Met Life's third-highest-paid employee, earning $1.1 million as manager of the branch. With such a performance history, the stuff of legends, he became the company's star, a person to look up to and to inspire trainees and other employees.

His was the passion of a TV evangelist: "Most people go through life being told why they can't accomplish something. If they would just believe, then they would be halfway there. That's the way I dream and that's what I expect from my people."[2] He soon became known as the "Master Motivator," and increasingly was the guest speaker at Met Life conferences.

On the Monday after that Christmas, the dire prediction came to pass. He was summoned to the office of William Groggans, the head of Met Life's Southeast territory, and was handed a letter by the sober-faced Groggans. With trembling hands he opened it and read that he was fired for engaging in improper conduct.

The Route to Stardom

Unfortunately, the growth of his Tampa office could not be credited to simple motivation of employees. Urso found his vehicle for great growth to be the whole-life insurance policy. This was part life insurance and part savings. As such, it required high premiums, but only part earned interest and compounded on a tax-deferred basis; the rest went to pay for the life insurance policy. What made this so attractive to company sales reps was the commission: A Met whole-life policy paid a 55 percent first-year commission. In contrast, an annuity paid only a 2 percent first-year commission.

Urso found the nurses' market to be particularly attractive. Perhaps because of their constant exposure to death, nurses were easily convinced of the need for economic security. He had his salespeople call themselves "nursing representatives." And his Tampa salespeople carried their fake retirement plan beyond Florida, eventually reaching 37 states. A New York client, for example, thought she had bought a retirement annuity. But it turned out to be life insurance even though she didn't want such coverage because she had no beneficiaries.[3]

As the growth of the Tampa agency became phenomenal, his budget for mailing brochures was upped to nearly $1 million in 1992, ten times that of any other Met Life office. This gave him national reach.

---

[2] Weld F. Royal, "Scapegoat or Scoundrel," *Sales & Marketing Management* (January 1995), p. 64.

[3] Jane Bryant Quinn, "Yes, They're Out to Get You," *Newsweek* (January 24), 1994, p. 51.

Urso's own finances increased proportionately because he earned a commission on each policy his reps sold. In 1989, he was paid $270,000. In 1993, as compensation exceeded $1 million, he moved his family to Bay Shore Boulevard, the most expensive area of Tampa.

End of the Bonanza

A few complaints began surfacing. In 1990, the Texas insurance commissioner warned Met Life to stop its nursing ploy. The company made a token compliance by sending out two rounds of admonitory letters. But nothing apparently changed. See the following Information Box about the great deficiency of token compliance without follow-up.

An internal Met Life audit in 1991 raised some questions about Urso's pre-approach letters. The term *nursing representative* was called a "made-up" title. The auditors also questioned the term *retirement savings policy* as not appropriate for the product. However, the report concluded by congratulating the Tampa office for its contribution to the company. Not surprisingly, such mixed signals did not end the use of misleading language at that time.

In the summer of 1993, Florida state regulators began a more in-depth examination of the sales practices of the Urso agency. As a result of this investigation, Florida Insurance Commissioner Tom Gallagher charged Met Life with several violations. Now Met Life began more serious investigation.

INFORMATION BOX

THE VULNERABILITY OF COMPLIANCE, IF IT IS ONLY TOKEN

A token effort at compliance to a regulatory complaint or charge tends to have two consequences, neither good in the long run for the company involved:

1. Such tokenism gives a clear message to the organization: "Despite what outsiders say, this is acceptable conduct in this firm." Thus is set the climate for less than desirable practices.

2. Vulnerability to future harsher measures. With the malpractice continuing, regulators, convinced that the company is stalling and refusing to cooperate, will eventually take more drastic action. Penalties will move beyond warnings to become punitive.

Actually, the firm may not have intended to stall, but that is the impression conveyed. If the cause of the seemingly token effort is really faulty controls, one wonders how many other aspects of the operation are also ineptly controlled so that company policies are ignored.

Discuss what kinds of controls Met Life could have imposed in 1990 that would have made compliance actual and not token.

The crux of the investigations concerned promotional material Urso's office was sending to nurses nationwide. From 1989 to 1993, millions of direct-mail pieces had been sent out. Charges finally were leveled that this material disguised the product agents were selling. For example, one brochure coming from Urso's office depicted the Peanuts character Lucy in a nurse's uniform. The headline described the product as "retirement savings and security for the future a nurse deserves." Nowhere was insurance even mentioned, and allegations were that nurses across the country unknowingly purchased life insurance when they thought they were buying retirement savings plans.

As the investigation deepened, a former Urso agent, turned whistleblower, claimed he had been instructed to place his hands over the words "life insurance" on applications during presentations.

MET LIFE CORRECTIVE ACTIONS

With Florida regulators now investigating, the company's attitudes changed. At first, Met Life denied wrongdoing. But eventually it acknowledged problems. Under mounting public pressure, it agreed to pay $20 million in fines to more than 40 states as a result of unethical sales practices of its agents. It further agreed to refund premiums to nearly 92,000 policyholders who bought insurance based on misleading sales information between 1989 and 1993. These refunds were expected to reach $76 million.

Met Life fired or demoted five high-level executives as a result of the scandal. Urso's office was closed, and all seven of his managers and several reps were also discharged. Life insurance sales to individuals were down 25 percent through September 1994 over the same nine-month period in 1993. And Standard & Poor's downgraded Met's bond rating based on these alleged improprieties.

Shortly after the fines were announced, the Florida Department of Insurance filed charges against Urso and 86 other Met Life insurance agents, accusing them of fraudulent sales practices. The insurance commissioner said, "This was not a situation where a few agents decided to take advantage of their customers, but a concerted effort by many individuals to dupe customers into buying a life insurance policy disguised as a retirement savings plan."[4]

The corporation, in attempting to improve its public image, instituted a broad overhaul of its compliance procedures. It established a corporate ethics and compliance department to monitor behavior throughout the company and audit personal insurance sales offices. The department was also charged to report any compliance deficiencies to senior management and to follow up to ensure the implementation of corrective actions.

In Met Life's *1994 Annual Report*, Harry Kamen, CEO, and Ted Athanassiades, president, commented on their corrective actions regarding the scandal:

> We created what we think is the most effective compliance system in the industry. Not just for personal insurance, but for all components of the company. We installed systems

---

[4] Sean Armstrong, "The Good, The Bad and the Industry," *Best's Review, P/C* (June 1994), p. 36.

to coordinate and track the quality and integrity of our sales activities, and we created a new system of sales office auditing.

Also, there were organizational changes. And, for the first time in 22 years, we assembled all of our agency and district managers—about a thousand people—to discuss what we have done and need to do about the problems and where we were going.[5]

Meantime, Rick Urso started a suit against Met Life for defamation of character and for reneging on a $1 million severance agreement. He alleged that Met Life made him the fall guy in the nationwide sales scandal.

The personal consequences on Urso's life were not inconsequential. More than a year later he was still unemployed. He had looked for another insurance job, but no one would even see him. "There are nights he can't sleep. He lies awake worrying about the impact this will have on his two teenagers." And he laments that his wife cannot go out without people gossiping.[6]

WHERE DOES THE BLAME LIE?

Is Urso really the unscrupulous monster who rose to a million-dollar-a-year man on the foundations of deceit? Or is Met Life mainly to blame for encouraging, and then ignoring for too long, practices aimed at misleading and even deceiving? Probably the final reckoning will not be reached outside the courtroom. And who can say that the judgment then rendered will be completely valid?

The Case Against Met Life

Undeniably Urso did things that smacked of the illegal and unethical. But did the corporation knowingly provide the climate? Was his training such as to promote deceptive practices? Was Met Life completely unaware of his distortions and deceptions in promotional material and sales pitches? There seems to be substantial evidence that the company played a part; it was no innocent and unsuspecting bystander.

At best, Met Life top executives may not have been aware of the full extent of the hard selling efforts emanating at first from Tampa and then spreading further in the organization. Perhaps they chose to ignore any inkling that things were not completely on the up and up, in the quest for exceptional bottom-line performance. "Don't argue with success" might have become the corporate mindset.

At the worst, the company encouraged and even demanded hard selling and tried to pretend that such could still be accomplished with the highest ethical standards of performance. If such ethical standards were not met, then, company top executives could argue, they were not aware of such wrongdoings.

There is evidence of company culpability (more will undoubtedly be introduced during Urso's suit). Take the training program for new agents. Much of it was designed to help new employees overcome the difficulties of selling life insurance. In

---

[5] *Met Life 1994 Annual Report*, p. 16.

[6] Royal, p. 65.

so doing, they were taught to downplay the life insurance aspects of the product. Rather, the savings and tax-deferred growth benefits were to be stressed.

In training new agents to sell insurance over the phone, they were told that people prefer dealing with specialists. It seemed only a small temptation to use the title *nursing representative* rather than *insurance agent*.

After the scandal, Met Life admitted that the training might be faulty. Training had been decentralized into five regional centers, and the company believed that this may have led to a less standardized and less controlled curricula. Met Life has since reorganized so that many functions, including training and legal matters, are now done at one central location.[7]

The company's control or monitoring was certainly deficient and uncoordinated during the years of misconduct. For example, the marketing department promoted deceptive sales practices while the legal department warned of possible illegality but took no further action to eliminate it.

An Industry Problem?

The Met Life revelations focused public and regulatory attention on the entire insurance industry. The Insurance Commissioner of Florida also turned attention to the sales and marketing practices of New York Life and Prudential. The industry itself seems vulnerable to questionable practices. With millions of transactions, intense competition, and a widespread and rather autonomous sales force, opportunity exists for misrepresentation and other unethical dealings.

For example, just a few months after the Tampa office publicity, Met Life settled an unrelated scandal. Regulators in Pennsylvania fined the company $1.5 million for "churning." This is a practice of agents replacing old policies with new ones, in which additional commissions are charged and policyholders are disadvantaged. Class-action suits alleging churning have also been filed in Pennsylvania against Prudential, New York Life, and John Hancock.

But problems go beyond sales practices. Claims adjusters may attempt to withhold or reduce payments. General agents may place business with bogus or insolvent companies. Even actuaries may create unrealistic policy structures.

With a deteriorating public image, the industry faces further governmental regulation, both by states and by the federal government. But cynics, both within and outside the industry, wonder whether deception and fraud are so much a part of the business that nothing can be done about them.[8]

ANALYSIS

We could have placed this case under the Ethics and Social Responsibility section. The choice to include it under Control Weaknesses and Strengths assumed a lapse in complete feedback to top executives. But maybe they did not want to know. After all,

---

[7] "Trained to Mislead," *Sales & Marketing Management* (January 1995), p. 66.

[8] Armstrong, p. 35.

nothing was life-threatening here, no product safety features were being ignored or disguised, nobody was in physical danger.

This raises a key management issue. Can top executives hide from less than ethical practices—and even illegal ones—under the guise that they did not know? The answer should be *No!* See the following Information Box for a discussion of management accountability.

So, we are left with top management of Met Life grappling with the temptation to tacitly approve the aggressive selling practices of a sales executive so successful as to be the model for the whole organization, even though faint cries from the legal staff suggested that such might be subject to regulatory scrutiny and disapproval.

The harsh appraisal of this situation is that top management cannot be exonerated for the deficiencies of subordinates. If controls and monitoring processes are defective, top management is still accountable. The pious platitudes of Met Life management that they have now corrected the situation hardly excuse them for permitting this to have developed in the first place.

Ah, but embracing the temptation is so easy to rationalize. Management can always maintain that there was no good, solid proof of misdeeds. After all, where do aggressive sales efforts cross the line? Where do they become more than simply puffing, and become outright deceptive? See the following Information Box regarding puffing, and this admittedly gray area of the acceptable. Lacking indisputable evidence of misdeeds,

---

INFORMATION BOX

THE ULTIMATE RESPONSIBILITY

In the Maytag case in Chapter 4 we examine a costly snafu brought about by giving executives of a foreign subsidiary too much rein. With Met Life the problem was gradually eroding ethical practices. In both instances, top management still had ultimate responsibility and cannot escape blame for whatever goes wrong in an organization. Decades ago, President Truman coined the phrase, "The buck stops here," meaning that in this highest position rests the ultimate seat of responsibility.

Any manager who delegates to someone else the authority to do something will undoubtedly hold them responsible to do the job properly. Still, the manager must be aware that his or her own responsibility to higher management or to stockholders cannot be delegated away. If the subordinate does the job improperly, the manager is still responsible.

Going back to Met Life, or to any corporation involved with unethical and illegal practices, top executives can try to escape blame by denying that they knew anything about the misdeeds. This should not exonerate them. Even if they knew nothing directly, they still set the climate.

In Japan, the chief executive of an organization involved in a public scandal usually resigns in disgrace. In the United States, top executives often escape full retribution by blaming their subordinates and maintaining that they themselves knew nothing of the misdeed. Is it truly fair to hold a top executive culpable for the shortcomings of some unknown subordinate?

INFORMATION BOX

WHERE DO WE DRAW THE LINE ON PUFFING?

Puffing is generally thought of as mild exaggeration in selling or advertising. It is generally accepted as simply the mark of exuberance toward what is being promoted. As such, it is acceptable business conduct. Most people have come to regard promotional communications with some skepticism—"It's New! The Greatest! A Super Value! Gives Whiter Teeth! Whiter Laundry!..." and so on. We have become conditioned to viewing such blandisments as suspicious. But dishonest, or deceptive? Probably not. As long as the exaggeration stays mild.

But it can be a short step from mild exaggeration to outright falsehoods and deceptive claims. Did Met Life's "nursing representatives," "retirement plans," and hiding the reality of life insurance cross the line? Enough people seemed to think so, including state insurance commissioners and the victims themselves. This short step can tempt more bad practices than if the line between good and bad were more definitive.

Do you think all exaggerated claims, even the mild and vague ones known as puffing, should be banned? Why or why not?

why should these executives suspect the worst? Especially since their legal departments, not centralized as they were to be later, were timid in their denunciations?

Turning to controls, a major caveat should be posed for all firms: In the presence of strong management demands for performance—with the often implicit or imagined pressure to produce at all costs, or else—the ground is laid for less than desirable practices by subordinates. After all, their career paths and even job longevity depend on meeting these demands.

In an organizational climate of decentralization and laissez faire, such abuses are more likely to occur. Such a results-oriented structure suggests that it's not how you achieve the desired results, but that you meet them. So, while decentralization is, on balance, usually desirable, it can, in the right environment of top management laxity of high moral standards, lead to undesirable—and worse—practices.

At the least, it leads to opportunistic temptation by lower- and middle-level executives. Perhaps this is the final indictment of Met Life and Rick Urso. The climate was conductive to his ambitious opportunism. For a while it was wonderful. But the clinks and the abuses of accepted practices could not be disguised indefinitely.

And wherever possible, top management will repudiate its accountability responsibilities.

WHAT CAN BE LEARNED?

Unethical and illegal actions do not go undetected forever. It may take months, it may take years, but a firm's dark side will eventually be uncovered. Its reputation may then be besmirched, it may face loss of customers and competitive position, it may face heavy fines and increased regulation.

The eventual disclosure may come from a disgruntled employee (a whistle-blower). It may originate from a regulatory body or an investigative reporter. Or it may come from revelations emanating from a lawsuit. Eventually, the deviation is uncovered, and retribution follows. Such a scenario should be—but is not always—enough to constrain those individuals tempted to commit unethical and illegal actions.

What made the Met Life deceptive practices particularly troubling is that they were so visible, and yet were so long tolerated. A clear definition of what was acceptable and what was not seemed lacking by much of the sales organization. Something was clearly amiss, both in the training and in the controlling of agent personnel.

The control function is best centralized in any organization. Where the department or entity that monitors performance is decentralized, tolerance of bad practices is more likely than when centralized. The reason is rather simple. Where legal or accounting controls are decentralized, the people conducting them are more easily influenced and are likely to be neither as objective nor as critical as when they are more at an arm's length. So, reviewers and evaluators should not be close to the people they are examining. And they should only report to top management.

A strong sales incentive program invites bad practices. The lucrative commission incentive for the whole-life policies—55 percent first-year commission—was almost bound to stimulate abusive sales practices, especially when the rewards for this type of policy were so much greater than for any other. Firms often use various incentive programs and contests to motivate their employees to seek greater efforts. But if some are tempted to cross the line, the end result of public scrutiny and condemnation may not be worth whatever increases in sales might be gained.

Large corporations are particularly vulnerable to public scrutiny. Large firms, especially ones dealing with consumer products, are very visible. This visibility makes them attractive targets for critical scrutiny by activists, politicians, the media, regulatory bodies, and the legal establishment. Such firms ought to be particularly careful in any dealings that might be questioned, even if short-term profits have to be restrained. In Met Life's case, the fines and refunds approached $100 million. Although the firm in its 1994 annual report maintained that all the bad publicity was behind, that there were no ill effects, still we can wonder how quickly a besmirched reputation can truly be restored, especially when competitors are eager to grab the opportunity.

The following Information Box describes criticisms of another kind regarding a competitor of Met Life.

CONSIDER

What additional learning insights do you see?

INFORMATION BOX

CRITICISMS OF PRUDENTIAL INSURANCE COMPANY

Prudential has long cultivated its image as the "Rock," using a logo of the Rock of Gibraltar, symbol of permanence and stability. But like Met Life, it faced investigations and litigation over deceptive sales practices that affected millions of policyholders in the 1980s and early 1990s, and its sales of life-insurance policies slowed markedly. The company set aside more than $2 billion to cover the costs of litigation, and took a $1.64 billion charge against 1997 earnings. To try to resurrect its tarnished image, it increased advertising expenditures to $130 million in 1996 and 1997.

In August 1998 it came under fire of another kind, with disclosures of hefty compensations paid its executives, this despite the performance downturn: The top 100 executives averaged $820,000 in 1997, up 30 percent from 1994. By contrast, Met Life's top hundred executives averaged $600,000 in 1997, and State Farm had less than three dozen earning $350,000 or more.[9]

The compensation criticisms probably would not have surfaced had Prudential not sought to end its mutual status and move to public ownership, which would enable it to raise money more easily for purposes such as acquisitions. But demutualization exposed Prudential to critical scrutiny by huge institutional investors, notably the California Public Employees' Retirement System, and TIAA-CREF, a giant pension fund. These major shareholders regularly examine executive-compensation records of publicly traded companies.

Should executives be richly compensated when their firms are not doing well? Is it right to criticize a firm whose executives are far more richly rewarded than others in the same industry? Is it right for institutional investors to criticize and try to change policies in firms they invest in?

[9] Scot J. Paltrow, "As a Public Company Prudential May Find Pay Scales Draw Fire," *Wall Street Journal* (August 14, 1998), pp. A1, A8.

QUESTIONS

1. Do you think Rick Urso should have been fired? Why or why not?

2. Do you think Met Life CEO and president should have been fired? Why or why not?

3. Why was the term *life insurance* seemingly so desirable to avoid? What is wrong with life insurance?

4. Given the widespread publicity about the Met Life scandal, do you think the firm can regain consumer trust in a short time?

5. "This whole critical publicity has been blown way out of proportion. After all, nobody was injured. Not even in their pocketbook. They were sold something they really needed. For their own good." Evaluate.

6. "You have to admire that guy, Urso. He was a real genius. No one else could motivate a sales organization as he did. They should have made him president of the company. Or else he should become an evangelist." Evaluate.

7. Do you think the arguments are compelling that the control function should be centralized rather than decentralized? Why or why not?

HANDS-ON EXERCISES

Before

1. It is early 1990. You are the assistant to the CEO of Met Life. Rumors have been surfacing that life insurance sales efforts are becoming not only too high-pressure but also misleading. The CEO has ordered you to investigate. You find that the legal department in the Southeast Territory has some concerns about the efforts coming out of the highly successful Tampa office of Urso. Be as specific as you can about how you would investigate these unproven allegations, and how you would report this to your boss, assuming that some questionable practices seem apparent.

2. It is 1992. Internal investigations have confirmed that Urso and his "magnificent" Tampa office are using deceptive selling techniques in disguising the life insurance aspects of the policies they are selling. As the executive in charge in the Southeast, describe your actions and rationale at this point. (You have to assume that the later consequences are completely unknown as this point.)

After

3. The s___ has hit the fan. The scandal has become well-publicized, especially with such TV programs as *Dateline* and *20/20*. What would you do as top executive of Met Life at this point? How would you attempt to save the public image of the company?

TEAM DEBATE EXERCISE

The publicity is widespread about the "misdeeds" of Met Life. Debate how you would react. One position is to defend your company and rationalize what happened and downplay any ill-effects. The other position is to meekly bow to the allegations and admit wrongdoing and be as contrite as possible.

INVITATION TO RESEARCH

How is Met Life faring after this extremely bad publicity? Do sales seem to be rebounding? Can you find any information on whether the image has improved, whether the situation has been forgotten by the general public? Can you find out whether Rick Urso found another job? Are Kamen and Athanassiades still the top executives of Met Life? What conclusions can you draw from your research?

CHAPTER TWENTY

McDonald's: The Paragon of Controls, But They Slipped as Other Strengths Emerged

Few business firms anywhere in the world have been able to match the sustained growth of McDonald's. Initially, it grew with one simple product, a hamburger, and while it has broadened its product mix today, it still remains uniquely undiversified.

The foundation for the success has always been the most rigid standards and controls to be found anywhere. It insisted these be adhered to by all outlets, company-owned as well as franchised, and therein lies the great example of the desirability of rigorous controls over all aspects of an operation.

For decades, no competitor could match the standards of quality, service, and cleanliness that made McDonald's unique. In recent years, however, these controls slipped while competitors countered its former advantage.

Today, foreign markets sustain McDonald's.

THE MCDONALD'S GROWTH MACHINE

In its *1995 Annual Report*, McDonald's management was justifiably proud. Sales and profits had continued the long trend upward, and even seemed to be accelerating. See Table 20.1. Far from reaching a saturation point, the firm was opening more restaurants than ever, some 2,400 around the world in 1995, up from 1,800 the year before. "We plan to add between 2,500 and 3,200 restaurants in both 1996 and 1997, with about two-thirds outside of the United States. In other words, we opened more than six restaurants per day in 1995; over the next two years, we plan to open eight a day."[1] And, "Our growth opportunities remain significant: on any given day, 99 percent of the world's population does not eat at McDonald's ... yet."[2]

Company management extolled the power of the McDonald's brand overseas, and how on opening days lines were sometimes "miles" long. "Often our challenge is to keep up with demand. In China, for example, there are only 62 McDonald's to

[1] *McDonald's 1995 Annual Report*, p. 8.

[2] *Ibid.*, p. 7.

TABLE 20.1   Growth in Sales and Profits, 1985–1995

	Sales (millions)	Percent Gain	Income (millions)	Percent Gain
1985	$11,011		$433	
1986	12,432	12.9%	480	12.2%
1987	14,330	15.3	549	14.4
1988	16,064	12.1	646	17.7
1989	17,333	7.9	727	12.5
1990	18,759	8.2	802	10.3
1991	19,928	6.2	860	7.2
1992	21,885	9.8	959	11.5
1993	23,587	7.8	1,083	12.9
1994	25,987	10.2	1,224	13.0
1995	29,914	15.1	1,427	16.6

Source: 1995 Annual Report.

Commentary: Of particular interest is how the new expansion policies have brought a burst of revenues and profits in the mid-1990s. How audacious we are to even question these growth policies. But we have.

serve a population of 1.2 billion."[3] By the end of 1995, the company had 7,012 outlets in 89 countries of the world, with Japan alone having 1,482. Table 20.2 shows the top ten countries in number of McDonald's units.

Sometimes in marketing its products in different cultures, adjustments had to be made. The following Information Box describes the changes McDonald's made for its first store in India, which opened October 13, 1996.

TABLE 20.2   Top Ten Foreign Markets in Number of Units at Year End, 1995

Japan	1,482 restaurants
Canada	902
Germany	649
England	577
Australia	530
France	429
Brazil	243
Mexico	132
Netherlands	128
Taiwan	111

Source: 1995 Annual Report.

Commentary: Is the popularity in Japan a surprise?

[3] *Ibid.*

INFORMATION BOX

MCMUTTON BURGERS FOR INDIA

No all-beef patties are to be found in McDonald's packed restaurant in Delhi, India. Ground lamb has been substituted in the "Maharaja Mac" and other 100 percent pure mutton burgers in deference to the Hindu majority's reverence for the cow. The first no-beef McDonald's in the world also serves no pork, since this would offend India's Muslim minority.

Vegetarians can choose between veggie burgers and "Vegetable McNuggets," all cooked by a separate staff who do not handle meat products, conforming to another taboo. Such "Indianizing" has brought heavy crowds—from families, to turbaned Sikhs, to young Western wannabes—to jam the three-floor restaurant. Yet, there are militant critics: "I am against McDonald's because they are the chief killers of cows in the world," said Maneka Gandhi, an animal-rights activist and daughter-in-law of assassinated prime minister Indira Gandhi. "We don't need cow killers in India."[4] But most customers were not concerned about this, and said their only complaint was that the burgers were too small and bland for hearty, spice-loving Indian palates.

A second McDonald's opened in Bombay a week after the Delhi opening. It drew more than 12,000 customers on its first day.

Should the militant activists become more violent about McDonald's "conducting a global conspiracy against cattle," do you think McDonald's should abandon the India market? Why or why not?

---

[4] "Delhi Delights in McMutton Burgers," *Cleveland Plain Dealer* (November 6, 1996), p. 3-D.

Growth Prospects in the United States

With 11,368 of its restaurants in the United States, wasn't McDonald's rapidly reaching a point of saturation in its domestic market, if not overseas? Top management vehemently disputed this conclusion. Rather, it offered a startling statistical phenomenon to support accelerating expansion. Called "Greenberg's law," after newly appointed McDonald's U.S. chairman Jack Greenberg, it maintained that the more stores McDonald's put in a city the more per-capita transactions will result. Thus, with two stores in a city there might be 16 transactions per capita per year. Add two or four more stores and the transactions will not only double, or quadruple, but may even do better than that. The hypothesized explanation for this amazing phenomenon seemingly rested on two factors: convenience and market share. With more outlets, McDonald's increased its convenience to consumers, and added to its market share at the expense of competitors. Hence the justification for the expansion binge.

In the quest for this domestic expansion the company over the last five years had been able to reduce the cost of building a new U.S. traditional restaurant by 26 per-

COST CONTROL

cent through standardizing building materials and equipment and global sourcing, as well as improving construction methods and building designs. But it had also found abundant market opportunities in satellite restaurants. These were smaller, had lower sales volume, and served simplified menus. This format proved cost efficient in such nontraditional places as zoos, hospitals, airports, museums, and military bases as well as in retail stores such as Wal-Mart, The Home Depot, and some other major stores. For example, such satellite restaurants were in some 800 Wal-Mart stores by the end of 1995, with more planned. In October 1996, a McDonald's Express opened in a 1,200 square-foot space in an office building in Lansing, Michigan, perhaps a harbinger of more such sites to come.

In its eager search for ever more outlets, McDonald's did something it had never done before. It took over stores from weak competitors. In late summer 1996, it bought 184 company-owned Roy Rogers outlets. "Here was an opportunity that was maybe once in a lifetime," Greenberg stated.[5] Earlier the same year, it acquired Burghy's, an 80-store fast-food chain in Italy. And in New Zealand, it added 17 restaurants from the Georgie Pie chain.

The new stores being opened were seldom like the old ones. The popularity of "drive-thru" windows generated 55 percent of U.S. sales, and in the process fewer seats were needed inside. This left more space available for gas stations or for indoor playgrounds—Ronald's Playplaces—to attract families. McDonald's made joint ventures with Chevron and Amoco to codevelop properties. And it signed an exclusive marketing deal with Disney for promoting each other's brands.

McDonald's had always been a big spender for advertising, and this has been effective. Even back in the 1970s, a survey of school children found 96 percent identifying Ronald McDonald, ranking him second only to Santa Claus.[6] In 1995, advertising and promotional expenditures totaled approximately $1.8 billion, or 6 percent of sales.[7]

Factors in the Invincibility of McDonald's

Through the third quarter of 1996, McDonald's could proudly claim 126 consecutive quarters of record earnings. Since its earliest days, the ingredients of success were simple, but few competitors were able to effectively emulate them. The basic aspects were:

- A brief menu, but having consistent quality over thousands of outlets
- Strictly enforced and rigorous operational standards controlling service, cleanliness, and all other aspects of the operation
- Friendly employees, despite a high turnover of personnel because of the monotony of automated food handling
- Heavy mass media advertising directed mostly at families and children

[5] Gary Samuels, "Golden Arches Galore," *Forbes* (November 4, 1996), p. 48.
[6] "The Burger That Conquered the Country," *Time* (September 17, 1973), pp. 84–92.
[7] *McDonald's 1995 Annual Report*, p. 9.

- Identification of a fertile target market—the family—and directing the marketing strategy to satisfying it with product, price, promotional efforts, and site locations (at least in the early years, the suburban locations with their high density of families)

However, by the end of 1996, international operations were the real vehicle of growth, providing 47 percent of the company's $30 billion sales and 54 percent of profits. Of no small concern, the domestic operation had not blossomed accordingly.

STORM CLOUDS FOR THE DOMESTIC OPERATION

Souring Franchisee Relations

In the market-share game, in which McDonald's dominated all its competitors, corporate management concluded that the firm with the most outlets in a given community wins. But as McDonald's unprecedented expansion continued, many franchisees were skeptical of headquarters' claim that no one loses when the company opens more outlets in a community since market share rises proportionately. Still, the franchise holder had to wonder how much his sales would diminish when another McDonald's opens down the street.

The 7,000-member American Franchisee Association, an organization formed to look after franchisees' rights, claimed that McDonald's operators were joining in record numbers.[8] Other franchisees formed a clandestine group called the Consortium, representing dissidents who felt present management was unresponsive to their concerns. They remembered a kinder and gentler company. See the following Information Box for contrasting franchisee views on the high-growth market share policy.

Another concern of franchisees was the new set of business practices developed by corporate headquarters, known as Franchising 2000. The company claimed it instituted this as a way to improve standards for quality, service, cleanliness, and value by giving franchisees better "tools." But some saw this as a blatant attempt to gain more power over the franchised operations. One provision revived a controversial A, B, C, and F grading system, with only franchisees that receive A's and B's eligible for more restaurants. Furthermore, McDonald's began using Franchising 2000 to enforce a single pricing strategy throughout the chain, so that a Big Mac, for example, would cost the same everywhere. The corporation maintained that such uniformity was necessary for the discounting needed to build market share. Those not complying risked losing their franchise.

Franchise relations should not be a matter of small concern to McDonald's. Table 20.3 shows the ratio of franchised restaurants to total restaurants both in the United States and outside the United States. As can be seen, franchises constitute by far the largest proportion of restaurants.

[8] Richard Gibson, "Some Franchisees Say Moves by McDonald's Hurt Their Operations," *Wall Street Journal* (April 17, 1996), pp. A1, A8.

INFORMATION BOX

THE CONTENTMENT OF TWO MCDONALD'S FRANCHISEES

In 1980, Wayne Kilburn and his wife, Mary Jane, took over the only McDonald's in Ridgecrest, California, a town of 26,000. The Kilburns prospered in the years to come. Then McDonald's instituted its "market-share plan" for Ridgecrest. Late in 1995 it put a company-owned restaurant inside the Wal-Mart. A few months later it built another outlet inside the China Lake Naval Weapons Center. A third new company-owned store went up just outside the naval base. "Basically, they killed me," *Forbes* reports Kilburn saying. And he claimed his volume dropped 30 percent.[9]

In its *1995 Annual Report,* corporate headquarters offered another view concerning franchisee contentment. Tom Wolf was a McDonald's franchisee with 15 restaurants in the Huntington, West Virginia and Ashland, Kentucky markets. He opened his first McDonald's in 1974, had eight by the end of 1993, and opened seven more in the last two years, including two McDonald's in Wal-Mart stores and another in an alliance with an oil company; in addition he added indoor Playplaces to two existing restaurants.

Has all this investment in growth made a difference? The *Annual Report* quotes Tom: "I wouldn't change a thing. Sales are up. I'm serving more customers, my market share is up and I'm confident about the future. Customers say that the Playplaces and Wal-Mart units are 'a great idea.' The business is out there. We've got to take these opportunities now, or leave them for someone else to take."[10]

"The high-growth, market share policy should not bother any franchisee. It simply creates opportunities to invest in more restaurants." Evaluate this statement.

[9] Samuels, *op. cit.*, p. 48.
[10] *McDonald's 1995 Annual Report*, p. 32.

TABLE 20.3 **Percent of Franchised to Total Traditional Restaurants, Selected Years, 1985–1995**

	1985	1988	1992	1995
Traditional restaurants				
Total	8,901	10,513	13,093	16,809
Operated by franchisees	6,150	7,110	9,237	11,240
Percent franchised to total	69.1%	67.6%	70.5%	66.9%

Source: Calculated from *1995 Annual Report.*

Commentary: While by 1995, the ratio of franchised to total restaurants had dropped slightly, still more than two-thirds are operated by franchisees. Perhaps this suggests that franchisee concerns ought to receive more consideration by corporate headquarters.

Menu Problems

Sales growth ↓

Since 1993, domestic per-store sales slumped from a positive 4 percent to a negative 3 percent by the third quarter of 1996, this being the fifth quarter in a row of negative sales gains. In part this decline was thought attributable to older customers drifting away: "Huge numbers of baby-boomers … want less of the cheap, fattening foods at places like McDonald's. As soon as their kids are old enough, they go elsewhere."[11]

In an attempt to garner more business from this customer segment, McDonald's with a $200 million promotional blitz launched its first "grownup taste" sandwich, the Arch Deluxe line of beef, fish, and chicken burgers. It forecast that this would become a $1 billion brand in only its first year. But before long, some were calling this a McFlop. In September 1996, Edward Rensi, head of U.S. operations, tried to minimize the stake in the new sandwich, and sent a memo to 2,700 concerned franchisees, "the Arch Deluxe was never intended to be a silver bullet."[12] On October 8, Rensi was replaced by Jack Greenberg. *Menu Problems*

ARCH DELUX

McDonald's domestic troubles were not entirely new. As far back as the late 1980s, competitors, including Pizza Hut and Taco Bell, were nibbling at McDonald's market share, and Burger King was more than holding its own. Even the great traditional strength of McDonald's of unsurpassed controlled standards over food, service, and cleanliness seemed to be waning: A 1995 *Restaurants and Institutions Choice in Chains* survey of 2,849 adults gave McDonald's low marks on food quality, value, service, and cleanliness. Top honors instead went to Wendy's.[13] *Competitors*

In 1991, McDonald's reluctantly tried discounting, with "Extra Value Meals," largely to keep up with Taco Bell's value pricing. But by 1995, price promotions were no longer attracting customers, and per-store sales began slumping. The new, adultoriented Deluxe line was not only aimed at older adults, but with its prices 20 percent more than regular items, the hope was to parry the discounting.

The company had had previous problems in expanding its line. The McDLT was notably unsuccessful despite heavy promotion. And more recently, the low-fat McLean, an effort to attract weight-conscious adults, was a complete disaster. In fact this beef and seaweed concoction sold so badly that some operators kept only a few frozen patties on hand, while others, as revealed in an embarrassing TV expose, sold fully fatted burgers in McLean boxes to the few customers asking for them. *!!*

Some years before, the company had tried but failed to develop an acceptable pizza product. It also was unable to create a dinner menu that would attract evening-hour traffic. Two other experiments were also abandoned: a 1950s-style cafe and a family-type concept called Hearth Express that served chicken, ham, and meatloaf. *Try New formats*

[11] Shelly Branch, "McDonald's Strikes Out with Grownups," *Fortune* (November 11, 1996), p. 158.

[12] *Ibid.*

[13] *Ibid.*

Stale Menu   Decline in Controls

THE SITUATION AT THE NEW MILLENNIUM

Jack Greenberg was promoted to CEO in August 1998, and then to Chairman of the Board in May 1999. There was hope that he would improve the alienation felt by many franchisees. He bought Donatos Pizza, a Midwestern chain of 143 restaurants, proclaiming: "We would like to make this a growth opportunity for our franchisees."[14] In imitation of its competitors, particularly Wendy's, the company installed a new cooking system to deliver sandwiches to order, "Made for You," which meant fresher with less waste compared with the old system of holding bins. "You don't grow this business by having clean washrooms," Greenberg said. "We will grow this business through food."[15]

Despite Greenberg's leadership, McDonald's domestic operations continued to falter. By 2001, it was averaging only 1 percent same-store sales growth, far behind the 4 percent average of Burger King and Wendy's. After 44 years as one of America's premier growth companies, market saturation seemed imminent. The main reason was thought to be a stale menu, but this was hardly a new insight.

Of perhaps just as much concern was the deterioration of the stringent controls that for decades had marked McDonald's as the paragon among all firms. A 2001 University of Michigan study on customer satisfaction showed that if anything conditions had not improved, indeed had gotten worse, from the 1995 survey giving McDonald's low marks on food, service, and cleanliness. This 2001 study also ranked McDonald's among the poorest-performing fast-food chains, with 11 percent of customers dissatisfied because of slow service, wrong orders, dirty stores, and rude and uncaring employees. Estimates were that unhappy customers could mean an average of $60,000 in lost sales per year per store. In efforts to improve customer satisfaction, "customer recovery teams" were planned along with better education of store managers and franchisees in handling complaints.[16]

Undoubtedly such problems reflected the difficulty many businesses had in hiring good help in the low unemployment of the late 1990s and beginning the new millennium. But other fast-food chains were doing better in this regard than McDonald's. Perhaps another factor contributed to the control problems. In recognition of franchisee complaints, Greenberg threw out the Franchise 2000 rulebook with its 80 pages of onerous regulations, and gave franchisees more say in their local menus.

The frenetic growth in outlets of the mid-1990s was over, as many angry franchisees saw their sales decline as much as 20 percent due to cannibalization. In 1999, only 150 new outlets were added, down sharply from the 1,100 of a few years before.

Increasingly Greenberg turned his attention to judicious food diversifications. He planned to grow the 143-store Donatos Pizza regional chain to a national one of 1,000 stores. He bought into Chipotle Mexican Grill, a popular Denver-based chain

[14] James P. Miller and Richard Gibson, "Did Somebody Say Pizza?," *Wall Street Journal* (May 1, 1999), p. A4.

[15] Kevin Helliker and Richard Gibson, "The New Chief Is Ordering Up Changes at McDonald's," *Wall Street Journal* (August 24, 1998), p. B4.

[16] Richard Gibson, Dow Jones News, as reported in "McDonald's Leaders Finding Rudeness, Slowness Are Costing Company Business," *Cleveland Plain Dealer* (July 16, 2001), p. C6.

of Mexican restaurants. The purchase of Aroma, a coffee-and-sandwich bar in London, England, showed perhaps the most promise. In the UK, the cold-sandwich market was almost double the size of the burger market and growing twice as fast, appealing to a mostly single, health-conscious and female customer-base, with practically no overlap with the burger crowd—therefore, no cannibalization. Some 150 stores were planned by 2002. In another major acquisition, the faltering Boston Market chain was acquired on May 26, 2000. About 100 underperforming Boston Market restaurants were closed, with others converted to McDonald's, Chipotle Mexican Grill, and Donatos Pizza. This still left more than 750 Boston restaurants that could challenge McDonald's management in achieving profitability.

In the major menu thrust beyond burgers, more new products were coming out of McDonald's test kitchens than ever before, many of these appealing regionally rather than nationally: for example, the McBrat, a $1.99 sandwich with sauerkraut and onion on the bratwurst, a big hit in Minnesota and Wisconsin; a McLobster Roll in New England; Homestyle Burger with hot mustard in Texas; the Brutus Buckeye Burger for Ohioans; and even bagel breakfast sandwiches, already doing well in 6,000 stores.[17]

Still, U.S. sales grew just 3 percent in 2000, while fourth-quarter net earnings declined 7 percent. McDonald's responded with a "New Tastes Menu," a collection of 44 items to be rotated four-at-a-time. An analyst noted, however, that these were mostly "tired old products with such startling innovations like a strip of bacon or a dollop of ranch dressing."[18]

The Attractiveness of McDonald's Franchises

Despite concerns about future promise and publicity about franchisee concerns, franchise applications in the United States were more than ten times the number of outlets available. McDonald's could still be very choosy in selecting franchisees. This popularity of franchises meant that retiring franchisees could count on buyers for their stores, while the difficulty of gaining a franchise assured only highly motivated people would be finalists.

Financial requirements were not for the marginal. Total price tag for a typical full-size McDonald's was around $500,000 in 1998, with labor, at 8 percent of sales, and rent the major expenses after opening. A prospective franchisee trained at least a year, working in restaurants without pay, even performing such tasks as scrubbing bathrooms. Usually when an opportunity finally came it involved pulling up stakes and moving.[19]

The Situation in the Rest of the World

In Europe, mad cow hysteria and currency woes were playing havoc, and McDonald's stock was at a two-year low. But non-U.S. restaurants continued to offer the best

---

[17] Bruce Upbin, "Beyond Burgers," *Forbes* (November 1, 1999), pp. 218–223.

[18] Brandon Copple, "Same Old, Same Old," *Forbes* (February 19, 2001), p. 60.

[19] Richard Gibson, "McDonald's Problems in Kitchen Don't Dim the Lure of Franchises," *Wall Street Journal* (June 3, 1998), pp. A1, A6.

opportunities, and by the end of 2000 foreign restaurants outnumbered U.S. outlets, 15,900 to 12,408 outlets in the United States. International business contributed 52 percent of total operating income by 2000.[20] The success of the international operations partly reflected McDonald's adaptation to foreign environments. (We saw an example of this earlier in the McMutton Burgers for India Information Box.)

Successful Foreign Adaptations

We will briefly describe adaptations in Yugoslavia during the NATO air war in 1999; in Egypt today; and in Japan, by far the biggest foreign market for McDonald's.

Serbia, 1999

The NATO air war lasted 76 days. At first the 15 McDonald's restaurants in Yugoslavia were closed due to angry mobs bent on vandalizing. Fanned by media attacks on "NATO criminals and aggressors," mobs of youth smashed windows and painted insults. But the restaurants soon reopened, downplaying the U.S. citizenship and presenting McDonald's as a Yugoslav company.

They promoted the McCountry, a domestic pork burger with paprika garnish. (Pork is considered the most Serbian of meats.) To cater to Serbian identity and pride, they brought out posters and lapel buttons showing the golden arches topped with a traditional Serbian cap called the *sajkaca*. Dragoljub Jakic, the 47-year-old managing director of McDonald's in Yugoslavia, noted that the cap "is a strong, unique Serbian symbol. By adding this symbol of our cultural heritage, we hoped to denote our pride in being a local company." They also handed out free cheeseburgers at anti-NATO rallies. One restaurant's basement in Belgrade even became a bomb shelter.

The result? In spite of falling wages, rising prices, and lingering anger at the United States, the McDonald's restaurants were thronged with Serbs.[21]

Egypt

McDonald's franchises introduced the traditional Arab snack—deep-fried patties of ground beans flavored with spices—on an American-style hamburger bun with tomato, lettuce, pickles, and a spicy tahini sauce. At about 38 cents, this McFalafel was one of the cheapest items on the menu, but it was more than three times what a falafel sandwich cost in thousands of shops around the country. The company also sought an authentic touch for its advertising, hiring Egyptian pop star Shaaban Abdel-Rahim to sing its praises with the jingle, "if you eat a bite, you can't stop before finishing the whole roll." Only months before, Abdel-Rahim helped fuel an anti-Israeli and anti-American campaign during Israeli–Palestinian battles, with the hit *I Hate Israel*.[22]

---

[20] Company public information.

[21] Robert Block, "How Big Mac Kept from Becoming a Serb Archenemy," *Wall Street Journal* (September 3, 1999), p. B3.

[22] From the Associated Press, "McDonald's Puts Arab Snack On a Bun," *Tri-City Herald* (June 24, 2001), p. B5.

Japan Inroads

McDonald's has been in Japan for 30 years. By the end of 1995 it had 1,482 restaurants there, by far the largest penetration of any foreign market. (See Table 20.2.) By the end of 1998, there were 2,852 restaurants, and by 2001 nearly 3,600. McDonald's changed the eating habits of the nation, making fast-food a part of everyday life and marking the birth of a business empire. McDonald's—*Maku* in Japanese shorthand—controlled about 65 percent of the fast-food burger market, with $3.5 billion in sales while serving 1.3 billion customers a year. The mad cow disease scare that had so severely affected demand in Europe was largely averted as Japan used Australian beef, where there had been no disease.

Through the years, McDonald's had walloped most of its competitors, including even Burger King, which pulled out of Japan. Price cutting was found to be a very effective strategy amid a decade-long economic slowdown. Part of the success came from adapting hamburgers to the Japanese palate. For example, the Teriyaki Mac Burger was cooked in an Oriental-flavored sauce, and the Calbee Burger featured a Korean-style taste.

On July 26, 2001, McDonald's Japan Co. became a publicly listed company with an initial public offering of $35 a share that would earn about $405 million. Now it raised its sights to another 10,000 outlets by 2010, and was gearing to tackle all rivals for eating out, such as *sjhops* offering beef-over-rice bowls, buckwheat noodles, and shushi.[23]

ANALYSIS

After decades of uninterrupted growth in sales, profits, and number of stores opened, the domestic operation's growth in the latter 1990s seemed endangered. Admittedly, there were good gains in revenues and income, but these reflected a sharp increase in number of stores. For example, in 1996 McDonald's opened 2,500 new stores, four times the number opened just four years before. However, same-store sales dropped 2.5 percent from 1994 to 1995 for U.S. restaurants—all this despite vigorous discounting and promotional efforts. The situation was hardly improved by 2001, except that the number of new stores had slowed drastically, partly in deference to franchisees who cringed at the increased competition, not so much with Wendy's, Burger King, and Taco Bell as from other McDonald's outlets.

Relations with franchisees, formerly best in the industry, deteriorated in the mid-1990s as corporate management pursued policies more dictatorial and selfish than ever before, policies that signaled the end of the kinder-and-gentler stance franchisees remembered. In particular, the new expansion policy aimed at increased market share, regardless of its effect on established franchisees, portended worsening relations and the start of an adversarial instead of supportive climate.

Top management saw the cost-benefit consequences of the aggressive expansion policy as in the company's best interest, especially with greater cost efficiencies of new

---

[23] Yuri Kageyama, Associated Press, as appearing in "McDonald's Shakes Up Japan with IPO Plan," *Cleveland Plain Dealer* (July 25, 2001), p. C4.

construction. If total market share could be substantially increased, despite same-store sales declining, the accounting analysis could support more stores. But was the tradeoff with unhappy franchisees worth it?

A major domestic challenge for a growth-minded McDonald's was the menu: how to appeal to adults and expand market potential. If the dinner market could be tapped, this offered a major growth opportunity. But the last successful menu expansion had been the breakfast menu, and that was decades ago.

What menu changes should be made? With a history of past failures, expectations could hardly be robust. Yet, McDonald's as with any chain organization whether fast-food or otherwise, can test different prices and strategies or different menus and different atmospheres in just a few outlets, and only if results are favorable expand further. By the new millennium, acquisitions of other restaurant chains seemed the best bet for menu diversification, but the assimilation of some of these—such as the Boston Market acquisition—offered no profit guarantees.

The latter half of the 1990s and the beginning of the millennium saw lagging enforcement of the highest standards and controls in the world over product quality and service, those imposed since the days of founder Ray Kroc. Even chairman Greenberg was guilty of saying, "You don't grow this business with clean restrooms. You grow it with food." Now in consumer satisfaction surveys, the cornerstone of the mighty McDonald's was being surpassed by its competitors.

The international market may save the growth of McDonald's. Albeit with some menu adaptations, people in practically all countries of the world are enamored with the hamburger, the symbol of the American way of life. As the *1995 Annual Report* noted, "Our growth opportunities remain significant: on any given day, 99 percent of the world's population does not eat at McDonald's ... yet."

WHAT CAN BE LEARNED?

It is possible to have strong and enduring growth without diversification. For more than four decades, since 1955, McDonald's has grown continuously and substantially. In all this time, the product was essentially the hamburger in its various trappings and accompaniments. Almost all other firms in their quest for growth have diversified, sometimes wisely and synergistically, at other times imprudently and even recklessly.

For such an undeviating focus, the product should have universal appeal, be frequently consumed, and have almost unlimited potential. The hamburger probably meets these criteria better than practically any other product, along with beer, soft drinks, and tobacco. And soft drinks, of course, are a natural accompaniment of the hamburger.

Eventually even the hamburger may not be enough for continued strong growth as the international market reaches saturation and the domestic market oversaturation. Then McDonald's may be forced to seek judicious diversifications or lose the growth mode.

The insight to be gained, however, is that firms in pursuit of growth often jump into acquisitions far too hastily when the better course of action would be to more fully develop market penetration of their existing products.

Beware the reckless drive for market share. A firm can usually "buy" market share, if it is willing to sacrifice profits in so doing. It can step up advertising and sales promotion. It can lower prices, assuming that lower prices would bring more demand. It can increase sales staff and motivate them to be more aggressive. Sales and competitive position then will usually rise. But costs may increase disproportionately. In other words, the benefits to be gained may not be worth the costs.

McDonald's, as we saw in its domestic operation in the mid-1990s, aggressively increased market share by opening thousands of new units. As long as development costs could be kept sufficiently low for these new units to be profitable and not cannibalize or take too much business away from other McDonald's restaurants, then the strategy was defensible. Still, the costs of damaged franchisee relations resulting in lowered morale, cooperation, and festering resentments could be real indeed. Interestingly, this market share growth strategy was toned down by early 2000.

Maintaining the highest standards requires constant monitoring. McDonald's heritage and its competitive advantage has long been associated with the highest standards and controls for cleanliness, fast service, dependable quality of food, and friendly and well-groomed employees. The following Information Box discusses strategy countering by competitors and the great difficulty in matching nonprice strengths.

INFORMATION BOX

MATCHING A COMPETITOR'S STRATEGY

Some strategies are easily countered or duplicated by competitors. Price-cutting is the most easily countered. A price cut can often be matched within minutes. Similarly, a different package or a warranty is easily imitated by competitors.

But some strategies are not so easily duplicated. Most of these involve service, a strong and positive company image, or both. A reputation for quality and dependability is not easily countered, at least in the short run. A good company or brand image is hard to match because it usually results from years of good service and satisfied customers. The great controls of McDonald's with its high standards would seem to be easily imitated, but they proved not to be, as no other firm fully matched them until recently.

The strategies and operations most difficult to imitate often are not the wildly innovative ones, nor the ones that are complex and well researched. Rather they seem to be the simple ones: simply doing a better job in servicing and satisfying customers and in performing even mundane operations cheerfully and efficiently.

What explanation can you give for competitors' inability for so long to match the standards of McDonald's?

Alas, in the last few years even McDonald's has apparently let its control of operational standards slip. We have seen that surveys of customer satisfaction in 1995 and 2001 gave McDonald's low marks on food quality, value, service, and cleanliness, with its competitors showing up considerably better. Why this lapse? Without doubt, maintaining high standards among thousands of units, company-owned as well as franchised, requires constant monitoring and exhortation. But this was successfully done for over four decades.

Can controls be too stringent? In a belated attempt to improve standards and tighten corporate control, McDonald's instituted the controversial Franchising 2000. Among other things this called for grading franchisees, with those receiving the lower grades being penalized. McDonald's also wanted to take away any pricing flexibility for its franchisees: All restaurants now had to charge the same prices, or risk losing their franchise. Not surprising, some franchisees were concerned about this new "get tough" management.

Can controls be too stringent? As with most things, extremes are seldom desirable. All firms need tight controls over far-flung outlets to keep corporate management alert to emerging problems and opportunities and maintain a desired image and standard of performance. In a franchise operation this is all the more necessary since we are dealing with independent entrepreneurs rather than hired managers. However, controls can be so rigid that no room is left for special circumstances and opportunities. If the enforcement is too punitive, the climate becomes more that of a police state than a teamwork relationship with both parties cooperating to their mutual advantage. This brings us to the next insight for discussion.

Is there room for a kinder, gentler firm in today's hotly competitive environment? Many longtime McDonald's franchisees remembered with sadness a kinder, gentler company, an atmosphere nurtured by founder Ray Kroc. To be sure, Kroc insisted that customers be assured of a clean, family atmosphere with quick and cheerful service. To Kroc, this meant strict standards, not only in food preparation but also in care and maintenance of facilities, including toilets. Company auditors closely checked that the standards were adhered to, under Kroc's belief that a weakness in one restaurant could have a detrimental effect on other units in the system. Still, the atmosphere was helpful—the inspectors were "consultants"—rather than adversarial. Kroc was proud that he was responsible for making more than 1,000 millionaires among the franchise holders.

Many franchisees traced the deterioration of franchiser–franchisee relations to the 1992 death of Gerald Newman, McDonald's chief accounting officer. He spent much time interacting with franchisees, sometimes encouraging—he had a reputation for a sympathetic ear—sometimes even giving them a financial break.[24]

So, is it possible and desirable to be a kind and gentle company? With franchisees? Employees? Suppliers? Customers? Of course it is. Organizations, and the people who run them, often forget this in the arrogance of power. They excuse

---

[24] Gibson, "Some Franchisees say…" p. A8.

a "get tough" mindset on the exigencies of competition and the need to be faithful to their stockholders.

Kind and gentle—is this an anachronism, a throwback to a quieter time, a nostalgia long past its usefulness? Let us hope not.

CONSIDER

Can you add other learning insights?

QUESTIONS

1. How do you account for the reluctance of competitors to imitate the successful efforts of another firm in their industry? Under what circumstances is imitation likely to be embraced?

2. To date McDonald's has shunned diversification into unrelated food retailing operations as well as nonfood options. Discuss the desirability of such diversifications.

3. "Eventually—and this may come sooner than most think—there will no longer be any choice locations anywhere in the world for new hamburger outlets. As a McDonald's stockholder, I'm getting worried." Discuss.

4. Does the size of McDonald's give it a powerful advantage over its competitors? How about Burger King in Japan? Why or why not?

5. What do you think is McDonald's near-term and long-term potential? What makes you think this?

6. Is it likely that McDonald's will ever find a saturated market for its hamburgers?

7. Discuss the importance of market share in the fast-food industry.

8. Discuss the desirability of McDonald's efforts to insist on the same price in all domestic restaurants.

9. Do you think McDonald's "adaptability" in such countries as Yugoslavia and Egypt went too far in repudiating U.S. values? Why or why not?

HANDS-ON EXERCISES

1. You have been given the assignment by Edward Rensi in 1993 to instill a recommitment to improved customer service in all domestic operations. Discuss in as much detail as you can how you would go about fostering this among the 10,000 domestic outlets.

2. As a McDonald's senior executive, what long-term expansion mode would you recommend for your company?

3. As a Burger King senior executive, what long-term expansion mode would you recommend for your company to combat a McDonald's maybe grown a bit vulnerable?

TEAM DEBATE EXERCISES

1. Debate this issue: McDonald's is reaching the limits of its growth without drastic change. (Note: The side that espouses drastic change should give some attention to the most likely directions for such, and be prepared to defend these expansion possibilities.)

2. Debate the issue of a "get-tough" attitude of corporate management toward franchisees even if it riles some, versus involving them more in future directions of the company. In particular, be prepared to address the challenge of bringing customer satisfaction up to traditional standards.

3. Debate this contention: Market share is overemphasized in this industry. (Both sides in their debate may want to consider whether this assertion may or may not apply to other industries.)

INVITATION TO RESEARCH

Is McDonald's becoming more vulnerable to competitors today? Does it have any emerging problems? Has it attempted any major diversifications yet? Is the international operation still overshadowing the domestic?

ENTREPRENEURIAL
ADVENTURES

CHAPTER TWENTY-ONE

OfficeMax:
Grasping the Ring

Michael Feuer had a passion to be an entrepreneur. He realized this passion was rather late in coming, but by age 42 he was bored with the corporate life. Still, perhaps it had been there all along, this passion.

He had started with Fabri-Centers of America, a 600-store chain, 17 years before, and had quickly rose through the ranks. He liked to describe himself in those days as suffering from the Frank Sinatra syndrome—"I wanted to do it my way." And he got tired of what he called CYB, "covering your backside," which he saw most executives spending too much of their time trying to do, at the expense of total effectiveness. If he only had his own business he could escape these drains on career satisfaction and constraints on his potential. However, he couldn't accept the common notion of the true entrepreneur as one who has enormous self-confidence, enough to give up the security of the paycheck and go off on his or her own. "I'm not a true entrepreneur because I suffer acutely from what I call 'F of F,' the fear of failure."[1]

In his pursuit of entrepreneurship, Feuer turned down a number of big-money corporate jobs and the perks that go with them. Increasingly he felt an overwhelming urge to be his own man, to succeed or fail on his own terms. He soon realized, however, the reality of starting a small business from scratch and the contrast with what might have been if he had chosen the corporate option.

THE START

Feuer found a partner, Robert Hurwitz, and the two recognized a flaw in the way office products were distributed and sold. The traditional channel of distribution for this merchandise was from manufacturers to wholesalers or distributors and finally to stationers, who were usually small retailers. This rather lengthy process imposed

[1] Until late 1993, little had been written about the success of OfficeMax. Much of the early material and quotes have come from speeches that Feuer made to various business and graduate business school classes.

293

markups at each stage of the distribution and resulted in relatively high prices for the end user. Feuer saw this as archaic, akin to the "old-time mom-and-pop groceries on every corner," which were eventually replaced by more efficient and much lower-priced supermarkets. These for the most part bypassed wholesalers and distributors and went directly to manufacturers.

Feuer and Hurwitz (who is no longer active in the firm on a full-time basis) were able to mass $3 million from 50 investors, some friends and family members as well as a number of doctors and lawyers. The two partners did not use any debt financing, nor did they seek venture capitalists. They shunned these most common sources of capital for new firms, not wanting to give up some control of their enterprise; neither did they want to answer to skeptics and defend every major decision. However, for many promising small businesses, venture capital can provide needed startup funds difficult to obtain otherwise. See the following Information Box for more discussion of venture capitalists and their role in fostering small enterprises.

While Feuer and Hurwitz recognized what seemed an attractive opportunity, they were not the only ones to do so. In May 1988 an industry trade paper listed all the embryonic firms in the emerging office products superstore industry. OfficeMax rated number 14 on a list of 15. "We would have been dead last, but another company had started a week later than we did, although neither one of us had any stores."[2]

Feuer and Hurwitz established headquarters offices in a tiny 500-square-foot brick warehouse. It had little heat or air conditioning. The company owned only a few pieces of office furniture, a coffee-maker, and a copy machine, but no fax. The restroom had to be unisex since there was only space for one toilet. They had recruited seven people who were only half-jokingly told that they needed to have small appetites because there was little money to pay them. But Feuer promised that they would share in the financial success of the company, and for these seven their faith and hope for the future was enough. Feuer likes to tell the story of how he reinterviewed a candidate for a vice president's position who had turned him down in 1988. Had he accepted the job then he would have been a multimillionaire by 1993.

THE FIRST YEAR

Even with $3 million of seed money from the 50 investors, OfficeMax had limited resources for what it proposed to do. A major problem now was to convince manufacturers to do business with this upstart firm in Cleveland. Most manufacturers were satisfied with the existing distribution channels and were reluctant to grant credit to a revolutionary newcomer with hardly a store to its name.

The key to winning the support of these manufacturers lay in convincing them that OfficeMax had such a promising future that it could offer them far more business potential than they would ever have with their present distributors—that OfficeMax would soon be a 30-, 50-, even 300-store chain in a few years. "We explained to them that it was in *their* best interest to help us today—to guarantee a place with us tomorrow."

---

[2] John R. Brandt, "Taking It to the Max," *Corporate Cleveland* (September 1988), p. 17.

INFORMATION BOX

VENTURE CAPITALISTS: AID TO ENTREPRENEURS

The biggest roadblock to self-employment is financing. Banks tend to be unreceptive to funding unproven new ventures, especially for someone without a track record. Given that most would-be entrepreneurs have limited resources from which to draw, where are they to get the financing needed?

Feuer and Hurwitz bypassed conventional sources of financing by finding 50 willing investors. For many other would-be entrepreneurs venture capitalists may be the answer.

Venture capitalists are wealthy individuals (or firms) looking for extraordinary returns for their investments. At the same time, they are willing to accept substantial risks. Backing nascent entrepreneurs in speculative undertakings can be the route to a far greater return on investment than possible otherwise—provided that the venture capitalist chooses wisely who to stake. This decision is much easier after a fledgling enterprise has a promising start. Then venture capitalists may stand in line for a piece of the action. But until then, the entrepreneur may struggle to get seed money.

How do these sources of funding choose among the many business ideas brought to them? "They look at the people, not the ideas," says Arthur Rock, one of the foremost venture capitalists. "Nearly every mistake I've made has been because I picked the wrong people, not the wrong idea."[3]

For a would-be entrepreneur seeking venture capital, then, the most important step may be in selling yourself, in addition to your idea. Intellectual honesty is sometimes mentioned by venture capitalists as a necessary ingredient. This may be defined as a willingness to face facts rigorously and not be deluded by rosy dreams and unrealistic expectations.

Those who win the early support of venture capitalists will likely have to give away a good piece of the action. Should the enterprise prove successful, the venture capitalists will expect to share in the success. Indeed, the funds provided by a venture capitalist may be crucial to even starting, or they may mean the difference in being adequately funded or so poorly funded that failure is almost inevitable.

Selling a definitive business plan to a prospective venture capitalist is usually a requirement for such financing. In the process, of course, you are selling yourself. You may want to do this exercise. Choose a new business idea, develop an initial business plan, and attempt to persuasively present it to a would-be investor.

---

[3] John Merwin, "Have You Got What It Takes?" *Forbes* (August 3, 1981), p. 61.

To make its message credible, OfficeMax needed to create an image of stability and of a firm poised to jump. To help convey this image, Feuer convinced a major Cleveland bank to grant the company an unsecured line of credit. There was only one condition: OfficeMax had to promise that it would never use it. But this impressive-looking line of credit, bespeaking the faith that a major bank seemingly had in the embryonic firm, brought respect from manufacturers. Then OfficeMax even went so far as to ask them for unheard-of terms of sale—such as 60, 90, even 120 days with a discount.

Xerox was somehow persuaded to grant a year's payment delay for purchases. Many other manufacturers also accepted the outlandish requests. The bold promise of growth was realized, and many manufacturers five years later found OfficeMax to be their best customer. OfficeMax became so important at Xerox that the account is now handled by a divisional president and chief financial officer.

The first store was opened July 5, 1988, three months after the enterprise itself was started. This was an amazingly short time to fine-tune the concept, find a site, remodel as needed, and merchandise and staff the store. Feuer explains that the firm urgently needed some cash to survive, hence the desperate efforts to bring the first unit on line. In addition to providing needed cash flow, the first store had to confirm the viability and promise of the superstore concept to investors and suppliers alike.

This the first store quickly did. Customers eagerly embraced the great variety yet lowest prices of the superstore, more commonly known today as a category killer store for office products. The only publicity had been a newspaper story two days before. Yet, the store racked up $6,400 in sales that first day.

In the next 90 days, stores two and three were opened, also in metropolitan Cleveland. The fourth store opened in Detroit, not far from the executive offices of Kmart, destined a few years later to become a majority shareholder. Within six months the company was breaking even before corporate expenses.

As Feuer describes his work schedule in those early days, he typically was in the corporate office from 7:00 A.M. to 7:00 P.M., stopping at his home just long enough to change into nondescript clothing before going to the first store, where he could inconspicuously observe the shopping activity and talk to customers, asking them what they liked and didn't like about the store. He likes to recount how he would even follow customers who left without buying anything out to the parking lot to ask them why OfficeMax did not meet their needs.

Following the example of Feuer, from its inception the company has had a strong commitment to its customers. For example, OfficeMax accepted collect calls from customers. Any complaints had to be resolved in less than 24 hours, complete with an apology from OfficeMax. The company's objective was to build loyalty. "We're not embarrassed to say that we were wrong—and the customer was right."

As the company began making a small profit, Feuer's worst nightmare was that the accounting had been "screwed up," and that OfficeMax was on the verge of bankruptcy without realizing it. With this tormenting thought, he went back to the existing shareholders after six months to raise additional capital. The early success of the enterprise enabled them to raise the per share price 75 percent over the original placement.

By the end of the first full year, OfficeMax had six stores operational in Ohio and Michigan, with total sales of $13 million. The stores were profitable due to undeviating cost-consciousness.

GROWTH CONTINUES

By early 1990, two years into the operation, OfficeMax had 17 stores in operation. Unexpectedly, Montgomery Ward proposed a merger between OfficeMax and Office World, a similar operation that Ward had funded along with a number of venture capitalists. Office World had been started with what seemed to OfficeMax executives as almost a king's ransom. But it proceeded to lose $10 million in a very short time. In the negotiations, OfficeMax was in the power position, and it acquired Office World and its seven Chicago locations on rather attractive terms: Its major concession was to relinquish 2 of its 10 board seats to Montgomery Ward and the venture capitalists, but it acquired along with the stores several million dollars in badly needed cash.

By the summer of 1990, OfficeMax had about $25 million in cash, with 30 stores in operation. It raised another $8 million in a third private placement, at a share price 600 percent higher than the original investors had paid just two years before. Corporate offices were now moved into a building with space for both men's and women's restrooms.

Feuer began an aggressive new expansion program, calling for opening 20 additional stores. Competition was heating up in this new superstore industry, and several competitors had gone public to raise funds for more rapid expansion. Several others had gone bankrupt.

The Kmart Connection

The biggest threat facing OfficeMax now came from news that Kmart was poised to roll out its new Office Square superstore chain, which would be a direct threat to OfficeMax. With all the resources of Kmart—financial, managerial, and real estate expertise and influence—Feuer and company saw themselves being crushed and driven into Lake Erie. Feuer consoled himself that being left penniless would at least be character building.

Mostly as a defensive strategy, Feuer sought to open talks with Kmart. Kmart top executives proved to be receptive, and in November 1990 an agreement was negotiated in which Kmart made an investment of about $40 million in return for a 22 percent equity stake in OfficeMax. As a part of the agreement, the feared Office Square became a possession of OfficeMax, and Kmart received one seat on the OfficeMax board.

Now the expansion program could begin accelerating, with Kmart's full cooperation and support. So good was the rapport that within 10 months of the initial transaction, discussions were started concerning a broader business relationship with Kmart.

As the original goals of the business were being realized, it was perhaps time to cash in some of the chips, Michael Feuer thought. Two options seemed appropriate for the original investors: (1) go public, or (2) structure a new deal with Kmart. The company decided to go with Kmart. Kmart agreed to buy out all of the shareholders, with the exception of 50 percent of the shares of Feuer and partner Hurwitz, for a total market capitalization of about $215 million. This was up from zero just 42 months earlier. What made the deal particularly attractive was the fact that while 92 percent of OfficeMax was sold to a well-heeled parent, it could still retain total autonomy.

Onward and Upward, Without Kmart

By the end of July 1995, OfficeMax had 405 superstores in more than 150 markets in 41 states and Puerto Rico. The typical store was 23,500 square feet and had 6,000 items. Faster growth had been achieved through two major acquisitions: the 46-store Office Warehouse chain and the 105-store BizMart chain.

Sales were primarily to small and medium-sized businesses employing between 1 and 100 employees, home office customers, and individual consumers. But institutions such as school boards and universities were also targets, and the low prices of OfficeMax were a powerful inducement. A new program was established for next-day delivery of office supplies, based on calls to telephone centers with toll-free lines.

The company was planning to open up to 20 new FurnitureMax stores, which were to be 8,000 to 10,000 square feet additions to existing OfficeMax stores devoted to office furniture. It also was testing five to ten new CopyMax stores. Along with a multimedia advertising strategy, the company now had a 220-page merchandise catalog featuring about 5,000 items with toll-free telephone ordering.

Meanwhile, Kmart was seeking additional money to provide badly needed facelifts for its stores in the desperate attempt to hold off the mighty Wal-Mart. This led Kmart to sell its 25 percent share of OfficeMax, as well as some of its other subsidiaries, in order to raise a needed $3 billion in cash. This was finalized in July 1995. OfficeMax sold through underwriters 24,555,375 common shares, including all of the 18,803,526 shares held by Kmart, at $19.875 a share. OfficeMax itself netted $110 million to be used to fund its store expansion. Its future as a public company rather than a subsidiary of Kmart now presented a heady dream to Feuer and his investors. The following Information Box discusses the prescription for great wealth in going public.

By fiscal 1995 (year ending January 31), revenues were over $1.8 billion. Net income was $30.4 million, up 181 percent from the year before. Figures 21.1 and 21.2 show the growth in sales and in number of stores.

INFORMATION BOX

THE PRESCRIPTION FOR GREAT WEALTH FOR ENTREPRENEURS

An entrepreneur often has much to gain by going public with an enterprise after a few years if it shows early success and a promising future. The entrepreneur keeps a portion of the stock and offers the rest to the public. With an attractive new venture, the offering price may be high enough to make the entrepreneur an instant multimillionaire.

Take Office Depot, for example. This was the largest office supply superstore chain in North America, although it is not that much bigger than OfficeMax. It was listed on the New York Stock Exchange and its 94,143,455 shares of common stock sold for about $39 a share, giving a total market value of about $3.7 billion. If OfficeMax went public and had a similar relative market value and if Feuer and Hurwitz held 8 percent of the total capitalization, they would be worth about $296 million or almost $150 million apiece.

What rationale do you see for Feuer's decision to structure a new deal with Kmart rather than go public? Do you agree with his rationale?

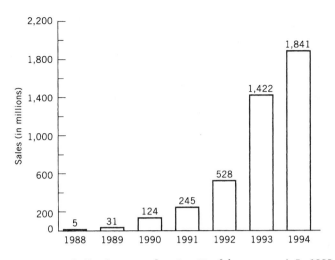

Figure 21.1 Sales growth (fiscal years ending Jan. 31 of the next year). In 1988, OfficeMax projected 1993 sales of less than $100 million; actual 1993 sales were 14 times larger.

STORM CLOUDS

In 1996, OfficeMax became only the fourth company up to that time to exceed $3 billion in revenues in less than nine years. As of September 1998, it had 769 stores in 48 states and Puerto Rico. Through joint ventures, it also had nine stores in Mexico and a first store in Japan. In addition, there were 129 CopyMax outlets

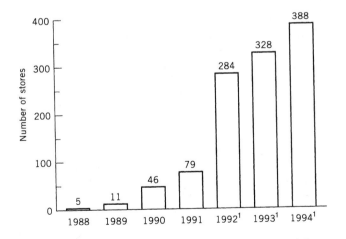

Figure 21.2 Growth in number of stores (fiscal years ending Jan. 31 of the next year). OfficeMax's 1988 business plan called for 50 stores by 1993; the company ended the year with nearly seven times that number.

[1] Includes BizMart stores.

targeting the estimated $9 billion "print-for-pay" industry, as well as 129 FurnitureMax stores tapping the estimated $12 billion office furniture industry.[4]

In 1999, it planned to open 120 new superstores in the United States on top of the 150 opened in 1998. Revenues had steadily climbed to $3.765 billion in 1997, while net income had grown to $89.6 million, an increase of 30 percent from 1996.[5] Over the three-year period from January 31, 1994 to January 31, 1997, OfficeMax's market share compared to its largest competitor, Office Depot, rose from 30.1 percent to 35.9 percent, as shown below:

	Fiscal Year 1997	1994
Office Depot revenues	$6.716 billion	$4.266 billion
OfficeMax revenues	3.765	1.841
Market share of OfficeMax relative to Office Depot	35.9%	30.1%

Yet, OfficeMax's stock price had fallen precipitously to under $10 a share by September 1998. By late 1998, analysts began attacking OfficeMax: It was showing up more poorly than competitors Office Depot and Staples. In particular, sales were lagging at its older stores, and OfficeMax warned that third- and fourth-quarter earnings would not hit expectations, mostly because of heavy price-cutting on computers. Critics were quick to point out that Office Depot and Staples were not so adversely affected.[6] Was this just a temporary aberration?

The situation was to worsen, as businesses began cutting back in a slowing economy in 2000, and the office-supply industry faced an oversaturated market: too many stores from years of vigorous expansion in the 1990s.

The fourth quarter of 2000, which should have been the strongest quarter of the year, was particularly nasty. OfficeMax posted an $85 million loss, while Office Depot and Staples posted $168 million and $112 million losses respectively. All announced sharp cuts in expansion and closings of underperforming stores. OfficeMax, now grown to 995 stores, planned 50 store closings.[7] Company stock was trading around $2 a share.

ANALYSIS

Here we see what initially was an outstanding entrepreneurial success. The growth rate in only a few years rivaled the best at that time. In the same year that OfficeMax was started, 685,095 other new businesses were also formed in the United States, but

---

[4] *1998 OfficeMax Annual Report.*

[5] *Ibid.*

[6] For example, Teresa Dixon Murray, "Office Max Predicts Shortfall in Earnings," *Cleveland Plain Dealer* (October 7, 1998), pp. 1C, 2C; and "OfficeMax Opens New Stores While Sales Lag at Old Ones," *Cleveland Plain Dealer* (October 29, 1998), p. 2C.

[7] Mya Frazier, "Bad Day at the Office [Supplier]," *Cleveland Plain Dealer* (March 7, 2001), p. C1.

more than half of these eventually failed. Of the survivors, only a small percentage would ever achieve a net worth over $50 million. Only a handful would ever reach $200 million. What made OfficeMax so uniquely successful?

It was not that it had identified a great idea and nurtured it exclusively. While OfficeMax launched on to a business opportunity arising from the archaic distribution structure of the office-supplies industry, it was far from unique in this identification. Indeed, the concept of category-killer stores was in the ascendancy for all kinds of retail goods.[8] The competition could become intense when category-killer stores competed with each other. Eventually, only three chains of superstores remained in the office-products industry, and OfficeMax was one of these, although the smallest. Why did OfficeMax succeed so well, while most of its competitors failed or were acquired?

Much of the success was due to the efforts of the principal founder, Michael Feuer. His vision was to retain control of the nascent enterprise by shunning venture capitalists and debt financing. While the money initially raised, $3 million, would seem adequate for most ventures, for a category-killer chain it was barely sufficient. But severe austerity combined with the promise of great future rewards motivated both employees and suppliers. This required optimism and an enthusiastic selling job by Feuer. And it also required a trusting relationship with investors, employees, and suppliers.

Great attention to customer service, to cost containment to the point of austerity, to the myriad details needed for opening stores with adequate employees and merchandise in severe deadline situations—all of these were part of the success package.

Building on the growth without losing sight of the austerity heritage was perhaps even more important as the enterprise grew from a few stores to 20, 50, and more.

Of particular interest for any growing enterprise is the opportunity to make attractive acquisitions of former competitors who have fallen into desperate straits. The successful firm is in a position to quickly build on the bones of former competitors who could not make it.

Alas, some of the early virtues of austerity and moderate borrowing (and consequent modest interest expenses) were disregarded in the heady rush to expansion in the late 1990s. A saturated market and an economic slowdown forced retrenchment, not only for OfficeMax but for its bigger competitors as well.

WHAT CAN BE LEARNED?

Successful entrepreneurship is not easy. Not many who opt to go into business for themselves expect this to be an easy road, a comfortable and lazy lifestyle. Yet the work ethic of successful entrepreneurs can be awesome, even for those prepared for long hours and worries in the night. Michael Feuer customarily put in 12- to 18-hour days between corporate headquarters and keeping in close touch with

---

[8] A *category-killer* store gets its name from the strategy of carrying such a huge assortment of merchandise at good prices in a particular category of goods that they practically destroy traditional merchants of such goods.

stores and customers and suppliers. He would wake up at 3 A.M. to stare at the ceiling while wondering if he made the right decision. He felt a responsibility to his employees, even after they had grown from the seven original ones whose jobs depended on his decisions. By the end of 1993, he had more than 19,000 reasons to worry in the night.

Would he have been less successful with a more moderate work ethic? Maybe. But the personal stake in a growing business drives many entrepreneurs to become workaholics even to the point of sacrificing other aspects of their lives, including family.

There is power in a growth image, even if it is only an illusion. In perhaps one of the most crucial moves taken in the early and most vulnerable months of the embryonic enterprise, Feuer and his people were able to sell both bankers and manufacturers on the great growth prospects for the company, that "we would rapidly become a 20-, 50-, or even 300-store chain. We explained that it was in *their* best interest to help us today—to guarantee a place with us tomorrow."

What makes a strong growth company so attractive to investors, creditors, suppliers, and employees? Part of the attractiveness certainly is that everyone likes to be associated with a winner. The greatest appeal of growth companies is their economic promise. This embraces investors, of course, because their investment grows with the business. Creditors and suppliers see more and more business coming their way as the company grows ever larger. And employees see great career opportunities continually opening up in a rapidly growing organization.

Perhaps in creating the image of OfficeMax as a company on the threshhold of great growth, Feuer was simply very persuasive. But perhaps many of the people he talked with were so eager to be convinced and to be offered the opportunity to get in on the ground floor of what might be the stuff of dreams that they would accept even grandiose conjecture.

Go the extra miles in customer relations. It is easy for an organization to proclaim its dedication to customer service and good customer relations. Too often, however, such is only lip service, pious pronouncements without real substance. OfficeMax went far beyond lip service. Feuer and his executives, at least in the early years, sought close contact with customers in stores, even to the point of following them to the parking lot to see what might have been lacking in the merchandise or service that discouraged a purchase. The company accepted collect calls from customers who might have problems or complaints or special needs. A promise of satisfaction of all complaints within 24 hours, the guiding "How can we make you happy?" question in all customer dealings, and readiness to apologize attest to a customer commitment beyond the ordinary. With few exceptions, all businesses depend on customer loyalty and repeat business for their success. Perhaps in office products, where many customers are businesses, customer loyalty is all the more important. But it is easy to delude yourself and an organization that the loss of any single customer is not all that important, and that the firm must guard against being taken advantage of by unreasonable customers. Where should a firm, particularly a retailer, draw the line? Can any retailer be too liberal in the handling of customer complaints?

Again, the power of "lean and mean." In several earlier cases we noted problems of bloated bureaucracies and/or uncontrolled spending, and the dire effect on profitability. We examined several highly successful firms, notably Southwest Airlines and Vanguard, that followed a policy of continued frugality despite increasing size. The temptation with great growth is to let down the barriers and open the spending spigots. OfficeMax resisted this urge in the early years, but then got caught up in the frenzy of opening stores as fast as it could.

Again, dedicated employees can give a powerful advantage. As with Southwest Airlines, OfficeMax in its early years was able to stimulate employees to move beyond individual concerns to a higher level of performance, a true team approach. This dedication, and the vague promise of future great expectations, brought employees to OfficeMax for very low wages, some turning down much higher paying jobs for the dream that might or might not come to pass. The dedication of these employees made possible opening the first store from scatch barely three months after the company was founded, with other stores quickly following.

The hope for great growth, a trusted leader, and an organization geared to a team effort seem to be most compatible in producing dedicated employees. One suspects there is also a close relationship in lean-and-mean organizations, where limited bureaucracy and management levels bring ease of communication. Unfortunately for a maturing OfficeMax, such motivational factors began to wane. The hope for great growth had to be more soberly appraised in a competitive environment where OfficeMax was number three behind two other aggressive competitors and in an almost-saturated market.

Beware market saturation. How many office-supply superstores can one metro area handle and still enable all outlets to prosper? Especially when there is little to choose from among the major competitors? OfficeMax, Staples, and Office Depot all have large box stores, widest possible assortment of goods, and reasonably low prices, and all push employees to be friendly, knowledgeable, and to provide the best possible service. In such an environment with little distinctiveness possible, market saturation or overstoring becomes a real problem. It hurts profitability, until weaker competitors leave the market, and certainly curbs the growth potential.

CONSIDER

Can you identify other learning insights coming from this case?

QUESTIONS

1. In the hiring process, how would you identify candidates who are most likely to become dedicated employees?
2. Can a firm be too liberal in handling customer complaints?
3. "OfficeMax is number three in its industry. This is a severe disadvantage, as it can never match the resources of its two larger competitors." Evaluate this assertion.

4. Do you think Feuer was being entirely ethical when he sold manufacturers on the desirability of doing business with OfficeMax in the very early days of the company? Why or why not?

5. Do you see any limitations to the future of category-killer stores?

6. Can you think of some types of merchandise where category-killer stores are unlikely to be successful?

7. Feuer regularly put in 12- to 18-hour days in the early years. Do you think he would have been as successful with less of a work ethic? Why or why not?

8. Do a SWOT analysis—analyzing strengths and weaknesses, opportunities and threats (see Chapter 17) for OfficeMax. What do you conclude as far as future prospects?

9. Would you like to work for OfficeMax today? (You may want to do a little investigation of job opportunities there to support your position.)

HANDS-ON EXERCISES

1. You own a small office-supply store. Business has been steady and sufficient for a good living for you and your family up to now. Now an OfficeMax has opened less than a mile away. Discuss how you possibly can compete against such a superstore when you cannot come close to matching their variety of goods or their prices.

2. You are the assistant to Feuer. He wants you to draw up plans for targeting large institutions and businesses. Be as specific as you can, making assumptions where needed, and persuasively support your recommendations.

TEAM DEBATE EXERCISE

On October 25, 1995, the largest office-products retailer, Office Depot, announced it was planning to open a dozen stores on OfficeMax's home turf, metropolitan Cleveland, where OfficeMax has its headquarters and 17 stores. "When we enter a major market, our usual policy is to go in rather quickly and saturate the market with 6 to a dozen to 20 stores within the first couple of years," Office Depot said. Michael Feuer was unfazed. "We think the advantage we have is such a fierce sense and focus of local pride. I don't think there will be much of a test," he said. Debate the challenge OfficeMax now faces: It should be badly worried, because the market already is close to saturation; it should not be worried since the market potential is still increasing and it can outperform Office Depot.[9]

---

[9] Bill Lubinger, "Office Depot Is Taking on OfficeMax," *Cleveland Plain Dealer* (October 25, 1995), p. C1.

INVITATION TO RESEARCH

What is the situation with OfficeMax today? Has it come back to profitability and growth? How does its price-earnings ratio compare with Office Depot and Staples?

Boston Beer: Leading
the Microbrewers

Jim Koch was obsessed with becoming an entrepreneur. He wasn't quite sure where he should do his entrepreneuring—maybe the brewing industry? Years before, his great-great-grandfather, Louis Koch, had concocted a recipe at his St. Louis brewery that was heavier, more full-bodied than such as Budweiser or Miller. However, it was much more expensive to produce than mass-market beers. It involved a lengthy brewing and fermentation process, as well as such premium ingredients as Bavarian hops that cost many times more than those regularly used by other brewers.

BCG MATRIX Jim had a well-paying job with the prestigious Boston Consulting Group. He had been with them for six-and-a-half years already, but still he was haunted by that dream of becoming his own man. Of late, the thought pursued him that maybe the brewing industry might be ripe for a new type of product and a new approach, a good-tasting brew something like his ancestor's. He wondered if he might have a strategic window of *TARGET* opportunity in a particular consumer segment: men in their mid-twenties and older who were beer aficionados and would be willing to pay a premium for a good-tasting beer. What he couldn't be certain of was how large this segment was, and he knew from his consulting experience that too small a segment doomed a strategy. So, were there enough such sophisticated drinkers to support the new company that he envisioned?

In 1984, he thought he detected a clue that this might indeed be the case: sales were surging for import beers such as Heineken and Beck's with their different tastes. Didn't this portend that enough Americans would be willing to pay substantially more for a full-bodied flavor?

NICHE As he studied this more, he also came to believe that these imports were very vulnerable to well-made domestic brews. They faced a major problem in maintaining freshness with a product that goes sour rather quickly. He knew that the foreign brewers, in trying to minimize the destructive influence of the time lag between production and consumption, were adding preservatives and even using cheaper ingredients for the American market.

Some small local brewers offered stronger tastes. But they were having great difficulty producing a lager with consistent quality. And he sensed they were squandering their opportunity. Although they could produce small batches of well-crafted

Micros lacked Q.C. &
mktg. savvy

beer, albeit of erratic quality, what they mainly lacked was ability and resources to aggressively market their products.

He decided to take the plunge, and gave up his job.

Amassing sufficient capital to start a new venture is the common problem with almost all entrepreneurs, and so it was with Koch. Still, he was better off than most. He had saved $100,000 from his years with Boston Consulting, and he persuaded family and friends to chip in another $140,000. But while this might be enough to start a new retail or service venture, it was far less than the estimated $10 million or more needed to build a state-of-the-art brewery.

Koch got around this major obstacle. Instead of building or buying he contracted an existing firm, Pittsburgh Brewing Company, to brew his beer. It had good facilities, but more than this, its people had the brewing skills coming from more than 20 years of operation. He would call his new beer Samuel Adams, after a Revolutionary War patriot who was also a brewer.

His strength was Marketing, Not Brewing

PROBLEMS

A mighty problem still existed, and the success of the venture hinged on this. Koch would have to sell his great-tasting beer at $20 a case to break even and make a reasonable profit. But this was 15 percent more than even the premium imports like Heineken. Would anyone buy such an expensive beer, and one that didn't even have the cachet of an import? See the following Information Box about the merits of a high-price strategy. *SKIMMING*

It fell to Koch as the fledgling firm's only salesperson to try to acquaint retailers and consumers with his new beer, this unknown brand with the very high price. "I went from bar to bar," he said. "Sometimes I had to call 15 times before someone would agree to carry it."[1] *Personal Selling*

He somehow conjured up enough funds for a $100,000 ad campaign in the local market. Shunning the advertising theme of the big brewers that stressed the sociability of the people drinking their brand, Koch's ads attacked the imports: "Declare your independence from foreign beer," he urged. And the name Samuel Adams was compatible with this cry for independence. Foreign brews were singled out as not having the premium ingredients and quality brewing of Samuel Adams. Koch appeared on most of his commercials, saying such things as: "Hi, I'm Jim Koch. It takes me all year to brew what the largest import makes in just three hours because I take the time to brew Samuel Adams right. I use my great-great-grandfather's century-old recipe, all malt brewing and rare hops that cost 10 times what they use in the mass-produced imports."[2]

Gradually his persistence in calling on retailers and his anti-import ads, some of which garnered national attention in such periodicals as *Newsweek* and *USA Today*, induced more and more bartenders and beer drinkers to at least try Samuel Adams. Many liked it, despite the high price. (Or, perhaps, because of it?) *Free P.R.*

[1] Jenny McCune, "Brewing Up Profits," *Management Review* (April 1994), p. 18.
[2] *Ibid.*, p. 19.

- little guy
- personal touch
- quality ingredients
- Buy American

Price Signalling (handwritten)

INFORMATION BOX

COMPETING ON PRICE, REVISITED: THE PRICE-QUALITY PERCEPTION

In the Southwest Air case, we examined the potent strategy of offering the lowest prices—if this could be done profitably due to a lower expense and overhead structure than competitors.

Here, Boston Beer is attempting to compete while having some of the highest prices in the industry. Is this crazy? Why would anyone pay prices higher than even the expensive imported beers, just for a different taste?

The highest price can convey an image of the very highest quality. We as consumers have long been conditioned to think this. With cars, we may not be able to afford this highest quality, such as an Infiniti, Lexus, or Mercedes convertible. But with beer, almost anyone can afford to buy the highest price brew sometimes, maybe to influence guests or to simply enjoy a different taste that we are led to think is better.

Sometimes such a price-quality perception sets us up. It might be valid, or might not be. Especially is this true where quality is difficult to ascertain, such as with beer and liquor, with bottled water, with perfume, as well as other products with hidden ingredients and complex characteristics.

Do you think you have ever fallen victim to the price-quality misperception? How does one determine quality for an alcoholic beverage such as vodka, gin, and scotch, as well as beer? By the taste? The advertising claims? Anything else?

DISTRIBUTION PROBLEMS (handwritten heading)

Now his problem became finding distributors, and this proved particularly troubling for a new firm in an industry where major brands often had a lock on existing wholesalers. The situation was so bad in Boston—no wholesaler would carry Samuel Adams, even though it was a local brand—that Boston Beer bought a truck and delivered the cases itself.

slow growth (handwritten) He slowly expanded his distribution one geographical area at a time, from Boston into Washington, D.C., then to New York, Chicago, and California, taking care that production could match the steady expansion without sacrificing quality. He brought in his secretary at Boston Consulting, Rhonda Kaliman, to assist him in building a sales organization. This grew from less than a dozen sales reps in 1989 to 70 nationwide by 1994, more than any other microbrewer and about the same number as Anheuser-Busch, the giant of the industry. Now Samuel Adams salespeople could give more personalized and expert attention to customers than competitors whose sales reps often sold many beverage lines. *large sales force* (handwritten)

Sales soared 63 percent in 1992 when the company went national and achieved distribution in bars and restaurants in 48 states. In a continual search for new beer ideas, Boston Beer added a stout, a wheat beer, and even a cranberry lambic, a type of beer flavored with fruit. Adding to the growing popularity were numerous industry awards and citations Samuel Adams had received since 1984. Not only was it

AWARDS (handwritten)

voted the Best Beer in America four times at the annual Great American Beer Festival, but it received six gold medals in blind tastings.

Jim Koch and two of his brewmasters were testing their entry into the Great American Beer Festival—"Triple Bock." They had not yet tried to market this creation, although their expectations were high. But this was so different. It boasted a 17 percent alcoholic content with no carbonation and they planned to package it in a cobalt blue bottle with a cork. It was meant to be sipped as a fine brandy. "It's a taste that nobody has ever put into a beer," Koch said.[3] Too innovative? Jim and his colleagues pondered this as they sipped on this beautiful day in April 1994.

THE BREWING INDUSTRY IN THE 1990s

In 10 years, the company had forged ahead to become a major contender in its industry and the largest U.S. specialty brewer. But a significant change in consumer preferences was confronting the industry in the 1990s. The big brands that had been so dominant, to the extent that smaller brewers could not compete against their production efficiencies, now were seeing their market shares decline. The brand images they had spent millions trying to establish were in trouble. Many were cutting prices in desperate attempts to keep and lure consumers. For example, special price promotions in some markets were offering 12-packs of Budweiser, Coors, and Miller for just $1.99.

The shifting consumer preferences, and the severe price competition with their regular brands, were compelling the big brewers to seek the types of beers that would command higher prices. Imports were still strengthening, growing at an 11 percent rate between 1993 and 1994. But microbrews seemed the wave of the future, with prices and profit margins that were mouth-watering to the big barons of the industry.

Consequently, the major breweries came up with their own craft brands. For example, Icehouse, a name that conveys a microbrewery image, was actually produced in megabreweries by Miller Brewing. So too, Killian's Irish Red, a pseudo-import, was made by Coors in Golden, Colorado. Killian's, stocked in retailer's import cases and commanding a high price, muscled its way abreast of Samuel Adams as the largest specialty beer in the United States.

The brewing industry was desperately trying to innovate. But no one saw anything revolutionary on the horizon, not like the 1970s, when light beer made a significant breakthrough in the staid industry. Now, "ice" beers became the gimmick. First developed in Canada, these are beers produced at temperatures a little colder than ordinary beer. This gives them a slightly higher alcohol content. Whether because of this, or the magic of the name *ice,* these products captured almost 6 percent of total industry sales in 1994, more than all the imports combined. But, still, the potential seems limited.

Anheuser-Busch, with a still dominant 44 percent of U.S. beer sales despite its 9 percent sales volume slide in the early 1990s, asserted its reluctance to change: "The breweries that we have are designed to produce big brands. Our competition can't

[3] McCune, p. 20.

compete with big brands. That's why they've had to introduce lots of little brands."[4] But even Anheuser, despite its words, was sneaking into microbrewing by buying into Redhook Ale Brewery, a Seattle microbrewery that sold 76,000 barrels of beer in 1993, versus Anheuser's 90 million. Anheuser's distributors applauded this move as a badly needed step in giving them higher-profit, prestige brands. When Anheuser tip-toed into this market, other giants began to look for microbreweries to invest in.

threat

This troubled Jim Koch: "I'm afraid of the big guys. They have the power to dom-inate any segment they want." Then he expressed his confidence: "Still, my faith is that better beer will win out."[5]

THE CONTINUING SAGA OF BOSTON BEER

IPO.

In August 1995, Boston Beer announced an initial public stock offering (IPO) of 5.3 million shares, of which 990,000 shares would be made available directly to the pub-lic through a coupon offer. This selling of shares to the general public was unlike any other IPO, and as such caught the fancy of the national press.

Free P.R.!

The company put clip-and-mail coupons on Samuel Adams six-packs and other beer packages. These offered customers a chance to buy 33 shares of stock at a maximum price of $15, or $495 total. Only one subscription was allowed per customer, and these were honored on a first-come, first-served basis. The success was overwhelming. First distributed in October, by the first of November the offering was oversubscribed. The company expected that the total funds generated from the IPO would be $75 million.[6] But when the new stock offering finally came out on November 20, 1995, heavy demand led to it being priced at $20 a share. Two days later it was selling on the New York Stock Exchange for $30. Interestingly, its stock symbol is SAM.

Boston Beer was riding a high. It reported an impressive 50 percent growth in 1994 over 1993, brewing 700,000 barrels and becoming the largest microbrewery in the country. The entire microbrewing industry was producing more than double the volume in 1990. By now Boston Beer had 12 different beers, including 6 seasonal, and was distributing in all 50 states through 300 wholesalers. Its newest beer, the 17-percent alcohol content Triple Bock, had been introduced to the market.[7]

The Down-side of Contract

Most of Boston Beer's production continued to be contract brewed. In early 1995, it did encounter difficulties with Pittsburgh Brewing, the first of the three con-tract breweries it was now using. Because of an alleged overdraft of $31 million by its owner, Michael Carlow, who was accused of fraud, the brewery was to be auctioned off. Jim Koch stoutly professed having no interest in buying the brewery and that any problems of Pittsburgh Brewery would have no effect on Boston Beer.[8] See the fol-lowing Information Box for a discussion of contracting out rather than building pro-duction facilities.

---

[4] Patricia Sellers, "A Whole New Ballgame in Beer," *Fortune* (September 19, 1994), p. 86.

[5] *Ibid.*

[6] "Boston Beer's Plan for Offering Stock," *New York Times—National Edition* (August 26, 1995), p. 20.

[7] "Little Giants," *Beverage-World* (December 1994), p. 26.

[8] "Sam Adams Brewer May Be On Block," *Boston-Business-Journal* (February 24, 1995), p. 3.

INFORMATION BOX

THE MERITS OF EXPANDING SLOWLY AND KEEPING FIXED COSTS TO A MINIMUM

There is much to be said for any enterprise, new or older, to keep its fixed overhead to a minimum. If it can escape having to commit large sums to physical plant and production facilities, its breakeven point is far less, which means that less sales are needed to cover expenses and interest payments, leaving more to go into profits. In the event of adversity, such a firm can retrench much more nimbly than if burdened with heavy overhead. In every such decision of renting or buying, the economics of the particular situation need to be carefully analyzed.

Arguments against such contracting out usually maintain that efficiency will be sacrificed, since direct control is lacking. So, this argument would maintain that Pittsburgh Brewing could not do as good a job as Boston Beer could have done itself. Yet, the empirical evidence is that Boston's contract brewers were giving it the high standards it wanted. It set the standards and insisted on them being met, or it would find another contract brewery.

Still, the "edifice complex" tantalizes most top executives, as well as hospital and school administrators, who see the stone and mortar of their buildings and factories as conveying tangible evidence of their own importance and accomplishments. They will claim that such is important to the public image of their organization.

Given the approximately $100 million that Boston Beer receives from its IPO, would you predict some of this will go for "stones and mortar"?

TOWARD THE MILLENNIUM

By 1998, Samuel Adams had become the seventh-largest brewer overall, and was the largest independent craft brewer, in the sector that had grown 39 percent in a five-year period, while U.S. beer total shipments remained virtually flat. Samuel Adams Boston Lager, the company's flagship product, grew faster than the overall craft beer sector, and accounted for the majority of Boston Beer's sales in 1997.

For 1997, revenues were $184 million, down 3.8 percent from the year before, but a major increase from the $77 million in 1994, the year before Boston went public. Net income at $7.6 million was a decline of 9.9 percent from the year before, but this compared with $5.3 million in 1994.

Boston Beer produced more than two dozen styles of beer, and was selling in all 50 states and several foreign countries. Its sales force was still the largest of any craft brewer, and one of the largest in the domestic beer industry.

The acute disappointment had to be the stock market valuation of its shares. An exuberant public reaction to the initial stock offering had bid the price up to $30 a share. Almost immediately, the share price began a slow decline. By late 1998, shares were trading around $8.

The situation had not improved significantly by the millennium. Indeed, the growth that had so bedazzled Koch and early investors seemed only an illusion. Samuel Adams had been the forefather of microbrews, but this specialty market had now spawned 3,000 microbrews, all competing within the $3 billion beer segment—a market that represented just 3 percent of the U.S. beer market—with a mind-boggling array of ciders, ales, stouts, and so-called better beers. "After people got inundated with so many choices ... they kind of stepped back," said one industry analyst.[9]

Koch drastically cut back his assortment of different brews, concentrating only on best sellers: the flagship lager and four seasonal brews. He went through four advertising agencies in six years trying to find the right pitch, but without much success. Experts were wondering if Koch would eventually sell out to a big brewer such as Miller. By mid-2001, the stock price ranged from $8 to $10 a share, still a disaster for its IPO investors.

ANALYSIS

Entreprenurial Character

Although many entrepreneurial opportunities come in the retail and service industries, mostly because these typically require less startup investment, Jim Koch saw the possibility in beer, even without a huge wallet. He started with $100,000 of his own money and $140,000 from friends and relatives. He had the beer recipe and determination. By contracting out the production to an existing brewery with unused production capacity, the bulk of the startup money could be spent on nonproduction concerns, such as advertising.

TRAITS His determination to gain acceptance of his beer, despite its high price and domestic origin, is characteristic of most successful entrepreneurs. They press on, despite obstacles in gaining acceptance. They have confidence that their product or concept is viable. They are not easily discouraged.

At the same time, Koch believed he had something unique, a flavor and quality that neither domestic nor imported brews could deliver. He had the audacity to further make his product unique by charging even higher prices than the imports, thus conveying an image of highest quality.

His search for uniqueness did not end with the product. He developed an advertising theme far different from that of other beers by stressing quality and aggressively attacking the imports: "Declare your independence from foreign beer." And he was the spokesman on TV and radio commercials, giving a personal and charismatic touch.

As Boston Beer moved out of regional into national distribution, he developed a sales force as large as Anheuser-Busch, the giant of the industry. His grasping of uniqueness even went to Boston Beer's initial public stock offering, in which customers were invited to buy into the company through coupons on six-packs. And it was oversubscribed in only a few weeks.

---

[9] Hillary Chura, "Boston Beer Crafts Strategy: Slumping Brewer Abandons Some of Its Specialty Beers," *Advertising Age* (November 8, 1999), p. 20.

Controlled Growth

The temptation for any firm, but especially for newer, smaller firms, when demand seems to be growing insatiably is to expand aggressively: "We must not miss this opportunity." Such optimism can sow the seeds of disaster, when demand suddenly lessens because of a saturated market and/or new competition. And our firm is left with too much plant and other fixed assets, and a burdensome overhead.

Controlled growth—we might also call this "aggressive moderation"—is usually far better. Now our firm is not shunning growth, even vigorous growth, but is controlling it within its present resources, not overextending itself. Boston Beer showed this restraint by expanding within its production capability, adding several more contract brewers as needed. It expanded market by market at the beginning, moving to a new geographical area only when it could supply it. First was Boston, then Washington DC, then New York, Chicago, California, and finally all 50 states.

Besides husbanding resources, both material and personnel, aggressive moderation is compatible with the tightness of controls needed to assure high-quality product and service standards. Even more than this, moderation allows a firm to build the accounting and financial standards and controls needed to prevent the dangerous buildup of inventories and expenses.

Limits on Potential

It is difficult to perceive, in the heady days of growth for a new firm, that the growth potential is sorely limited, without drastic and risky changes. Limits on potential usually are due to two factors:

1. Ease of entry into the industry, which encourages a host of competitors. This turned out to be especially true with the influx of microbrewers, to 3,000 in just a few years. (It was also a major factor in the devastation of the dot.coms as described in Chapter 15.)

2. Finite potential in demand. (This also affected the high-tech industry and the collapse of the Nasdaq at the turn of the millennium.) Demand for specialty beer, while at first robust and rising, was certainly not going to take over the mainsteam beer market.

Given the rush to microbreweries in an environment of limited demand, the aspirations of Jim Koch to be a dominant force in the brewing industry had to be curbed. He could still be a profitable firm and do well in his niche, but he would never be a challenge beyond that. Perhaps that is enough for most entrepreneurs. They can hardly expect to grasp the golden ring of complete market dominance.

WHAT CAN BE LEARNED?

The price-quality perception. We have a curious phenomenon today regarding price. More consumers than ever are shopping at discount stores because they supposedly offer better prices than other retailers. Airlines competing with lowest prices, such as Southwest and Continental, are greatly increasing airline traffic. Yet for many products, especially those that are complex and have hidden ingredients, a higher price than competitors is the major indicator of high quality. Boston Beer certainly confirms that higher price can successfully differentiate a firm. Especially if the taste is robustly different, and if the theme of highest quality is constantly stressed in advertising.

Perhaps the moral is that both low prices and high prices can be successful. A strategy of lowest prices, however, tends to be more vulnerable since competitors can so easily and quickly match these low prices (not always profitably, of course), while a high-price strategy stressing quality tends to attract fewer competitors. But it will also attract fewer customers, as with higher-priced goods such as office furniture (remember Herman Miller?). The high-price strategy should be more generally successful with products that are relatively inexpensive to begin with, such as beer, and ones where the image of prestige and good taste is attractive.

The challenge of the right approach to growth. In the analysis section we discussed the desirability of controlled growth or aggressive moderation and noted that Boston Beer practiced this well. There are some who would challenge such a slowness in grabbing opportunities. Exuberant expansion instead is advocated, when and if the golden opportunity is presented (some would call this "running with the ball"). Operations should be expanded as fast as possible in such a situation, some would say. But there are times when caution is advised.

Risks lie on all sides as we reach for these opportunities. When a market begins to boom and a firm is unable to keep up with demand without greatly increasing capacity and resources, it faces a dilemma: Stay conservative in the expectation that the burgeoning potential will be short-lived, and thereby abdicate some of the growing market to competitors, or expand vigorously and take full advantage of the opportunity. If the euphoria is short-lived, and demand slows drastically, the firm is then left with expanded capacity, more resource commitment than needed, high interest and carrying costs, and perhaps even jeopardized viability because of overextension. Above all, however, a firm should not expand beyond its ability to maintain organizational and accounting control over the operation. To do so is tantamount to letting a sailing ship brave the uncertainties of a storm under full canvas.

Keep the breakeven point as low as possible, especially for new ventures. Fixed investments in plant and equipment raise the breakeven point of sales needed to cover overhead costs and make a profit. Boston Beer kept its breakeven point low by using contract breweries. Now this would have been a mistake if the quality of production at these breweries was erratic or not up to Boston Beer expectations. These were indeed vital requirements if it were to succeed in selling its high-priced beer. But by working closely with experienced brewers, quality control apparently was no problem.

Certainly the lower breakeven point makes for less risk. And the future is always uncertain, despite research and careful planning. Mistakes will be made. The environment is constantly changing as to customer attitudes and preferences, and particularly in actions of competitors.

When a decision involves high stakes and an uncertain future—which translates into high risks—is it not wiser to approach the venture somewhat conservatively, not spurning the opportunity, but also not committing major resources and efforts until success appears more certain?

✗ The *importance of maintaining quality.* For a high-priced product, a brief letdown in quality control can be disastrous to the image. The story is told of Jim Koch ordering a draft of his own Samuel Adams at a restaurant across from Lincoln Center in New York City. He was horrified at the taste. He called the manager and they went to the basement and looked at the keg. "It was two-and-a-half months past its pull date." The manager quickly changed the past-its-prime keg, which the distributor, intentionally or not, had sold the restaurant.[10] Sometimes a lapse in quality is not the fault of the manufacturer, but of a distributor or dealer. Whoever is at fault, the brand image is tarnished. And it is difficult to resurrect a reputation of poor or uncertain quality.

✗ *For investors, consider the risk of initial public offerings (IPOs).* IPOs are often bid up to unreasonable prices in public enthusiasm with new offerings. While Boston Beer did well as a niche brewer, and dominated its niche, it has to be a major disappointment to its investors who bought in at the beginning. Perhaps the better investor strategy is to wait for public enthusiasm to calm down before taking a stake in a new enterprise.

CONSIDER

Can you think of other learning insights?

QUESTIONS

1. Have you ever tried one of the Boston Beer brews? If so, how did you like the taste? Did you think it was worth the higher price?

2. The investment community evidently thought Boston Beer had great growth probabilities to have bid up the initial price so quickly. Why do you suppose so many fell into this trap? Or was Jim Koch a poor executive in not bringing Boston Beer up to their expectations?

3. "The myriad specialty beers are but a fad. People will quickly tire of expensive, strong-flavored beer. Much of it is just a gimmick." Discuss.

4. What problems do you see retailers facing with the burgeoning number of different beers today? What might be the implications of this?

5. Playing the devil's advocate (one who takes an opposing view for the sake of argument and deeper analysis), critique the strategy of charging some of the highest prices in the world for your beer.

6. We saw the detection of a problem with the freshness of a beer at a restaurant by Jim Koch himself. How can Boston Beer prevent such incidents

[10] Example related in McCune, p. 16.

from happening again? Can such distributor negligence or short-sighted actions be totally prevented by Boston Beer?

7. Do you think Boston Beer can continue to compete effectively against the giant brewers who are now moving with their infinitely greater resources into the specialty beer market with their own microbrews? Why or why not?

8. In 1998, Boston Beer produced more than two dozen styles of beer. Do you see any problems with this?

HANDS-ON EXERCISES

1. You are Jim Koch. You have just learned that Michael Feuer, founder of OfficeMax, described in Chapter 21, has grown his entrepreneurial endeavor to a $1.8 billion enterprise in just seven years. It has taken you ten years to grow Boston Beer to a $50 million firm. You are depressed at this but determined to greatly increase your company's growth. How would you go about setting Boston Beer on this great growth path? Be as specific as you can. What dangers do you see ahead?

2. It is 1986 and Boston Beer is beginning its growth after hiring Pittsburgh Brewery to produce its beer. Jim Koch has charged you with coordinating the efforts at Pittsburgh Brewery, paying particular attention to assuring that your quality standards are rigidly maintained. How would you go about doing this?

TEAM DEBATE EXERCISE

Debate how Boston Beer should commit the $100 million it received in late 1995 from the public stock offering. In particular, debate whether the bulk of the proceeds should go to building its own state-of-the-art brewery, or something else.

INVITATION TO RESEARCH

How is Boston Beer faring today? Has its expansion accelerated or stalled? Is it facing any particular problems? Has the stock price risen to the $30 initial issuance price?

PART EIGHT

LAPSES IN ETHICAL AND SOCIAL RESPONSIBILITY

CHAPTER TWENTY-THREE

ADM: Price Fixing, Political Cronyism, and a Whistleblower

In June 1995, a whistleblower informed federal agents of the scheme of a giant multi-national conglomerate, Archer-Daniels-Midland, to control sales of a widely demanded food additive and thus keep prices high worldwide. For three years, he had been secretly recording meetings of the firm's senior executives with Asian and European competitors. The whistleblower, Mark E. Whitacre, was revealed to ADM by an attorney who was supposedly conferring with him as a possible client.

Repercussions quickly followed. The company charged him with stealing from the firm and fired him. The plot became more complicated. But overhanging all was the role of the corporation and its 77-year-old top executive: Did they truly act unethically and illegally, or were the allegations ballooned out of all proportions? What kind of a person was this whistleblower, a hero or a villain?

THE WHISTLEBLOWER, MARK E. WHITACRE

Mark Whitacre joined Archer-Daniels in 1989, and spent about half his career there helping antitrust investigators. He was a rising star, recruited to head the fledgling BioProducts division, where he rose to become a corporate vice president and a leading candidate to become the company's next president while still in his thirties.

He had been recruited from Degussa AG, a German chemical company where he was manager in organic chemicals and feed additives. However, his resume inflated his credentials with the title executive vice-president; he was only a vice-president.

While at ADM, he earned a business degree from a home-study school in California. Later ADM issued biographical material crediting him with an MBA from Northwestern University and the prestigious J.L. Kellogg School of Management. In an interview, Whitacre admitted the claims about his MBA were inflated to impress Wall Street analysts, but he blamed ADM: "I feel bad about it. I, along with other executives that speak at analysts meetings, cooperated ... it's a common practice."[1]

---

[1] "ADM Informant Faces Widening Allegations; He Attempts Suicide," Wall Street Journal (August 14, 1995), p. A4.

His ambition was to become president of ADM, which he claimed was promised him repeatedly.[2] How becoming a governmental informer would help him with this ambition seems murky.

Over three years he secretly helped investigators obtain videotapes revealing two senior executives meeting with Asian and European competitors in various places around the world. The executives were vice-chairman Michael D. Andreas, son and heir apparent of the 77-year-old Dwayne Andreas, chairman and chief executive; and vice president Terrance Wilson, head of the corn-processing division. Sometimes Whitacre would wear a hidden microphone to obtain the incriminating evidence of price-fixing. We will follow the later travails of Whitacre, but let us examine whistle-blowing in general in the following Information Box.

INFORMATION BOX

WHISTLEBLOWING

A whistleblower is an insider in an organization who publicizes alleged corporate miscon-duct. Such misconduct may involve unethical practices of all kinds, such as fraud, restraint of trade, price-fixing, bribes, coercion, unsafe products and facilities, and violations of other laws and regulations. Presumably, the whistleblower has exhausted the possibilities for changing the questionable practices within the normal organizational channels and, as a last resort, has taken the matter to government officials and/or the press.

Since whistleblowing may result in contract cancellations, corporate fines, and lost jobs, those who become whistleblowers may be vilified by their fellow workers and fired and even framed by their firms. This makes whistleblowing a course of action only for the truly courageous, whose concern for societal best interest outweighs their concern for themselves.

However, there is sometimes a thin line between an employee who truly believes the public interest is jeopardized and the individual who has a gripe or is a fanatic. There are some who believe management is condoning misconduct when in fact such miscon-duct is isolated and without management awareness or acceptance. And some see whistleblowing as a means of furthering their own interests, such as gaining fame or even advancing their careers.

Ralph Nader, in a 1972 book on whistleblowing, suggested that corporate employees have a primary duty to protect society that exists over and above secondary obligations to the corporation. He give examples of whistleblowing heroes, as well as courses of action for other would-be whistleblowers.[3]

Do you think you could ever be a whistleblower? Under what circumstances?

---

[1] "ADM Informant Faces Widening Allegations; He Attempts Suicide," *Wall Street Journal* (August 14, 1995), p. A4.

[2] *Ibid.*

[3] Ralph Nader, Peter Petkas, and Nate Blackwell, *Whistleblowing* (New York: Bantam Books), 1972.

FBI agents on the night of June 27 entered the headquarters of the huge grain-processing company in Decatur, Illinois. They carted off files and delivered grand jury subpoenas seeking evidence of price collusion of ADM and competitors. Whitacre was one of the executives subpoenaed, and met with an attorney recommended by the company's general counsel's office, a common practice when companies face governmental inquiries.

Shortly after this meeting, the attorney disclosed to ADM that Whitacre was the federal informant in their midst, thus imperiling Whitacre's position in the company. This seemed a clear ethical violation of the confidentiality of lawyer/client relations. But the attorney, John M. Dowd of a prominent law firm doing business with ADM, claimed that Whitacre authorized him to do so. Whitacre and his new attorney angrily denied any such authorization.

In any case, now the company had the knowledge to retaliate. They fired him, accused him of stealing $2.5 million, and reported these findings to the Justice Department. Later the company increased the amount it claimed Whitacre had stolen to $9 million. They charged that he had been embezzling money by submitting phony invoices for capital expenditures, then channeling the payments into off-shore bank accounts.

The Justice Department saw the credibility of their key witness being weakened by such allegations, especially since Whitacre acknowledged that he had indeed participated in the bogus invoice schemes, although he said the payments were made with the full knowledge and encouragement of company higher-ups. Nevertheless, he and as many as 12 other ADM executives came under criminal investigation for evading taxes. The Justice Department's criminal fraud section further examined allegations that the off-the-books payments were approved by top management.[4]

A few days later, Whitacre tried to kill himself. At dawn, he drove his car into the garage of his home, closed the door, and left the engine running. On this morning he was supposed to fly to Washington to meet with federal authorities. He had arranged for the gardener to come to work late that morning, but the gardener arrived shortly after seven and found Whitacre unconscious in his car.

Shortly before the suicide attempt, Whitacre had written a letter to the *Wall Street Journal*, acknowledging that he had received money from ADM through unusual means: "Regarding overseas accounts and kick-backs; and overseas payments to some employees. Dig Deep. It's there! They give it; then use it against you when you are their enemy."[5]

On September 13, F. Ross Johnson, an ADM board member, in a talk at Emory University's Goizueta Business School commented on Whitacre's suicide attempt: "You know, he tried to commit suicide. But he did it in a six-car garage, which, I think, if you're going to do it, that's the place to do it. [The audience laughed.] And the gardener just happened to come by. So now he is bouncing around."[6]

---

[4] Ronald Henkoff, "Checks, Lies and Videotape," *Fortune* (October 30, 1995), p. 110.

[5] "ADM Informant Faces…" *Ibid.*, p. A 1.

[6] "ADM and the FBI 'Scumbags'," *Fortune* (October 30, 1995), p. 116.

Whether the suicide attempt was genuine or contrived, Whitacre apparently faced a traumatic period in his life. He wound up in a suburban Chicago hospital with no job and no place to live. He had money problems, being unable to touch any of the funds in his overseas accounts. He and his wife had moved out of their $1.25 million estate near Decatur, Illinois, after contracting to buy a house near Nashville for $925,000. After the suicide attempt, they attempted to back out of the deal, only to be sued for breach of contract.

With all this, somehow Whitacre seemed to have landed on his feet by early October. True, he and his family were living in a rented house in the Chicago area, but he had become chief executive of Future Health Technologies, a startup biotechnology firm, at a six-figure salary comparable to what he earned legally at ADM.

THE ALLEGATIONS AGAINST THE COMPANY

By fall 1995, three grand juries were investigating whether ADM and some of its competitors conspired to fix prices. Three major product lines of ADM were allegedly involved: lysine, high-fructose corn syrup, and citric acid. Lysine is an amino-acid mixed with feed for hogs and chickens to hasten the growth of lean muscles in the animals. High-fructose corn syrup is a caloric sweetener used in soft drinks. Citric acid, like lysine, is a corn-derived product used in the detergent, food and beverage industries.

The importance of these products in the total product mix of ADM is indisputable. For example, while lysine is virtually unknown to the public, it is a key ingredient in the feed industry. About 500 million pounds are produced annually. Prices since 1961 have been averaging more than $1 a pound. So millions of dollars are at stake to manufacturers. With modern facilities at its sprawling complex in Decatur, Illinois, ADM can produce about half the world's purchases of lysine annually. And this is one of the company's highest profit products.

The sweetener, high-fructose corn syrup, is a major product for ADM, with a $3 billion-a-year market worldwide. Soft drinks account for more than 75 percent of annual production.

ADM entered the citric-acid business in 1991 when it acquired a unit of Pfizer. Today it is the primary U.S. maker of this additive. One of the largest customers is Procter & Gamble, which uses it for detergents.

As one example of the seemingly incriminating evidence of price fixing uncovered in videotapes, Michael Andreas is shown during a meeting he attended with lysine competitors at the Hyatt Regency Hotel at Los Angeles International Airport. There the participants discussed sales targets for each company as a means of limiting supply. This would destroy the free supply/demand machinations of the market and would permit prices to be kept artificially high, thus increasing the profits of the participants.[7] Although the evidence seemed to be substantial, still success at beating

---

[7] Reported in "Investigators Suspect a Global Conspiracy in Archer-Daniels Case," *Wall Street Journal* (July 28, 1995), pp. A1 and A5.

the price-fixing charges might well depend on how well ADM could convince that Whitacre, the government's star witness, was a liar and a thief.

With the charges and countercharges of Whitacre and the company, investigations went beyond price-fixing to tax-evasion for high-level executives sanctioned by top management. Whitacre may have been the tip of the iceberg. The criminal-fraud division of the Justice Department began investigating whether the company illegally paid millions of dollars in off-the-books compensation to an array of company executives through foreign bank accounts. If so, then the culpability of Whitacre would be muted, and his value as a witness greatly enhanced.

It is worth noting the severity of the penalties if suits successfully come to pass. Fines for price fixing can range into the hundreds of millions of dollars, and some executives could even be given jail sentences. Furthermore, class-action suits by shareholders and customers can result in heavy damage awards. See the following Information Box for a discussion of the famous price-fixing conspiracy of 1959 that set the precedence for jail sentences for executives involved.

INFORMATION BOX

THE FAMOUS PRICE-FIXING CONSPIRACY OF 1959

In 1959, the biggest conspiracy of its kind in U.S. business history impacted the nation's thinking regarding business ethics.

Twenty-nine companies, including such giants as General Electric, Westinghouse, and Allis-Chalmers, were found guilty of conspiring to fix prices in deals involving about $7 billion of electrical equipment. The products involved in the conspiracy included power transformers, power switchgear assemblies, turbine generators, industrial control equipment, and circuit breakers. The companies were fined $1,924,500. Of particular note in this case, 52 executives (none of these top executives) were prosecuted and fined about $140,000. Even more startling, seven of the defendants received jail sentences. This was a first under federal antitrust laws.

On top of all that, almost 2,000 private-action, treble-damage cases were brought as a result of the court findings. In one of these alone, damages of $28,800,000 were awarded.

Incentives for the illegal actions stemmed from several sources. Without doubt, top management was exerting strong pressure on lower executives to improve their performance. Collusion with executives in other firms seemed to be a practical way to do this, especially in an environment rather blasé toward antitrust collusion. This attitude changed with the harsh penalties imposed by Judge J. Cullen Ganey.

Those executives who lost their jobs and went to jail were readily offered equivalent jobs in other corporations. The business community accepted them with open arms. Do you think they deserved such acceptance?

TABLE 23.1   ADM Revenues, 1986–1995

Year ending June 30	Sales (millions)	Year-to-Year Percent Increase
1986	$5,336	
1987	5,775	10.8
1988	6,798	11.8
1989	7,929	11.6
1990	7,751	(2.2)
1991	8,468	9.3
1992	9,232	9.0
1993	9,811	6.5
1994	11,374	15.9
1995	12,672	11.4
Gain since 1986		137.5%

Source: Adapted from 1995 ADM Annual Report.

ADM AND DWAYNE ANDREAS

The story of Archer-Daniels-Midland Co. is really the story of its chairman, Dwayne O. Andreas. In 1947, ADM chairman, Shreve Archer, died after choking on a chicken bone. Dwayne Andreas was a vice-president at Cargill, a rival firm. For the next 18 years he advanced steadily in the industry and became wealthy, while Archer-Daniels showed little growth. In 1966, at age 47, Andreas was asked to become a director at ADM. The founding families sold him a sizable amount of stock and proposed to groom him for the top spot. Four years later, he was named chief executive officer.

In 1995, Andreas was still firmly in command and running the publicly traded company almost as a personal dynasty. In 25 years he had built up the firm into the nation's biggest farm-commodity processor, with $12.7 billion in annual revenue. Table 23.1 shows the steady growth of revenues since 1986, while Table 23.2 shows the growth of earnings, not quite as steady but still almost two and a half times greater than in 1986.

POLITICAL MANEUVERING

Although company headquarters were at Decatur, Illinois, Andreas's influence in Washington was probably unparalleled by any other business leader. ADM led corporate America in political contributions; it contributed hundreds of thousands of dollars to both parties. Furthermore, Andreas supported Jimmy Carter's campaign—ADM even bought his struggling peanut farm in 1981. But Andreas also contributed generously to Ronald Reagan and George Bush. During the Reagan years, when U.S. firms were entering the Soviet market, ADM was in the vanguard. Andreas became

TABLE 23.2   ADM Net Earnings, 1986–1995

Year ending June 30	Earnings (millions)	Year-to-Year Percent Increase
1986	$230	
1987	265	15.2
1988	353	33.2
1989	425	20.3
1990	484	13.9
1991	467	(3.5)
1992	504	7.9
1993	568	12.7
1994	484	(14.8)
1995	796	64.5
Gain since 1986		246.1%

Source: Adapted from 1995 *ADM Annual Report.*

close to then-Soviet president, Mikhail Gorbachev. But as a hedge, he also courted Boris Yeltsin, Gorbachev's emerging rival.

Perhaps his greatest political supporter became Senator Robert Dole, who is from the farm state of Kansas. When Dole's wife, Elizabeth Dole, took over administration of the American Red Cross, Andreas donated $1 million to the cause. Dole also was given use of an ADM corporate plane, for which he paid the equivalent of a first-class ticket. An added factor in the friendship and rapport was the proximity of their vacation homes: Dole and his wife own a unit in Sea View, Florida, as do David Brinkley, a renowned TV newsman, and Robert Strauss, an ADM board member, and, of course, Dwayne Andreas.[8] Interestingly, President Clinton also regarded Andreas as an ally.

Such political presence has brought great rewards to the company. ADM is a major beneficiary of federal price supports for sugar. Because such supports have kept sugar prices artificially high, ADM's sweetener, high-fructose corn syrup, has been attractive for giant companies such as CocaCola. Estimates are that fructose generates about 40 percent of ADM's earnings.[9]

Archer-Daniels also benefits from the 54-cent-a-gallon excise-tax break on ethanol, being the major producer of this corn-based fuel additive. Indeed, it is doubtful if the ethanol industry would exist without this tax break, and Bob Dole has been its most ardent congressional supporter.

Despite all the campaign contributions and personal rapport with the seats of power in Washington, Andreas and ADM have done little direct lobbying. Rather,

---

[8] Reported in "How Dwayne Andreas Rules Archer-Daniels By Hedging His Bets," *Wall Street Journal* (October 27, 1995), p. A8.

[9] *Ibid.*

such efforts have been done indirectly through various commodity and trade associations. For example, the American Peanut Shellers Association, with ADM support, handles the lobbying on peanut price supports.[10]

The Board of Directors

The investigations and the charges and countercharges drew fire from some of the major institutional holders of ADM stock. For example, the California Public Employees Retirement System—Calpers, as it is known, and owner of 3.6 million shares of Archer-Daniels—complained, charging that the board was too closely tied to Chairman and CEO Dwayne Andreas. "The ADM board is dominated by insiders, many of whom happen to be related to the CEO," Calpers complained. Calpers also criticized the ADM board for approving a 14 percent pay raise for Andreas, "rather than demand the CEO's resignation."[11] Other institutional investors also joined the criticisms: for example, the United Brotherhood of Carpenters, the Teamsters Union, and New York's major pension funds.

Shareholders had several other major criticisms of the board. It was supposed to authorize all capital expenditures above $250,000. The alleged claims for offshore pay were disguised as requests for spending on plant and equipment, and these the board passed with no hesitation. As to the charges of price-fixing and the allegations against major executives, the board was conspicuously uncritical, and finally made some token efforts to look further into the charges.

Brian Mulroney, former prime minister of Canada, co-chaired the special committee charged with coordinating the company's response to the federal investigations. One would think that part of his job was to safeguard the interests of shareholders. But major institutional shareholders doubted his objectivity, and noted his very close relations to Dwayne Andreas. Critics contended that what was needed was not a rubber-stamp special committee but "a team of experts to lead a full-blown, independent investigation."[12]

Regarding the composition of the board, critics seemed to have a case: the board was hardly objective and unbiased toward company top management; rather, it was highly supportive and dominated by insiders, many of whom were related to the CEO. For example, 4 of Archer-Daniels 17 directors were members of the Andreas family. An additional 6 directors were retired executives or relatives of senior managers. The outside directors also had close connections to Andreas, such as Robert S. Strauss, the Washington lawyer whose firm represented ADM, and Mulroney, who was also with a law firm used by the firm. Even Harvard University Professor Ray Goldberg, a member of the board, had strong ties with Andreas, dating back to his dissertation.

---

[10] *Ibid.*

[11] Joann S. Lublin, "Archer-Daniels-Midland Is Drawing Fire from Some Institutional Holders," *Wall Street Journal* (October 11, 1995), p. A8.

[12] Henkoff, p. 110.

While close bonds of boards with management are not unusual with many companies, such cozy relations can be detrimental to shareholders' best interests.

ANALYSIS

ADM's Conduct

Was ADM guilty of unethical conduct, and even illegalities? At the time this first was written, three grand juries were investigating the price fixing. The Department of Justice was looking into the tax-evasion charges. But nothing had been decided or proven. Perhaps ADM was guilty of price fixing, and perhaps not. Maybe the firm was guilty of nefarious practices to enable its high-level executives to avoid some income taxes through off-the-books compensation. If proven, such practices would not only be unethical, but also illegal and subject to harsh penalties.

Certain other activities of this giant company posed some ethical controversies even if they were not illegal—for example, packing the board with cronies dedicated to preserving the establishment at the expense of stockholders; the great quest for preferential treatment in the highest corridors of power; and just perhaps, the setting up of Whitacre. Let us examine these ethical issues.

Packing the board so that it is exceptionally supportive of the entrenched management may be condemned as not truly representing the rights of stockholders. But in its 25 years with Andreas at the helm, ADM's stock value rose at an annual average rate of 17 percent over the last decade. Few stockholders could dispute Andreas's contribution to the firm, even though they might fume at his riding roughshod over his critics—especially institutions holding large amounts of stock. Of course, if grand juries do return indictments, the autocratic tactics of Andreas will bring him down if it is proven that he knew of any such illegal activities.

Some would maintain that the courting of favoritism and special treatment from high-level Washington politicians may have gone too far. But should not any organization have the right to do its best to push for beneficial legislation and regulation? Of course, some will be more effective than others in doing so. Is this so much different from competition in the marketplace?

Whitacre's Role

Why did Whitacre choose to be a government mole? Still in his thirties, Whitacre had advanced to high position in the company, with corresponding substantial compensation (enough to afford an estate valued at more than a million dollars), and who was at least one of the top candidates for the presidency of the firm. And yet he had been secretly taping supposedly illegal discussions. Why? What did he have to gain? There was so much to lose.

Added to this, he must have been a very capable executive, yet he was naive enough to leave himself vulnerable by accepting, and maybe even initiating, illegal scams through false invoices and overseas bank accounts. And he apparently naively confessed to a company lawyer his involvement as an informant for the FBI, not just recently but for three years. It doesn't make much sense, does it?

UPDATE

In October 1996, ADM pleaded guilty to criminal price-fixing charges and paid a record $100 million fine and nearly that amount again to settle lawsuits by customers and investors. But ADM's troubles were not ended.

Early in December 1996, a federal grand jury charged Michael Andreas, earning $1.3 million annually as the number-two executive at ADM and heir apparent to his father to run the company, and Terrance Wilson, former head of ADM's corn-processing division, with conspiring with Asian makers of lysine to rig the price of the livestock feed additive. Andreas took a leave of absence with full pay, and Wilson retired. It was thought that any conviction or guilty plea by Michael Andreas would destroy his chances of continuing his family's three-decade-long reign over ADM. However, Dwayne Andreas could yet preserve the patrimony: His nephew, G. Allen Andreas, a 53-year-old lawyer, was one of three executives named to share Dwayne Andreas's responsibility in a newly formed office of chief executive.

In a surprising twist to the case, Mark Whitacre, the whistleblower, was also indicted.

The Verdict

The verdicts came in late 1998. After a week of deliberation in a two-month trial, the jury found Andreas, Wilson, and Whitacre guilty in a landmark price-fixing case, thereby giving the Justice Department its biggest convictions in a push against illegal global cartels. The federal prosecutors had been thwarted in how to rebuild the case after their mole, Whitacre, had been convicted of embezzlement and was already serving a 9-year prison sentence. The problem was solved by wringing confessions from Asian executives who were also involved in the conspiracy.

The bizarre behavior of Whitacre, after initially providing documentation of the birth of a price-fixing scheme, was unexpected and almost disastrous, and hard to explain even given that he was a big spender who openly pined to become president of ADM.

The End of the Andreas Dynasty

On August 13, 2001, ADM announced that Dwayne Andreas, 83 years old, was leaving its board and that his imprisoned son would not have a job there waiting for him. Five directors who had been handpicked by Andreas for their seats in the boardroom also were being ousted. His son, Michael Andreas, 52, still serving a three-year sentence, agreed to repay $8 million of the legal expenses ADM accumulated defending him as the most prominent U.S. business executive ever sent to prison on price-fixing charges. "This closes a chapter on six difficult years," the company said.[13]

---

[13] Scott Kilman, "ADM Says Ex-Chief Dwayne Andreas Will Leave Board," *Wall Street Journal* (August 13, 2001), p. A6.

WHAT CAN BE LEARNED?

Price fixing is one of the easiest cases to prosecute. Conspiracies to fix prices are direct violations of the Sherman Act. The government does not need to prove that competition was injured or that trade was restrained. All that needs to be proven is that a meeting took place with agreements to fix prices, bids, or allocate market share.

The penalties for price conspiracies have greatly increased since the celebrated electrical equipment industry conspiracy of 1959. Given the ease of prosecution, one would think that no prudent executive would ever take such a risk. Yet, there have been sporadic instances of price-fixing since then, and maybe we have it here with Michael Andreas, the son of Dwayne. Is there no learning experience?

Is political patronage necessary? We know that ADM sought political patronage and preferential treatment to an extraordinary degree—perhaps more than any other firm. Is this so bad?

Purists argue that this distorts the objectivity of our governmental institutions. Others say it is part of the democratic process in a pluralistic society. It might be so vital to our type of government that it cannot be eliminated—at best, can only be curbed.

On the other hand, it simply adds one more dimension to the competitive environment. Other firms can be invited to flex their muscles in the halls of government.

But when it comes to violations of the law, which supposedly reflects the wishes of society, then no firm is immune from the consequences. Even if its political patronage has been assiduously cultivated, it cannot escape the consequences of its illegal actions. The press, and the legal establishment, see to that.

Beware the "shareholder be damned" attitude. Some shareholders of ADM suspect that ADM had this attitude. As a consequence, the company faced at least two dozen shareholder lawsuits. As it approached the 1995 October annual meeting, nine big institutional investors announced plans to vote against reelecting ADM directors. But the move was largely symbolic, since their combined shares represented only 4.9 percent of the 505 million outstanding shares.[14] And their views received little attention in the meeting. Nor, apparently did those of other shareholders. The *Wall Street Journal* reported that at the meeting Andreas squelched criticisms of the issue of the antitrust probe and other allegations as he "summarily cut off a critic by turning off his microphone: 'I'm chairman. I'll make the rules as I go along,' Mr. Andreas said."[15]

A cozy relationship with the board encourages such attitudes. And when operating performance is continually improving, such shareholder criticisms may be seen as merely gnats striving for attention, and thus worthy of being ignored. If the top executive is inclined to be autocratic, then the environment is supportive.

---

[14] "Probe Tears Veil of Secrecy at Archer Daniels Midland," *Cleveland Plain Dealer* (October 18, 1995), p. 3-C.
[15] "How Dwayne Andreas Rules..." p. A1.

But is this wise? I think not. Should adversity set in, sometime in the future, then such attitudes toward investors can be self-destructive, even with a supportive board. If performance deteriorates, no board can maintain its sheeplike support for incumbent management, not in the face of vehement shareholders (especially large institutional investors) or major creditors.

But does adversity have to come? Only the profoundest optimist can think that success is forever. In ADM's case, adversity may be on the threshold, if Justice Department investigations result in grand jury indictments.

An organization's ethical tone is set by top management. If top management is unconcerned about ethical conduct, or if it is an active participant in less than desirable practices, this sets the tone throughout the organization. It promotes erosion of acceptable moral conduct in many areas of the operation. It becomes contagious as even those inclined to be more morally scrupulous join their colleagues. Then we have the "follow-the-leader" mindset.

In such an unhealthy environment, a few whistleblowers may arise and attempt to right the situation, often unsuccessfully and at great personal risk. Others who cannot tolerate the decline in moral standards, but don't have the courage to be whistleblowers, will leave the company. Almost inevitably, the misconduct will come to light, and repercussions of the severest kind result. Perhaps top management can escape the blame, though lower-level executives will be sacrificed. Occasionally, top management also comes under fire, and is forced to resign. Unfortunately, too often with healthy retirement benefits.

CONSIDER

Can you think of other learning insights?

QUESTIONS

1. What is your position regarding top management's culpability for the misdeeds of their subordinates?

2. Do you think ADM's efforts at gaining political favoritism went too far? Why or why not?

3. "If Dwayne's son is found guilty of price-fixing, there's no way that the big man himself cannot be found guilty." Evaluate this statement.

4. "With all the false invoices and persons involved in these millions of dollars of payouts off-the-books, there's no way the company could not have known what was going on." Evaluate.

5. Speculate on what would lead Whitacre to "betray" his company. If a number of possibilities are mentioned, which do you think is most compelling?

6. With the severe penalties and ease of prosecution of price-fixing cases, why would any firm or any executive attempt it today?

7. Why do you suppose, with all its efforts to gain preferential treatment through courting the mighty in government, ADM has not resorted to direct lobbying? Has it missed a golden opportunity to further its causes?

HANDS-ON EXERCISES

Before

1. Assume that Dwayne Andreas wants to maintain high ethical standards in his organization. Describe how he should go about this.

After

2. Assume that several key executives have indeed been found guilty of price-fixing; assume further that there are also indictments of illegal payments to certain executives. Further, the Senate ethics committee is investigating whether there have been improprieties in dealings with some members of Congress. How would you as CEO attempt damage control?

TEAM DEBATE EXERCISE

Debate the ethics of aggressively courting prominent politicians and government administrators. The two extreme positions would be: (1) going as far as you can short of being charged with outright bribery; (2) limiting relationship building to a few token contributions to trade association lobbying efforts.

INVITATION TO RESEARCH

Has ADM's public image been badly tarnished by all this publicity, or can you determine this? Has the firm continued to grow and prosper?

CHAPTER TWENTY-FOUR

The Great Firestone/Ford Tire Disaster

*P*roduct defects that lead to customer injuries and deaths through manufacturer carelessness constitute serious ethical and social responsibility abuses. Far worse, however, is when the manufacturer knows about safety problems and conceals such information, or denies it.

This case is unique in that two manufacturers are culpable, but each blames the other. As a result, Firestone and Ford have been savaged by the press, public opinion, the government, and a host of salivating lawyers. Massive tire recalls destroyed the bottom line and even raised concerns about the viability of Bridgestone/Firestone, while sales of the Ford Explorer, the world's best-selling sport-utility vehicle, plummeted 22 percent in April 2001 from the year before; at the same time domestic sales of SUVs overall climbed 9 percent.

A HORROR SCENARIO

Firestone tires mounted on Ford Explorers were linked to more than 200 deaths from rollovers in the United States, as well as more than 60 in Venezuela and a reported 14 fatalities in Saudi Arabia and neighboring countries. A widely publicized lawsuit took place in Texas in the Summer of 2001. It had been thought beforehand that the jury would settle the controversy of who was most to blame for the deaths and injuries from Explorers outfitted with Firestone tires.

Ford settled its portion of the suit for $6 million one month before the trial began. While Firestone now became the sole defendant, jurors were asked to also assess Ford's responsibility for the accident.

The lawsuit was brought by the family of Marisa Rodriguez, a mother of three who was left brain-damaged and paralyzed after the steel belt and tread of a Firestone tire tore apart during a trip to Mexico in March 2000. As a result, the Explorer rolled over three times, crushing the roof above Mrs. Rodriguez in the rear seat, and also injuring her husband Joel, who was asleep in the front passenger seat. The live picture of Mrs. Rodriguez in a wheelchair received maximum coverage by network TV.

After the federal court jury in the Texas border town of McAllen had been dead-locked for four days, a settlement was reached with Bridgestone/Firestone for $7.85 million. (The plantiffs originally had asked for $1 billion.)

The settlement out of court with both Ford and Firestone did not resolve the issue of who was most to blame for this and the hundreds of other injuries and deaths. But a lawyer for the Rodriguez family predicted that sooner or later a verdict would emerge: "There's going to be trials and there's going to be verdicts. We've got Marisa Rodriguezes all over the country."[1]

ANATOMY OF THE PROBLEM

The Ford/Firestone Relationship

Ford and Firestone have had a long, intimate history. In 1895, Harvey Firestone sold tires to Henry Ford for his first automobile. In 1906, the Firestone Tire & Rubber Company won its first contract for Ford Motor Company's mass-produced vehicles, a commitment that continued through the decades.

Henry Ford and Harvey Firestone became business confederates and best friends who went on annual summer camping trips, riding around in Model T's along with Thomas Edison and naturalist John Burroughs. Further cementing the relationship, in 1947 Firestone's granddaughter, Martha, married Ford's grandson, William Clay Ford, in a dazzling ceremony in Akron, Ohio that attracted a *Who's Who* of dignitaries and celebrities. Their son, William Clay Ford Jr., was to become Ford's chairman.

In 1988, Tokyo-based Bridgestone Corporation bought Firestone, 20 years after the Japanese company sold its first tires in the United States under the Bridgestone name. In 1990, Ford introduced the Explorer sport-utility vehicle to replace the Bronco II in the 1991 model year. It became the nation's top-selling SUV, and the Explorer generated huge profits for more than a decade. Bridgestone/Firestone was the sole supplier of the Explorer's tires.

The Relationship Worsens

The first intimation of trouble came in 1999 when Ford began replacing tires of Explorers in Saudi Arabia and nearby countries after 14 fatalities. The tire failures were blamed on hot weather and underinflated tires. At the time, overseas fatalities did not have to be reported to U.S. regulators, so the accidents received scant attention in the media.

The media caught the scent in early 2000 when television reports in Houston revealed instances of tread separation on Firestone's ATX tires, and the National Highway Traffic Safety Administration (NHTSA) started an investigation. By May, four U.S. fatalities had been reported, and NHTSA expanded the investigation to 47 million ATX, ATXII, and Wilderness tires.

---

[1] "Firestone Agrees to Pay $7.5 Million in Tire Suit," *Cleveland Plain Dealer* (August 25, 2001), pp. A1, A13; also, Milo Geyelin and Timothy Aeppel, "For Firestone, Tire Trial Is Mixed Victory," *Wall Street Journal* (August 27, 2001), pp. A3, A4.

In August 2000, as deaths began mounting leading to increasing pressure from consumers and multiple lawsuits, Firestone voluntarily recalled 14.4 million 15-inch radial tires because of tread separation. The plant in Decatur, Illinois was implicated in most of these accidents. Ford and Firestone agreed to replace the tires, but estimated that 6.5 million were still on the road. Consumer groups sought a still wider recall, charging that Explorers with other Firestone tire models were also prone to separation leading to rollovers.

In December 2000, Firestone issued a report blaming Ford for the problems, claiming that the Explorer's design caused rollovers with any tread separations. On April 20, 2001, Ford gave NHTSA a report blaming Firestone for flawed manufacturing.

In May 2001, Ford announced that it was replacing all remaining 13 million Firestone Wilderness AT tires on its vehicles, saying that the move was necessary because it didn't have confidence in the tires' safety. "We feel it's our responsibility to act immediately," Ford CEO Jacques Nasser said. Ford said the move would cost the automaker $2.1 billion, although it hoped to get this back from Firestone.

Firestone Chairman and CEO John Lampe defended his tires, saying "no one cares more about the safety of the people who travel on our tires than we do. When we have a problem, we admit it and we fix it."[2]

The Last Days

It is lamentable when a long-lasting, close relationship is severed. But on May 21, 2001, Lampe abruptly ended the 95-year association, accusing Ford of refusing to acknowledge safety problems with its vehicle, thus putting all the blame on Firestone.

The crisis had been brewing for months. Many Firestone executives did not trust Ford, and even exchanging documents was done with rancor, with major differences in interpreting the data. Firestone argued that tread-separation claims occurred 10 times more frequently on Ford Explorers than on Ranger pickups with the same tires, thus supporting their contention that the Explorer was mostly at fault. Ford rejected Firestone's charges about the Explorer, saying that for 10 years the model "has ranked at or near the top in terms of safety among the 12 SUVs in its class." It stated that 2.9 million Goodyear tires mounted on more than 500,000 Explorers had "performed with industry-leading safety."[3]

The critical time came in a May 21 meeting of Mr. Lampe and a contingent of Ford officials, in which each side held firm that the other was to blame. Discussions broke down on how the two companies could work together to examine Explorer's role in the accidents. At that point, Lampe sent a letter to Ford's Nasser ending their relationship. Both sides then were left with the task of defending themselves before Congress and the court of public opinion, and ultimately a siege of lawsuits. See the following Information Box for a discussion of how emotion drives consumers in their perception, good and bad, of companies.

---

[2] Ed Garsten, Associated Press, as reported in "Ford Tire Tab $2.1 Billion," *Cleveland Plain Dealer* (May 23, 2001), pp. 1C, 4C.

[3] Timothy Aeppel, Joseph B. White, and Stephen Power, "Firestone Quits as Tire Supplier to Ford," *Wall Street Journal* (May 22, 2001), pp. A3, A12.

INFORMATION BOX

HOW EMOTION INFLUENCES COMPANY REPUTATION

The second annual corporate-reputation survey conducted by the Harris market-research firm and the Reputation Institute involving 26,011 respondents found that Emotional Appeal—trust, admiration and respect, and generally good feelings toward—was the driving force in how people rated companies. The survey found that advertising doesn't necessarily change opinions. Despite a $100 million advertising campaign about what a good citizen Philip Morris Company was in feeding the hungry and helping victims of domestic violence, the company still received low marks on trust, respect, and admiration. But the most recent poll showed that Philip Morris no longer had the worst reputation in America. This title went to Bridgestone/Firestone, with Ford receiving the lowest reputation rating among auto companies.

Once lost, a company's reputation or public image is usually difficult to regain. For example, Exxon Mobil's reputation for environmental responsibility was still given low grades more than a decade after the destructive Alaskan oil spill involving the oil tanker Exxon Valdez.

Do you think Firestone can ever fix its reputation after the massive recall and publicity involving the failure of its tires? If so, how?

Source: Ronald Alsop, "Survey: Emotion Drives Public Perception of Companies," *Wall Street Journal* (February 11, 2001), p. 5H.

Advantage to Competitors   *if they can take it!*

Major competitors Goodyear and Michelin and smaller competitors and private-label tire makers predictably raised tire prices 3 to 5 percent. Goodyear now tried to increase production robustly to replace the millions of Firestone tires recalled or soon to be, but it was trying to avoid overtime pay to bolster profits. In a written statement, Goodyear said, "We are working very closely with Ford to jointly develop an aggressive plan to address consumers' needs as quickly as possible."[4]

The slowdown in auto sales in the slowing economy that began in 2000 had led Goodyear to production cutbacks, including cutting worldwide workers by 7,200, as it posted an 83 percent decline in profits in 2000. Now it faced a challenge in gearing up to handle the windfall of the ending of the Ford/Firestone relationship.

WHERE LIES THE BLAME?

In years to come, courts and lawyers will sort out the culpability amid controversy. The final outcome is unpredictable, but the finger of blame points to a number of

---

[4] Thomas W. Gerdel, "Goodyear, Michelin Raising Consumer Tire Prices," *Cleveland Plain Dealer* (May 23, 2001), pp. 1C, 4C.

sources, though the weighting of the blame is uncertain. While major responsibility should be shared by Ford and Firestone, the National Highway Traffic Safety Administration (NHTSA) and the motoring public were hardly blameless.

Ford

Whether the design of Ford's Explorer made it more prone to rollover than other SUVs will be decided in the courtroom arena. One thing seems clear: Ford recommended a low inflation level for its Firestone-equipped tires, and this would subject them to more flex in the sidewall and greater heat buildup. With high-speed driving in hot weather, such a high-profile vehicle would have more risk of rolling over with any tire trouble, especially with inexperienced drivers. For example, Ford's recommended tire pressure was 26 pounds, and this would bring the car's center of gravity lower to the ground, which would seem good, but only at first look. Ford was alone among SUV makers in equipping the Explorer with c tires rather than the more heat-resistant b tires that were the near-universal standard on most sports utility vehicles. To make the c grade, tires only had to withstand two hours at 50 mph when properly inflated and loaded, plus another 90 minutes at speeds up to 85 mph. This standard dated back to 1968 when sustained highway speeds were much lower than today. Now, people drive hour after hour at speeds well above 70 mph.

The c-rated Firestones were used on millions of Ford pickup trucks without problems. However, in contrast with SUVs, most pickup trucks are not taken on long-haul, high-speed road trips filled with family and luggage.

Ford CEO Jacques Nasser justified replacing 13 million tires by claiming the Firestones were failing at a rate higher than Goodyears mounted on two million Explorers in the mid-1990s. But the Goodyears carried the b rating. The dangerous effect of heat buildup was shown by most Explorers' accidents taking place in hot Southern states and other hot-climate countries with high speed limits.

Ford engineers should have been aware of these dangers, if not immediately, certainly after a few years, and adapted the Explorer to customers who drive fast, pay little attention to tire maintenance, and are prone to panic with a blowout and flip the car. Unfortunately, the American legal environment, the tort system, makes the manufacturer vulnerable to lawsuits and massive damage claims should it acknowledge in retrospect that it had made a bad mistake in its tire selection and pressure recommendation. So the temptation was to blame the tiremaker, and spend millions to create it as a media monster.

Bridgetone/Firestone

Firestone tires were far from blameless. Early on, investigations of deadly vehicle accidents linked the causes to tire failure, notably due to shoddy manufacturing practices at the Firestone Decatur, Illinois plant; the 6.5 million tire recall by Firestone was of the 15-inch radial ATX and ATX11 tires and Wilderness AT tires made in this plant. In June 27, 2001, the company announced the plant would be closed. But Firestone's poorly controlled manufacturing process proved not to be limited to this single operation. See the following Information Box about the whistleblower who exposed another plant's careless disregard of safe tire production.

Still, there were contrary indications that the fault was not all Bridgestone/Firestone's, that Ford shared the blame. General Motors had detected no problems with Firestones it used as standard equipment in 14 of its models. In fact, in July 2001 GM named Firestone as its supplier of the year for the sixth consecutive time. Honda of America was also loyal to Firestones, which it used on best-selling Civics and Odysseys.[5]

On September 14, 2001, months after all Firestones had been recalled from Ford Explorers, an apparently skilled driver, a deputy bailiff driving home from the Cleveland Municipal Court, was killed when he lost control of his Explorer and it flipped over a guardrail, slid down an embankment and rolled over several times.[6]

INFORMATION BOX

A WHISTLEBLOWER "HERO"

Alan Hogan was honored in June 2001 by the Civil Justice Foundation for exposing how employees at a Bridgestone/Firestone plant in North Carolina routinely made defective tires. This consumer advocacy group, founded by the Association of Trial Lawyers of America, bestowed similar "community champion" awards on tobacco whistleblower Jeffrey Wigand, and on Erin Brockovich, who exposed hazardous-waste dangers and was the subject of a popular movie.

With his insider's knowledge of shoddy tire-building practices, Hogan was widely credited with bringing about the first recall. He testified at a wrongful-death lawsuit in 1999 that he witnessed the crafting of countless bad tires built with dried-out rubber and wood bits, cigarette butts, screws and other foreign materials mixed in. Hogan, who had quit the company and opened an auto-body shop in his home town, became a pariah among many people for his revelations about the major employer of the community, and company attorneys looked into his work and family life for anything they could use to discredit him. They tried to portray him as a disgruntled former employee. An anonymous fax accused him of spreading "vicious, malicious allegations" about the company. Employees were warned not to do business with car dealerships that dealt with his body shop.

But he persevered, and eventually won recognition and accolades. "I'm surprised it took this long," he said. "Maybe now people will see this is the way it's been since 1994, 1995, when they started covering this up." His whistleblowing credentials were now in high demand as an expert witness in other lawsuits.

Do you see any reasons why Hogan may not have been completely objective in his whistleblowing efforts?

Source: Dan Chapman, Cox News, as reported in "Firestone Ex-Worker Called Hero in Recall," *Cleveland Plain Dealer* (May 29, 2001), p. 1C.

---

[5] Ed Garten, Associated Press, as reported in "Ford Tire Tab, $2.1 Billion," *Cleveland Plain Dealer* (May 23, 2001), pp, 1C, 4C; and Alison Grant, "Bridgestone/Firestone Faces Struggle to Survive," *Cleveland Plain Dealer* (August 5, 2001), pp. H1, H5.

[6] "SUV Flips, Killing Deputy Bailiff, 24," *Cleveland Plain Dealer* (September 15, 2001), p. 85.

Government

Public Citizen and other consumer groups were critical of the government, maintaining that it was too slow in completing its initial Firestone investigation and had dragged its feet in any investigation of the Explorer. A Public Citizen study saw the use of the specific Firestone tires as coming from cost- and weight-saving miscalculations and gambles by Ford, "making what was already a bad problem into a lethal one." Not just the companies were at fault, but Federal regulators were lax in not toughening standards on SUVs to prevent roofs from collapsing in rollover crashes. "The human damage caused is barbaric and unnecessary," President Joan Claybrook said.[7]

The Driver

There is little doubt that consumers contributed to accidents by neglecting tire pressure so that it was often below even the low recommendations of Ford, by heavily loading vehicles, and by driving too fast over long periods of time so that heat could build up to danger levels. Added to this, the lack of driving expertise to handle emergency blowouts was often the fatal blow. Yet, could a carmaker, tiremaker, or government really expect the average consumer to act with strict prudence? Precautions, be they car standards or tire standards, needed to be imposed with worst scenarios in mind as to consumer behavior.

CONSEQUENCES

Each company maneuvered primarily to cast blame on the other. Ford announced in May 2001 it would triple the size of the Firestone recall, a $2.8 billion prospect, a cost Ford wanted to shift to the tiremaker. Firestone, at that point, severed its long relationship with Ford by refusing to supply the company with more tires. CEO Lampe maintained Ford was trying to divert scrutiny of the rollover-prone Explorer by casting doubt on the safety of Firestone tires.

Both parties suffered in this name-calling and passing-the-buck. By Fall 2001, sales of Explorers were off sharply, as consumers wondered whether the hundreds of Explorer crashes were due to the SUV's design, or Firestone tires, or both. Ford lost market share to Toyota and other foreign rivals in the SUV market. In July 2001, it reported its first loss from operations since 1992. It also faced 200 product-liability lawsuits that involved Explorer rollovers. Still, Ford was big enough to absorb problems with one of its models.

Smaller Bridgestone/Firestone faced a more dangerous situation. In 2000, its earnings dropped 80 percent, reflecting the costs of recalling millions of tires, as well as a special charge to cover legal expenses. The Firestone unit, which accounted for 40 percent of the parent company's revenue, posted a net loss of $510 million after it took a $750 million charge for legal expenses. Sales were forecast to plunge 20

---

[7] Alison Grant, "Government, Goodyear Still Navigating a Bumpy Road," *Cleveland Plain Dealer* (August 5, 2001), p. H5.

percent in 2001, and costs of lawsuits could eventually reach billions of dollars, to the point where some analysts doubted Firestone as a brand could survive.[8]

Options Firestone Faced

This esteemed brand, launched more than a century ago, had been the exclusive tire supplier to the Indy 500. Now its future was in doubt, despite decades of brand loyalty. The brand faced three options:

Option #1

Some thought the company should try to deemphasize Firestone, and push business to the Bridgestone label. This would likely result in some loss of market segmentation and the flexibility of having distinct low-end, mid-level, and premium tires. Others thought such a half-hearted approach would simply prolong the agony of hanging on to a besmirched brand.

Option #2

Obliterate the Firestone name, it being irretrievable. "Firestone should just give up," said one public relations analyst. "They've damaged themselves so severely." A University of Michigan Business School professor called the brand dead: "Can you imagine any jury claiming that somebody who's suspected of building bad tires is innocent?"[9]

Option #3

Try to salvage the brand. Some questioned the wisdom of abandoning the century-old Firestone name, with its rich tradition and millions of cumulative advertising dollars. They thought that with money, time, and creative advertising, Bridgestone/Firestone should be able to restore its image. But to do so, Roger Blackwell of Ohio State University thought the company needed to make an admission of regret: "The lawyers will tell them not to admit blame.... But they need to do what Johnson & Johnson did when when someone was killed by their product [cyanide-tainted Tylenol]. A credible spokesman got on TV and had tears in his eyes when he spoke." An independent tire dealer who lost $100,000 in sales in 2000 but was confident of a rebound, supported this option: "The American public is quick to forget," he said.[10]

POSTMORTEM

Buyers of Ford Explorers with Firestone tires for years faced far higher risks of deaths and injuries, both in the United States and abroad, than they would have from

---

[8] Akiko Kashiwagi, "Recalls Cost Bridgestone Dearly; Firestone's Parent's Profit Drops 80%," *Washington Post* (February 23, 2001), p. E03.

[9] "Struggle to Survive," p. H5.

[10] *Ibid.* .

other models. The *New York Times* reported that the tire defects, and their contribution to accidents, were known in 1996.[11] Not until August 1999 did Ford begin replacing tires on Explorers in Saudi Arabia, calling the step a "customer notification enhancement program." Fourteen fatalities had already been reported. Not until March 2000, after television reports of problems, did federal regulators and the two manufacturers take all this seriously.

Ford, in its concern with the bottom line, stubbornly refused to admit that anything was wrong with its SUV, while Firestone couldn't seem to clean up its act in the Decatur, Illinois plant, and even some other plants, where carelessness and lack of customer concern prevailed. Minor ethical abuses became major when lives were lost, but the foot-dragging continued until lawyers came on the scene. Then these two tried to cover their mistakes with finger pointing, while a vulnerable public continued to be in jeopardy. Throughout this whole time, saving lives did not apparently have a very high priority. Eventually the consequences came back to haunt the companies, with hundreds of lawsuits, millions of tire recalls, and public images denigrated.

How could this have been permitted to happen? After all, top management were not deliberately vicious men. They were well intentioned, albeit badly misguided. Perhaps their worst sin was to at first ignore, and then refuse to admit and try to cover up increasingly apparent serious risk factors.

Part of the problem was the stubborn mindset of top executives that nothing was wrong: A few accidents reflected driver carelessness, not a defective product. Neither would assume the worst scenario: that this was a dangerous product used on a dangerous product that was killing people, and neither Ford nor Firestone could escape blame.

Forty years ago a somewhat similar situation occurred with the GM Corvair, a rear-engine car that exhibited instability under extreme cornering conditions causing it to flip over. Ralph Nader gained his reputation as a consumer advocate in his condemnation of this "unsafe" car with a best-selling book, *Unsafe At Any Speed.* But GM executives refused to admit there was any problem, until eventually the evidence was overwhelming and lawsuits flourished, and the federal government stepped in with the National Traffic and Motor Vehicle Safety Act of 1966 that among other things required manufacturers to notify customers of any defects or flaws later discovered in their vehicles.

GM executives, like those of Ford and Firestone 40 years later, were honorable men. Yet, something seems to happen to the conscience and the moral sensitivity of top executives. They commission actions in their corporate personas that they would hardly dream of doing in their private lives. John DeLorean, former GM executive, was one of the first to note this dichotomy:

> These were not immoral men who were bringing out this car [the Corvair]. These were warm, breathing men with families and children who as private individuals would never have approved [this project] for a minute if they were told, "You are going to kill and injure people with this car." But these same men, in a business atmosphere, where everything is

[11] Keith Bradsher, "SUV Tire Defects Were Known in '96 But Not Reported; 190 Died in Next 4 years," *New York Times* (June 24, 2001), p. 1N.

reduced to terms of costs, corporate goals, and production deadlines, were able to approve a product most of them wouldn't have considered approving as individuals.[12]

We have to raise the question: Why this lockstep obsession with sales and profits at all costs? See the following Information Box for a discussion of this issue.

INFORMATION BOX

THE GROUPTHINK INFLUENCE ON UNETHICAL BEHAVIOR

The callousness about "killer" cars would, as John DeLorean theorized, probably never have prevailed if an individual was making the decision outside the corporate environment. But bring in *groupthink*, which is decision-by-committee, and add to this a high degree of organizational loyalty (versus loyalty to the public interest), and such callousness can manifest itself. Why can the moral standards of groupthink be so much lower than individual moral standards?

Perhaps the answer lies in the "pack mentality" that characterizes certain committees or groups highly committed to organizational goals. All else then becomes subordinated to these goals, being a single-minded perspective. Within any committee, individual responsibility for decision is diluted since this is a committee decision. Furthermore, without the contrary arguments of a strong "devil's advocate" (i.e., one who argues the opposing viewpoint, sometimes simply to be sure that all sides of an issue are considered), a follow-the-leader syndrome can take place, with no one willing to oppose the majority views.

But there is more to it than that. Chester Barnard, a business executive, scholar, and philosopher, noted the paradox: People can have a number of private moral codes that affect behavior in different situations, and these codes are not always compatible. Codes for private life, regarding family and religion, may be far different from codes for business life. Throughout the history of business, it has not been unusual to find that the scrupulous and God-fearing churchgoer is far different when he or she conducts business during the week: A far lower ethical standard prevails during the week than on the Sabbath. Nor has it been unusual to find that a person can be a paragon of love, understanding, and empathy with his or her family but be totally lacking in such qualities with employees or customers.[13] We might add that even tyrants guilty of the most extreme atrocities, such as Hitler and Saddam Hussein, have been known to exude great tenderness and consideration for their intimates.

What does it take for a person to resist and not accept the majority viewpoint? What do you think would be the characteristics of such a person? Do you see yourself as such a gadfly?

---

[12] J. Patrick Wright, *On a Clear Day You Can See General Motors* (Grosse Point, MI: Wright Enterprises, 1979), pp. 5–6.

[13] Chester I. Barnard, *The Functions of the Executive* (Cambridge, MA: Harvard University Press, 1938), p. 263.

WHAT CAN BE LEARNED?

A firm today must zealously guard against product liability suits. Any responsible executive needs to recognize that product liability suits, in today's litigious environment, can even bankrupt a firm. The business arena has become more risky, more fraught with peril for the unwary or the naively unconcerned. Consequently, any firm needs careful and objective testing of any product that can affect customer health and safety. Sometimes such testing may require that production be delayed, even if competition gains some advantage from this delay. The risks of putting an unsafe product on the market outweigh competitive concerns.

Suspicions and complaints about product safety must be thoroughly investigated. We should learn from this case that immediate and thorough investigation of any suspicions or complaints must be undertaken, regardless of the confidence management may have in the product or of the glowing recommendations of persons whose objectivity could be suspect. To procrastinate or ignore complaints poses what should be unacceptable risks.

Sometimes the root of the problem is not obvious, or is more complex than first thought. In this Ford/Firestone case, objective research should have focused on both the Explorer and the Firestone tires, and how the situation could be remedied to minimize rollovers and save lives.

The health and safety of customers is entirely compatible with the well-being of the firm. It is a lose/lose situation if this is ignored: The customer is jeopardized, but eventually the firm is, too, as lawsuits grow and damages increase. Why, then, the corporate mindset of "us versus them"? There should be no conflicting goals. Both win when customer welfare is maximized.

In the worst scenario, go for a conciliatory salvage strategy. Ford and Firestone faced a crossroads by late 1999 and early 2000. Reports of fatalities linked to Ford Explorers and Firestone tires were trickling in, the first occurring in the hot climate of Saudi Arabia, and these were in a matter of months to become a flood. How should a company react?

A salvage strategy can be attempted by toughing it out, trying to combat the bad press, denying culpability, blaming someone else, and resorting to the strongest possible legal defense. This essentially was what Ford opted to do, as it blamed Firestone for everything, and spent millions advertising to promote this contention.

Firestone was more vulnerable since its shredded tires could hardly be denied, and it was forced to recall millions of tires, although it stoutly maintained that the cause of the shredding was underinflation and the wrong quality of tire, as well as the Explorer itself. At stake were company reputations, economic positions, and even viability for Firestone—but also the lives of hundreds of users.

Conciliation usually is the better salvage strategy. This involves recognition and full admission of the problem and removal of the risk, even if this involved a full-market withdrawal until the source of the problem could be identified and correction made. Expensive, yes, but far less risky for the viability of the company and certainly for the health of those customers involved.

Neither strategy is without substantial costs. But the first course of action puts major cost consequences in the future, where they may turn out to be vastly greater as legal expenses and damage awards skyrocket. The second course of action poses an immediate impact on profitability, and will not avoid legal expenses, but may save the company and its reputation and return it to profitability in the near future.

Where blame is most likely shared, the solution of the problem lies not in confrontation but in cooperation. This is the most grievous component of the violations of the public trust by Ford and Firestone: denial and confrontation, rather than both parties working together to solve the problem of product safety.

CONSIDER

Can you think of additional learning insights?

LATE-BREAKING NEWS

Bridgestone/Firestone agreed to replace more defective Wilderness AT tires as the NHTSA closed its investigation. The tires were produced at two plants before 1998, and had been linked to 25 fatalities. Estimates placed 885,000 of these tires still on the road. The recall was far less than Ford had hoped, so that Firestone would not be obligated to cover the cost of Ford's replacement program of 13,000,000 tires. Fatalities by October 2001 had reached 271 involving Firestone tires. Firestone still sought a formal investigation of the Explorer, insisting that its design contributed to the accidents.[13]

On October 30, 2001, the announcement came that Henry Clay Ford Jr. 44, would replace Jacques Nasser as CEO. The move puts a Ford family member in charge for the first time since 1979 when Henry Ford II resigned. Nasser had been under pressure for months for Ford's loss of market share and tumbling profitability and the adverse publicity of the Explorer with its Firestone tires. Ford is the son of William Clay Ford Sr., who is the grandson of founder Henry Ford and brother of Henry Ford II.[14]

The newly-designed 2002 Ford Explorer received a top score in a crash test from the Insurance Institute for Highway Safety in December 2001. Changes in the 2002 Explorer to improve passenger protection were part of the automaker's "commitment to continuous improvements," a Ford spokesperson said.[15]

---

[13] Timothy Aeppel, Stephen Power, and Norihiko Shirouzu, "Firestone Broadens Recall of Defective Tires," *Wall Street Journal* (October 5, 2001), pp. A3, A4.

[14] Ed Garsten, Associated Press, as reported in "Ford CEO to Again Be Ford Family Member," *Cleveland Plain Dealer* (October 30, 2001), p. C1.

[15] Christopher Jensen, *Cleveland Plain Dealer* (December 12, 2001), pp. C1 and C4.

QUESTIONS

1. Can a firm guarantee complete product safety? Discuss.

2. Based on the information we presented, whom do you think is most to blame for the deaths and injuries? What led you to your conclusion?

3. "If an Explorer driver never checks the tire pressure and drives well above the speed limit, he has no one to blame but himself in an accident—not the vehicle and not the tires." Discuss.

4. Do you think the government should be blamed in the Explorer deaths and injuries? Why or why not?

5. Would you give credence to the "community champion" awards bestowed by a consumer advocacy group founded by the Association of Trial Lawyers, and given to Alan Hogan in June 2001 for exposing careless tire production? Why or why not?

6. "Admittedly the groupthink mindset may be responsible for a few unethical and bad decisions, but isn't this mindset more likely to consider the consequences to the company of delivering unsafe products, and be opposed to not taking aggressive corrective action?" Evaluate this.

7. Have you had any experience with a Ford Explorer? If so, what is your perception of its performance and safety?

8. Have you had any experience with Firestone tires? What is your perception of their performance and safety?

HANDS-ON EXERCISES

1. Place yourself in the position of John Lampe, CEO of Firestone, as the crisis worsens and accusations mount. Discuss how you would try to change the climate with Jacques Nasser of Ford from confrontational to cooperative. Be as specific as you can. Do you think you would be successful?

2. Firestone is on its knees after massive tire recalls and monstrous damage suits. You are a consultant brought in to help the firm recover. Be as specific as possible in recommendations, and in the priority of things to do. Make any assumptions you need to, but keep them reasonable. Defend your recommendations.

TEAM DEBATE EXERCISE

Debate the issue of dropping or keeping the Firestone name. Defend your position and attack the other side.

INVITATION TO RESEARCH

Has the safety record of the Explorer improved, and what was done to improve it?

Was the Firestone name kept, and has it recouped its reputation?

Can you find statistics as to how competing tire companies, particularly Goodyear and Michelin, have fared during and after the Firestone recall?

Are Ford and Firestone friends again? How costly have the damage suits been to both firms?

CONCLUSIONS

CHAPTER TWENTY-FIVE

What Can Be Learned?

In considering mistakes, three things are worth noting: (1) Even the most successful organizations make mistakes but survive as long as they maintain a good "batting average" of satisfactory decisions; (2) mistakes should be effective teaching tools for avoiding similar errors in the future, and (3) firms can bounce back from adversity, and turn around.

We can make a number of generalizations from these mistakes and successes. Of course, management is a discipline that does not lend itself to laws or axioms; exceptions to every principle or generalization can be found. Still, the decision maker does well to heed the following insights. For the most part they are based on specific corporate experiences and are transferable to other situations and other times.

INSIGHTS REGARDING OVERALL ENTERPRISE PERSPECTIVES

Importance of Public Image

The impact, for good or bad, of an organization's public image was a common thread through a number of cases—for example, Continental, Harley Davidson, Southwest Airlines, United Way, Boston Beer, Perrier, Johnson & Johnson, and the Ford Explorer and Firestone tires.

Continental Airlines is a case for hope. It shows that a reputation in the pits, not only with employees but with the general public, can be resurrected and revitalized, even over a short period of time, but it takes inspired leadership to do so. And this its new CEO, Gordon Bethune, supplied.

Harley Davidson, the cycle maker, showed an image turnaround also, only it took decades to accomplish. The image of the black-jacketed motorcyclist was a disaster, but in the 1980s this turned around to become even a status symbol. Harley executives helped develop the new mystique, and then exploited it.

Southwest's image of friendliness, great efficiency, and unbeatable prices propelled it to an unassailable position among short-haul airlines. Now it seeks to expand its image to longer hauls.

The nonprofit United Way was brought to its knees by revelations about the excesses of its long-time chief executive, William Aramony. Donations dwindled and local chapters withheld funds from the national organization as the reputation of the largest charitable organization was sullied.

Johnson & Johnson gained a great image of undeviating concern for its customers, regardless of cost. At the other extreme, both Ford and Firestone showed their callousness and refusal to take responsibility for product deficiencies that resulted in hundreds of deaths.

Other examples of capitalizing on a positive image were Vanguard and Boston Beer. On the other hand, Perrier and Met Life let their images slip.

The importance of a firm's public image is undeniable, yet some firms continue to disregard this and either act in ways detrimental to image or else ignore the constraints and opportunities that a reputation affords.

Power of the Media

We have seen or suspected the power of the media in a number of cases. Coca-Cola, United Way, IBM, Perrier, and Ford and Firestone are obvious examples. This power is often used critically—to hurt a firm's public image. The media can fan a problem or exacerbate an embarrassing or imprudent action. In particular, this media focus can trigger the herd instinct, in which increasing numbers of people join in protests and public criticism. And the media in their zeal can sometimes cross the line, as did the media in England in denigrating Maytag for the ill-advised promotion of its Hoover Europe subsidiary.

We can make these generalizations regarding image and its relationship with the media:

1. It is desirable to maintain a stable, clear-cut image and undeviating objectives.
2. It is difficult and time-consuming to upgrade an image.
3. In order to satisfy negative media mindset, in dire circumstances new top management may be needed if image is to be more quickly upgraded.
4. A good image can be quickly lost if a firm relaxes in an environment of aggressive competition, or else has an episode of product-safety concerns.
5. Well-known firms, and not-for-profit firms dependent on voluntary contributions, are especially vulnerable to critical public scrutiny and must use great care in safeguarding their reputations.

No Guarantee of Success

That success does not guarantee continued success or freedom from adversity is a sobering realization that must come from examining these cases. Many of the mistakes occurred in notably successful organizations, such as Harley Davidson, IBM, Euro Disney, Boeing, Maytag, Met Life, United Way, even Coca Cola. How could things go so badly for such firms conditioned to success? The three C's mindset offers an explanation for this perversity.

The Three C's Mindset

We can also call this "the king of the hill" syndrome. With such an organizational climate, success actually brings vulnerability. The three C's—complacency, conservatism, and conceit—can blanket leading organizations. To avoid this, a constructive attitude of never underestimating competitors can be fostered by:

- Bringing fresh blood into the organization for new ideas and different perspectives
- Establishing a strong and continuing commitment to customer service and satisfaction
- Conducting periodic corporate self-analyses designed to detect weaknesses as well as opportunities in their early stages
- Continually monitoring the environment and being alert to any changes (more about this later)

The environment is dynamic, sometimes with subtle and hardly recognizable changes, at other times with violent and unmistakable changes. To operate in this environment, an established firm must be on guard to defend its position.

Adversity Need Not Be Forever

Just as a dominant firm can lose its momentum and competitive position, so can a faltering organization be turned around. If a faltering firm can at least maintain some semblance of viability, as some of the dot.coms and telecoms barely did, then it has hope. So significant and even inspiring is this possibility, that we devoted Part III to great comeback firms: Continental Airlines, Harley Davidson, and IBM.

PLANNING INSIGHTS

What Should Our Business Be?

An organization's business, its mission and purpose, should be thought through, spelled out clearly, and well communicated by those involved in policy making. Otherwise, the organization lacks unified and coordinated objectives, which is akin to trying to navigate without a map.

Good judgment suggests choosing safe rather than courageous goals. But in the heady optimism for high-techs in the 1990s, few such firms could resist the temptation to go for the moon, and spend and plan accordingly with no semblance of frugality. This same mindset wrecked saving and loans a decade earlier.

Determining what a firm's business is or should be gives a starting point for specifying goals. Several elements help with this determination.

The firm's *resources and distinctive abilities and strengths* should play a major role in determining its goals. It is not enough to wish for a certain status or position if resources and competence do not warrant this. To take an extreme example, a railroad company can hardly expect to transform itself into an airline, even though both may be in the transportation business. A Wal-Mart is hardly likely to successfully imitate a Neiman Marcus.

Environmental and competitive opportunities ought to be considered. The initial inroads of foreign carmakers in the United States stemmed from environmental opportunities for energy-efficient vehicles at a time when U.S. carmakers had ignored this area. Southwest Air similarly found opportunity in lowest prices for short hops that its bigger competitors could not match without losing money.

The Right Growth Orientation

The opposite of a growth commitment is a status quo philosophy, one uninterested in expansion or the problems and work involved. Harley Davidson was content, despite being pushed around by foreign competitors, until eventually a new management reawakened it decades later.

In general, how tenable is a low-growth or no-growth philosophy? Although at first glance it seems workable, such a philosophy sows the seeds of its own destruction. More than four decades ago the following insight was pointed out:

> Vitality is required even for survival; but vitality is difficult to maintain without growth, at least in the American business climate. The vitality of a firm depends on the vigor and ambition of its members. The prospect of growth is one of the principal means by which a firm can attract able and vigorous recruits.[1]

Consequently, a firm not obviously growth-minded finds it difficult to attract able people. Customers see a growing firm as reliable, eager to please, and constantly improving. As we saw with OfficeMax, suppliers and creditors tend to give preferential treatment to a growth-oriented firm because they hope to retain it as a customer and client when it reaches large size.

But emphasizing growth can be carried too far. The growth must be kept within the abilities of the firm to handle. Several cases, such as McDonald's, Southwest Air, and Vanguard, showed how firms can grow rapidly without losing control. But we also have the bungled growth efforts of Maytag's Hoover Division in the UK, and Euro Disney, where controls were loosened far too much for foreign subsidiaries. Not to be outdone, there was the unethical growth climate at Met Life. Good financial judgment and decent ethical behavior must not be sacrificed to the siren call of growth. With relatively new firms, such as the high-tech startups, growth can easily outpace management competence and the ability to effectively utilize mass infusions of investment capital.

We can make these generalizations about the most desirable growth perspectives:

1. Growth targets should not exceed the abilities and rsources of the organization. Growth at any cost—especially at the expense of profits and financial stability—should be shunned. In particular, tight controls over

---

[1] Wroe Alderson, *Marketing Behavior and Executive Action* (Homewood, IL: Irwin, 1957), p. 59.

inventories and expenses should be established, and performance should be closely monitored.

2. The most prudent approach to growth is to keep the organization and operation as simple and uniform as possible, to be flexible in case sales do not meet expectations, and to seek a low breakeven point, especially for new and untried ventures.

3. Rapidly expanding markets pose dangers from both too-conservative and overly optimistic sales forecasts. The latter may overextend resources and jeopardize viability should demand contract; the former opens the door to more aggressive competitors. There is no right answer to this dilemma, but management should be aware of the risks and the rewards of both extremes.

4. A strategy emphasizing rapid growth should not neglect other aspects of the operation. For example, older stores should not be ignored in the quest to open new outlets, as OfficeMax had to be careful of in its rapid opening of new stores. The giant aircraft producer, Boeing, found itself unable to cope with burgeoning demand partly because of too much attention given to assimilating McDonnell Douglas.

5. Decentralized management is more compatible with rapid growth than centralized, because it puts less strain on home office executives. However, delegation must have well-defined standards and controls as well as competent subordinates. Otherwise, the Maytag Hoover fiasco may be repeated.

6. The integrity of the product and the firm's reputation must not be sacrificed in pursuit of rapid growth. This is especially important when customers' health and safety may be jeopardized.

Search for Uniqueness

Most firms seek some differential advantage or uniqueness over existing competitors. Some never find it, or they rely on gimmicks, such as a new package or some product feature of little consequence to customers. All the successes we examined had uniqueness: Southwest Air, Herman Miller, Johnson & Johnson, McDonald's, Vanguard, even Harley Davidson at last, with its fortuitous mystique.

Uniqueness, though, may not be long-lasting. Snapple, the ill-fated acquisition of Quaker Oats, soon found its uniqueness that had permitted a higher price waning. Perrier, the premium bottled water, found publicity about contamination at a plant destroying its advantage. Boston Beer and Herman Miller faced the danger of losing their premium product advantage. Even McDonald's, for decades unique in its control of product quality and service, is no longer unique among its competitors.

So, uniqueness is widely sought, but not always achieved or maintained. It is a mistake to believe that uniqueness has to come from a distinctive product. It can come from simply doing some things better, such as better service, better quality control, greater dependability, or greater efforts toward pleasing customers.

We can make these generalizations regarding finding opportunities and strategic windows:

1. Opportunities often exist when a traditional way of doing business has prevailed in the industry for a long time—maybe the climate is ripe for a change.

2. Opportunities often exist when present firms are not completely satisfying customers' needs.

3. Innovations are not limited to products but can involve customer services as well as such things as methods of distribution.

4. For industries with rapidly changing technologies—usually new industries—heavy research and development expenditures are usually required if a firm is to avoid falling behind its competitors. But heavy R&D expenditures do not guarantee being in the vanguard, as shown by the tribulations of IBM despite its huge expenditures.

Power of Judicious Imitation

Some firms are reluctant to copy successful practices of their competitors; they want to be leaders, not followers. But successful practices or innovations may need to be copied if a firm is not to be left behind. Sometimes the imitator outdoes the innovator. Success can lie in doing the ordinary better than competitors.

Michael Feuer with OfficeMax took a format similar to other category-killer stores, but did things better, at least in the beginning. On the other hand, many competitors of McDonald's long ignored its successful format, even though the high standards and rigid controls were obvious to all. The same has been true of the low prices and great quality of Vanguard and Southwest Airlines. These two firms defy competitors to match their prices and efficiency. Admittedly, it is not easy to develop high standards and to insist that they be followed, or to become so efficient that prices can be lowered to the point where competitors cannot match them without losing money. We can make this generalization:

- It makes sense for a company to identify the characteristics of successful competitors (and even similar but noncompeting firms), and then to adopt these characteristics if they are compatible with its resources. Let someone else do the experimenting and risk taking. The imitator faces some risk in waiting too long, but this usually is far less than the risk that the innovator faces.

EXECUTION INSIGHTS

The Austerity Mindset

Four of the firms we studied exemplified this philosophy to the fullest. Two were rather new firms, Boston Beer and OfficeMax, but with greater size they released the austerity reins. Another firm, Southwest Airlines, shows no signs of changing its successful austerity format, nor does Vanguard, which steadfastly adheres to the frugality of its founder, John Bogle.

We have seen the opposite in the organizational bloat of an IBM, and in the often-fatal excesses of the dot.coms and other high-tech firms that joined the savings and loans of a generation earlier. Besieged Scott Paper and Sunbeam, reeling from the drastic cuts of Al Dunlap, deserved some of this because their organizations had grown cumbersome. Chrysler, at the time of its merger with Daimler, also brought with it a recently bloated organization.

Lean and mean is the order of the day with many firms. The problem with the lemming-like pursuit of the lean-and-mean goal is knowing how far to downsize without cutting into bone and muscle, which then becomes counterproductive. As thousands of managers and staff specialists can attest, the loss of jobs and destruction of career paths has been traumatic for individuals and society alike. So it is much better not to become bloated in the first place.

Resistance to Change

People, as well as organizations, are naturally reluctant to embrace change. Change is disruptive, it destroys routines and muddies interpersonal relationships with subordinates, coworkers, and superiors. Previously important positions may be downgraded or even eliminated, and persons who view themselves as highly competent may be forced to assume unfamiliar duties, with the fear that they cannot master the new assignments. When the change involves wholesale terminations in a major downsizing, such as the ones Dunlap engineered and the restructuring that the new German top brass forced on Chrysler, resistance and fear of change can become so great that overall efficiency is seriously jeopardized.

Normal resistance to change can be combatted by good communication with participants about forthcoming changes. Without such communication rumors and fears may be blown far out of proportion. Acceptance of change is facilitated if employees are involved as fully as possible in planning the changes, if their participation is solicited and welcomed, and if assurance can be given that positions will not be impaired, only changed. Gradual rather than abrupt changes also make a transition smoother.

In the final analysis, however, possible negative repercussions should not deter making needed changes and embracing different opportunities, as Herman Miller found in a suddenly different environment for office furniture, and Disney found confronting it in Europe. If change is desirable, as it usually is with long-established bureaucratic organizations, it should be initiated. Individuals and organizations can adapt to change—it just takes some time.

Beware the Rush to Merge

Mergers create the most disruption. Even mergers that seem to combine similarities often miss serious relationship subtleties, as Quaker Oats with its costly acquisition of Snapple found out too late. When a merger involves an acquisition of an old and cherished U.S. firm by a foreign firm, a onetime enemy in World War II, the resistance to change is all the greater. When subterfuge is added to such a merger, with U.S. management mistakenly expecting this to be a "merger of equals," personnel and assimilation problems become all the greater. As this is written, DaimlerChrysler has still not smoothed out this merger of unequals.

Studies increasingly show that most mergers and acquisitions do not meet expectations. For example, a study of 78 deals over a two-year period done by the consulting firm Booz Allen & Hamilton found that in mergers of similar size companies the failure rate was 67 percent. If the acquirer was more than twice the size of the target company, the failure rate was still 38 percent. Reasons given for the failures were loss of key staff members, culture clashes, poor or clumsy integration, and the loss of key customers.[2]

Prudent Crisis Management

Crises are unexpected happenings that pose threats to the organization's well-being, ranging from modest to catastrophic. A number of cases involved crises: for example, United Way, Maytag, Euro Disney, Herman Miller, Coca-Cola, ADM, Met Life, Perrier, Boeing, Ford and Firestone, and Johnson & Johnson. Some handled their crises reasonably well, such as United Way, Euro Disney, and the paragon of crisis management, J&J., although we can question in the first two cases how such crises were allowed to happen in the first place. However, Maytag, ADM, Perrier, Boeing, Ford/Firestone, and Met Life either overreacted or else failed badly in salvaging the situation.

Most crises can be minimized if a company practices risk avoidance, has contingency plans, and is alert to changes in the environment. For example, it is prudent to prohibit key executives from traveling on the same plane; it is prudent to insure key executives so their incapacity will not endanger the organization; it is prudent to set up contingency plans for a strike, an equipment failure or plant shutdown, the loss of a major customer, unexpected economic conditions, or a serious lawsuit; and it is prudent to back up records and, for financial firms in particular, to have such backups in distant locations. With contingency plans, it is best to work backward from a worst-case scenario. Some crises can be anticipated, such as a looming oil embargo, a shortage of certain raw materials, a growing union militancy in the industry. When the environment looks particularly troubling, as was the case after the destruction of the World Trade Center on September 11, 2001, a firm in a vulnerable industry might consider organizing a crisis management team.

Insurance usually covers certain risks, but the mettle of any organization can be severely tested by an unexpected crisis not covered adequately by insurance, for example, a major product recall because of serious safety or health risks. Such may have major impact on profits, as Johnson & Johnson found with its Tylenol recall, and Perrier lost market share never to be regained. Crises may necessitate some changes in the organization and the way of doing business, but they need not cause the demise of the company if alternatives are weighed and actions taken only after due deliberation. Firms should avoid making hasty disruptive changes or, the other extreme, making too few changes too late.

Don't Rock the Boat

This philosophy advocates not making changes unless problems warrant it. If things are going well, even if not as well as desired, don't tamper, since the consequences

---

[2] Janet Whitman, Dow Jones News, as reported in "Mergers Often Look Better on Paper, Consultant's Study of 78 Deals Finds," *Cleveland Plain Dealer* (August 5, 2001), p. H3.

might be worse. This is also commonly known as the "if it's not broke, don't fix it" philosophy. The Coca-Cola case is the strongest confirmation of this idea: Changing the flavor of Coke slightly did not improve demand but simply aroused condemnation.

As with most things, however, this admonition of not changing that which seems to be satisfactory should not be graven in stone. An operation may be improved through fine-tuning; an alternative may be better. The dilemma of Herman Miller suggests that unchanging policies and strategies of the past need to be rethought. IBM, Boeing, and United Way were slow in making changes and severe problems caught up with them. Scott Paper and Sunbeam likewise needed to make changes long before Dunlap brought his drastic ones. Continuance of the status quo is usually just a wistful fancy, one that deludes any organization not geared to the possibility of change.

Environmental Monitoring

A firm should be alert to changes in the business environment: changes in customer preferences and needs, in competition, in the economy, in government regulation, and even in international events such as nationalism in Canada, NAFTA, OPEC machinations, changes in Eastern Europe and South Africa, economic developments in the Far East, and the threats and consequences of terrorist activities here and abroad. IBM, Harley Davidson, and Boeing failed to detect and act upon significant changes in their industries. Disney encountered different customer attitudes in Europe than it had experienced before.

How can a firm remain alert to subtle and insidious or more obvious changes? It must have *sensors* constantly monitoring the environment. The sensor may be a marketing or economic research department, but in many instances such a formal organizational entity is not really necessary to provide primary monitoring. Executive alertness is essential. Most changes do not occur suddenly and without warning—but we well know this still can happen, the danger exists, and should not be disregarded. Feedback from customers, sales representatives and suppliers; news of the latest relevant projections in business journals; and even simple observations of what is happening in stores, advertising, prices, and new technologies can provide information about a changing environment. Unfortunately, in the urgency of handling day-to-day operating problems, managers may miss clues of imminent changes in the competitive environment.

Following are generalizations regarding vulnerability to competition:

1. Initial market advantage tends to be rather quickly countered by competitors.
2. Countering by competitors is more likely when an innovation is involved than when the advantage comes from more commonplace effective management, such as superb cost controls or customer service.
3. An easy-entry industry is particularly vulnerable to new and aggressive competition, especially if the market is expanding. In new industries, severe price competition usually weeds out the marginal firms.
4. Long-dominant firms tend to be vulnerable to upstart competitors because of their complacency, conservatism, and conceit. They frequently are resistant to change, and myopic about the environment.

5. Careful monitoring of performance at strategic control points can detect weakening positions needing corrective action before situations become serious. (This will be further discussed shortly.)

6. In expanding markets it is unwise to judge performance by increases in sales rather than by market share; an increase in sales may hide a deteriorating situation as competitors increase sales more.

7. A no-growth policy invites competitive inroads.

The Power of Giving Employees a Sense of Pride and a Caring Management

The great turnaround of Continental from the confrontational days of Lorenzo has to be mainly attributed to the people-oriented environment fostered by Bethune. The marvel is how quickly it was done, starting with such a simple thing as an open-door policy to the executive suite, and encouragement of full communication with employees.

Still, Continental was not unique is this enlisting of employees to the team. Other successful firms have done so, although perhaps none so strikingly or so suddenly. Kelleher of Southwest Airlines certainly developed an esprit de corps, and this helped account for the great cost advantage of Southwest. Ray Kroc of McDonald's fostered this as McDonald's began its great charge, although in recent years relations with franchisees grew more fragile under new top management. Michael Feuer gained dedicated employees in the early growth years of OfficeMax and John Bogle imbued Vanguard with his concept of frugality and customer service.

Then we have the other extreme, the mechanistic handling of employees by Al Dunlap. Any temporary improvement of profits, through cutting expenses to the bone with vast layoffs, finally came to roost as he himself was fired at Sunbeam.

Boeing's problems with its peaks and valleys of layoffs and hiring destroyed pride and esprit de corps of employees, except perhaps for a nucleus. This sense of pride was certainly latent with such a prestigious product, but without workplace stability a great opportunity was lost to cement employee morale.

In addition to a people-oriented management, another key factor, in cultivating employee morale and teamwork lies in the perceived growth prospects of the firm. Where growth prospects look good, even coming back from the adversity of Continental, then employees can grasp that extra measure of enthusiasm and motivation.

CONTROL INSIGHTS

Delegation Overdone

Good managers delegate as much as possible to subordinates. By giving them some freedom and as much responsibility as they can handle, future leaders are developed. More than this, delegation allows higher executives to concentrate on the most important matters. Other areas of the operation need come to their attention only where performance deviates significantly from what is expected at *strategic control points*. This is known as *management by exception*.

Management by exception failed, however, with Maytag and its overseas Hoover division. The flaw lay in failing to monitor faulty promotional plans. By the time results were coming in, it was too late. Admittedly, with diverse and far-flung operations it becomes more difficult to closely monitor all aspects, but still there should be strategic control points to warn of impending dangers. At the least, home office approval of expenditures above a certain amount must be enforced.

We found delegation problems in other cases. The ridiculous acquisition of Snapple—a product at the end of its faddish life cycle and incompatible with the existing distribution structure of Gatorade—smacks of dependence on incompetent researchers to whom too much responsibility was delegated.

The Euro Disney difficulties may have resulted from not enough autonomy: The European operation did not adjust well to a somewhat different playing field, in which customers were far more price-conscious than had been experienced before.

At the top executive level, United Way found the excesses of its chief, Aramony, to be unacceptable. Here, the board of directors could be faulted for being far too tolerant of a chief executive's questionable behavior. This raises another issue: How closely should the board exercise control?

Board-of-Directors Patsies

A board of directors can monitor top management performance closely and objectively. Or it can be completely supportive and uncritical. In the latter situation, the board exercises no controls on top management; in the former, it becomes an important control factor at the highest level.

Given the potential control power of the board, top executives find their own interests best served by packing the board with supporters. Dwayne Andreas of ADM succeeded in doing so and found virtual freedom to run the company as he saw fit. Even large institutional shareholders could not muster enough support to thwart his dictatorship. Aramony of United Way also had a sympathetic and supportive board that permitted his excesses to go unmonitored, until investigative reporters blew the whistle.

Instead of assuming the status of watchdogs for investors' best interests, such patsy boards disserve them.

Systematic Evaluations and Controls

Organizations need feedback to determine how well something is being done, whether improvement is possible, where it should occur, how much is needed, and how quickly it must be accomplished. Without feedback or performance evaluation, a worsening situation can go unrecognized until too late for corrective action.

As firms become larger, the need for better controls or feedback increases, because top management can no longer personally monitor all aspects of the operation. Mergers and diversifications, which often result in loosely controlled decentralized operations—for example, again, Maytag and its overseas Hoover division—all the more need systematic feedback on performance.

Financial and expense controls are vital. After all, if costs and inventories get severely out of line—and worse, if this is not recognized until late—then the very viability of the firm can be jeopardized. Many of the exuberant high-tech enterprises, and the savings and loans before them, found that their heedless extravagances hastened their demise.

Performance standards are another critical means of control for widespread operations. Unless operating standards are imposed and enforced, uniformity of performance is sacrificed, resulting in unevenness of quality and service and a lack of coordination and continuity among the different units. Even unethical and illegal practices may ensue, as we saw with Met Life. Instead of running a tight ship, managers face a loose and undisciplined one. McDonald's had long been the model of a tight ship, with its enduring insistence on the tightest standards in the industry.

INSIGHTS REGARDING SPECIFIC STRATEGY ELEMENTS

Appeal of Price

In several cases we have seen an anomaly regarding the effective use of price. Southwest Airlines owes its great strategic advantage to offering the lowest prices in its industry and doing so profitably with a cost structure lower than other air carriers. Similarly, mutual fund giant Vanguard brought frugality and lowest prices to investors while still giving them the best service in the industry.

Yet, Continental Air found that the low-price strategy of Frank Lorenzo almost destroyed it in the absence of good service and morale. Discount stores base their customer appeal in offering lower prices than conventional retailers. Undoubtedly customers are strongly attracted by low prices, but low prices must not be at the expense of reasonable customer service and product quality.

Yet, we saw several cases where high prices attracted. Entrepreneur Jim Koch targeted Boston Beer as having a robust flavor with the highest prices in the industry. Harley Davidson customers were willing to wait months to obtain its high-priced bikes. Herman Miller for decades had a secure market niche with its premium-quality innovative office furniture, although the niche began eroding in the 1990s. Perrier led the bottled-water industry with its charging high prices for the simple commodity of water, and this was successful until the contamination exposé.

On the other hand, high prices did not work to Disney's advantage in Euro Disney. The French and most other Europeans were more frugal than Disney executives expected; only when prices were cut significantly was viability more certain. Quaker Oats also found high prices of Snapple left it vulnerable to lower-priced competitors.

With price it seems we face the twin appeals of bargains and highest quality. Although more customers are attracted to bargains and low prices, some will pay a lot more for something they believe is the highest quality. And the great majority of customers believe that high price equates with high quality—which it does sometimes, but not always.

Can Advertising Do the Job?

We are left with contradictions regarding the power and effectiveness of advertising. Boston Beer, despite its larger competitors and its own rather modest expenditures for advertising, carved a significant niche in the beer market with an unusual theme. At the time of Coca-Cola's blunder with its New Coke it was spending $100 million more for advertising than Pepsi, and all the while was losing market share. Does advertising have much relationship with success?

The right theme can bring success, although with the sheer volume of advertising, finding an appealing and unique theme is a mighty challenge. Of course, you can give the store away, as Maytag Hoover's promotional campaign almost did: It certainly created great attention and interest.

Thus we see the great challenge of advertising. One never knows for sure how much should be spent to get the job done, to reach the planned objectives of perhaps increasing sales or market share by a certain percentage. However, despite the inability to measure directly the effectiveness of advertising, it is the brave—or foolhardy—executive who stands pat in the face of aggressive increased promotions by competitors. We draw these conclusions:

- There is no assured correlation between expenditures for advertising and sales success. But the right theme or message can be powerful.

- In most cases, advertising can generate initial trial. But if the other elements of the strategy are relatively unattractive, customers will be neither won nor retained.

Analytical Management Tools

We identified several of the most useful analytical tools for decision making. In Euro Disney we discussed breakeven analysis, a highly useful means for making go/no-go decisions about new ventures and alternative business strategies. In Maytag, the cost-benefit analysis was described, which might have prevented the bungled promotion in England. And we encountered the SWOT analysis in the Southwest Airlines case. While these analyses do not guarantee best decisions, they do bring order and systematic thinking into the art of management decision making.

ETHICAL CONSIDERATIONS

A firm tempted to walk the low road in search of greater short-run profits may eventually find the risks far outweigh the rewards. We have examined more than a few cases dealing with ethical controversies, for example, ADM's indictment for price fixing and its more subtle efforts to gain special influence in the halls of government. Then there was Met Life's indictment for deceptive sales practices, and the exposés of undesirable practices by United Way. Nor can we forget the callousness toward life and injury by Ford and Firestone regarding Explorers fitted with Firestone tires. While we cannot delve very deeply into social and ethical issues,[3] several insights are worth noting:

---

[3] For more depth of coverage, see R. F. Hartley, *Business Ethics* (New York: Wiley, 1993).

1. A firm can no longer disavow itself of the possibility of critical scrutiny. Activist groups and/or investigative reporters often publicize alleged misdeeds long before governmental regulators will. Legal actions may follow.

2. Public protests may take a colorful path, with marches, picketing, billboard whitewashing, and the like, and may enlist public and media support for their cause.

Should a firm attempt to resist and defend itself? The overwhelming evidence is to the contrary. The bad press, the adversarial relations, and the effect on public image are hardly worth such a confrontation. The better course of action may be to back down as quietly as possible, repugnant though such may be to a management convinced of the reasonableness of its position.

Most ethical problems we saw came with hostile media. Sensationalism, exaggeration, and taking sides against the big corporation usually sell more copies or gain more audience. Many executives are uncomfortable and even hostile toward an inquisitive press. So, they create a bad impression, frequently one of trying to hide something. Even worse is confrontation, as the tobacco industry has long practiced.

Johnson & Johnson's secret for gaining rapport with the media was corporate openness and cooperation. After the Tylenol catastrophe, it sought good two-way communication with media furnishing information from the field while J&J gave full and honest disclosure of its own investigation and actions. To promote good rapport, company officials were readily available to the press.

GENERAL INSIGHTS

Impact of One Person

In many cases one person had a powerful impact on the organization. Ray Kroc of McDonald's converted a small hamburger stand into the world's largest restaurant operation. Herb Kelleher of Southwest became the tormentor of the mighty airlines. John Bogle of Vanguard started a crusade against the high-priced mutual funds of competitors, and led his firm to become the biggest of all. Less well known are the entrepreneurs Jim Koch of Boston Beer and Michael Feuer of OfficeMax.

For turnaround accomplishments, Gordon Bethune, who turned around a demoralized Continental Airlines, stands tall, as does Lou Gerstner of IBM, with Vaughn Beals of Harley Davidson no slouch.

One person can also have a negative impact on an organization. Al Dunlap, the decimator of sick companies, who finally got his comeuppance with Sunbeam, is perhaps best known. Then there is William Aramony who almost destroyed United Way by his high living and arrogance. Less well-known is Dwayne Andreas, the longtime CEO of ADM who set the climate for illegalities both embarrassing and reprehensible. The impact of one person, for good or ill, is one of the recurring marvels of history, whether business history or world history.

Prevalence of Opportunities for Entrepreneurship Today

Despite the maturing of our economy and the growing size and power of many firms in many industries, opportunities for entrepreneurship still abound. This last decade witnessed the greatest proliferation ever of entrepreneurship. Much of this came in the high-tech arena, with technological advances proliferating and thousands of entrepreneurs, many in their twenties, jumping into the arena only to crash. Still, opportunities exist not only for the changemaker or innovator, but also for the person who only seeks to do things a little better than existing, and complacent, competition.

Most entrepreneurial successes are unheralded, although dozens are widely publicized. While we dealt specifically with new business ventures in Part VII, with such rising stars as Boston Beer and OfficeMax, two other cases are not so many years away from their beginnings: for example, Vanguard and Southwest Airlines. Bill Gates of Microsoft is the premier entrepreneur.[4] Opportunities are there for the dedicated. Venture capital to support promising new businesses helped many fledgling enterprises, and became a flood during the wild boom of the 1990s. As a new business shows early promise, initial public offerings (IPOs) (i.e., new stock issues) become important sources of capital, as we saw with Boston Beer, OfficeMax, and the dot.coms and telecoms.

But entrepreneurship is not for everyone. In prudent times, the great venture capitalists look at the person, not the idea. Typically they distribute their seed money to resourceful people who are courageous enough to give up security for the unknown consequences of their embryonic ventures, who have great self-confidence, and who demonstrate a tremendous will to win.

CONCLUSION

We learn from mistakes and from successes, although every management problem and opportunity seems cast in a somewhat different setting. But there are still common elements. One author has likened business strategy to military strategy:

> Strategies which are flexible rather than static embrace optimum use and offer the greatest number of alternative objectives. A good commander knows that he cannot control his environment to suit a prescribed strategy. Natural phenomena pose their own restraints to strategic planning, whether physical, geographic, regional, or psychological and sociological.[5]

He later adds:

> Planning leadership recognizes the unpleasant fact that, despite every effort, the war may be lost. Therefore, the aim is to retain the maximum number of facilities and the

---

[4] This case is described in R. F. Hartley, *Marketing Mistakes,* 7th ed. (New York: Wiley, 1998), pp. 217–233.

[5] Myron S. Heidingsfield, *Changing Patterns in Marketing* (Boston: Allyn & Bacon, 1968), p. 11.

basic organization. Indicators of a deteriorating and unsalvageable total situation are, therefore, mandatory... No possible combination of strategies and tactics, no mobilization of resources ... can supply a magic formula which guarantees victory; it is possible only to increase the probability of victory.[6]

Thus, we can pull two concepts from military strategy to help guide business strategy: the desirability of flexibility in an unknown or changing environment and the idea that a basic core should be maintained in crises. The first suggests that the firm should be prepared for adjustments in strategy as conditions warrant. The second suggests that there is a basic core of a firm's business that should be unchanging; it should be the final bastion to fall back on for regrouping if necessary. Harley Davidson stolidly maintained its core position, even though it let expansion opportunities slither away. IBM had a solid core that it was able to maintain and from which it could mount a resurgence.

In regard to the basic core of a firm, every viable firm has some distinctive function or "ecological niche" in the business environment:

> Every business firm occupies a position which is in some respects unique. Its location, the product it sells, its operating methods, or the customers it serves tend to set it off in some degree from every other firm. Each firm competes by making the most of its individuality and its special character.[7]

Woe to the firm that loses its ecological niche.

QUESTIONS

1. Design a program aimed at mistake avoidance. Be as specific, as creative, and as complete as possible.
2. Would you advise a firm to be an imitator or an innovator? Why?
3. "There is no such thing as a sustainable competitive advantage." Discuss.
4. How would you build controls into an organization to ensure that similar mistakes do not happen in the future?
5. Array as many pros and cons of entrepreneurship as you can. Which do you see as most compelling?
6. Do you agree with the thought expressed in this chapter that a firm confronted with strong ethical criticism should abandon the product or the way of doing business? Why or why not?
7. We have suggested that the learning insights discussed in this chapter and elsewhere in the book are transferable to other firms and other times. Do you completely agree with this? Why or why not?

[6] *Ibid.*
[7] Alderson, p. 101.

HANDS-ON EXERCISE

Your firm has had a history of reacting rather than anticipating changes in the industry. As the staff assistant to the CEO, you have been assigned the responsibility of developing adequate sensors of the marketplace. How will you go about developing such sensors?

TEAM DEBATE EXERCISE

Debate the extremes of forecasting for an innovative new product: conservative versus aggressive.